Lecture Notes in Computer Science 7040

Commenced Publication in 1973
Founding and Former Series Editors:
Gerhard Goos, Juris Hartmanis, and Jan van !

David V. Keyson   Mary Lou Maher
Norbert Streitz   Adrian Cheok
Juan Carlos Augusto   Reiner Wichert
Gwenn Englebienne   Hamid Aghajan
Ben J. A. Kröse (Eds.)

Ambient Intelligence

Second International Joint Conference, AmI 2011
Amsterdam, The Netherlands, November 16-18, 2011
Proceedings

 Springer

Volume Editors

David V. Keyson, Delft University of Technology, The Netherlands
E-mail: d.v.keyson@tudelft.nl

Mary Lou Maher, University of Maryland, College Park, MD, USA
E-mail: marylou.maher@gmail.com

Norbert Streitz, Smart Future Initiative, Frankfurt, Germany
E-mail: norbert.streitz@smart-future.net

Adrian Cheok, National University of Singapore, Singapore
E-mail: adriancheok@mixedrealitylab.org

Juan Carlos Augusto, University of Ulster, Newtownabbey, UK
E-mail: jc.augusto@ulster.ac.uk

Reiner Wichert, Fraunhofer-Institut für
Graphische Datenverarbeitung IGD, Darmstadt, Germany
E-mail: reiner.wichert@igd.fraunhofer.de

Gwenn Englebienne, University of Amsterdam, The Netherlands
E-mail: g.englebienne@uva.nl

Hamid Aghajan, Stanford University, Stanford, CA, USA
E-mail: aghajan@stanford.edu

Ben J. A. Kröse, University of Amsterdam and
Amsterdam University of Applied Sciences, The Netherlands
E-mail: b.j.a.krose@hva.nl

ISSN 0302-9743   e-ISSN 1611-3349
ISBN 978-3-642-25166-5   e-ISBN 978-3-642-25167-2
DOI 10.1007/978-3-642-25167-2
Springer Heidelberg Dordrecht London New York

Library of Congress Control Number: 2011940005

CR Subject Classification (1998): I.2, H.4, H.3, C.2.4, H.5, I.2.11, K.4

LNCS Sublibrary: SL 3 – Information Systems and Application, incl. Internet/Web
and HCI

Typesetting: Camera-ready by author, data conversion by Scientific Publishing Services, Chennai, India

Printed on acid-free paper

Springer is part of Springer Science+Business Media (www.springer.com)

Preface

This volume contains the papers and posters selected for presentation at the International Joint Conference on Ambient Intelligence (AmI-11) held in Amsterdam in November 2011. Ambient intelligence (AmI) represents a vision of the future in which products and services will be responsive to the user context, offering a rich variety of applications in the professional and consumer domains. AmI combines concepts of ubiquitous technology, intelligent systems and advanced user interface design putting humans in the center of technological developments.

Starting as the European Symposium on Ambient Intelligence in 2003 the conference has grown to an annual international event that brings together researchers and serves as a forum to discuss the latest trends and solutions.

Following the publication of early scenarios on ambient intelligence in 2001 by the European Commission's Joint Research Centre, the theme of AmI-11 focused on the "The Road Ahead, Shaping the Next 10 Years."

For this we had two keynote speakers focusing on this theme. On the first day a presentation was given by Margaret Morris, of Intel Research, who in her presentation "Left to Our Own Devices" described the role of mobile phones as gateway to ubiquitous computing. The closing keynote was given by Albrecht Schmidt, who presented "Beyond Ubicomp—Computing Is Changing the Way We Live."

The conference represented many "firsts" for the AmI community; for the first time the conference was held in Amsterdam, a rich and culturally diverse city that maintains the charms of an old city while being a modern thriving world city. For the first time a special track was held in the area of ambient-assisted living, reflecting the number of scientific investigations focusing on increasing the viability of seniors living longer while maintaining quality of life, independently at home. As a new element of the AmI program, a doctoral consortium track combined with an expert panel enabled PhDs to share findings and approaches to research.

After a solid review process, 50 papers and 8 workshops were accepted. To ensure the quality of work presented, 63% of regular and late-breaking paper submissions were rejected. Three independent reviewers were matched by expertise area to the topic of each paper. The Chairs handled borderline cases, and requested additional reviews when needed. A special thanks goes to the dedicated work of the 80 Program Members involved in the review panel who came from Asia, Europe, South America and North America, reflecting the spirit of AmI participation. Their names are published in the conference program.

Based on previous years, there appeared to be a growing trend of field studies, which suggests recognition of the need to validate new technologies, evaluations and design approaches to ambient systems. The range of papers dealing with novel interaction techniques and smart environments and sensing demonstrate the gains to be achieved in real-world settings. A number of late-breaking papers examine the power of ambient systems in terms of affecting human behavior, raising issues related to trust and privacy, which were topics touched upon in the conference, but deserve further attention in future research on ambient intelligence.

Apart from the main conference we had a record number of workshops organized on the day before the conference. We also had a doctoral colloquium in which PhD students met and discussed their work with each other and a panel of experienced AmI researchers and practitioners. The workshop and the doctoral colloquium papers are published in the proceedings in the Springer's *Communications in Computer and Information Science* series.

AmI-11 was made possible by contributions from Philips Research, IIP Create, Noldus Information Technology, the City of Amsterdam, Ministry of Economic Affairs through AgentschapNL, the University of Amsterdam and Hogeschool van Amsterdam.

In closing we would like to thank the conference Organizing Committee for their dedicated support and all of the paper presenters and conference participants who contributed to the vibrant discussions, panels, and workshops held at AmI 2011.

November 2011   David Keyson
                                                            Ben Kröse

Organization

The 5th European Conference on Ambient Intelligence, AmI 11, was held in Amsterdam, The Netherlands.

Organizing Committee

General Chair

Ben J.A. Kröse — University of Amsterdam and Amsterdam University of Applied Sciences, The Netherlands

General Co-chair

Hamid Aghajan — Stanford University, USA and Ghent University / IBBT, Belgium

Program Chairs

David Keyson — Delft University of Technology, The Netherlands

Mary Lou Maher — University of Maryland, USA

Late-Breaking Results

Norbert Streitz — Smart Future Initiative, Germany

Adrian Cheok — Keio University, Japan and National University Singapore

AAL Special Session

Martijn Vastenburg — Delft University of Technology, The Netherlands

Thomas Visser — Delft University of Technology, The Netherlands

Landscape Chair

Juan Carlos Augusto — University of Ulster, UK

Workshops

Reiner Wichert — Fraunhofer IGD, Germany

Kristof Van Laerhoven — TU Darmstadt, Germany

Jean Gelissen — Philips Research, The Netherlands

Doctoral Colloquium

Natalia Romero

Delft University of Technology,
   The Netherlands

Agnieszka Szóstek

Institute for Information Processing, Poland

Demos and Exhibitions

Richard Kleihorst

VITO NV, Belgium and Ghent University,
   Belgium

Vanessa Evers

University of Twente, The Netherlands

Publications

Gwenn Englebienne

University of Amsterdam,
   The Netherlands

Marije Kanis

Amsterdam University of Applied Sciences,
   The Netherlands

Publicity

Albert Ali Salah

University of Amsterdam, The Netherlands

Program and Reviewing Committee

Dionisis Adamopoulos   University of Piraeus, Greece
Pablo Anton   Universidad de Malaga, Spain
Juan Carlos Augusto   University of Ulster, UK
Asier Aztiria   Mondragon Unibertsitatea, Spain
Sander Bakkes   Amsterdam University of Applied Sciences,
                                 The Netherlands

Eugen Berlin   TU Darmstadt, Germany
Ulf Blanke   TU Darmstadt, Germany
Aaron Bobick   Georgia Tech, USA
Juan Antonio Botia Blaya   Universidad de Murcia, Spain
Marko Borazio   University of Technology Darmstadt, Germany
Jörg Cassens   University of Lübeck, Germany
Federico Castanedo   University of Deusto, Spain
Andreu Català   Technical University of Catalonia, Spain
Adrian David Cheok   Interactive & Digital Media Institute,
                                 Singapore
Maurice Chu   PARC, USA
Fulvio Corno   Politecnico di Torino, Italy
Cristina De Castro   IEIIT-CNR, Italy
Mark de Graaf   Eindhoven University of Technology,
                                 The Netherlands
Marc de Hoogh   Delft University of Technology,
                                 The Netherlands

Boris de Ruyter	Philips Research Europe, The Netherlands
Sebastian Denef	Fraunhofer FIT, Germany
Anind Dey	Carnegie Mellon University, USA
Berry Eggen	Eindhoven University of Technology, The Netherlands
Babak A. Farshchian	SINTEF, Norway
Owen Noel Newton Fernando	Mixed Reality Lab, UK
Doug Fisher	Vanderbilt, USA
Sven Fleck	SmartSurv Vision Systems GmbH, Germany
Kaori Fujinami	Tokyo University of Agriculture and Technology, Japan
Nikolaos Georgantas	INRIA, France
Björn Gottfried	Universität Bremen, Germany
Nuno Guimarães	University of Lisbon, Portugal
Nick Guldemond	Delft University of Technology, The Netherlands
Dirk Heylen	Universiteit Twente, The Netherlands
Juan Jimenez	Delft University of Technology, The Netherlands
Bjoern Joop	University of Duisburg-Essen, Germany
Ralf Jung	DFKI, Germany
Dietrich Kammer	Technische Universität Dresden, Germany
Evangelos Karapanos	Madeira Interactive Technologies Institute
David Keyson	Delft University of Technology, The Netherlands
Shinichi Konomi	University of Tokyo, Japan
Ben Kröse	University of Amsterdam, The Netherlands
Antonio Krüger	DFKI, Germany
Philippe Lalanda	Grenoble University, France
Jun Liu	University of Ulster, UK
Mary Lou Maher	University of Maryland, USA
George Margetis	Foundation for Research & Technology — Hellas, Greece
Davide Merico	Università degli Studi di Milano-Bicocca, Italy
Alexander Meschtscherjakov	University of Salzburg, Austria
Dorothy Monekosso	University of Ulster, UK
Christian Mueller-Tomfelde	Commonwealth Scientific and Industrial Research Organisation, Australia
Antonio Muãoz	Universidad de Málaga, Spain
Gabriele Oligeri	ISTI-CNR, Italy
Eila Ovaska	VTT Technical Research Centre of Finland
Don Paterson	University of California Irvine, USA
Ronald Poppe	University of Twente, The Netherlands
Chris Poppe	University of Ghent, Belgium
Davy Preuveneers	Katholieke Universiteit Leuven, Belgium
Gilles Privat	Orange Labs, France

Andreas Riener	Johannes Kepler Universität Linz, Austria
Aitor Rodriguez	Centre d'Accessibilitat i Intelligència Ambiental de Catalunya, Spain
Natalia Romero Herrera	Delft University of Technology, The Netherlands
Elham Saadatian	Mixed Reality Lab, UK
Michael Schneider	DFKI, Germany
Norbert Streitz	Smart Future Initiative, Germany
Janienke Sturm	Eindhoven University of Technology, The Netherlands
Gita Sukthankar	University of Central Florida, USA
Guillermo Talavera	Centre d'Accessibilitat i Intelligència Ambiental de Catalunya, Spain
Hiroshi Tanaka	Kanagawa Institute of Technology, Japan
Andrew Vande Moere	University of Leuven, Belgium
Martijn Vastenburg	Delft University of Technology, The Netherlands
Carlos A. Velasco	Fraunhofer Institute for Applied Information Technology FIT, Germany
Thomas Visser	Delft University of Technology, The Netherlands
Kate Wac	University of Geneva, Switzerland
Xuan Wang	Mixed Reality Lab, UK
Jun Wei	Mixed Reality Lab, UK
Reiner Wichert	Fraunhofer IGD, Germany
Sabine Wildevuur	Waag Society, The Netherlands
Jan Wojdziak	Technische Universität Dresden, Germany
Olga Zlydareva	Eindhoven University of Technology, The Netherlands
Alessio Vecchio	University of Pisa, Italy
Evert van Loenen	Philips Research, The Netherlands

Sponsors

Philips Research Europe
IIP Create
Noldus Information Technology
City of Amsterdam
Ministry of Economic Affairs AgentschapNL IOP-MMI
University of Amsterdam
HvA University of Applied Science
Foundation Innovation Alliance SIA

Table of Contents

Novel Interaction Technologies

Affecting Human Behaviour

Privacy and Trust

Landscape

Ambient Assisted Living

Poster Papers

Workshop Summaries

HapticArmrest:
Remote Tactile Feedback on Touch Surfaces Using Combined Actuators

Hendrik Richter, Sebastian Löhmann, and Alexander Wiethoff

University of Munich, Germany
{hendrik.richter,sebastian.loehmann,
alexander.wiethoff}@ifi.lmu.de

Abstract. Interactive surfaces form an integral component of intelligent environments. In the paper, we describe HapticArmrest, a simple tactile interface that communicates tactual surface characteristic and form of interactive elements on direct touch surfaces. Spatially separating manual touch input and active tactile output allows for the combination of various types of tactile actuators for versatile haptic feedback. In a preliminary experiment, we indicate that our approach enables a reliable discrimination of virtual elements on touch surfaces solely based on tactile representations. We also assessed the hedonic and pragmatic qualities of the generated tactile stimuli by applying methods from the field of usability research.

Keywords: interactive surfaces, haptics, tactile feedback, touch, actuators.

1 Introduction

Due to advances in display technology and sensing devices, surfaces responsive to direct manual touch are all around. The flexibility of touch-based graphical user interfaces allow for devices in a multitude of sizes and forms (mobile phones, tablet PCs, tabletops, public displays etc.). Interactive surfaces are used in dynamic scenarios that could involve personal and public use, noise or high visual and cognitive load. Despite the ubiquity of touch input and the benefits of multimodal signals in ubiquitous scenarios, most touch interfaces still lack tactile output. Touch screens only present a flat, uniform surface to the interacting user's hand; all GUI elements provide the same reduced cutaneous (i.e. tactile) impression.

Scientific approaches to provide versatile tactile sensations to the human skin are in existence. Evaluations show that users of touch surfaces greatly benefit from tactile feedback. This is true for both objective measures and emotional aspects of the interaction [10, 15, 5, 20]. Still, haptic sensations are underused as a redundant information channel in the fields of mobile interaction or pervasive and physical computing [24]. A possible reason is a lack of haptic signal generators that are versatile and effective, but at the same time small and non-expensive [8]. Current high-bandwidth

D. Keyson et al. (Eds.): AmI 2011, LNCS 7040, pp. 1–10, 2011.

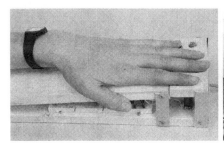

Fig. 1. The HapticArmrest (left) communicates tactile patterns and movements to the user's non-dominant hand. When touching an interactive element with the opposite hand, the user feels the form and surface characteristics of this item (right).

solutions mostly entail technical complexity and space issues. A potentially high number of bulky, complex and power consuming tactile actuators have to be implemented into the touch interface (see part 3). This impedes the application of tactile cues as an additional channel of information in ubiquitous scenarios.

To cope with these challenges, we propose the spatial separation of manual touch and resulting tactile feedback. By doing so, we may be able to combine cheap and simple haptic actuators for nonetheless meaningful and rich tactile feedback on touch interfaces. Additionally, our approach may help to reduce the complexity and size of used actuators and is applicable on arbitrary interactive surfaces. We built a prototypical haptic interface (see Figure 1) with dual type touch feedback by combining different actuators. Thus, we provide both haptic (movement of fingers) and tactile (vibrations on the skin) sensations. In a first evaluation (see part 5.1), we show that users are able to reliably discriminate visually identical interactive elements solely depending on the generated remote tactile stimuli. Additionally, in order to assess the hedonic and pragmatic qualities of the conveyed tactile stimuli, we applied methods from the field of usability research (see part 5.2). Here, the users indicate the livening and positive nature of the designed stimuli and give rise to improvements of the prototype.

2   Remote Tactile Feedback and Combined Actuators

As stated before, we spatially separate manual touch input and resulting tactile output. We believe that this approach of having remote tactile feedback provides three main consequences:

(1) We can combine actuators that differ in size, complexity and stimulus characteristics.
(2) We can produce combined tactile feedback for the communication of meaningful and rich content such as form and abstract state of interactive elements.
(3) Any surfaces can be augmented with remote tactile impressions as the surface itself does not have to be modified; the electromechanical infrastructure is not restricted to the size and form of the surface.

In order to assess the feasibility of our approach, we designed a prototypical tactile interface, the HapticArmrest (see Figure 1). Our prototype comprises two types of actuators:

a) Eccentric Motors: This low-complexity type of actuator generates structured vibrotactile patterns that can be dynamically modified by altering signal parameters such as amplitude, frequency or rhythm. The user perceives the stimuli as rhythmic vibrations on the skin.
b) Linear Solenoids: This off-the shelf component communicates highly dynamic stimuli such as changes of pressure or movement. The user recognizes a sudden change of height of the object under his fingertips.

Feedback occurs in three different situations. First, the edges of an object can be touched directly. Second, the user can slide his finger onto a virtual object (rollover) or leave the object (rollout), which includes cutting across an edge. Third, surface textures of virtual objects can be explored. This system behavior is based on common state models to describe interactions with direct manipulation interfaces [4]. Technical details on actuators and stimulus design are specified in part 4.

Instead of augmenting the user with wearable technology, we decided to instrument the user's direct environment. In this case, it is possible for the user to lift his arm from the device to use both hands for the interaction or to stop exploring the surface. When thinking of scenarios such as office areas or cars in which the users tend to remain in direct contact with chairs, seats or tables, it is easier to implement the actuator technology in the user's direct environment. For scenarios involving interactive tables or walls, remote tactile feedback may even be conveyed by actuators in the frame of the device or even in the floor. In this case, every single user may feel distinct and personal tactile stimuli that is responsive to the specific context of the user. Tactile actuators similar to our prototype may be implemented in a frame of a public interactive table and could communicate characteristics of virtual elements and acknowledgements for activations in order to reduce visual load.

We tested the basic potential of our approach in a preliminary experiment. Our interest was twofold. We wanted to assess if people are able to use the additional channel of tactile information on touch surfaces despite the spatial separation of manual action and resulting stimulus. Therefore, we designed a setup in which participants had to identify interactive GUI-elements solely based on tactile information. Furthermore, we wanted to look at the usability and hedonic quality of the tactile stimuli we created by combining sensations from the motors and solenoids. Methods for the evaluation of tactile stimuli are sparse [14]. Therefore, we transferred methods from usability research such as AttrakDiff [9] for the comparison and summative evaluation of the two different stimuli.

3   Related Work

Thanks to technological advances in the development of interfaces (processing power, sensors, actuators), the interest in the use of multimodal information processing is constantly growing [18]. Multimodal interaction is beneficial in highly dynamic scenarios with environmental factors such as noise, vibration or narrowness [7]. The redundant use of multiple senses helps to improve the interaction as a whole [11]. With touch interfaces being the most commonly used interfaces in dynamic scenarios, the use of haptics comes into play.

The communication of actively generated tactile information to the human's skin has been studied for a long time in fields such as virtual reality, accessibility and Sensory Substitution [8]. Researchers utilize artificial haptic stimuli to transmit either abstract information such as warnings, acknowledgements or system states or palpable characteristics of virtual elements such as form or malleability onto the user's skin [8,16].

Interfaces that provide tactile feedback for direct touch mostly fall into one of three categories: First, miniature actuator system such as [19] move the mobile device or the device's screen as a whole. Thereby only a single point of touch input can be supported by tactile stimuli. The approach does not scale for tabletops or interactive walls. Systems such as Tesla Touch [2] convey tactile signals based on electrical stimuli, but also only provide single touch input. Second, a form of tactile interface that is used for a long time is a tactile display such as FEELEX [12]. The interactive surface is segmented into individually movable 'tactile pixels'. Currently, this approach results in a reduced tactile and visual resolution due to mechanical complexity and size of the individual actuators. Third, tangible user interfaces atop the interactive surface such as [16] could help to communicate versatile stimuli using various types of actuators. All of these approaches postulate in essence that tactile feedback for an interaction should be applied directly to the body part that is in contact with the screen, i.e. mostly the fingertip.

By contrast, we try to evaluate the feasibility of remote tactile feedback. Few researchers have incorporated distal tactile stimuli before [21]. However, they presented promising impacts on interaction speed and text entry [17]. The more general approach of tactile sensory relocation has been researched and used before in the fields of accessibility and Sensory Substitution [1]. For example, Clippinger et al. [6] describe a sensory feedback system for an upper-limb amputation prosthesis. Here, sensors in the gripper-like prosthesis capture the level of closing pressure. This information is communicated to remote parts of the user's body using electrotactile actuators. This approach of tactile sensory relocation helps the user to precisely control the force used for grasp and pinch with the artificial hand.

4   HapticArmrest: Technical Details

The decision to design an armrest was influenced by an observation made by Ryall et al. [22]. When interacting with direct-touch tabletops, people tend to lean on the surface with their non-active hand or arm. This leads to accidental inputs and thus to confusing reactions of the system. Haptic Armrest offers a placement area for the user's idle arm.

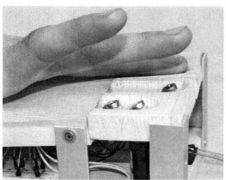

Fig. 2. View of the two types of actuators on the HapticArmrest. Eccentric motors (left) and linear solenoids (right).

4.1   Actuators

HapticArmrest incorporates two types of actuators (see Figure 2). Solenoids provide haptic feedback by lifting the user's fingers, while vibration motors, commonly used to shake mobile phones, apply vibrotactile stimuli to the fingertips. We used the number of single actuators of every type as an additional parameter to design the abstract stimuli.

Eccentric Motors
As the prototype can be used by both left- and right-handed persons, altogether six vibration motors have been installed. Four of them provide feedback to all fingers of the right hand besides the thumb. Because of the different length of little and index finger, two more motors are needed for left-handed users. Each motor can be triggered separately, which allows for a stimulation of an arbitrary number of fingertips at the same time. This kind of tactile feedback can be used to simulate the exploration of an object's surface texture. These textures do not resemble materials of the real world, but are designed for articulate distinction.

Solenoids
Each of the two built-in solenoids is connected to a wooden pad, which can be lifted by up to four millimeters. Each pad includes two cavities giving the user a hint where to place the fingers. This kind of feedback was used during the evaluation to simulate the touch of an object's edges, including rollover and rollout.

4.2   Signals

For both types of feedback, so called tactons (tactile icons) [3] where used to create different feedback patterns. The varying parameters were rhythm, duration and the combination of different actuators. Considering the vibration motors, three rhythms were used: permanent vibrations, alternating activation and deactivation of the motors and, what we called "wave", activating the four motors one after another, starting with the small finger. The duration of the stimuli was either 200 or 400 milliseconds

[13]. The vibrations were applied to the small finger, the index finger or all fingers besides the thumb. Given these parameters, we created twelve different feedback patterns. We followed the same procedure with the two solenoids by lifting different fingers with a certain duration and rhythm.

The combination of both types of haptic feedback, vibrations and lifting the fingers, allow for a fourth parameter and thus for the creation of new patterns and possibly even new haptic stimuli.

5   Evaluations

With our evaluation, we wanted to verify that users are able to utilize the remote tactile stimuli as an additional and synchronous channel of information when manipulating and exploring interactive elements. Therefore, we designed a task in which participants had to discriminate virtual elements using tactile signals created by the EdgeMatrix. Touch feedback can have a strong emotional impact [23], so we tried to assess hedonic quality and usability of our signals and the system by applying standard measures from the field of usability research (see part 5.2).

5.1   Discrimination Task

The experimental setting is depicted in Figure 1. We conducted the experiment using a touch based tablet PC which depicted 6 gray squares (4 x 4cm). A touch on a square resulted in two types of feedback (edges, areas) generated by the HapticArmrest (see part 4). During each test trial, two of the six elements shared a common tactile characteristic.

Twelve volunteers (6 female), ranging in age from 20 to 27, were recruited for the experiment. All participants were right handed. They wore earmuffs to isolate environmental noise. After an introduction and a training phase, each participant completed six trials. During a trial, the participant was free to touch and explore the depicted elements. He was asked to point out to the pair of elements with the same tactile impression. In three of the six trials, a pair of elements with identical tactile 'surface-impression' was depicted. In the other three trials, a pair of elements with identical tactile 'edge-impression' had to be identified. Elements that were not part of the pair had randomly selected tactile characteristics. The order of the tactile representation was counterbalanced. Each tactile pattern representing a pair of elements was only presented once for every participant. In total over all participants, 72 pairs of GUI elements had to be identified (36 for each actuator technology).

Results.
The results in Figure 3 show that all pairs of elements with identical remote vibrotactile feel could be identified by the participants. For the pairs of elements with tactile edges using vertically moving solenoid actuators, in six out of 36 trials participants were not able to identify one pair of elements out of three. This results in a discrimination rate of 83.33 percent for the solenoid actuator technology.

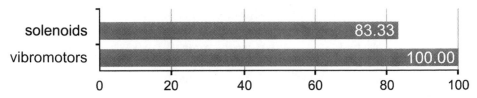

Fig. 3. Percentage of correctly identified pairs of tactile GUI elements for each actuator technology (solenoids = edge feedback, vibromotors = surface feedback)

5.2 Hedonic and Pragmatic Qualities

As this type of feedback modality is still emerging from the research environment we also investigated the hedonic qualities users connected with the feedback. Therefore we conducted an evaluation based on AttracDiff [9] by Hassenzahl et al. This scientific method is targeted towards revealing additional to the general usability and performance of the system the *emotional and hedonic quality* of an interaction modality. Pairs of opposing adjectives (semantic differentials) are presented to the participant who is asked to rate the system based on this measure on a scale from -3 to +3. We tested and evaluated two signal types: (a) vibrotactile stimuli, represented in Figure 4 through squares and (b) pressure plus movement indicated in figure 4 with circles.

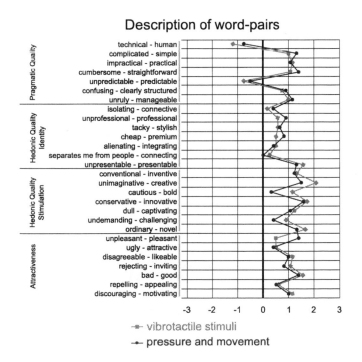

Fig. 4. Results of AttrakDiff

The most noticeable results from the test indicated that both feedback modalities were perceived as rather *technical* (mean=-1.0) vs. *human* by the users (see Figure 4). Further, the approach of providing such feedback signal types was recognized as being quite *creative* (mean=2.0) compared to *uninspired* on the other side of the spectrum. A difference between the approaches was stated regarding the feedback type (a), which led to the result of being *pleasant* compared to rather *unpleasant* (mean=0.5) for feedback type (b) with a mean of 1.5.

In general, the closeness of the results of both signal types (see figure 4) can be interpreted in a way that the participants did not perceive the two stimuli as completely separate feedback types. This supports our assumption that we can convey tactile stimuli resulting from multiple combined remote actuators. Regarding the technicality of our approach, we will further substantiate this issue in future case studies by applying different immaterialities to the housing of the actuator technology (e.g. organic user interfaces). The general *pleasance* and perceived *creative* nature of both approaches seem worthwhile investigating, for example by applying different actuator technologies, thus increasing the pleasance of use.

6   Discussion

Considering the results of both studies, we can state the following: The HapticArmrest has been a valuable device for the exploration of the potential of remote tactile feedback and the combination of tactile stimuli. We used low-cost and low-complexity actuators to communicate two different types of stimuli to haptically augment interactive graphical elements. Yet, we did not measure the influence of noise and (subjectively unnoticeable) latency produced by our off-the shelf components. Still, due to their reduced complexity, the actuators may easily be implemented in tactile interfaces and the user's direct environment. Furthermore, our results indicate that it is possible for the user to reliably identify interactive elements based on stimuli that are created by this type of low-complexity actuators.

The distinctive feature of our approach is the spatial separation of touch-based input and artificial tactile output. Thus, any surface might be augmented with remote tactile feedback. Our results indicate that even with the remote application of tactile stimuli, the simultaneous feedback is still understandable and usable during an interaction.

Due to the aforementioned impact of tactile stimuli on the human emotion system, we also have to evaluate the usability and hedonic quality of the tactile stimuli designed in this way. Quantitative empirical evaluations for the analysis of tactile perception across the body surface or the effects of tactile feedback on error rates are well established (e.g. in [10]). In contrast, we lack standard methods to evaluate qualitative aspects of artificial tactile stimuli. Such methods could help to repeat and validate our investigations. For a start, we used methods from the field of usability research such as AttrakDiff (see part 5.2).

With AttrakDiff, the participants rated the stimuli based on semantic differentials, i.e. pairs of opposing adjectives (see Figure 4). However, some of these pairs (such as *cautious vs. bold*) do not quite fit. Participants stated their difficulties to use these adjectives to describe emotional or perceived aspects of artificial sensations to touch. However, word-pairs such as *cheap vs. premium* or *pleasant vs. unpleasant* do cover tactile feedback well and enable us to improve the design of future tactile interfaces and stimuli. In general, the most distinctive results can be found in the sections *Hedonic Quality - Stimulation* and *Attractiveness*. For future evaluations, we plan to extend these sections in order to cover the special characteristics of tactile stimuli. A more customized evaluation method covering the hedonic qualities of non-visual stimuli could give rise to the design of future interfaces.

7 Conclusion and Future Work

With the HapticArmrest we introduced an inexpensive hardware design for a device that allows for the exploration of remote tactile feedback on touch surfaces. Our prototype incorporates cheap and simple off-the-shelf actuators such as vibrational motors and linear solenoids. We applied sudden movement and diffuse vibrotactile stimuli to express both form and surface characteristics of virtual button-like screen elements. In a preliminary experiment, we explore the effectiveness and usability of remotely applied feedback.

In the future, we intend to further advance our user interface. We already received valuable comments that suggest to reduce the noise or to alter the form of our interface. By using smaller and less conspicuous actuators, our interface could blend into the user's direct environment. We also think about using other locations of the user's body to place the actuators. The areas of the human skin differ in two-point, frequency and amplitude discrimination thresholds. Thus, more pressure would be needed to create the same amount of tactile stimulation. However, large usable areas such as the human back lend itself for the application of tactile stimuli. Adding other somatosensoric modalities such as the perception of heat or moisture by using appropriate actuators could further enrich and improve the interaction.

In summary, our work questions the assumption that tactile feedback has to be given at the interacting fingertip or hand. With remote tactile feedback, we can augment touch surfaces no matter what technology, form or size. The integration of different forms of actuators creating tactile stimuli which complement one another may become possible. Novel forms of multimodal interfaces may help us in enhancing and enriching the dynamic interaction with ubiquitous and multimodal interfaces.

References

1. Bach-y-Rita, P., Kercel, S.W.: Sensory substitution and the human-machine interface. Trends in Cognitive Sciences 7(12), 541–546 (2003)
2. Bau, O., Poupyrev, I., Israr, A., Harrison, C.: TeslaTouch. In: Proc. UIST 2010, pp. 283–292 (2010)
3. Brewster, S., Brown, M.: Tactons: structured tactile messages for non-visual information display. In: Proc. AUIC 2004, vol. 28, pp. 15–23 (2004)

4. Buxton, W.: A three-state model of graphical input. In: Proc. INTERACT 1990, pp. 449–456. North-Holland Publishing (1990)
5. Chang, A., O'Sullivan, C.: Audio-haptic feedback in mobile phones. In: Proc. CHI 2005, pp. 1264–1267 (2005)
6. Clippinger, F., Avery, R., Titus, B.: A sensory feedback system for an upper-limb amputation prosthesis. Bulletin of Prosthetics Research, 248–258 (1974)
7. Cohen, P.R., McGee, D.R.: Tangible multimodal interfaces for safety-critical applications. Communications of the ACM 47, 41–46 (2004)
8. Gallace, A., Tan, H.Z., Spence, C.: The Body Surface as a Communication System: The State of the Art after 50 Years. Presence: Teleoperators & Virtual Environments 16(6), 655–676 (2007)
9. Hassenzahl, M., Tractinsky, N.: User experience – a research agenda. Behavior & Information Technology 25(2), 91–97 (2006)
10. Hoggan, E., Brewster, S.A., Johnston, J.: Investigating the Effectiveness of Tactile Feedback for Mobile Touchscreens. In: Proc. CHI 2008, pp. 1573–1582 (2008)
11. Hoggan, E., Crossan, A., Brewster, S.A., Kaaresoja, T.: Audio or tactile feedback: which modality when. In: Proc. CHI 2009, pp. 2253–2256 (2009)
12. Iwata, H., Yano, H., Nakaizumi, F., Kawamura, R.: Project FEELEX: adding haptic surface to graphics. In: Proc. SIGGRAPH 2001, pp. 469–476 (2001)
13. Kaaresoja, T., Linjama, J.: Perception of short tactile pulses generated by a vibration motor in a mobile phone. In: Proc. EuroHaptics 2005, pp. 471–472 (2005)
14. Koskinen, E., Kaaresoja, T., Laitinen, P.: Feel-good touch. In: Proc. IMCI 2008, pp. 297–304 (2008)
15. Leung, R., MacLean, K., Bertelsen, M.B., Saubhasik, M.: Evaluation of Haptically Augmented Touchscreen GUI Elements under Cognitive Load. In: Proc. ICMI 2007, pp. 374–381 (2007)
16. Marquardt, N., Nacenta, M., Young, J., Carpendale, S., Greenberg, S., Sharlin, E.: The Haptic Tabletop Puck: Tactile Feedback for Interactive Tabletops. In: Proc. ITS 2009, pp. 93–100 (2009)
17. McAdam, C., Brewster, S.: Distal tactile feedback for text entry on tabletop computers. In: Proc. of BCS-HCI 2009, pp. 504–511 (2009)
18. Oviatt, S.: Multimodal interfaces. In: Jacko, J.A., Sears, A. (eds.) The Human-Computer Interaction Handbook, pp. 286–304 (2002)
19. Poupyrev, I., Maruyama, S., Rekimoto, J.: Ambient touch: designing tactile interfaces for handheld devices. In: Proc. UIST 2002, pp. 51–60 (2002)
20. Richter, H., Ecker, R., Deisler, C., Butz, A.: HapTouch and the 2 + 1 State Model. In: Proc. AutomotiveUI 2010, pp. 72–79 (2010)
21. Richter, H.: Multi-Haptics and Personalized Tactile Feedback on Interactive Surfaces. In: EuroHaptics 2010 (2010)
22. Ryall, K., Forlines, C., Shen, C., Morris, M.R., Everitt, K.: Experiences with and observations of direct-touch tabletops. In: Proc. TABLETOP 2006, pp. 89–96 (2006)
23. Salminen, K., Surakka, V., Lylykangas, J., Raisamo, J., Saarinen, R., Raisamo, R., et al.: Proc. CHI 2008, pp. 1555–1562 (2008)
24. Wright, A.: The touchy subject of haptics. Communications of the ACM 54(1), 20–22 (2011)

Interacting with the Steering Wheel: Potential Reductions in Driver Distraction

Sebastian Osswald, Alexander Meschtscherjakov,
David Wilfinger, and Manfred Tscheligi

Christian Doppler Laboratory "Contextual Interfaces", ICT&S Center
University of Salzburg, Sigmund Haffner Gasse 18, 5020 Salzburg, Austria

Abstract. Driving a car has become a challenge for many people despite the fact that evermore technology is built into vehicles in order to support the driver. Above all, the increasing number of in-vehicle information systems (IVIS) is a main source of driver distraction. The fragmentation of IVIS elements in the cockpit increases the attention demand and cognitive load of the driver. In this paper, we present an approach to integrate most in-car interaction possibilities into a steering wheel, by combining a multi-button row with a single touch in an intelligent steering wheel. We performed an online study (N=301) to investigate the pre-prototype user acceptance of the three different steering wheel modalities (single touch, multi button, combi touch) as well as a lab-based driving simulator study (N=10) to assess the practicability of the single touch interaction. The results of the online study showed that especially the single touch was highly accepted by the participants. The driving simulator study revealed that touch-based interaction on a steering wheel is feasible for low demand tasks in terms of driver distraction. Especially, the single touch embedded into the steering wheel is a promising approach for ambient information in the automotive context.

Keywords: automotive user interfaces, touch interaction, steering wheel, driver distraction, acceptance, user studies.

1 Introduction

It is well recognized that driver distraction is a contributing factor in many road accidents. Recent research revealed the usage of mobile phones, for instance, as one of the most distracting issues in the car [15]. Thus, many states enacted laws, banning the use of mobile devices while driving. Regarding the increasing number of functionalities, developing interaction modalities that reduce the distraction and lower the driver's workload is becoming a central issue in HCI research. The integration of pervasive technology and ambient intelligence (AmI) could be a major contributor to increase safety on the roads. Therefore, different interaction modalities (input and output) have to be investigated. Regarding input and output modalities, research and industry so far have focused on the visual and auditive channel. Voice input and output has been mainly used to

D. Keyson et al. (Eds.): AmI 2011, LNCS 7040, pp. 11–20, 2011.
© Springer-Verlag Berlin Heidelberg 2011

control the telephone or other tertiary tasks. Status information (e.g. speed, revolutions per minute, hazard lights) is often visualized in the dashboard or more recently on head-up displays. In-vehicle information systems (IVIS) such as radio, navigation, and climate control are mainly controlled via buttons all over the cockpit or on the steering wheel as well as by utilizing touch screens in the center stack. Other promising approaches to reduce driver distraction combined IVIS in the center console with multifunctional interaction devices (e.g. BMW iDrive, Audi MMI).

Most of these systems have two drawbacks. First, except for buttons on the steering wheel, they force the driver to bridge distances from the steering wheel to the input device by moving the arm. Second, the ever-increasing number of knobs and switches leads to a high fragmentation of interactive elements in the cockpit. We therefore propose to combine aspects of direct manipulation with the positioning of centralized interactive elements within the steering wheel.

Based on an intelligent steering wheel prototype with multi-button and single touch, which was developed by our partner AudioMobil Elektronik GmbH (http://www.audio-mobil.com) in the Christian-Doppler-Laboratory for Contextual Interfaces we conducted two user studies. The first study aimed at evaluating user acceptance of every single interaction modality as well as the user acceptance of the combi touch (buttons and touch). The second study aimed at investigating driver distraction through the single touch on the steering wheel by means of a simulator based lab study. This paper describes the prototype as well as the setup and results of both user studies.

2   Background Literature

2.1   AmI in the Automotive Context

The automotive context has been recently researched by the AmI community. Information about the environmental context, other drivers and social contacts is increasingly available for drivers, whereas the question of where information is displayed and the devices are operated in the best way is still unanswered. Schmidt et al. emphasize the challenging importance for pervasive computing research concerning the interaction with pervasive computing systems in the car [14]. Due to the increasing range of services that can be accessed in the car, Feld et al. stated that the claim of personal experience for the driver and the passengers can be satisfied by combining ambient speech and mobile personal devices [7]. Their approach uses speaker recognition to identify the passenger's position in the car to put the user in control. To make taxi transportation more efficient, [12] propose an ambient map-based service platform that provides real time environmental information about the availability of taxi transportation, predicting the number of vacant taxis for customers and operators. Displaying ambient information in the car requires meaningful devices that meet the safety standards of the car context. We believe that an interaction surface on the steering wheel can meet these requirements.

2.2 Interaction Modalities

Recently, many studies assessed the need of new concepts to deal with the complexity of current in-vehicle information systems. There are numerous studies comparing different interaction modalities for IVIS (see for example Harbluk et al. [8]). To reduce the visual demand of the driver, Ecker et al. developed a new concept using pie menus that serve as a visualization of gestures to interact with an IVIS [6]. For applying touch screens as an interaction modality in the car, Rydstrom et al. evaluated and compared three different IVIS, two operated by a rotary switch and one by a touch screen. A usability test with ten different tasks was conducted with the result that the naive users interacted more rapidly with the touch screen interface [13]. Gesture-, touch- and tactile-based interaction techniques have been investigated by [1]. Touch interaction presented itself as the fastest and easiest in supporting the driver. Investigating interaction techniques that aim to make it easier to interact with a IVIS, Doering et al. utilized the steering wheel as additional interaction surface. A developed set of multi-touch gestures was applied and compared with conventional user interfaces in terms of distraction, showing that the driver's visual demand is reduced significantly by the gestural interaction [5].

2.3 Driver Distraction and User Acceptance

Besides supporting the driver, IVIS can also be distracting. Distraction can concern different channels of sensory perception what increases the cognitive load [15]. Regarding the nature of tasks entering a navigation destination was most distracting. An increased distraction can even be observed for simply listening to the radio, without actual action on the driver's side. Regarding distraction related to input modalities, voice control turned out to be consistently less distracting than control via a display. Burnett et al. even assume a direct connection between the sheer availability of an IVIS and increasing unnecessary usage as well as an increasing distraction [3]. When developing novel interactive systems, it is necessary besides considering the driver distraction to address to what extent potential users will accept the system and its design. User acceptance (UA) in the context of information technology is described as the willingness of users to employ information technologies for their tasks. The technology acceptance model (TAM), which allows measuring and describing UA, is widely used. The TAM questionnaire delivers valid data on UA in a pre-prototype state of system development by measuring three scales, namely Perceived Usefulness (PU), Perceived Ease of Use (EOU) and Behavioral Intention of Use (BI) [4]. The importance of UA in the context of mobile and automotive user interfaces was besides others already identified by [11].

3   Intelligent Steering Wheel Prototype

To address the issue of accepting IVIS in the car context, this work introduces three design alternatives. Nowadays, many new cars have buttons on the steering wheel, some already have a touch screen in the central console. Thus, integrating and combining these elements in the steering wheel seems promising and that is why the single touch, multi-button and combi touch steering wheel concepts were designed (see section 3.1). First, the capabilities and features of the concepts were roughly described for the acceptance evaluation. The available features vary between the concepts from basic interaction like volume control via buttons to more complex interaction like starting a navigation. For the second study, an elaborated prototype was developed to address the issue of distraction (see section 5). The overall focus was inspired by the potential of the steering wheel as an easy interaction surface [5] and the promising results for steering wheel interaction techniques like handwriting recognition described by Kern et. al. [9]. We believe that the steering wheel can make an important contribution for instance in interacting with an intelligent agents who sense and react act upon the environment.

3.1   Design Concepts

- The *single touch (c1)* design concept allows direct manipulation of displayed interface elements. Common IVIS tasks can be performed like choosing a radio station as well as more sophisticated tasks. For example, navigation tasks can be performed directly on a scrollable map. The navigation to a desired city can be started by only tapping on the city name.
- The *multi-button (c2)* design concept contains short term interaction aspects like buttons for indicating or light control.
- The *combi touch (c3)* allows the driver to see additional information on the display while pressing an element of the multi-button row. For example the fuel gauge button not only indicates low fuel it rather displays customizable trip and distance information on the screen.

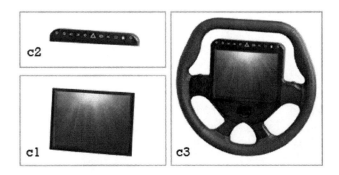

Fig. 1. Steering wheel design concepts: single touch (c1) multi-button (c2) and combi touch (c3)

3.2   Research Goals

The main aim of our study was to investigate the user acceptance of an intelligent steering wheel embodying an ambient device for contextual information.

RG1: Evaluate user acceptance of the design concepts in a pre-prototype stage.
RG2: Identify the distraction of tasks conducted with the single touch (c1).

It is addressed to which extent the user acceptance of three steering wheel design concepts differs and if there are other factors influencing the acceptance. Besides the measured acceptance of the presented modality concepts, the touch display steering wheel is chosen and applied in an end user study as it allows for more complex interaction.

4   Pre-prototype Technology Acceptance Study

4.1   Study Setup

To investigate how the three design concepts were perceived, we conducted an online survey measuring the user acceptance of the three design concepts with the help of the TAM scales. The TAM questionnaire was added for each design concept, who were distinctly explained to give the participant a good overview about the potential functionality of every modality. For a better understanding, every description was also accompanied by an explanatory picture. Recruiting the participants, the invitations for the online questionnaire were sent using a type of "snowball" sample. At first, known email distribution lists were used followed by announcements on two social networking sites as well as threads were started on five different car-related websites. These invitations not only asked to answer the questions, but also to pass it to other people who might be interested. After the first few days with less than 100 responses the "snowball" picked up momentum and we received 413 responses (fully and partially completed). The data from this study were used to calculated the TAM scales and to conduct a qualitative analysis.

4.2   Results

301 Participants (115 female, 186 male) fully completed the questionnaire for all three TAM scales. The participant age ranged from 17 to 76 (M= 28.55 years; SD = 9.46 years). Before computing the TAM scales (PU, EOU, BI) the internal consistency was computed (Cronbach's alpha: > 0.8). To calculate the differences in acceptance between the three design concepts, a repeated measures ANOVA was conducted. The results show a significant main effect for the within subject factor ($F[12.576] = 15.571$, $p < 0.005$) resulting in a greater acceptance of the single touch (c1). Factors influencing acceptance emerged from the general low values for EOU and BI in contrast to a high PU value. Related to the strong participant apprehensions found in the qualitative data, the analysis shows that perceived functionality, perceived security and perceived quality cover most of the users' apprehensions towards all innovative input modalities.

5   Touch Screen Steering Wheel Distraction Study

The following study was designed to investigate the effect of IVIS-related tasks on the primary driving performance. Putting the focus on the highly accepted and promising touch display approach, it was decided not to investigate the two other concepts. Studying the driving performance, ten secondary tasks were designed (seven single touch related tasks and three other not IVIS related tasks) and evaluated. The seven single touch tasks were: music source change (change the music source by choosing music from the hard drive); navigation entry (insert city name by entering the letters and start navigation); make phone call (open address book and call Steve), radio station (save the designated radio station); map navigation (search city on the map and start navigation); sound adjustment (set the volume fader settings to front), climate control (increase the ventilation setting). The three other tasks not IVIS related tasks were: take coins (take 3 coins with 30 cent out of a purse), unfold tissue (unfold a tissue and put it on the passenger seat) unwrap candy (unwrap a candy to eat it).

As proposed by Harbluk et al. the single touch tasks were separated in three different levels of complexity (low, medium and high demand) [8]. The classification was justified through a pretest and rated by the task durance, interaction steps and combination of different interaction styles (e.g. point and touch, drag and drop). In order of their increasing difficulty the tasks were assigned to the demand levels I-III.

5.1   Study Setup

Since the tasks were considered to be highly distracting for the subjects and therefore dangerous, a driving simulator was chosen. The presented study used a fixed-base driving simulator consisting of a driving seat, a steering wheel (including the prototype), pedals and a 50" monitor mounted on a console. One PC with a high performance graphic card was used for visualizing the lane change test (LCT) simulation. Another PC was needed for the software prototype on the steering wheel, while a third PC enabled a video surveillance of the simulator setup (see figure 2). To explore the distraction of touch interaction on a steering wheel, we implemented a fully functional piece of software within a touchscreen steering wheel prototype. The prototype consists of a flash-based software program (enables the interaction with e.g. music player, navigation, phone) and the hardware configuration (touch display 6,5" & steering wheel framework) the interaction characteristics were derived from state of the art in-car touch screen IVIS as well as the interface design. We measured the driver distraction with the standardized Lane Change Test (LCT), an assessment methodology that is easy to implement and quick to conduct [10]. The LCT simulates a straight three-lane road with a track distance of three kilometers. The driving speed is constantly limited to 60km/h to avoid speeding related distraction. Frequently appearing signs (18 in total) are marking the correct line the subjects have to use. Therefore, the subjects were instructed to change the lane as soon as they could recognize the designated sign. Simultaneously, they performed IVIS related tasks on the

Fig. 2. LCT test setup with a fixed-base driving simulator

steering wheel. As a result, it is assumed that the mean lane deviation from the ideal driving line provides the metric for comparison between the three different task demand levels (low, medium, high). Following the standardized LCT setup requirements, the driving performance under dual task conditions (driving & interaction) is calculated against a normative model of primary task performance to measure distraction. As a result the impaired lateral control (Mdev) reflects the extent to which each of the three demand levels results in increased distraction. A more in-depth description about the LCT can be found in Bruyas et al. [2]. The conduction of the ten secondary tasks were expected to influence the primary task performance (driving) according to their complexity. Hence a comparison with other IVIS designs seems fruitful to examine the distraction of the prototype. However, the study would mainly result in a rating of different IVIS in relation to their distraction level, a comparison with a baseline in-car distraction was considered as more promising in a first step. A standard driving task without performing any secondary task was defined as a baseline (no IVIS distraction) for comparison. The distraction caused by the three physical tasks (coin, tissue, candy) was determined as a second baseline for in-car distraction to be compared with the distraction of the secondary interaction tasks.

5.2   Experimental Design

The simulator part of the experiment was divided into three main stages. First, we acquainted the subjects with the simulator environment and allowed them to familiarize themselves with the simulator controls (about 3 minutes). Second, a complete turn (3 kms) was performed by each subject according to the lane change requirements to get a baseline condition without interaction influences. Third, they performed the ten secondary tasks. Assistance was given at the beginning of every task and the subjects could practice the task repeatedly until they felt comfortable with it. At the end of every task, the LCT software was reset and a new track was randomly chosen (different starting positions).

To investigate the subjective perceptions regarding the acceptance towards the touch screen steering wheel, we designed a questionnaire based on the same key elements as used in the first questionnaire study. The secondary task demand was the within subject factor. The learning effects did not need to be considered, since the scenarios did not involve any unexpected simulated traffic scenarios.

5.3   Analysis and Results

We invited 5 female and 5 male participants. The age ranged from 23 to 36 and their driving experience from 2 to 18 years. In terms of mileage, the subjects varied from below 5000 to 40000 kms annual distance travelled. We experienced no case of simulator sickness within our sample group. As a measure of distraction the deviation between a normative model and the driven path of the subject was calculated (as an example, figure 3 shows the normative model data (green line) the driven path (outer red line) and the deviation (red area)). The calculated deviation data represents the quality of the driver's performance, namely the perception (delayed or failed perception of the road signs), the quality of the maneuver (larger deviation trough slower lane changes) and lane keeping quality (unsteady lane keeping also results in increased deviation).The mean duration for task completion varied widely from 2.7s to 87.3s. We determined the participants' average deviation (see figure 4(a)) and carried out an Analysis of Variance (ANOVA). The main effect between the groups was significant ($F(2.48) = 64.3$, $p < 0.001$) indicating the affection by the different conditions (descriptives see figure 4(b)). Multiple comparisons (Post Hoc Scheffe) revealed significant differences between the baseline condition and all task demand levels ($p < 0.001$). Therefore, all tasks can be described as distracting. No difference in distraction appeared between baseline I & II and between baseline II and task demand level I (easy interaction). The results also revealed significant differences between all connections of task demand level I, II and III ($p < 0.001$). Based on the significant differences in lateral deviation (see figure 3), the task demand levels II (Mdev=0.71) & III (Mdev=1.03) turned out to decrease driving performance most. The analysis of the subsequently completed questionnaire revealed that the subjects rated the touch interaction on the steering wheel high (4,11 on a 5-point Likert scale). Based on the TAM questionnaire, the high acceptance of the touch display (c1) could be assessed.

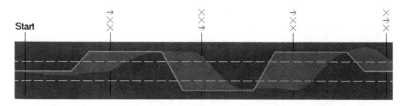

Fig. 3. Graphical representation of the lateral deviation between the normative model and the driven path

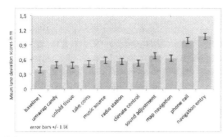

LCT Deviation			
Condition	Mean (m)	SD	SD Error
Baseline I	0.39	0.08	0.02
Baseline II	0.49	0.09	0.03
Task D. Level I	0.55	0.94	0.03
Task D. Level II	0.71	0.09	0.03
Task D. Level III	1.03	0.14	0.04

(a) Calculated mean lane deviation by tasks

(b) Mean lateral deviation for baselines and task demand levels

Fig. 4. Lateral mean deviation for single tasks and combined demand levels

6   Conclusion and Future Work

In this paper, we proposed the reduction of driver's distraction by applying automotive interaction modalities that can be found on the steering wheel. For all three systems, differences in user acceptance regarding all three UA factors were found, with the overall better rated single touch (c1). Focusing on concept (c1), the second study revealed enhanced distraction for the medium and high demand levels tasks. Low demand tasks showed distraction on the same level as the physical tasks. So we conclude that low demand tasks (e.g. list selection) on a touch screen steering wheel can be performed without increased standard distraction and hence such a device is ideal for an ambient environment.

Our findings show that the integration of a single touch in the steering wheel is a promising approach to centralize input and output modalities on one place. It provides the user with the possibility to interact with a IVIS without the need to move the hand off the steering wheel. So far we have focused on already existing tertiary task in the car (e.g. navigation entry). Another possibility of the touch screen is the visualization of ambient information like the adaption of information visualization on the context (e.g. a tachometer changes size or color depending on speed or the driver's condition). Regarding the range of available context information we are optimistic that this will bring the development of the intelligent steering wheel a step further.

In future work we plan to support the reliability of our results with a prototype iteration. While the simulator study reported in this paper focused on differences in task demands, another benefit might have a bigger impact on the deployment of ambient information: By separating physical input and visual output, the driver is supported in focusing on the primary driving task. The limitation of the peripheral sight through the acute viewing angle on the steering wheel could be abrogated trough the positioning of an ambient display as visual output in the top of the central console. This constellation allows the driver to control the IVIS via touch on the steering wheel while having the ambient output in the road related field of view.

Acknowledgements. The financial support by the Federal Ministry of Economy, Family and Youth and the National Foundation for Research, Technology and Development is gratefully acknowledged (Christian Doppler Laboratory for Contextual Interfaces).

References

1. Bach, K.M., Jaeger, M.G., Skov, M.B., Thomassen, N.G.: You can touch, but you can't look: interacting with in-vehicle systems. In: CHI 2008: Proc. SIGCHI on Human Factors in Computing Systems, pp. 1139–1148. ACM, NY (2008)
2. Bruyas, M., Brusque, C., Auriault, A., Tattegrain, H., Aillerie, I., Duraz, M.: Impairment of lane change performance due to distraction: effect of experimental contexts. In: Proc. of Humanist 2008 (2008)
3. Burnett, G., Summerskill, S.J., Porte, J.: On-the-move destination entry for vehicle navigation systems: unsafe by any means? Behaviour and Information Technology 23, 265–272 (2004)
4. Davis, F., Venkatesh, V.: Toward preprototype user acceptance testing of new information systems: implications for software project management. IEEE Engineering Management 51(1), 31–46 (2004)
5. Döring, T., Kern, D., Marshall, P., Pfeiffer, M., Schöning, J., Gruhn, V., Schmidt, A.: Gestural interaction on the steering wheel: reducing the visual demand. In: Proc. of CHI 2011, pp. 483–492. ACM, NY (2011)
6. Ecker, R., Broy, V., Butz, A., De Luca, A.: Pietouch: a direct touch gesture interface for interacting with in-vehicle information systems. In: Proc. of MobileHCI 2009, pp. 1–10. ACM, NY (2009)
7. Feld, M., Schwartz, T., Müller, C.: This Is Me: Using Ambient Voice Patterns For In-Car Positioning. In: de Ruyter, B., Wichert, R., Keyson, D.V., Markopoulos, P., Streitz, N., Divitini, M., Georgantas, N., Mana Gomez, A. (eds.) AmI 2010. LNCS, vol. 6439, pp. 290–294. Springer, Heidelberg (2010)
8. Harbluk, J., Mitroi, J., Burns, P.: Three navigation systems with three tasks: using the lane-change test (LCT) to assess distraction demand. In: Human Factors in Driver Assessment, Training and Vehicle Design (2009)
9. Kern, D., Schmidt, A., Arnsmann, J., Appelmann, T., Pararasasegaran, N., Piepiera, B.: Writing to your car: handwritten text input while driving. In: Proc Human Factors, CHI EA 2009, pp. 4705–4710. ACM, New York (2009)
10. Mattes, S.: The lane change task as a tool for driver distraction evaluation. In: Strasser, H., Rausch, H., Bubb, H. (eds.) Quality of Work and Products in Enterprises of the Future, pp. 57–60. Ergonomia Verlag, Stuttgart (2003)
11. Meschtscherjakov, A., Wilfinger, D., Scherndl, T., Tscheligi, M.: Acceptance of future persuasive in-car interfaces towards a more economic driving behaviour. In: Proc. of AutomotiveUI 2010, pp. 81–88. ACM (2009)
12. Phithakkitnukoon, S., Veloso, M., Bento, C., Biderman, A., Ratti, C.: Taxi-Aware Map: Identifying and Predicting Vacant Taxis in the City. In: de Ruyter, B., Wichert, R., Keyson, D.V., Markopoulos, P., Streitz, N., Divitini, M., Georgantas, N., Mana Gomez, A. (eds.) AmI 2010. LNCS, vol. 6439, pp. 86–95. Springer, Heidelberg (2010)
13. Rydström, A., Bengtsson, P., Grane, C., Broström, R., Agardh, J., Nilsson, J.: Multifunctional systems in vehicles: a usability evaluation. In: Proc. of CybErg 2005, pp. 768–775(8). Ergonomics Association Press, Johannesburg (2005)
14. Schmidt, A., Spiessl, W., Kern, D.: Driving automotive user interface research. IEEE Pervasive Computing 9(1), 85–88 (2010)
15. Strayer, D.L., Drews, F.A.: Cell-phone induced driver distraction. Current Directions in Psychological Science 16(3), 128–131 (2007)

Table-Top Interface Using Fingernail Images and Real Object Recognition

Kenta Hara[1], Noriko Takemura[1], Yoshio Iwai[2], and Kosuke Sato[1]

[1] Graduate School of Engineering Science, Osaka University,
Machikaneyama 1-3, Toyonaka, Osaka 560-8531, Japan
[2] Graduate School of Engineering, Tottori University,
4-101, Koyamachominami, Tottori-shi, Tottori, Japan 680-8552
{hara,takemura,sato}@sens.sys.es.osaka-u.ac.jp,
iwai@ike.tottori-u.ac.jp

Abstract. Many researchers have proposed the development of table-top interfaces in the last decade. In a table-top system, for user satisfaction, they must be able to operate digital and analog media seamlessly. In this paper, we propose a table-top interface system that allows users to intuitively operate digital media by gesture recognition. The proposed system can capture the image of an object placed on the table by recognizing pressing gestures from fingernail images, and can transfer digital content by recognizing user's shaking gestures. The evaluation experiments show that users can intuitively operate the proposed system without being aware of the data transmission.

Keywords: table-top interface, object recognition, gesture recognition, fingernail image.

1 Introduction

Recently, many researchers have proposed the development of table-top interfaces and electronic book (e-book) devices, especially to support the wide distribution of e-book among the generic public. However, when a user simultaneously interacts with digital and physical media through an e-book device, complicated operations of data transmission to and from the e-book device adversely affect user convenience and satisfaction. This is because of the difference in operations between the physical space and the digital space. For example, when a user handles an object such as a document on the table-top display that shows digital content, a burdensome operation of transmission, such as scanning, prevents the user from intuitively operating the digital media as if it were physical media.

Ways of data exchange between users differ in digital and physical media. They can place physical documents on a table and pick them up easily; however, in order to exchange digital data, users have to transmit them by sending an e-mail or using some type of storage media such as USB flash drives and SD cards. In order to bridge the gap in data transmission between digital and physical media, a system that provides intuitive operations for data transmission is required.

D. Keyson et al. (Eds.): AmI 2011, LNCS 7040, pp. 21–30, 2011.

In this paper, we propose a system that allows users to interact with digital content by using physical gestures that will help in modeling the operations of document handling on a table. The proposed system recognizes a pressing gesture captured from a user's fingernail image by a high-mounted camera, of which the user is unaware. The system also recognizes shaking and tapping gestures from sensors incorporated in an e-book device that trigger data transmission between digital and physical media.

2   Related Studies

2.1   Gesture Recognition

A touch panel, such as a table-top system, has been conventionally used for integrating input and output spaces, and several other systems that use touch panel have been proposed. Sugita et al. proposed a method for detection of contact on a surface and estimation of the direction of fingertip pressure by detecting a change of fingernail color when the fingertip touches a hard object[1]. When the user's finger pressed a surface, the fingernail color turned white and the brightness of the fingernail image varied significantly. Therefore, whether the finger stayed – in contact or not – was determined by the variance threshold. The pressing direction was estimated by detecting the origin of pressure change on the fingertips. Although this method enables touch sensing everywhere, there is a hardware restriction because this method requires a high-resolution fingertip image. Enhanced Desk, proposed by Oka et al., recognized user gestures by processing images using a camera[2]. However, this system did not attempt to recognize whether the user touched the surface. Han et al. proposed an input method based on frustrated total internal reaction (FTIR) phenomenon[3]. This system not only supported multi touch gestures but could also be applied to larger equipments. However, it could not detect gestures when a hand was not in contact with the surface of this system. Currently, touch panels are certainly inexpensive and already available in the general consumer market. However, their sensing area is limited to the surface of the display.

In our system, fingernail image analysis is adopted to detect not only positions but also states of fingers. By limiting the system to pressing gesture recognition and by introducing a novel method for estimating fingertip states, the proposed system can recognize states from low-resolution images. Thus, high-resolution images are not required; a camera can be mounted at a high position so that the user is not aware of it. Moreover, this method enlarges the sensing area of the surface of not only the display but also the object placed on a table.

2.2   Table-Top Systems

When users work in an environment where physical and digital media are combined, they prefer to use an intuitive interface that maps a movement in the real world to digital operations. Various systems that attempt to achieve this capability have been proposed(e.g., [4], [5]). These systems projected digital documents and images on real-world objects or used a table as a display which allowed users to operate them with their fingers.

Hartmann et al. proposed a system that supported collaborative work by capturing images of real objects placed on a desk and projecting it[6]. When an object was recognized, digital handles were projected around the corners of the object; the user could capture the object's image onto the table by dragging the handle with his or her finger. However, this system required a complicated hardware setting, and it did not support a more intuitive operation of pointing to the object itself rather than that to the digital handle. Snap Table, proposed by Koshimizu et al., enabled users to transfer digital documents or images displayed on a table to an e-paper device by using physical gestures[7]. A photo-addressable e-paper was used so that digital media could be immediately transferred to the e-paper device. However, this system required prior access to digital documents, because it did not support capturing data from real media.

As mentioned above, our proposed system can recognize pressed states of fingertips, such that the user can directly press down a real object placed on a table into a display that is digital space. Moreover, this system provides a novel feedback to users, which is not provided by the conventional method. Moreover, as an extension of the operations performed with documents placed on the table, this system allows users to transfer digital media between the table and an e-book device by using gestures. Through these processes, the proposed system enables users to interact more seamlessly with physical and digital space.

3 System Overview

3.1 Process Flow

Fig. 1. shows the process flowchart of the proposed system. Images of a table-top display are captured by a camera mounted high over the table. The system estimates the positions of an object placed on a table, a user's fingertip, and an e-book device. From the captured images, the system also estimates the state of the fingertip by recognizing pressing gestures and the relationship of the e-book device and the object on the table. Using this information, the system interacts with the user by updating the table-top display and communicating with the e-book device.

3.2 Pressing Gesture Recognition

First, the system extracts the skin region H from the captured image. In this paper, we assume that region H is regarded as the region of the hand. Fingertip region T is determined from region H. Finger positions are defined as the centers of each fingertip region T, and sub images of each fingertip region T are normalized into an image H_f with a size of 10×10 [pixels]. The fingertip image H_f is defined as a 300-dimensional feature vector (10×10 [pixels]$\times$RGB). The state of a fingertip is determined by a linear discriminant function that is generated by the support vector machine (SVM) (Fig. 2). In the SVM-based method,

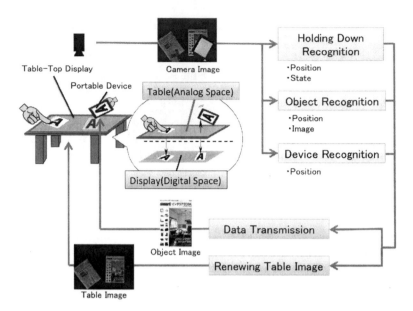

Fig. 1. Process flow of proposed system

the maximum-margin hyperplane can be obtained and suitable generalization performance can be achieved.

T is determined by scanning region H in raster-scan order using an $n \times n$ window R as follows:

$$T = \left\{ (x,y) \, \middle| \, [(x,y) \in H] \wedge \left[t_{min} < \frac{1}{n^2} \sum_{p=x-\frac{n}{2}}^{x+\frac{n}{2}-1} \sum_{q=y-\frac{n}{2}}^{y+\frac{n}{2}-1} g(p,q) < t_{max} \right] \right\} \quad (1)$$

where t_{min} and t_{max} are determined empirically and $g(p,q)$ is defined as

$$g(p,q) = \begin{cases} 1 & \text{if } (p,q) \in H, \\ 0 & \text{if } (p,q) \notin H. \end{cases} \quad (2)$$

The number of skin-color pixels in window R is counted in real time because the system uses an integral image technique[8].

(a)   Non-pressed   (b) Pressed

Fig. 2. Change in fingernail color with pressing gesture

3.3   Table Image Update

When an object is placed on a table, the region of the object is extracted from an input color image by background subtraction using V-value in the HSV color space. When the difference between the centroid points of the region in the current frame and those in the previous frame is smaller than a certain threshold, the captured region is determined to be the object region. The system stores the captured image in the storage for future use.

When the system is in this state, the user can select an object from the ones placed on the table by pressing the object on the table surface. The pressing gesture is recognized from H_f described in the previous section. In order to reduce errors in recognition, the system recognizes the user's pressing gesture only when the discrimination function recognizes pressing gestures during a certain time t_{step}. When the system recognizes the user's pressing gesture, the system updates the table-top image by using the captured object image described in the previous section. In this way, the proposed system uses an intuitive operation that allows an object placed on the table to be captured from the table-top by using a pressing gesture.

3.4   Bidirectional Transmission between Table and E-Book Device

Four color markers are attached at each corner of an e-book device in order to estimate the position of the e-book device from a captured image. The e-book device is detected when the distance and angle between same color markers are smaller than certain threshold values. This process is required to distinguish the device from objects on the table. When the e-book device is detected, the position of the e-book device, P_{pad}, is estimated from the geometry of the markers.

After the position estimation, the system starts a session to communicate between the e-book device and the table. The communication application in the e-book device has two modes – receive and send – and these modes get activated by shaking or tapping gestures. A shaking gesture is recognized by using an accelerometer in the e-book device, while a tapping gesture is recognized by using a touch sensor in the e-book device.

During the receive mode, the user selects an object from the table-top image and holds the e-book device over the object while performing a shaking gesture. When the system detects the e-book device and estimates its position P_{pad}, it retrieves an object image corresponding to P_{pad} from the storage. When the e-book device recognizes a shaking gesture or a touching gesture, it receives the retrieved object image from the table-top system through a wireless network and displays the image (Fig. 3 (a)).

During the send mode, the user selects an image on the e-book device that has to be sent and then performs a shaking gesture over any position on the table. When the e-book device recognizes the shaking gesture, it sends the image to the table-top system through a wireless network. When the table-top system receives the image, it displays the image at position P_{pad} (Fig. 3 (b)).

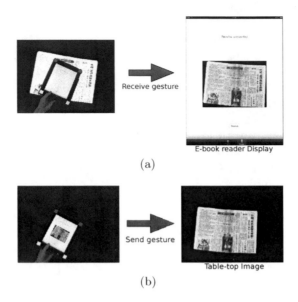

(a)

(b)

Fig. 3. Bidirectional transmission

4 Evaluation

4.1 Experimental Setup

Fig. 4. shows the configuration of the proposed system. Since the camera is installed at a height of two meters, images of the entire display can be captured, which enables users to interact easily with any part of the display. The table-top interface is developed by attaching a clear acrylic plate onto the display. The resolution of the camera is 800×600 [pixels] and the frame rate is 15 [fps]. The Apple iPad is used as the e-book device.

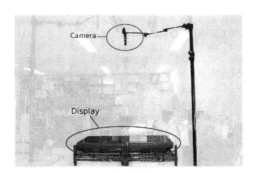

Fig. 4. Overview of experimental system

4.2 Experiments of Pressing Gesture Recognition

In order to confirm the effectiveness of our discrimination method, we conducted experiments with 14 subjects and compared our method to the conventional method[1]. Nine thousand fingernail images were obtained as training data from eight men and women in their 20s. Tables 1. and 2. show the recognition rate of subjects whose data was gathered during training and that of the other subjects, respectively. These tables indicate that our method performs better than the conventional method. The recognition rate of subjects whose data was obtained during training is 90.2%, which confirms the effectiveness of our method.

We also examined the relationship between the gesture recognition rate and the time needed for recognition t_{step}(Fig. 5.). A pressing gesture and a non-pressing gesture were performed for 30 [s] by five of the subjects whose data was used for training, and these gestures were recognized with each t_{step} varied from 0 [s] to 5 [s] at intervals of 0.25 [s]. The recognition rate varies with changes in t_{step}, and when t_{step} is 1 [s], up to 98% recognition rate was obtained.

Table 1. Recognition rate(trained subjects)

	Press	Non-press	Average
Proposed	**92.8%**	**87.7%**	**90.2%**
Conventional	73.2%	87.1%	80.2%

Table 2. Recognition rate(untrained subjects)

	Press	Non-press	Average
Proposed	**88.8%**	79.3%	**84.1%**
Conventional	72.9%	**87.4%**	80.2%

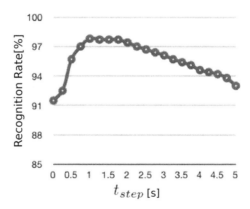

Fig. 5. Recognition rate of each t_{step}

4.3 Evaluation of System Usability

In these experiments, 14 subjects performed two tasks: capturing objects and transferring contents between the table and the iPad. The system was evaluated subjectively by a questionnaire.

In the operation of capturing objects, the subjects captured several objects sequentially. We compared three methods used to capture objects : (1) capturing by pressing the table (the proposed method), (2) pointing to out of reach objects, and (3) using a mouse to click on an object image displayed on an additional window. The subjects performed the task using these three methods. In the operation of transferring content between the table and the iPad, the subjects transferred the captured image on the display to the iPad and then transferred the transferred image in the iPad to the table. We employed a tapping gesture on the display of the iPad and a shaking gesture of the iPad as gestures for triggering the transfer. The subjects performed both gestures in this experiment.

After the tasks were completed, the system was evaluated subjectively with the following questionnaire for each of the two tasks. The subjects selected a number along a scale, like "1" for very dissatisfied and "5" for very satisfied.

Q1. Was it easy to remember how to perform the operations?
Q2. Could you perform the operations as wanted to?
Q3. Do you feel that the operating action was natural?
Q4. Could you perform the operations without detecting digital processing?
Q5. How attractive was the operation you performed?

According to the results, the responses to Q4 are significantly different between the methods in terms of both capture operation and communication operation (Fig. 6.). When the subjects answered the questions about the capture operation, the responses to Q1 and Q2 were high in all the methods and there was not much difference between them. The evaluations of Q3 and Q5 in the proposed method were higher compared to the others, and there was a 5% level of significant difference. When the subjects answered the questions about communication, the shaking gesture was evaluated higher than the button operation in Q4 responses. And, responses to Q5 are higher than their median in both.

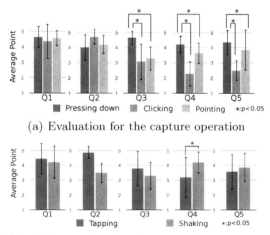

(a) Evaluation for the capture operation

(b) Evaluation for the communication operation

Fig. 6. Questionnaire responses for system usability

5   Discussion

From the experimental results in Section 4.2, we observed that the proposed system is advantageous over the previous system because the recognition rate of the proposed system is higher than that of the previous system regardless of the fact that the data were collected during training. In the previous system, the recognition of a pressing gesture was performed using a fingertip image that had a size of 20×20 [pixels]. Although the image size was 10×10 [pixels] in the proposed system, the proposed system shows better recognition performance than the previous system. Moreover, the results show that the proposed system can even handle small fingertip images.

As shown in Table 2., the recognition rate for untrained subjects is 84.1%, which is lower than that for trained subjects, but it is higher than that of the previous method. For some subjects, however, the recognition rate is very low because there was no fingernail color variation in the fingertip images of these subjects, which is considered as a different situation in the training data.

Because the accuracy of recognition of pressing gestures depends on the training data, the accuracy is degraded when the color variation is very different from the training data. In real-life situations, the number of users of a desk is limited. When the users are identified in advance, training data are collected from them and the recognition rate reaches 90%, as shown in Table 1. Fig. 5. shows an improvement in the recognition rate, which occurred by changing the duration time t_{step}; when t_{step} is set to around 1 [s], the recognition rate reaches 98%.

Pointing and pressing gestures have the same performance results as mouse operations for typical computer applications because the evaluation of an operation in the proposed system is equal to that in the conventional systems, as demonstrated from the results in Q1 and Q2 in Section 4.3. The recognition rate of pressing gestures is large enough to satisfy the user and does not prevent operability. As shown in Fig. 6. (a), the capturing of an object using a pressing gesture is similar to a user's mental model that an object is pressed onto the table by pushing the object. The users can perform an operation without discomfort and the system is evaluated highly in Q5 for the above reason.

The responses for the communication operation are significantly different with 5% error level, as shown in Fig. 6. (b), and the shaking gesture is evaluated highly because the user can seamlessly perform the operation without being aware of any digital process. The use of gestures is effective in concealing digital processes. The evaluations of both shaking and pressing gestures are attractive, as shown by the results of Q5, and the method used to select an object by holding the iPad over the object is naturally accepted. Three of the subjects failed to hold the iPad over a real object before the system captured an image of the object. From this observation, we realized that some subjects did not differentiate between real objects and object images during the experimental tasks. This phenomenon fulfilled our final goal of this study, which is filling the usability gap between real objects and digital data.

6 Conclusion

In this paper, we have proposed an interface in which mental models in the real world can be applied to an operation against digital data in an environment consisting of a table-top display and an e-book device.

In the proposed system, digital media and a real object can be dealt with simultaneously without a feeling of unfamiliarity. The system allows the user to interact with digital media using specific predefined gestures such as pressing a finger on a table-top display and shaking gestures of a device. In this system, we proposed a method for recognizing a pressing gestures on the basis of a fingernail image with a size of 10×10 [pixels]. We built a prototype system and confirmed that our recognition method is effective and that our interaction method does not cause users to feel unfamiliar or uncomfortable.

Improving the recognition accuracy and speed are our future goals. We also aim to improve the method for achieving a more comfortable interaction.

References

1. Sugita, N., Iwai, D., Sato, K.: Touch Sensing by Image Analysis of Fingernail. In: SICE Annual Conference, pp. 1520–1525 (2008)
2. Koike, H., Sato, Y., Kobayashi, Y.: Integrating Paper and Digital Information on EnhancedDesk: A Method for Realtime Finger Tracking on a Augmented Desk System. ACM Transactions on Computer-Human Interaction 8(4) (December 2001)
3. Han, J.Y.: Low-cost Multi-touch Sensing through Frustrated Total Internal Reflection. In: Symposium on User Interface Software and Technology, pp. 115–118 (2005)
4. Kane, S.K., Avrahami, D., Wobbrock, J.O., Harrison, B., Rea, A., Philipose, M., LaMarca, A.: Bonfire: A Nomadic System for Hybrid Laptop-Tabletop Interaction. In: Symposium on User Interface Software and Technology, pp. 129–138 (2009)
5. Iwai, D., Sato, K.: Limpid Desk: See-Through Access to Disorderly Desktop in Projection-Based Mixed Reality. In: Symposium on Virtual Reality Software and Technology, pp. 112–115 (2006)
6. Hartmann, B., Moriss, M.R., Benko, H., Wilson, A.D.: Pictionaire: Supporting Collaborative Design Work by Integrating Physical and Digital Artifacts. In: Conference on Computer Supported Cooperative Work, pp. 421–424 (2010)
7. Koshimizu, M., Hayashi, N., Hirose, Y.: SnapTable: Physical Handling for Digital Documents for Electronic Paper. In: The Third Nordic Conference on Human Computer, pp. 401–404 (2004)
8. Viola, P., Jones, M.: Rapid object detection using a boosted cascade of simple features. In: IEEE Computer Society Conference on Computer Vision and Pattern Recognition, pp. 511–518 (2001)

Discrimination of Multiple Objects and Expanding Positioning Area for Indoor Positioning Systems Using Ultrasonic Sensors

Hikaru Sunaga, Takashi Hada, Masaki Akiyama,
Shigenori Ioroi, and Hiroshi Tanaka

Kanagawa Institute of Technology,
1030 Shimo-ogino, Atugi-shi, Kanagawa, Japan
{s1085033,s1085046,s1185006}@cce.kanagawa-it.ac.jp,
{ioroi,h_tanaka}@ic.kanagawa-it.ac.jp

Abstract. This paper describes new concepts and techniques for an indoor positioning system that uses ultrasonic signals to enhance practicability. This indoor positioning system can be applied to the location detection of a moving object such as a person or a goods trolley over a wide indoor area. The proposed system works by means of ultrasonic signals. This makes it easy to avoid multipath effects because the propagation velocity of ultrasonic signals is much slower than that of radio waves. In addition, ultrasonic signals are not restricted by radio regulations that may differ from country to country. The main feature of our system, developed and presented last year, is that it does not require synchronization between the transmitting and receiving units. This paper describes a system for accommodating multiple moving objects and expanding positioning area. Two techniques, the allocation of a specific ID to each positioning object and the use of a virtual receiving point for ultrasonic signals, were investigated in order to realize the required functions and make the proposed system more practical. The effectiveness of these techniques was confirmed by experiments carried out using ultrasonic sensors installed in the ceiling and model railway trains acting as moving objects on the floor below.

Keywords: Indoor positioning, Ultrasonic signal, FPGA, Area expansion, Moving objects.

1 Introduction

The global positioning system (GPS) is widely used for determining position in outdoor areas. It has become a universal system and the location information provided by GPS is widely used in navigation devices and many other service systems [1]-[2]. However, for indoor positioning applications, no common system has yet been established and various possibilities are being investigated. Position information is an indispensable requirement for the realization of "smart space", which can, for example, be used to assist navigation for the visually impaired and can supply helpful information to people

D. Keyson et al. (Eds.): AmI 2011, LNCS 7040, pp. 31–40, 2011.

regarding appropriate location and timing for various indoor activities.   Many
applications can make use of location information.

Fig.1 summarizes the different categories of indoor positioning system currently
available, taking positioning accuracy and positioning range into consideration.   The
received signal strength of RF signals from wireless LANs (WLAN) etc., using the so
called "Received Signal Strength Indicator" (RSSI), has been used to determine
position in an indoor area [3]-[4].   However, signal strength is heavily influenced by
multipath effects and it is quite difficult to accurately identify the distance between
the receiving unit and the transmitting unit.   Consequently, the positioning accuracy
that is derived from such distance information is quite low.   In addition, the actual
multipath effects are dependent on the room layout.   As a result, this type of system
cannot be applied for practical use in situations where accurate positioning is
required.   An alternative system based on the propagation time difference and the use
of ultra wide band (UWB) has been proposed, but accuracy is not yet adequate for
pedestrian navigation and product tracking in indoor areas.   A system using RFIDs
could be one solution, but since the propagation distance is quite short a lot of RFID
tags would be needed to construct a suitable positioning system over a wide area.

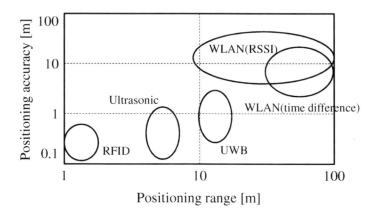

Fig. 1. Categories of indoor positioning systems

Positioning systems based on the use of ultrasonic signals seem to be a promising
alternative. Conventional systems are usually based on the principle of trilateration [5],
in which, the distance between two points is measured by the difference in propagation
time of radio signals and ultrasonic signals [6].   The propagation time of radio signals
can be neglected in this system.   Therefore, the difference of arrival time between radio
signals and ultrasonic signals become propagation time of ultrasonic signal between two
points.   Alternatively, time synchronization between transmitting and receiving units
can be implemented in order to detect the propagation time [7]. However, because these
systems use radio devices, they are rather complicated and must satisfy existing radio
regulations, which often differ from country to country.

Instead, we have adopted inverse GPS methods [8], in which the arrangement of
transmitting and receiving units is the reverse of that used in GPS. We have

developed an indoor positioning system based on this method and its effectiveness and positioning accuracy have been evaluated [9].   This paper describes the techniques used to realize the proposed system and the steps needed to make it more practical.

First, the use of ID transmission via an infrared signal was adopted to accommodate multiple moving objects and increase the application area of the system.   This technique makes use of an ultrasonic transmitter that is installed on the moving object and only emits an ultrasonic transmission when it receives its own ID signal.   Second, since it is desirable to expand the effective positioning area and enlarge the receiving field for ultrasonic signals (thereby reducing the number of ultrasonic detection ports required) the concept of a virtual reception point was also adopted.   An experimental system utilizing infrared devices and ultrasonic receiving units was built to verify the effectiveness of these methods.   Ultrasonic receiving sensors were installed in the ceiling and the model railroad trains moving on tracks on the floor below were used to evaluate the system experimentally.

2   Positioning Method and System Architecture

2.1   Positioning Method and System Architecture

The system configuration proposed involves the use of ultrasonic receiving sensors connected to a receiving unit embedded in the ceiling and an ultrasonic transmitter attached to a moving object below.   The basic operating principle is shown in Fig.2 [9].   Conventional positioning systems are usually based on trilateration, in which time synchronization between the transmitting unit and the receiving unit is required in order to detect the propagation time between the two components. Consequently, some mechanism is needed to establish synchronization.   However, in the proposed system, the clock of the transmission unit is independent of the receiving unit. Therefore, the propagation time cannot be obtained and only the delay times of each receiving sensor can be detected.   Here, the delay time refers to the amount of time elapsed after the first receiving sensor detects the ultrasonic signal.   Three delay times (t_1, t_2 and t_3) can be obtained from four receiving sensors as shown in Fig.2. The synchronization of all receiving sensors is maintained because they are all connected to a single receiving unit in which one clock governs all timing.

The following mathematical equations can be derived by considering the distance and propagation time.   Here, x_i, y_i, and z_i are the positions of the receiving sensors and are determined when they are embedded in the ceiling.   The constant, c, is the ultrasonic signal velocity (dependents on temperature).   The variable, t, is the propagation time from the transmitter to the receiving sensor that is the first of all the receiving sensors to receive the ultrasonic signal signal (an unknown value).   The variables t_1, t_2 and t_3 are the delay time at each receiving sensor (determined as described above).   The variables x, y, and z are the coordinates giving the position of the moving object that is attached to the transmitter (these values need to be solved). Since there are four unknown quantities (x, y, z and t), at least four receiving sensors are required in order to solve the following equations:

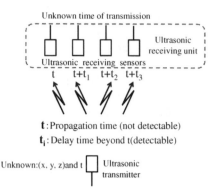

Fig. 2. Basic positioning principle

$$\sqrt{(x-x_0)^2+(y-y_0)^2+(z-z_0)^2} = ct$$

$$\sqrt{(x-x_1)^2+(y-y_1)^2+(z-z_1)^2} = c(t+t_1)$$

$$\sqrt{(x-x_2)^2+(y-y_2)^2+(z-z_2)^2} = c(t+t_2)$$ (1)

$$\sqrt{(x-x_3)^2+(y-y_3)^2+(z-z_3)^2} = c(t+t_3)$$

2.2   Prototype System Configuration

The prototype system used for verifying the effectiveness of the design proposed in this paper is shown in Fig.3, which illustrates the three components of the positioning system: the ultrasonic receiving unit, the ultrasonic transmitters (#1, #2), and the signal processing PC used for position calculation.

The ultrasonic receiving unit consists of ultrasonic receiving sensors, a FPGA and a H8 microcomputer. The output signal of each receiving sensor (Murata MA40S4R units with a diameter and height of 10mm and 7mm, respectively) is amplified by each receiving unit using an amplifier and comparator, and is detected as the arrival of the ultrasonic pulse.

An FPGA captures the ultrasonic signals from each sensor via the receiving unit and generates count values which indicate the elapsed time between ultrasonic reception and the designated time. The FPGA is capable of receiving signals from a large number of ports.   These values are then sent to the PC via the H8 microcomputer and the RS485 interface. A thermistor is used to monitor the ambient temperature since temperature information is needed to compensate for changes in the ultrasonic signal propagation velocity.

The ultrasonic transmitter installed on the moving object has an infrared light receiving sensor attached and each ultrasonic receiving unit also incorporates an infrared light emission unit. The role of this receiver and transmitter is described in the next section.

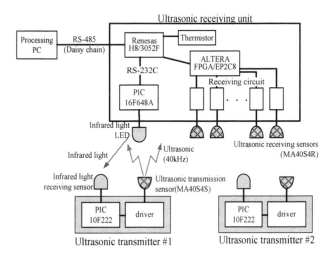

Fig. 3. System configuration

3   Accommodation of Multiple Objects

If the system proposed above is to be of any practical use, it must be able to accommodate multiple moving objects. Distinguishing each individual object is essential in order to satisfy this requirement. Therefore, an infrared signal is used to transmit a designated ID from the ultrasonic receiving unit and the ultrasonic transmitter emits ultrasonic pulses when it receives its own ID. This enables the system to distinguish each individual ultrasonic transmitter that is installed on each positioning object.

The system sequence used to obtain the received times (count values) from multiple moving objects in order to derive the delay time in expression (1) is indicated in Fig.4. The count starts when the ultrasonic receiving unit sends a trigger signal to the ultrasonic transmitter causing it to emit an ultrasonic signal. The count values are then stored in the FPGA in the receiving unit when the associated sensor connected to the receiving circuit receives the ultrasonic signal. These values are sent to the PC via the H8 microcomputer which calculates the delay times that are then used for the positioning calculations. Although only one input capture sequence is described in this figure, multiple count values are obtained from the corresponding ports connected to each ultrasonic sensor.

The delay times, t_i, shown in expression (1) are calculated from these count values by taking the clock time of the receiving unit into account. Each count value is reduced by the count value of the first sensor to receive the ultrasonic pulses (i.e., the minimum count value) in order to convert the counts into delay times. The position calculation is then carried out by taking account of the temperature, obtained as a voltage value from the thermistor, in order to determine the ultrasonic signal velocity, c. The entire sequence, from trigger signal to position calculation, is then repeated for all subsequent iterations, as shown in Fig.4.

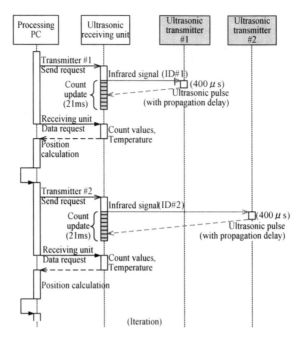

Fig. 4. System sequence

4   Expansion of Receiving Region

In order to make such a system cost effective, it is necessary to expand the receiving region. The receiving region for a single ultrasonic sensor is restricted by the receiving angle. However, if multiple sensors are combined the receiving range can be expanded. The method we used is shown in Fig.5, which illustrates how the receiving range can be expanded without having to increase the number of receiving ports for the FPGA and the number of connections from the receiving unit to the FPGA. This simplifies system installation because multiple sensors can be dealt with just as easily as a single sensor. The signals that are received from all four sensors are then composed by an OR circuit. Therefore, if anyone of the four sensors receives the ultrasonic signals, this is detected by the receiving unit.

Pre-evaluation testing confirmed that this configuration enlarges the receiving area 1.7 times, compared with the conventional method using a single sensor, when measured at a distance of 2 m from the transmitter.

When this technique is applied to the system described above, the concept of a virtual receiving point is used for position calculation. This means that although the real receiving point is the actual sensor location, a virtual receiving point is used for the positioning calculation, as shown in Fig.6. This virtual receiving point represents the location of the four receiving sensors. The following expression (2) needs to be solved whenever the receiving unit is changed in order to expand the receiving area. Here, r refers to the sensor attachment radius and r/c refers to propagation time from

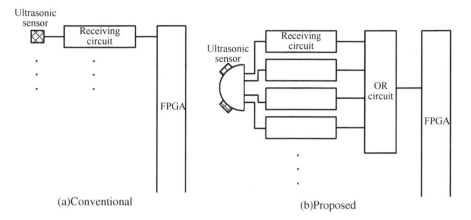

(a)Conventional   (b)Proposed

Fig. 5. Proposed method for expansion of the reception field

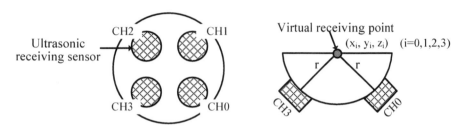

Fig. 6. Virtual receiving point

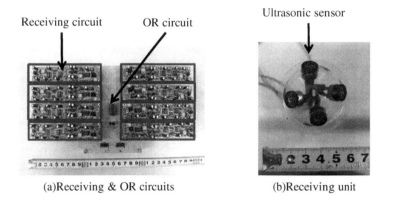

(a)Receiving & OR circuits   (b)Receiving unit

Fig. 7. Receiving circuits and receiving unit

the receiving sensor and the virtual point. The virtual point is set at the center of the sphere to which the four sensors are attached.

An illustration of the receiving circuits and the OR circuit is shown in Fig.7 (a). The four receiving sensors are built into a single receiving unit, as indicated in Fig.7 (b). The OR circuit composes the output signal from the four sensor outputs and its signal is sent to the FPGA to provide the reception timing for the ultrasonic pulse.

$$\sqrt{(x-x_0)^2+(y-y_0)^2+(z-z_0)^2}=ct$$

$$\sqrt{(x-x_1)^2+(y-y_1)^2+(z-z_1)^2}=c(t+t_1+\frac{r}{c})$$

$$\sqrt{(x-x_2)^2+(y-y_2)^2+(z-z_2)^2}=c(t+t_2+\frac{r}{c})$$ (2)

$$\sqrt{(x-x_3)^2+(y-y_3)^2+(z-z_3)^2}=c(t+t_3+\frac{r}{c})$$

5   Confirmation Experiment

5.1   Static Test for Accuracy Evaluation

The validity of the methods proposed above was confirmed by experiment. A comparison of the obtained, using expression (1) and expression (2), is shown in Table 1, including the averaging error and standard deviation. The measurement target was set up on the floor and its position was measured using the two methods described earlier. Five fixed points were set for evaluation purposes. The results indicate that positioning accuracy is not degraded by the introduction of virtual receiving points.

Table 1. Positioning accuracy

Position	Conventional(one sensor)			Proposed(four sensors)		
	Average	Positioning error	Standard deviation	Average	Positioning error	Standard deviation
X = 0	3.6	3.6	3.6	19.9	19.9	8.9
Y = 0	-18.5	18.5	4.5	-39.4	39.4	11.3
Z = 50	50.1	0.1	0.0	50.3	0.3	0.1
X = 0	12.8	12.8	3.4	-32.9	32.9	8.5
Y = 700	819.1	119.1	11.0	669.3	30.7	9.6
Z = 50	56.4	6.4	0.4	52.1	2.1	0.2
X = 0	-19.4	19.4	4.4	-48.8	48.8	10.5
Y = -700	-777.1	77.1	2.8	-720.3	20.3	15.4
Z = 50	59.4	9.4	0.1	57.7	7.7	0.4
X = 700	777.6	77.6	7.2	678.8	21.2	6.2
Y = 0	21.0	21.0	1.2	-44.3	44.3	10.5
Z = 50	59.0	9.0	0.3	56.3	6.3	6.3
X = -700	-763.8	63.8	6.5	-717.6	17.6	6.6
Y = 0	9.2	9.2	0.3	-9.4	9.4	11.1
Z = 50	55.0	5.0	0.2	53.3	3.3	0.2

(mm)

5.2   Dynamic Test for Moving Object

The practical usefulness of positioning for multiple moving objects was confirmed by experiment. The experimental apparatus used is shown in Fig.8. In this system, two model trains, each with a transmitter attached, are used as moving objects on a model railway track. The virtual positions of each receiving sensor are as indicated in the figure. The z position of the sensors installed on the frame has four locations because positioning accuracy degrades if all sensors are put in the same plane.

The experimental results obtained using this apparatus are shown in Fig.9, which illustrates the shape of the railway tracks and the positioning results (with an output

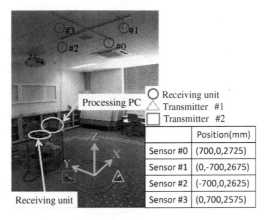

	Position(mm)
Sensor #0	(700,0,2725)
Sensor #1	(0,-700,2675)
Sensor #2	(-700,0,2625)
Sensor #3	(0,700,2575)

Fig. 8. Experimental apparatus

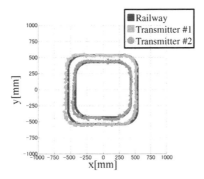

Fig. 9. Experimental results for moving objects

interval of approximately 0.5 seconds/object). The PC used in this experiment incorporated a Celeron processor and a 1.86 GHz clock rate. Consequently, if we used a higher clock rate, the output interval would be reduced because positioning calculation time is dominant. It was confirmed that the positioning error was within about 100mm in the xy plane. This should be sufficiently accurate to monitor the location of a moving person or goods trolley in an indoor area.

The possible causes of positioning error also (as shown in Table 1) are thought to be the fluctuation in count values from the FPGA that indicates the time delay, and attachment errors for the receiving sensors in the ceiling. Overall, it has been verified that the proposed system architecture and methodologies make it possible to apply the techniques described to the position detection of multiple moving objects and to expand the positioning area without degrading accuracy or increasing the number of FPGA receiving ports.

6   Conclusions

We have proposed a new positioning system for indoor use over a wide area. This system can be used to detect the position of people or moving vehicles in a factory.

The main feature of this system is that it does not require synchronization between transmitting and receiving units. Two different methods have been considered in order to make the system more practical. One of these methods involves improved discrimination to cope with the presence of multiple objects. This can be is realized by allocating a specific ID to each object and transmitting these IDs as IR signals. In addition, the concept of a virtual receiving point has also been proposed in order to expand the receiving area without increasing the number of FPGA receiving ports. A verification system was built and the validity of these methods was confirmed by experiment. This verified that the level of accuracy is sufficient to monitor the location of a person or goods vehicle within a factory, etc. The application of this system to indoor navigation for the visually impaired is a topic deserving further study. In order to produce an effective indoor navigation system, however, further expansion of the positioning area, an increase in the number of receiving sensors, and further evolution of the IR communication function used for sending navigation information will be required.

References

1. Harpter, A., Hopper, A., Steggles, P., Ward, A., Webster, P.: The Anatomy of a Context-Aware Application. Wireless Networks 8, 187–197 (2002)
2. Khalid, M., Xiaodong, L., Yuji, H., Kinji, M.: Autonomous Pull-Push Community Construction Technology for High-Assurance. IEICE Transactions on Information and Systems E92.D(10), 1836–1846 (2009)
3. Xiang, Z., Song, S., Chen, J., Wang, H., Huang, J., Gao, X.: A Wireless LAN-based Indoor Positioning Technology. IBM Journal of Research and Development 48, 617–626 (2004)
4. Gwon, Y., Jain, R., Kawahara, T.: Robust Indoor Location Estimation of Stationary and Mobile Users. In: Proceedings of the IEEE Conference on Computer Communications (INFOCOM 2004), Hong Kong, China (2004)
5. Berle, F.J.: Mixed Triangulation/trilateration Technique for Emitter Location. IEE Proc. 133(F.7), 638–641 (1986)
6. Priyantha, N., Miu, A., Balakrishnan, H., Teller, S.: The Cricket Compass for Context-aware Mobile Applications. In: Proceedings of the 7th Annual International Conference on Mobile Computing and Networking (MobiCom 2001), Rome, Italy, pp. 1–14 (2001)
7. Ward, A., Jones, A., Hopper, A.: A New Location Technique for the Active Office. IEEE Personal Communications 4(5), 42–47 (1997)
8. Homma, Y., Moriya, J., Hasegawa, T.: Comparative Experiments on Inverse GPS Based Systems Using Audible Sound or Ultrasonic Waves. IEICE Transactions on Fundamentals of Electronics, Communications and Computer Sciences J91-A(1), 139–142 (2008) (in Japanese)
9. Hada, T., Sunaga, H., Akiyama, M., Ioroi, S., Tanaka, H.: Investigation and Demonstration of Local Positioning System Using Ultrasonic Sensors for Wide Indoor Areas. In: de Ruyter, B., Wichert, R., Keyson, D.V., Markopoulos, P., Streitz, N., Divitini, M., Georgantas, N., Mana Gomez, A. (eds.) AmI 2010. LNCS, vol. 6439, pp. 280–284. Springer, Heidelberg (2010)

A Wearable User Interface for Measuring Reaction Time

Burcu Cinaz, Christian Vogt, Bert Arnrich, and Gerhard Tröster

ETH Zurich, Electronics Laboratory, Gloriastrasse 35, 8092 Zurich, Switzerland
Burcu.Cinaz@ife.ee.ethz.ch

Abstract. Reaction time (RT) tests are known as simple and sensitive tests for detecting variation in cognitive efficiency. RT tests measure the elapsed time between a stimulus and the individual's response to it. A drawback of existing RT tests is that they require the full attention of a test person which prohibits the measurement of cognitive efficiency during daily routine tasks. In this contribution we present the design and the evaluation of a wearable RT test user interface which can be operated throughout everyday life. We designed a wearable watch-like device which combines the generation of a haptic stimulus and the recognition of subject's hand movement response. In order to show to what extent the wearable RT test is convenient to measure reaction times, we designed an experiment in which we measured the reaction times of ten subjects from two different setups. In the first half of the experiment, the participants performed a desktop-based RT test whereas in the second half of the experiment they performed the wearable RT test. In order to measure changes in the duration and variability of reaction times we induced additional cognitive load in both setups. We show that individual changes of reaction times occurred due to the cognitive load manipulation are similar for both desktop-based and wearable RT test. Additionally we investigate the subjective ratings of perceived workload. We conclude that the presented wearable RT test allows to measure changes in reaction times occurred due to additional cognitive load and hence would allow the assessment of changes in cognitive efficiency throughout everyday life.

Keywords: reaction time, wearable user interface, cognitive efficiency.

1 Introduction and Motivation

Reaction time (RT) tests measure how rapidly information can be processed and a response to it can be activated [14]. In other words, RT tests measure the elapsed time between a stimulus and the individual's response to it. According to Jensen [10], RT tests are well suited for cognitive assessment tests since in comparison to conventional psychometric techniques, RT tests offer a high sensitivity for detecting variation in cognitive efficiency and they can be virtually unlimited repeated. Several desktop-based RT tests have been developed in which users have to respond to visual stimuli by using keyboard, mouse or special buttons. An extensive review about computer-based cognitive tests can be found in [20]. There are several examples on applying RT tests to assess cognitive functioning: early detection of cognitive decline such as

D. Keyson et al. (Eds.): AmI 2011, LNCS 7040, pp. 41–50, 2011.

dementia or Alzheimer's disease in elderly; determining the ability to manage complex activities such as driving, piloting or search and rescue; identifying of children with intellectual disabilities such as Attention Deficit Hyperactive Disorder (ADHD).

The main drawback of existing desktop-based RT tests is the requirement of the full attention of the subject, i.e. the subject has to interrupt his daily routine for several minutes in order to perform the task on the computer. This restriction prohibits the measurement of cognitive efficiency during daily routine tasks, e.g. to determine the ability to manage complex activities such as piloting. Our goal is to develop reaction time tests which can be operated throughout everyday life by means of wearable devices. An important step in the development is to ensure that wearable reaction time tests are suitable to measure changes in reaction times similar to desktop-based approaches.

In this paper, we present the design and the evaluation of a wearable RT test user interface. We designed a wearable watch-like device which combines the generation of haptic stimuli and the recognition of subject's responses. Haptic stimulus is generated by a vibration motor. The subject's responses to a stimulus are performed by a hand movement which is recognized with an inertial measurement unit (IMU). For the evaluation of the wearable interface, we conducted an experiment to investigate to what extent we can measure the user's reaction time with our interface compared to desktop-based tests.

2   Related Work

Three kinds of RT tests are commonly employed in literature [11]: simple, recognition and choice RT tests. Simple RT tests consist of one stimulus and one response. For instance the subject has to press a button as soon as the letter "X" appears at a predefined position or as soon as a light or sound appears. In recognition RT tests, the subject has to respond to a stimulus (target) and ignore other stimuli (non-target). This is sometimes called as "go/no-go" RT task. Recognition of a particular sound or symbol belongs to this category. Lastly, choice RT tests include multiple stimuli and multiple responses. The subject has to respond to each stimulus with a corresponding response, e.g. by pressing a certain key whenever a corresponding letter appears on the screen. A detailed series of recommendations on how to conduct experiments using reaction times and how to analyze the collected data can be found in [14], [10], [19].

Increasing age and age-related diseases like cognitive impairment are important factors which influence length and variability of reaction times [11]. It has been known that with increasing age, reaction times become more variable and longer. Gorus et al. showed that persons with cognitive deterioration demonstrated more intra-individual performance variability and more slowing in their reaction times than cognitively healthy elderly [5]. Braverman et al. showed in a clinical setting that the test of variables of attention (TOVA) is an accurate predictor of early attention complaints and memory impairments [2]. The effect of stress was investigated in an experiment which examines the cognitive performance under psychosocial stress [17]. The results showed that participants under stress were slower in their reaction times.

Another application area of RT tests is the Attention Deficit Hyperactive Disorder (ADHD) patients. Children with ADHD have often difficulties in focusing on tasks and one of the most consistent findings is increased moment-to-moment variability in reaction time [18].

Most of the studies have in common that RT tests are operated with a computerized test which requires the full attention of the subject. Since the user has to interrupt his current activity to perform the test, most of these techniques are not feasible to be used during normal life activities. There exist only a few studies which measure one's cognitive performance continuously during everyday activities. Lieberman et al. implemented visual stimuli (3 LEDs), auditory stimuli (a miniature speaker) and two push buttons on a wrist-worn device to assess vigilance [13]. Ivorra et al. implemented a haptic stimulus to interrogate the central nervous system in a minimally obtrusive way [8]. As the response, the detection of a wrist movement is defined. By doing so, they showed that a simple RT test can be continuously administered throughout the course of normal life activities. However, a comparison of the wearable implementation with desktop-based RT tests is missing.

3   Materials and Methods

3.1   Design of the Wearable Reaction Time Test

The wearable user interface to measure reaction times consists of two main modules: the stimuli module to generate haptic stimuli and the inertial measurement unit (IMU) module for detecting wrist movements. According to the literature, the wrist is a recommended stimulus site for wearable tactile displays [3], [12], [15], [16]. Therefore we designed a wrist-mounted tactile display in order to deliver the stimulus information to the user. For generating vibro-tactile stimuli, we used a coreless mini DC vibration motor with a diameter of 6mm and a resonant frequency around 200 Hz (manufactured by Precision Microdrives Ltd.). In order to maximize the vibration amplitude and to ensure a proper sense of the vibration, we placed the motor in a separate plastic enclosure resulted in WxLxH dimensions of 90x55x30mm which can be attached to the wrist of the user by using a strap. The stimuli module has its own battery supply. The vibration motor needs a continuous current of 83mA and a start current of 150mA. In a conservative calculation (continuous current of 150 mA, single stimulus duration 500ms, 160 stimuli in 12 minutes), a total of 400 mAh would be required to perform a continuous reaction time test over 24 hours. In order to guarantee a continuous operation during at least one day, we have selected a lithium ion battery with 650mAh. In addition, we have integrated an audio driver (MAX4410 by Maxim Inc.) in order to allow the generation of auditory stimuli through headphones. The IMU module consists of the ETH Orientation Sensor (ETHOS) which was developed in our laboratory [6]. The ETHOS includes a 3D accelerometer and gyroscope which allows to recognize the subject's gesture response.

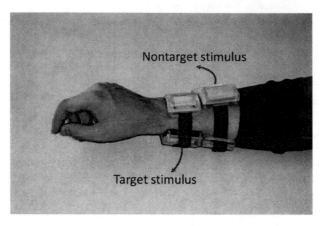

Fig. 1. Wearable implementation of a go/no-go RT test. The left module generates the target stimuli as vibrations on the lower side of the wrist, whereas the right module generates non-target stimuli on the upper side of the wrist. For both modules, the IMU is placed on the opposite side of the vibration motor to recognize the user's hand gesture response.

The accelerometer and gyroscope were sampled with a frequency of 128Hz. The detailed description of the ETHOS hardware platform can be found in [6]. We modified the firmware version of the ETHOS to control the vibro-tactile component. An implementation of a go/no-go task which is comprised of two wearable user interfaces to induce target and non-target stimuli can be seen in Fig. 1.

In order to automatically recognize a predefined hand gesture response to the haptic stimulus, we performed a preliminary experiment. Similar to the wearable RT test presented in [8], we have defined the response gesture as a fast rotation of the wrist. Three subjects performed a RT test on the wearable device during three different conditions. In the first condition, the subject was sitting on a chair while the arms were heading towards the floor. In the second condition, the arms were placed on the table. In the third condition, the subject was walking with a moderate speed (4km/h) on a treadmill. In each condition we recorded 3d acceleration and gyroscope data. Based on a visual inspection of the recorded data, we manually labeled each wrist response. For all conditions, it was clearly visible that the wrist-turn axis of the gyroscope (x-axis) was the most sensitive axis for detecting the fast rotation of the hand. In order to define a threshold for automatically detecting this hand gesture, we computed the correctly identified responses for different thresholds. With a threshold of 0.5rad/sec, we could correctly detect the occurrence of this hand gesture response in all conditions. The raw gyroscope data and the occurrence of haptic stimuli are exemplary shown in Fig. 2. According to the simple threshold approach mentioned above, we compute the time point when the user was assumed to have reacted.

3.2   Experiment: Comparison of Wearable and Desktop RT Tests

Ten healthy subjects (6 male, 4 female, average age 26.15 years) participated in our experiment. All participants were paid 30 Swiss Francs for participating in one session of approximately 70 minutes. The goal of this experiment was to evaluate our

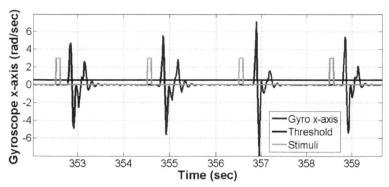

Fig. 2. X-component (wrist-turn axis) of the gyroscope data while reacting to four stimuli with a fast rotation of the hand. Based on the threshold approach the time point when a subject has reacted was computed.

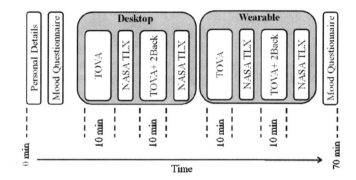

Fig. 3. Experimental procedure including two conditions (*baseline* as TOVA single task and *cognitive load* as TOVA+2Back dual-task) for each setup (desktop based RT and wearable RT)

wearable user interface by comparing the reaction times obtained by the wearable reaction time test with a desktop-based approach.

Experimental Setup. For the desktop-based reaction time test we used a free version of the TOVA test which is implemented with the psychology experiment building language (PEBL) [1]. The implementation of the test is based on the description in [4]. A white square appears briefly on the screen, with a black square within it. Participant must respond only to targets (the black square on top) and ignore the non-targets (the black square on the bottom). Each stimulus is presented for 100 ms at 2000 ms intervals. For the wearable RT test, we placed two RT modules on the dominant wrist of the user as shown in Fig. 1. The left module generates the haptic target stimuli on the lower side of the wrist (volar side), whereas the right module generates haptic non-target stimuli on the upper side of the wrist (dorsal side). Similar to the desktop-based RT test, each stimulus is generated for 100 ms at 2000 ms intervals. For recognizing the user's wrist turn response, we only use the data collected with the IMU placed opposite to the left module.

Experimental Procedure. Each setup (wearable and desktop-based) consists of two experimental conditions: (i) single-task in which the subject has to respond to the target stimulus, and (ii) dual-task in which the subject has to solve a cognitive task in parallel to the single-task. Each condition lasts 10 minutes and contains 320 stimuli (160 targets and 160 non-targets). This leads to a total of 640 reaction times for each subject (160 targets x 2 setup x 2 conditions). As cognitive task we employed a variant of the N-Back test, the so-called "Audio 2-Back" [9] as explained in the following. The four phases used for each subject are:

- *Desktop-based RT (single-task):* The subject has to respond to each target stimulus by pressing the space bar on the keyboard and ignore non-target stimuli types. This is the typical variant of the test of variables of attention (TOVA).
- *Desktop-based RT with N-Back (dual-task):* In this condition a second task is added to the traditional desktop-based TOVA test. The subject has to solve an Audio 2-Back task which is presented to the user simultaneously with the TOVA test. Thereby a letter is presented to the subject via an audio message and the subject has to respond if the currently pronounced letter is the same as the one that was pronounced 2 positions back. The response to the Audio 2-Back was done by saying "match" whenever a sound match occurs. The investigator controls if the subject answers correctly and gives feedback continuously to the user about correct and false answers to keep him concentrated on both of the tasks.
- *Wearable RT (single-task):* The subject has to respond to each target stimulus generated on the wrist by performing a wrist movement and ignore the non-target stimuli types.
- *Wearable RT with N-Back (dual-task):* The subject has to respond to target stimuli with hand movements, and solve Audio 2-Back task simultaneously.

In the following, we denote the single task of each setup as *"baseline"* and dual task as *"cognitive load"* condition. Directly after each condition for both settings, each subject was asked to indicate his perceived workload by completing the multidimensional assessment tool NASA Task Load Index (TLX) [7]. The rating consists of the following six scales: mental demand, physical demand, temporal demand, own performance, effort and frustration. Based on the ratings, the total workload was computed as a weighted average. The experimental procedure can be seen in Fig. 3.

4   Results

4.1   Reaction Times

For the analysis, the mean reaction time and the standard deviation are considered as evaluation metrics. In Table 1 and Fig. 4 the means and standard deviations of the reaction times for all subjects in each condition are presented. First, it can be observed that for both desktop and wearable RT test, the mean reaction time is always increased during the *cognitive load* condition compared to the *baseline* condition. Mean reaction times of the desktop-based RT test are significantly correlated with the wearable RT test for the *baseline* condition (r = 0.8336, P < 0.01) as well as for the *cognitive load* condition (r = 0.7070, P < 0.05). Second, it can be observed that the increase in mean reaction times from *baseline* to *cognitive load* conditions is similar within subjects for both desktop and wearable setting. The relative difference (mean RT during *cognitive load* minus mean RT during *baseline condition*) between desktop and wearable setting are significantly correlated (r = 0.7095, P <0.05). Consistently, the variability of reaction times was always higher in the *cognitive load* condition compared to the *baseline* condition for both desktop and wearable setting. No signifi-cant correlations were observed for the standard deviation of reaction times. Besides, it can be observed that for most subjects the mean reaction time in the wearable set-ting is lower compared to the desktop-based approach during *baseline* (exception is subject 9). In the *cognitive load* condition the mean wearable reaction times are again lower for most subjects (exceptions are subjects 1, 2 and 9). This might be explained by the fact that the transduction of a visual stimulus takes generally longer than the perception of a haptic stimulus as known from literature [10].

Table 1. Comparison of mean reaction times including standard deviation for the four experimental conditions

Subjects	Desktop-based Reaction Times		Wearable Reaction Times	
	Baseline[ms]	Cog. Load[ms]	Baseline[ms]	Cog. Load[ms]
1	455 (102)	560 (217)	408 (103)	574 (208)
2	375 (93)	400 (173)	351 (89)	423 (173)
3	339 (68)	455 (208)	314 (80)	429 (134)
4	317 (62)	475 (192)	257 (44)	429 (182)
5	336 (94)	401 (123)	263 (83)	333 (115)
6	398 (70)	439 (135)	348 (57)	424 (133)
7	350 (59)	513 (229)	347 (142)	498 (187)
8	338 (91)	417 (132)	303 (111)	373 (185)
9	311 (42)	367 (129)	321 (49)	471 (170)
10	334 (59)	432 (181)	302 (70)	418 (147)

Mean (Standard Deviation)

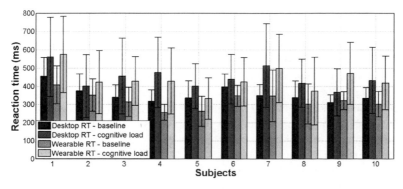

Fig. 4. Mean reaction times for each subject collected from two conditions in each setting. Error bars indicate standard deviation.

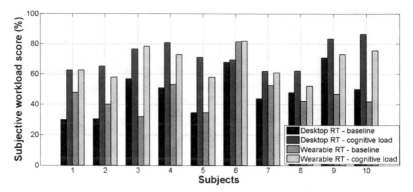

Fig. 5. Subjective workload scores of each subject obtained from the NASA task load index for each condition

4.2   Subjective Ratings

Fig. 5 shows the subjective NASA task load index for each subject. As intended from the experiment design, it can be observed that for both desktop and wearable RT test, the subjective ratings of the *cognitive load* condition are higher than the respective *baseline* condition. A comparison between both tests shows that 50% of the subjects perceived higher total workload during *baseline* condition when using the wearable device. This is due to the fact that 90% of all subjects rated the "physical demand" item of NASA-TLX with higher values for the wearable setting since additional physical demand was required for responding with the wrist movement. However, the comparison between both *cognitive load* conditions shows that 70% of the subjects perceived lower workload when using the wearable device. These results indicate that operating the wearable device results in lower perceived mental load when the user is engaged in a primary task which requires a certain amount of information processing.

5   Conclusion and Outlook

In this paper, we presented our experimental design and initial results in measuring reaction times of a person using a wearable RT test. In order to show to what extent a wearable interface is convenient to measure reaction times, we designed an experiment in which we measured response times of ten subjects from two different setups. In the first half of the experiment, the participants performed a desktop-based RT test whereas in the second half of the experiment they performed the wearable RT test. In order to measure changes in the duration and variability of reaction times we induced additional cognitive load in both setups. Besides the recording of reaction time data, subjective ratings of perceived workload were collected with the NASA-TLX. In a comparison of the obtained wearable reaction times with desktop-based reaction times, we showed that individual changes of reaction times due to the cognitive load are similar for both desktop-based and wearable RT test. According to the subjective ratings of the participants, we could show that all participants perceived the induced cognitive load as intended from the experiment design. Furthermore, subjective ratings showed that operating the wearable RT test interface under cognitive load results in lower perceived mental load compared to desktop-based reaction time test. These results suggest that the wearable RT test is more appropriate when the user is engaged in a second task which requires a certain amount of information processing. Based on the achieved results, we conclude that wrist-mounted reaction time tests seem feasible to measure factors which influence length and variability of reaction times and would allow the measurement of variation in cognitive efficiency throughout everyday life where the individuals are engaged in multiple tasks.

In our future work, we will perform statistical comparisons of different wearable RT setups, e.g. generation of the target/non-target stimulus on the dominant/non-dominant hand. In addition we are going to conduct long-term measurements of reaction times throughout daily life as cognitive performance indicator. We are planning to measure reaction times in real time from employers which have to perform complex intellectual tasks like flight operators. The obtained reaction times would allow us to identify loss of cognitive efficiency and to reduce the risk of cognitive overload.

Acknowledgements. This research has been partly funded by the European FP7 project ProFiTex, grant agreement number CT-TP 228855-2.

References

1. Pebl, http://pebl.sourceforge.net/
2. Braverman, E.R., Chen, A.L., Chen, T.J., Schoolfield, J.D., Notaro, A., Braverman, D., Kerner, M., Blum, S.H., Arcuri, V., Varshavskiy, M., Damle, U., Downs, B.W., Waite, R.L., Oscar-Berman, M., Giordano, J., Blum, K.: Test of variables of attention (TOVA) as a predictor of early attention complaints, an antecedent to dementia. Neuropsychiatr. Dis. Treat. 6, 681–690 (2010)
3. Chen, H.-Y., Santos, J., Graves, M., Kim, K., Tan, H.Z.: Tactor Localization at the Wrist. In: Ferre, M. (ed.) EuroHaptics 2008. LNCS, vol. 5024, pp. 209–218. Springer, Heidelberg (2008)
4. Forbes, G.B.: Clinical utility of the Test of Variables of Attention (TOVA) in the diagnosis of attention-deficit/hyperactivity disorder. J. Clin. Psychol. 54, 461–476 (1998)
5. Gorus, E., De Raedt, R., Lambert, M., Lemper, J.C., Mets, T.: Reaction times and performance variability in normal aging, mild cognitive impairment, and Alzheimer's disease. J. Geriatr. Psychiatry Neurol. 21, 204–218 (2008)
6. Harms, H., Amft, O., Winkler, R., Schumm, J., Kusserow, M., Tröster, G.: Ethos: Miniature orientation sensor for wearable human motion analysis. In: Proceedings of IEEE Sensors Conference. IEEE (2010)
7. Hart, S.G., Stavenland, L.E.: Development of NASA-TLX (Task Load Index): Results of empirical and theoretical research. In: Hancock, P.A., Meshkati, N. (eds.) Human Mental Workload, ch. 7, pp. 139–183. Elsevier (1988)
8. Ivorra, A., Daniels, C., Rubinsky, B.: Minimally obtrusive wearable device for continuous interactive cognitive and neurological assessment. Physiol. Meas. 29, 543–554 (2008)
9. Jaeggi, S.M., Buschkuehl, M., Jonides, J., Perrig, W.J.: Improving fluid intelligence with training on working memory. Proc. Natl. Acad. Sci. USA 105, 6829–6833 (2008)

10. Jensen, A.R.: Clocking the mind: Mental chronometry and individual differences. Elsevier (2006)
11. Kosinski, R.J.: A literature review on reaction time (August 2009)
12. Lee, S.C., Starner, T.: BuzzWear: alert perception in wearable tactile displays on the wrist. In: CHI 2010: Proceedings of the 28th International Conference on Human Factors in Computing Systems, pp. 433–442. ACM, New York (2010)
13. Lieberman, H.R., Matthew Kramer, F., Montain, S.J., Niro, P.: Field assessment and enhancement of cognitive performance: Development of an ambulatory vigilance monitor. Aviation, Space, and Environmental Medicine 78 (2007)
14. Duncan Luce, R.: Response Times: Their Role in Inferring Elementary Mental Organization. Oxford University Press (1986)
15. Matscheko, M., Ferscha, A., Riener, A., Lehner, M.: Tactor placement in wrist worn wearables. In: International Symposium on Wearable Computers (ISWC), pp. 1–8 (2010)
16. Oakley, I., Kim, Y., Lee, J., Ryu, J.: Determining the feasibility of forearm mounted vibrotactile displays. In: Haptic Interfaces for Virtual Environment and Teleoperator Systems, HAPTICS 2006 (2006)
17. Scholz, U., Marca, R.L., Nater, U.M., Aberle, I., Ehlert, U., Hornung, R., Martin, M., Kliegel, M.: Go no-go performance under psychosocial stress: Beneficial effects of implementation intentions. Neurobiology of Learning and Memory 91(1), 89–92 (2009)
18. Vaurio, R.G., Simmonds, D.J., Mostofsky, S.H.: Increased intra-individual reaction time variability in attention-deficit/hyperactivity disorder across response inhibition tasks with different cognitive demands. Neuropsychologia 47(12), 2389–2396 (2009)
19. Whelan, R.: Effective analysis of reaction time data. The Psychological Record 58, 475–482 (2008)
20. Wild, K., Howieson, D., Webbe, F., Seelye, A., Kaye, J.: Status of computerized cognitive testing in aging: A systematic review. Alzheimer's and Dementia 4(6), 428–437 (2008)

Using Constraint Optimization for Conflict Resolution and Detail Control in Activity Recognition

Chrysi Filippaki, Grigoris Antoniou, and Ioannis Tsamardinos

Computer Science Department, University of Crete,
Institute of Computer Science, Forth-ICS, Heraklion, Greece
{filipaki,antoniou,tsamard}@ics.forth.gr

Abstract. In Ambient Assisted Living and other environments the problem is to recognize all of user activities. Due to noisy or incomplete information a naïve recognition system may report activities that are logically inconsistent with each other, e.g., the user is sleeping on the couch and at the same time is watching TV. In this work, we develop a rule-based recognition system for hierarchically-organized activities that returns only logically consistent scenarios. This is achieved by explicitly formulating conflicts as Weighted Partial MaxSAT clauses to be satisfied. The system also has the ability to adjust the desired level of detail of the scenarios returned. This is accomplished by assigning preferences to clauses of the SAT problem. The system is implemented and evaluated in a real Ambient Intelligence experimental space. It is shown to be robust to the presence of noise; the level of detail can easily be adjusted by the use of two preference parameters.

Keywords: Conflict Resolution, Rule-based, Activity recognition.

1   Introduction

Activity recognition is receiving increasing attention among computer scientists, due to the wide spectrum of applications where it can be used. Potential applications of our activity recognition system include Ambient Assisted Living (AAL), intelligent workspaces, hospitals, classrooms etc. For example, in an AAL environment recognition of user's activities is important to provide assistance services.

Some prior work on activity recognition focuses on identifying all occurrences of a specific type of activity, e.g., people abandoning their luggage in an airport [12]. In more general activity recognition settings however, a system should identify all of user activities and their relations, e.g. their temporal sequence or subsumption (for activities hierarchically organized). In the later case, it is important for the system to report activities that are logically consistent and avoid reported scenarios, such as the user is sleeping on the couch and at the same time is watching TV.

Another consideration is deciding the level of detail granularity of the reported activities, depending on the context of use. Some applications may require very detailed recognition (1-hour TV-watching, 1′ phone-call, 1-hour TV-watching), while other coarser (2-hour TV-watching, or 2-hour relaxing at home). For example, a nurse

D. Keyson et al. (Eds.): AmI 2011, LNCS 7040, pp. 51–60, 2011.
© Springer-Verlag Berlin Heidelberg 2011

requesting a report from an AAL system on a patient may be interested in all of her daily activities and their exact temporal duration in order to determine whether and when the patient is taking her medication and whether she needs help with some activities or not. A doctor considering the patient lifestyle may only be interested in her sleep patterns, amount of rest, exercise and regularity of eating schedule.

This paper proposes a logic and rule-based system that deals with noisy sensors, and uncertainty of primitive event detection, resolves conflicts of the identified activities and reports logically consistent scenarios; finally, the system takes parameters that adjust the preferences for the level of abstraction and the amount of detail of the recognized activities. To the extent of our knowledge, this is the first system that addresses both activity conflicts and preferences about the level of detail.

The system input is a list of recognized atomic, instantaneous events (e.g., sit-on-chair, turn-on-TV, start-slideshow), also called *atomic activities*, from the sensors and their timing. *Complex activities* are recognized based on predefined hierarchical rules, which express temporal and spatial patterns between lower-level activities. Uncertainty is addressed by allowing the presence of optional activities: a complex activity may be detected even if some optional primitive activity is not detected. The presence of the optional activities increases the confidence of the recognition, expressed as a confidence factor. The temporal aspects of our rules are explicitly represented; the intervals of the recognized complex activities are computed and saved in our knowledge base for further processing. Both the confidence factors and the temporal intervals of the complex activities are computed from the factors and intervals of their constituent lower-level activities.

The system first creates a list of all potential complex activities and then detects all pairs of conflicting activities. The problem of resolving the conflicts is converted into a weighted partial maximum satisfiability problem (Weighted Partial MaxSAT) such that any solution to it corresponds to a set of identified activities (scenario) that do not conflict. The system also has the ability to adjust the desired level of detail in the scenarios returned. In order to achieve this, preferences (weights) are assigned to clauses of the Weighted Partial MaxSAT problem. Each complex activity's weight is calculated by taking into account its confidence, temporal duration and number of used atomic activities. Then the optimal solution is found by maximizing an objective function. We note that the optimization techniques presented could accommodate other types of preferences and be generalized to other settings.

The system is implemented and evaluated in a real Ambient Intelligence experimental space: a real user interacted with the system for a period of time and her activities are accurately recognized. The level of detail of the recognized scenario is demonstrated to be easily controlled by the use of two preference parameters. The system is shown to be robust to noisy inputs with simulation studies.

2   An Application Scenario

We now present a motivating as well as running-example scenario to use for modeling and recognition of user activities:

Running Example Scenario: Mary is relaxing in her home after a long day at work. She first lies in her bed for a while. Then she watches TV until the telephone rings. She answers the call and a colleague is asking her to watch a slideshow he prepared, for a project they are working on. She goes to the next room where she watches the slideshow and then she returns to her bedroom and watches again TV. All of her activities could be considered a type of a more general activity "User is relaxing at home", except for the activity were she is watching a slideshow about her work.

3   Reasoning Framework

The activity recognition system has three levels. The first is the recognition of every possible complex activity, based on the atomic activity, using a set of predefined rules implemented in the Java Expert System Shell (JESS) [11]. The second is the detection of all the conflicts between the recognized complex activities. The final step is conflict resolution and optimization of activity recognition according to preferences for the level of detail.

3.1   Identification of Plausible Occurrences of Activities

As a first step, the system identifies all plausible activities that may have taken place. The final scenario reported is a subset of these that maximizes preferences while also resolving all conflicts.

An *activity instance* (or simply, activity) is denoted by $E[t_1,t_2]_{cf}$, where E is a unique identifier of the activity, t_1 is its start time, t_2 is its end time and cf is the confidence value we have for this activity. Activity instances have the t_1, t_2, and cf values bound. *An atomic activity E* is defined as an instantaneous activity:

$$E\left[t_1,t_2\right]_{cf} \text{ is atomic activity} \Leftrightarrow t_1 = t_2 \qquad (1)$$

The input to the system is a *dataset* of detected atomic activities; the parameters t_1, t_2, and cf are obtained by the sensors. Complex activities are constructed recursively from the atomic and lower-level activities. The construction is based on an event algebra over *activity types*: any pattern of activities that matches an algebra rule produces a new activity. The algebra operators define the time interval of the recognized new activity. The operators are formalized as follows:

1. **Negation as failure NAF** (not): used to derive not E (i.e., that E is assumed not to hold) from failure to derive E.
2. **Disjunction operator** $(\vee)$: at least one of the specified instances has to occur. Disjunction of two activities E_1 and E_2 occurs when E_1 occurs or E_2 occurs.
3. **Conjunction operator** $(\wedge)$: the specified activity instances must occur at the same interval. Conjunction of two activities E_1 and E_2 occurs when both E_1 and E_2 occur, irrespective of their order of occurrence.

4. **Optional-activity operator** (optional): an optional activity still allows the recognition of higher-level activities that may depend on it, with smaller confidence: an activity is still recognized, if flagged as optional, with 0 confidence, even if it never occurred

$$optional\left(\,E[t_s,t_e]\,\right)_0 \leftarrow not\left(E[t_s,t_e]_{cf}\right) \tag{2}$$

$$optional\left(\,E[t_s,t_e]\,\right)_{cf} \leftarrow E[t_s,t_e]_{cf} \tag{3}$$

5. **Sequence operator (;):** the activity $(E_1 ; E_2)$ is recognized when E_1 and E_2 occur in this order. The activities have to follow each other within at most w time-units from each other. This precludes the situation the set is recognized from activities separated by an arbitrarily long time interval.

$$((E_1;E_2)\,[t_{1s},t_{2e}]/w)_{cf} \leftarrow E_1[t_{1s},t_{1e}]_{cf1}\,,\,E_2[t_{2s},t_{2e}]_{cf2}\,,$$
$$t_{1e}<t_{2s},(t_{2s}<t_{1e}+w) \tag{4}$$

$$((E_1\,;optional(E_2))\,[t_{1s},t_{1e}]/w)_{cfa} \leftarrow E_1[t_{1s},t_{1e}]_{cf1}\,,optional(\,E_2[t_{2s},t_{2e}])_0\,,$$
$$t_{1e}<t_{2s},(t_{2s}<t_{1e}+w) \tag{5}$$

$$((E_1\,;optional(E_2))\,[t_{1s},t_{2e}]/w)_{cfb} \leftarrow E1[t_{1s},t_{1e}]_{cf1}\,,optional(\,E2[t_{2s},t_{2e}])_{cf2}\,,$$
$$t_{1e}<t_{2s},(t_{2s}<t_{1e}+w) \tag{6}$$

where $cfa<cfb$.

6. **Set operator (set):** the activity $set(E_1,E_2)$ is recognized when both E_1 and E_2 occur in any order. The activities have to follow each other within at most w time-units from each other.

$$set((E_1,E_2)[min(t_{1s},t_{2s}),max(t_{1e},t_{2e})]/w)_{cf} \leftarrow E_1[t_{1s},t_{1e}]_{cf1}\,,E_2[t_{2s},t_{2e}]_{cf2}\,,$$
$$max(t_{1s},t_{2s})<min(t_{1e},t_{2e})+w \tag{7}$$

The definition of set operator in combination with the optional operator is similar to (5) and (6).

The confidence values cf of the complex activities are computed as follows. For a first level activity, the cf is sum of the confidences of its atomic activities normalized to [0, 100], where 100 is achieved when all activities, including optional ones, are recognized with the highest confidence. For a second and higher level activity, the cf is the sum of the cf of the component lower-level activities. Given this definition, a second level activity $(E_1 ; E_2)$ is equally preferable (same cf) to recognizing E_1 and E_2 as distinct activities, everything else being equal.

The definitions of two complex activities from our running example, based on the previous operators can be seen in Table 1. Note that the complex activity "User is relaxing at home" is a second level complex activity as it is recognized based on other complex activities.

Table 1. Two examples of complex activity types from the running example (Section 2)

Complex Activity Types Definitions

1.

$$UserIsWatchingTv \leftarrow TurnOnTv \; ;$$
$$set \left(optional \left(ChangeTvChannels\right), optional \left(ChangeTvVolume\right)\right) ;$$
$$TurnOffTv$$

2. $UserIsRelaxingAtHome \leftarrow set \begin{pmatrix} optional \; (UserIsRestingOnBed), \\ optional \; (UserIsWatchingTv), \\ optional \; (UserIsTalkingOnTelephone), \\ optional \; (UserIsWatchingSlideshow) \end{pmatrix}$

3.2   Conflict Detection

Obviously there are some pairs of activities that a user cannot perform at the same time e.g. "User is relaxing at home" and "User is watching slideshow". As a result an activity recognition system has to detect these conflicts, and select to report a sequence of recognized activities that is logically consistent. One way to detect conflicts is to define conflicting pairs of activity types, e.g., relaxing vs. working. However, this approach complicates knowledge engineering: whenever a new type is defined, all conflicting predefined types should be declared.

Instead, we follow an approach based on the concept of *activity resources* that facilitates knowledge representation. For each activity type a list of activity resources is specified. Resources can be split into tangible and intangible. Tangible resources are those which have actual physical existence e.g. a chair, whereas intangible resources are those that are present but cannot be grasped or contained e.g. user's attention.

We consider that two complex activities are in conflict, if their time-intervals overlap and they use common resources. The formal definition for the conflict detection between two recognized complex activities $E_1[t_{1s}, t_{1e}]_{cf1}$ and $E_2[t_{2s}, t_{2e}]_{cf2}$ is:

$$conflict(E_1, E_2) \Leftrightarrow t_{1s} \leq t_{2e}, \; t_{2s} \leq t_{1e},$$
$$\begin{pmatrix} \left(\exists r : r \in resources(E_1), r \in resources(E_2)\right) \vee \\ \begin{pmatrix} \exists E_n, E_k : E_n \in usedActivities(E_1), \; E_k \in usedActivities(E_2), \\ conflict(E_n, E_k) \end{pmatrix} \end{pmatrix}$$

$$(8)$$

Where:

- *resources(E_i)*: the set of resources complex activity $E_i [t_{is}, t_{ie}]$ $_{cfi}$ uses.
- *usedActivities(E_i)*: the set of activities we used to recognize complex activity $E_i [t_{is}, t_{ie}]$ $_{cfi}$.
- *r*: a resource that both complex activities use.

3.3 Conflict Resolution and Preference Optimization

Let us denote with B_i a propositional (binary) variable denoting whether a recognized activity E_i is selected in the final output. When two activities E_i and E_j are conflicting, only one of them should be selected for the returned scenario. This statement corresponds to the constraint $(\neg B_i \vee \neg B_j)$ on the propositional variables. Thus, resolving all conflicts is equivalent to solving a satisfiability problem (SAT) of the form:

$$(\neg B_k \vee \neg B_m) \wedge ... \wedge (\neg B_i \vee \neg B_j) \qquad (9)$$

where a clause is included in the formula for each identified conflict. Unfortunately, this problem has the trivial solution of setting all B_i to false, thus not returning any activities and avoiding all conflicts. Instead, one would like to give preference to solutions recognizing as many activities as possible, or even better, high-confidence activities that "explain" a large percentage of the user's time and atomic activities.

To obtain optimal solutions we convert instead to a Weighted Partial MaxSAT problem (WP-Max-SAT), which is a generalization of the SAT problem. In a WP-Max-SAT some clauses are specified as hard constraints (must be satisfied), while other ones are soft constraints (desirable to be satisfied). In the soft constraints, weights are assigned. Every weight represents the penalty to falsify the clause. Optimal solution for a Weighted Partial MaxSAT instance is an assignment such that satisfies all the hard clauses, and the sum of the weights of the falsified soft clauses is minimal. We used Sat4j, an open source library of SAT-solvers [10]. Specifically, for each plausible activity E_i (Section 3.1) we define the following:

- B_i : a binary variable denoting the selection of E_i in the output
- $D(E_i)$: the temporal duration of E_i
- $C(E_i)$: the confidence of E_i
- $A(E_i)$: the number of atomic activities we used to recognize (explained-by) E_i

For each conflict between E_i and E_j we create the clause $(\neg B_i \vee \neg B_j)$ as a hard constraint. For each activity E_i, we create the singleton clause B_i as a soft constraint. The weight given to B_i is

$$w_i = a \cdot D(E_i) + b \cdot C(E_i) + c \cdot A(E_i) \qquad (10)$$

where $a, b, c > 0$ are preference parameters. Thus, the preference given to selecting E_i increases with its confidence factor, the number of atomic activities it encompasses, and its temporal duration. The relative weight of these factors depends on the preference parameters. Consequently if $E_1,...,E_n$ are all the plausible activities we have recognized, our Weighted Partial MaxSAT problem is going to have the form:

Fig. 1. Screenshots from demonstration of the running example of Section 2. From left to right: a) Resting on bed b) Watching TV c) Talking on telephone d) Watching slideshow in a different room e) Watching TV (not shown).

$$B_1^{w_1} \wedge ... \wedge B_n^{w_n} \wedge (\neg B_k \vee \neg B_m) \wedge ... \wedge (\neg B_i \vee \neg B_j) \qquad (11)$$

where the superscripts of B_i denote the corresponding weight. Thus, the Weighted Partial MaxSAT solves the following optimization problem:

$$\max_{B_1 \cdots B_n} \sum_{i=1}^{n} w_i \cdot B_i \qquad (12)$$

s.t., all conflicts are resolved

4   Experimental Results

We have implemented the recognition system and integrated it within the ICS-FORTH "AmI SandBox" [13]. The facility includes a complex of three rooms equipped with state of the art AmI hardware, made available through a middleware infrastructure. A colleague of ours (not otherwise participating in this work) was given the instructions to enter the facility and perform the actions stated in the running example of Section 2. The user was not given any other instructions or guidance. A video of the demo is freely available[1]. Screenshots are shown in Fig. 1 at the representative moments: the system correctly identifies all of user activities.

To demonstrate the system's ability to report activities at different levels of detail we run the recognition algorithm with various settings of the preference parameters:

- When setting the preference parameters in formula (10) to (a=0.1, b=0.1, c=0.8) higher preference is given to scenarios that explain more atomic activities, i.e., detailed scenarios. In this case, the system returns the scenario of Fig. 2: "Resting on bed", "Watching TV", "Talking on Telephone", "Watching Slideshow", "Watching TV". Mary's activities are described in detail, as we asked the system to explain the maximum possible number of atomic activities.
- When setting the preference parameters to (a=0.85, b=0.1, c=0.05) higher preference is given to scenarios with activities of longer temporal duration, even if some

---

[1] http://139.91.189.213/ics/ami/videos/AmI%20Demo%209-5-11.wmv Some machines have to be operated through software for some atomic activities to be registered.

atomic activities are not explained (do not participate in any recognized complex activity). In this case, the system returns a single activity "User is relaxing at home". This is explained as follows: a plausible activity "User is relaxing at home" is identified encompassing the activities ("Resting on bed", "Watching TV", "Talking on Telephone", "Watching TV") *with duration the whole demo length*. Notice that, the "relaxing" activity is plausible even though the "Watching Slideshow" activity is interleaved, is also recognized and obviously conflicts with it.

To evaluate the robustness of the system, we conducted a number of simulation studies by running 40 datasets containing 1592 atomic activities. The activity types in the datasets are the same as in the scenario presented in section 2. We generated the datasets and then added randomly different percentages of noise. Noise can be split into random atomic activities that are inserted into our datasets and lost atomic activities. For a given level l of noise, $l \times 10\%$ of total atomic activities in the datasets is deleted (lost activities) and $l \times 90\%$ random atomic activities are inserted in the dataset.

The evaluation results are shown in Fig. 3. As expected the accuracy, precision and recall values decrease as the percentage of noise in the datasets increases (Fig. 3-right). But even with high level of noise (e.g. 50%) activities are accurately recognized (accuracy equal to 0.83). So the system has been proven robust to noise. As illustrated in Fig. 3-left from the total of activities correctly recognized (True Positives) the percentage with temporal errors (incorrect recognized start time or end time) is also affected by the noise levels in the datasets.

5   Related Work

There are three main approaches in activity recognition frameworks logic-based, probabilistic-based and combinations of them. In probabilistic systems, such as [7] and [8] where Hidden Markov Models (HMMs) and Hierarchical HMMs have been used respectively, noise and uncertainty are handled well. They require training data while our system requires knowledge engineering. However they do not cope with conflicts or abstraction preferences. Logic-based systems on the other hand, do not deal with missing activities and noise [1], [2]. They also lack the ability to handle conflicts or adjust the desired level of detail in their results.

There are various approaches trying to combine logic with probabilities. Shet and his colleagues proposed in a system that uses logic programming (Prolog) for activity recognition and they extended it with the bi-lattice framework to detect humans under partial occlusion, based on the output of parts based detectors [3].

Systems using Markov Logic Networks (MLNs) [4] are useful for handling noisy activity streams, as they combine the strengths of logical and probabilistic inference. There are some works that use Markov logic-type relational models for activity recognition based on video such as Tran and Davis [5] that used MLNs to probabilistically infer activities in a parking lot. Helaoui et al. [9] use MLNs as a declarative framework for recognizing interleaved and concurrent activities incorporating input from sensors and common-sense background knowledge. Our system can recognize interleaved and concurrent (but not unknown) activities as long as they do not use common resources. Finally in [6] Biswas et al. introduce a first-order probabilistic model that combines multiple clues to classify human activities from video data and is implemented as a Dynamic Markov Logic Network. The main drawback of all the aforementioned approaches is that they focus on recognizing the occurrences of specific activities instead of scenarios. Therefore they may report activities that are logically inconsistent with each other. Furthermore unlike our system they can not detect the conflicting activities or adjust the level of detail in their results.

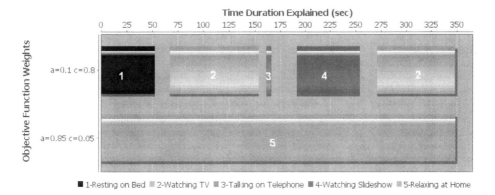

Fig. 2. Controlling the level of detail of the recognized activities with the use of preference parameters a, b, and c (Eq. 10). From top to bottom the times lines correspond to the recognized scenario when higher preference ($c = 0.8$, $a = 0.1$, $b = 0.1$) is given to the atomic activities "explained" by the scenario, recognized scenario when higher preference is given to recognizing longer complex activities ($a = 0.85$, $c = 0.05$, $b = 0.1$).

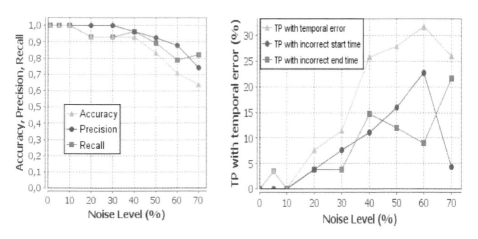

Fig. 3. Robustness of activity recognition in the presence of noise. (Left) Accuracy, precision and recall of the system as a function of noise level l. (Right) True Positives (TP) with temporal errors (incorrect start or end time) as a function of noise level l.

6   Conclusions and Future Work

We have presented a rule-based recognition system for hierarchically-organized complex activities that returns only logically consistent scenarios. An implemented scenario in an AmI environment demonstrated that the system is efficiently working and that the level of detail can be easily adjusted according to our preferences. Moreover experimental results have shown that the system is robust to noise. In the future we plan to improve the system's performance, by decreasing its computational time and to include more preference factors for controlling the scenarios' abstraction levels.

References

1. Artikis, A., Sergot, M., Paliouras, G.: A Logic Programming Approach to Activity Recognition. In: Proc. of ACM International Workshop on Events in Multimedia (2010)
2. Dousson, C., Maigat, P.L.: Chronicle recognition improvement using temporal focusing and hierarchisation. In: Proceedings of International Joint Conference on Artificial Intelligence (IJCAI), pp. 324–329 (2007)
3. Shet, V., Neumann, J., Ramesh, V., Davis, L.: Bilattice-based logical reasoning for human detection. In: Proc. of IEEE Computer Vision and Pattern Recognition, CVPR (2007)
4. Richardson, M., Domingos, P.: Markov logic networks. Machine Learning 62(1-2), 107–136 (2006)
5. Tran, S.D., Davis, L.S.: Event Modeling and Recognition using Markov Logic Networks. In: Forsyth, D., Torr, P., Zisserman, A. (eds.) ECCV 2008, Part II. LNCS, vol. 5303, pp. 610–623. Springer, Heidelberg (2008)
6. Biswas, R., Thrun, S., Fujimura, K.: Recognizing Activities with Multiple Cues. In: Elgammal, A., Rosenhahn, B., Klette, R. (eds.) Human Motion 2007. LNCS, vol. 4814, pp. 255–270. Springer, Heidelberg (2007)
7. Yamato, J., Ohya, J., Ishii, K.: Recognizing Human Action in Time-Sequential Images Using Hidden Markov Model. In: Proc. Computer Vision and Pattern Recognition, pp. 379–385 (1992)
8. Nguyen, N.T., Phung D.Q., Venkatesh, S., Bui, H.H.: Learning and detecting activities from movement trajectories using the hierarchical hidden Markov model. In: Proceedings of IEEE International Conference on Computer Vision and Pattern Recognition (CVPR), San Diego, pp. 955–960 (2005)
9. Helaoui, R., Niepert, M., Stuckenschmidt, H.: Recognizing Interleaved and Concurrent Activities: A Statistical-Relational Approach. In: Proceedings of the 9th Annual IEEE International Conference on Pervasive Computing and Communications (2011)
10. Le Berre, D., Parrain, A.: The Sat4j library, release 2.2. Journal on Satisfiability, Boolean Modeling and Computation (JSAT) 7, 59–64 (2010)
11. Friedman-Hill, E.: Jess in Action: Rule-Based Systems in Java. Manning Publications Co. (2003)
12. Liao, H.H., Chang, J.Y., Chen, L.G.: A localized Approach to abandoned luggage detection with Foreground –Mask sampling. In: Proceedings of 5th IEEE International Conference on Advanced Video and Signal based Surveillance, Santa Fe, pp. 132–139 (2008)
13. Grammenos, D., Zabulis, X., Argyros, A.A., Stephanidis C.: FORTH-ICS internal RTD Programme 'Ambient Intelligence and Smart Environments'. In 3rd European Conference on Ambient Intelligence, Salzburg (2009)

Knowledge-Based Systems for Ambient Social Interactions

Xiang Su[1], Ekaterina Gilman[1], Paweł Kwiatkowski[2], Tomasz Latkowski[2], Alma Pröbstl[1], Bartłomiej Wójtowicz[2], and Jukka Riekki[1]

[1] Department of Computer Science and Engineering and Infotech Oulu, University of Oulu, Finland
[2] Department of Electronics, Military University of Technology, Warsaw, Poland

Abstract. The development of ambient social applications brings challenges to aggregate information from heterogeneous sources, like users, physical environments, and available services. We propose a framework for aggregating information from different sources, and utilize a novel representation, Entity Notation (EN), as a starting point of connecting all information to knowledge-based systems, which offers good possibilities to support ambient social intelligence. In this paper, we present the framework, our EN representation, and an implementation of a map reminder service to demonstrate the usability of our framework.

Keywords: Knowledge-based Systems, Ambient Social Interactions, Entity Notation, Rule-based Reasoning.

1 Introduction

Nowadays, user-centric mobile applications are becoming more and more popular. They bring a new fashion of ambient social interactions among people [1]. Ambient social interactions benefit from information aggregation from the social information of users, available services, physical environment, etc. This aggregation can improve the usability and enable new functionalities for mobile social applications. However, such aggregation brings challenges due to several reasons; for example, different sources support different communication models and incompatible representations.

Semantic Web technologies enable information interchange between different sources. Heterogeneous information, like user profiles, shared community information and real time sensor measurements can be integrated into knowledge-based systems using Semantic Web technologies. Semantic Web technologies offer good possibilities to support intelligent ambient social interactions. For example, real time inference over social information, like the shared goals of a community, and physical environment information, like location, can enable ambient intelligent social interactions for individuals sharing common tasks and duties in communities. One main challenge is that social content and sensor data have no representation compatible with Semantic Web languages. Hence, it is difficult to semantically aggregate these information sources.

D. Keyson et al. (Eds.): AmI 2011, LNCS 7040, pp. 61–71, 2011.

Semantic Web technologies and social data processing require large amount of computing resources, which conflict with limited memory, computing, and communication resources available by mobile devices. Hence, most social applications have servers for storing and processing the information. However, server side communications challenge the usability of ambient social applications, as they are expected to be always available, regardless of the quality of network communications.

In this paper, we present our work towards building knowledge-based systems with Semantic Web technologies for ambient social interactions. A knowledge-based ambient social interaction framework will be suggested to bridge the gap between heterogeneous information sources. This framework offers large potential for implementing ambient social intelligence based on knowledge. Moreover, we utilize an innovated representation, Entity Notation (EN), in this framework as a starting point of connecting all information together, including sensor data, social content, Semantic Web-based inference, etc. EN is a Semantic Web languages compatible serialization, which stems from the basic semantics of RDF and ontologies. It is expressive for representing knowledge structures, and can be serialized by any sensor and application straightforwardly. EN is a promising solution to connect mobile applications with the knowledge-based systems on the server side, as it significantly reduces communication overhead. In order to verify our framework, we implement an application that reasons over social content produced by users and real-time location data to enable intelligent interactions among multiple users. We demonstrate a location-based reminder service, which presents reminders and maps to mobile users based on their needs.

The rest of this article is organized as follows. Section 2 presents related work and section 3 discusses the general framework to build knowledge-based systems for ambient social interactions. We introduce more details of EN, and our implementation details in section 4 and section 5 respectively. We conclude the paper in section 6.

2   Related Work

Most current mobile social applications simply extend the web interfaces of social software to mobile devices. That is, one can connect to his favorite online social network sites through his mobile phone, like Facebook Mobile [2], and LinkedIn Mobile [3]. Location-based mobile services provide interesting functionalities to facilitate social interactions. For example, Foursquare [4] is a location-based social networking software for mobile devices. It enables mobile users to explore the city, find friends, mark visited places, etc. Google Latitude [5] allows mobile phone users to share their locations with other users. Gbanga game [6] builds a virtual world according to real user locations facilitating different social interactions between users. More mobile applications, like WhozThat [7], Social Serendipity [8] and CenceMe [9] focus on finding new friends through short range communication techniques, like bluetooth.

On the other hand, applying semantics, such as ontologies, in location based services has been reported in [10] [11], but these efforts focus more on location-based navigation. Though knowledge-based systems would enable lots of intelligent functions for ambient social interactions, not much work has been done in this direction. In comparison with related work, we concentrate on building knowledge systems to aggregate information sources, which will facilitate ambient social interactions. This enhances the basic features of ambient social computing that utilize context information. Context is recognized from sensor data and by matching content and applications to current situation and needs of users. [12]. EN is suggested as a key enabler for ambient social interactions, and it is compared with other representations in [13].

3   A Framework for Building Knowledge-Based Systems for Ambient Social Interactions

Figure 1 presents a general framework to build knowledge-based systems for mobile social interactions. Information from heterogeneous sources, such as social information, physical environments, and available services are aggregated to knowledge-based systems. Social information includes the aspects of single person and communities. Communities are groups of people with common roles, interests or tasks. Social information can be extracted from their profiles, subscriptions, social networks, etc. Physical environments offer information about the physical surroundings of users, like location, time, noise level, temperature, etc. This information can be both quantitative and qualitative. Quantitative information is acquired by digital objects, like sensors, which measure environment and provide these measurements for knowledge bases. Qualitative information includes geographical, ethnographic and other information. Available services are other important sources for knowledge-based systems. Services provide more complex and processed data, for instance from networked sensors.

Knowledge-based systems are key enablers for ambient social intelligence. They include knowledge bases and reasoners. Knowledge bases store formal models of knowledge. In practice these knowledge models consist of a terminology part and an assertion part. The terminology part, the so called T-Box, defines formal models of concepts and states additional constraints among concepts. The assertion part, the so called A-Box, describes the concrete individuals of T-Box concepts and their relations with each other. Reasoners are software components able to infer new logical relations from the knowledge base. There are many different techniques that can be applied for reasoners, and the most popular ones are First Order Logic, Description Logic and probability theory. We utilize ontology models to represent knowledge in the knowledge base. Ontologies serve as a formal representation that machines can understand and interpret, which facilitate advanced knowledge processing, such as reasoning. Ontological knowledge bases support Description Logic (DL)-based and rule-based reasoning. Meanwhile, there are possibilities to support hybrid reasoning mechanisms when the knowledge bases of other representations are available. Hence, ontology models provide a flexible solution to support the complex relations of social interactions.

Users and applications are considered as actors in our framework. Users and applications consume deduced results produced by knowledge-based systems. However, they can also act as sources of social information, as sensors observe them in their activities.

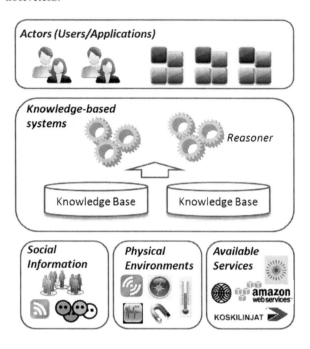

Fig. 1. The framework for building knowledge-based systems for ambient social interactions

Knowledge-based systems facilitate ambient social interactions by providing a formal grounding for all information sources. When such a common formal grounding is available, user specific social information, sensor produced data, and all other information can be aggregated based on the same grounding. That is, knowledge-based systems establish the common meaning of entities and their interactions. Interacting entities are able to share not only data, but semantics, for ambient social intelligence. Knowledge-based systems provide mechanisms to identify implicit logical connections and enable semantic interoperability straightforwardly and unambiguously.

Knowledge-based systems require a lot of computing resources from the hosting devices. A knowledge base can consume large amount of memory, which is not available from mobile devices, while reasoning is resource consuming process and only a limited set of currently available mobile devices can perform this operation constantly. Hence, it is a common practice to build big knowledge bases and complex reasoning processes on the server side. However, there is a possibility to deploy partial knowledge base and affordable reasoning on mobile devices. This will enable faster response time, enhanced privacy, and avoidance of the uncertainty, caused by communication issues of environments.

4   Entity Notation

Aggregation of heterogeneous information from different sources requires a powerful and flexible representation. In this section, we suggest utilizing EN [13] [14], to interconnect all information. EN was designed as a lightweight serialization of knowledge models. It is expressive to serialize ontologies and RDF models straightforwardly, and on the other hand, it is so simple that any sensor and application can compose EN packets. EN is compatible with Semantic Web languages, like RDF/XML and OWL. Hence, it can be interoperated with popular social contents, like RSS and FOAF ontology easily. Sensors can compose EN packets with minimal computing resources, and still the data can be transferred into RDF knowledge. Moreover, EN can be the payload of underlying protocols, like HTTP; hence, information from available services can be expressed and transferred.

Generally, an EN packet depicts an entity and its relationships with values and other entities. To fulfill the expressibility and lightweight requirements, we define two EN formats: the complete format, and the short format. The complete format has enough expressibility and has the following format:

```
EntityType EntityID
 PropertyName PropertyValue
 ...
 PropertyName PropertyValue
```

We utilize square brackets and angle brackets to identify the level of knowledge an EN packet should be mapped to. When an entity packet is wrapped in square brackets ([and]), this EN packet should be transferred to A-Box knowledge. When an entity description is wrapped in angle brackets (< and >), this EN packet should be transferred to T-Box knowledge. Here are two examples of EN complete packets. In the first packet, Alice is sharing a task with Bob, which is to pick someone up at University of Oulu (social information). The second packet represents locationsensor measurement of Alice (physical environments information).

```
[http://ee.oulu.fi/o#SharedTask http://ee.oulu.fi/o#pickupSharedTask101
http://ee.oulu.fi/o#ownerID  "Alice"
http://ee.oulu.fi/o#peerID  "Bob"
http://ee.oulu.fi/o#interestingPlace
http://ee.oulu.fi/o#universityofoulu]


[http://ee.oulu.fi/o#LocationSensor http://ee.oulu.fi/o#locaSensor767
http://ee.oulu.fi/o#ownerID  "Alice"
http://ee.oulu.fi/o#longitude  "25.468"
http://ee.oulu.fi/o#latitude "65.058"]
```

Lightweight short packets can support resource-constrained devices and slow communication links. The short EN format uses templates and prefixes to shorten packets. The basic idea is that a template contains a description of the constant part of a sequence of EN packets and placeholders for variable items. Prefixes are used to shorten URI references. Similar to complete packets, square and angle brackets are utilized to wrap the following descriptions depending on the level of knowledge, and we utilize UUIDs to identify templates:

```
UUID PropertyValue  ... PropertyValue
```

With templates and prefixes, we can shorten the examples above to:

```
[urn:uuid 76eac2 "Alice" "Bob" EE#universityofoulu]
```

```
[urn:uuid 539ea2 "Alice" "25.468" "65.058"]
```

Compared with other knowledge serializations, EN packets can be very compact, hence the communication overhead over server and mobile client communication links can be significantly reduced. This enables building knowledge-based systems on the server side, and still keep low overhead as possible.

5   Event Map Implementation for Ambient Social Interactions

To prove the usefulness of our designed framework we have implemented an ambient social application, which provides the reminder support for mobile users. This application enables rendering mobile maps and reminders to users according to ambient information, including fixed points of users' interests (PoIs), the geographical locations of mobile devices, and shared tasks of users. Application is executed in the background and the user can perform normal mobile phone activities. Ambient maps with reminders come to the foreground when there is important information to be shown to the users. We demonstrate two scenarios in our implementation. In the first one two persons are sharing a task of buying pizza for them at noon, and the one who is closer to the pizza restaurant (that is the PoI) will get an alert with a corresponding map to visit the restaurant. The second scenario tells about family. The wife specifies a shared task with her husband to pick up their kids from a school (that is the PoI). The couple has decided to pick up their kids as early as possible, so at the predefined time, the one who is closer to the school gets a reminding alert with a map on his or her mobile phone to pick up their kids.

Figure 2 presents the architecture of the implemented system, which consists of two main parts: a client side and a server side. The client side is a Java ME application, consisting of a task generator and a GPS receiver to process location data. With task generator users can specify their preferences or settings about which reminder to show, when to show, and whom to share the task with. Both location data and specified tasks are sent with short EN packets to the server to minimize communication payloads. An example of these packets are presented in section 4. The server side consists of an EN decomposer, a domain ontology, a

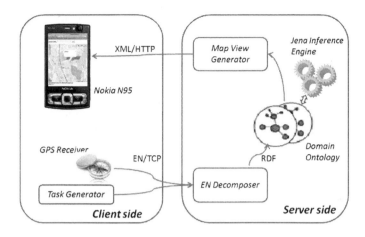

Fig. 2. Implemented architecture of ambient social interactions

reasoning engine and a map view generator. The EN decomposer transforms EN packets into RDF statements. These RDF triplets are added into the domain ontology and trigger the inference engine. We define a domain ontology, which includes predefined PoIs (such as restaurants and schools), user profiles, shared tasks, and other facts relevant to the system. The inference engine is a rule-based system which constantly checks if any task defined by any user can be executed and triggers corresponding rules. Rules are considered as instructions for actions that can be applied to a certain situation. If the task is executed, the map view generator renders the map according to the task settings. This map is sent to the specific person at specified time.

Our implemented prototype fully realizes the framework presented in Figure 1. We utilize user locations and shared tasks (social information in communities) as suppliers to the knowledge-based system. As can be seen from Figure 2, the knowledge-based system in our implementation consists of domain ontology and inference engine components. The domain ontology is a small knowledge base containing T-Box and A-Box knowledge. Our reasoning engine is a Jena rule-based system and it utilizes pre-designed rules to infer conclusions from the premises. Users act in the environment and operate with the application.

Table 1 shows some rules defined for our application scenarios. The left column describes the rule in natural language and the right column presents the Jena rules, applied to the domain ontology.

The left picture in Figure 3 is a screenshot from an emulator, which demonstrates the picking up kids scenario. A red mark specifies the target location and a blue mark specifies the current location of the user. Also a textual reminder of this task is shown to the user. The right picture captures the real user interaction with the application during our field test, which is a shared task for visiting a pizza restaurant.

Table 1. Social Interaction Rules for Event Map Implementation

Rule description	Reasoning rule
Alice creates the task and shares it with Bob. This task is supposed to be executed for one (Alice or Bob) who is closer to certain point of interest. This rule checks for the shared task (?sharedTask) whether Bob (?user) is closer to the point of interest (?place).	[rule1_check_closest_user: (?sharedTask rdf:type sw:SharedTasks) (?sharedTask sw:hasPersonToGo ?person) (?sharedTask sw:smallestDistance ?smallestDistance) (?sharedTask sw:hasSharingMember ?user) (?user sw:X ?userX)(?user sw:Y ?userY) (?sharedTask sw:hasPlace ?place) (?place sw:X ?placeX)(?place sw:Y ?placeY) countDistance(?userX, ?userY, ?placeX, ?placeY, ?distance) lessThan(?distance, ?smallestDistance) noValue(?smallestDistance sw:firedFor2 ?sharedTask) —> remove(1,2) (?sharedTask sw:smallestDistance ?distance) (?sharedTask sw:hasPersonToGo ?user) (?smallestDistance sw:firedFor2 ?sharedTask) hide(sw:firedFor2)]
This rule checks if the current time (?currentTime) is within the shared task validity time (?validity), if it is then the task is ready to be executed, hence its transmission property becomes "transmission_succeded". Also, the new time for task execution is set according to task repetition property.	[rule2_set_transmission_for_shared_task: (?sharedTask rdf:type sw:SharedTasks) (?sharedTask sw:time ?time) (?sharedTask sw:transmission 'no_transmission') now(?currentTime) validityTime(?time, ?validity) le(?time, ?currentTime) ge(?validity, ?currentTime) (?sharedTask sw:repetition ?repetition) setTime(?repetition, ?time, ?newtime) (?sharedTask sw:hasPlace ?place) (?place sw:X ?placeX)(?place sw:Y ?placeY) (?sharedTask sw:hasPersonToGo ?user) (?user sw:X ?userX)(?user sw:Y ?userY) noValue(?user sw:firedFor3 ?task) —> remove(1,2) (?sharedTask sw:time ?newtime) (?sharedTask sw:transmission 'transmission_succeded') (?user sw:firedFor3 ?sharedTask) hide(sw:firedFor3)]
This rule gathers all necessary information for the shared task (?sharedTask) which is ready to be executed (transmission property equals "transmission_succeded"). This information is obtained to generate the map with the reminder.	[rule3_send_map_for_shared_task: (?sharedTask rdf:type sw:SharedTasks) (?sharedTask sw:time ?time) (?sharedTask sw:transmission 'transmission_succeded') (?sharedTask sw:repetition ?repetition) (?sharedTask sw:hasPlace ?place) (?place sw:X ?placeX)(?place sw:Y ?placeY) (?sharedTask sw:hasPersonToGo ?user) (?user sw:X ?userX)(?user sw:Y ?userY) (?sharedTask sw:comment ?comment) —> mapInfo(?sharedTask,?comment,?user,?userX, ?userY,?place,?placeX,?placeY,?repetition,?time)]

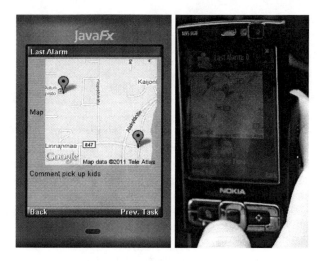

Fig. 3. Application screenshots

We implemented our client on Nokia N95 mobile phones and tested it with panOulu open access network. The user test has demonstrated the usability of our system. The application runs in the background, allowing users to perform their daily routine and appears at the foreground only if the execution time of the task (which was specified by the user) is reached. The concepts of tasks, points of interests and the logic of application were clear to the users and they could easily manage tasks by themselves. The field test also demonstrated that users are eager to share their location and task information *"as long as I [Test user] am in control what and when and to whom I share it with"*. The overall application was considered as a nice system which actually could be used as *"part of a calendar application"*.

6   Discussion

In this paper, we presented our work towards building knowledge-based systems for ambient social interactions. We discussed a general framework to enable Semantic Web technologies in ambient social interactions and details of EN. Scenario implementations demonstrate the usability of our framework. The aggregation of different information sources for ambient social intelligence is challenging since it requires the confluence of previously separated lines of research. We expect that Semantic Web technologies are promising solutions to connect heterogeneous information sources. In this article, we proposed a general framework and EN that serve as a starting point for advanced ambient intelligence features.

By their nature, ambient social applications must be available for users everytime and everywhere. Moreover, they are expected to be lightweight (consume few resources), allow normal mobile phone routine (like, phone calls), and respond fast. Knowledge-based systems facilitate different social behavioral interactions, even though it is a challenge to utilize the server back end communication for mobile applications, because of delays, connectivity, etc. We consider EN as a good solution to minimize communication overheads. Moreover, EN is an ideal candidate for playing important roles as an underlying representation for different information sources. It is expressive for representing information from social and physical contexts.

Building knowledge-based systems for social applications brings clear separation of the functionality between system components. That is, main advantage of this approach is that we isolate the application logic from the system. The application logic is mainly performed by rules which can be easily modified and extended on the fly, without a recompilation of the system. Hence, the functionality of the system can be easily changed. This is a very important issue especially for mobile applications, where users are not so eager to install application updates.

Our current implementation is limited in its consideration of privacy and security issues, because we reason all private information on the server side. Moreover, we could consider enabling more dynamic interactions, for instance allow users to trigger tasks when a certain friend is nearby, which is not supported in the current implementation.

As future work, we will consider deploying knowledge-based systems on mobile devices. This is one big step for realizing privacy-protected and fast ambient social interactions. Moreover, we will consider other possibilities of social information; for example, aggregating FOAF ontology and RSS feeds to enable intelligent functions for ambient social intelligence.

Acknowledgments. This work was funded by MOTIVE research project program of the Academy of Finland. The first author would thank the funding from NOKIA Foundation, and the second author would thank the funding from GETA (Graduate School in Electronics, Telecommunications and Automation). We would also thank Timo Saloranta and Dazhuo Li for being our volunteers of user tests.

References

1. de Ruyter, B.: Socail Interactions in Ambient Intelligent Environments, PhD thesis, Eindhoven University of Technology (2010)
2. Facebook Developer Documentation, http://developers.facebook.com/docs/
3. LinkedIn Professional Network, http://linkedin.com
4. Foursquare, https://foursquare.com/
5. Google Latitude, https://www.google.com/latitude
6. Gbanga, http://gbanga.com/
7. Beach A., Gartrell M., Akkala S., Elston J., Kelley J., Nishimoto K., Ray B., Razgulin S., Sundaresan K., Surendar B., Terada M., Han R.: WhozThat? Evolving an Ecosystem for Context-Aware Mobile Social Networks. IEEE Network, 50–55 (July/August 2008)

8. Eagle N., Pentland A.: Social Serendipity: Mobilizing Social Software. IEEE Pervasive Computing, 28–34 (April/June 2005)
9. Miluzzo, E., Lane, N.D., Eisenman, S.B., Campbell, A.T.: CenceMe – Injecting Sensing Presence into Social Networking Applications. In: Kortuem, G., Finney, J., Lea, R., Sundramoorthy, V. (eds.) EuroSSC 2007. LNCS, vol. 4793, pp. 1–28. Springer, Heidelberg (2007)
10. Tryfona, N., Pfoser, D.: Data Semantics in Location-Based Services. In: Spaccapietra, S., Zimányi, E. (eds.) Journal on Data Semantics III. LNCS, vol. 3534, pp. 168–195. Springer, Heidelberg (2005)
11. Kolomvatsos K., Papataxiarhis V., Tsetsos V.: Semantics Location Based Services for Smart Spaces. In: Metadata and Semantics, Part 7, pp. 515–524. Springer Press, Heidelberg (2009)
12. Vos, D.H., Haaker, T., Teerling, M.: Consumer Value of Context Aware and Location Based Mobile Services. In: 21st Bled eConference eCollaboration: Overcoming Boundaries through Multi-Channel Interaction, pp. 50–62 (2008)
13. Su, X., Riekki, J., Haverinen, J.: Entity Notation: Enabling Knowledge Representations for Resource-Constrained Sensors. Personal and Ubiquitous Computing (accepted, 2011)
14. Su, X., Riekki, J.: Transferring Ontologies between Mobile Devices and Knowledge-based Systems. In: 8th IEEE/IFIP International Conference on Embedded and Ubiquitous Computing, pp. 127–135. IEEE Press (2010)

Augmenting Mobile Localization with Activities and Common Sense Knowledge

Nicola Bicocchi[1], Gabriella Castelli[2], Marco Mamei[2], and Franco Zambonelli[2]

[1] Dipartimento di Ingegneria dell'Informazione, Universitá di Modena e Reggio Emilia
[2] Dipartimento di Scienze e Metodi dell'Ingegneria, Universitá di Modena e Reggio Emilia
`name.surname@unimore.it`

Abstract. Location is a key element for ambient intelligence services. Due to GPS inaccuracies, inferring high level information (i.e., being at home, at work, in a restaurant) from geographic coordinates in still non trivial. In this paper we use information about activities being performed by the user to improve location recognition accuracy. Unlike traditional methods, relations between locations and activities are not extracted from training data but from an external commonsense knowledge base. Our approach maps location and activity labels to concepts organized within the ConceptNet network. Then, it verifies their commonsense proximity by implementing a bio-inspired greedy algorithm. Experimental results show a sharp increase in localization accuracy.

1 Introduction

Ambient intelligence services ubiquitously need to perceive and understand their operating environment to achieve adaptable and flexible behaviors. The recent introduction of powerful mobile platforms allowed a plethora of innovative user-centric services [18,12] to be developed. These services, considered as a whole, aim to improve users' experience by making use of contextual information gathered from the environment.

Location is a key aspect concurring in context definition. The embedding of GPS receivers in modern mobile devices allows millions of people to acquire their position is terms of geographical coordinates. However, this representation is not actually informative. Applications, and consequently users, make greater use of higher level representations such as being at *home*, at *work*, in a *grocery shop* or in a *bank*.

A straightforward way to achieve this result is to feed a geocoding service with a GPS signal. For example, given a point and a search radius, Google Maps returns a list of locations of interest contained within the searched area. Unfortunately, to avoid false negatives (i.e., locations outside the search area) and deal with GPS inaccuracies, the search radius must range around 250m [15]. Due to this, especially in dense urban settings, the number of retrieved locations is often not negligible. Furthermore, urban environments are extremely patchy. Even a small (few meters) physical movement might imply logically different contexts (opposite sides of the wall separating the coffee shop and the bank). To improve localization accuracy (i.e., filtering irrelevant results), Ofstad et al. argued to perform localization across both *physical* and *logical* domains [16].

In this paper we propose to use recent activity recognition results [5] paired with commonsense reasoning to augment localization. Specifically, locations are filtered on

D. Keyson et al. (Eds.): AmI 2011, LNCS 7040, pp. 72–81, 2011.

the basis of their commonsense proximity with the activities performed by the user. How to collect relations between activities and locations? A well-known solution is based on collecting large bodies of training data. Then, eventual correlations among different features can be observed. However, this approach is inefficient and time-consuming. Alternatively, we propose to extract well-know relations from an external commonsense knowledge base. Specifically, a bio-inspired algorithm has been used to compute proximity among activities and locations within ConceptNet.

This paper presents the following contributions and insights: *(i)* it proposes to augment localization with activity recognition capabilities; *(ii)* it proposes to use external commonsense knowledge sources to extract relations between activities and locations; and *(iii)* it discusses experimental results collected from a real-world case study.

Accordingly, the rest of the paper is organized as follows: Section 2 discusses other works concerning augmented localization. Section 3 illustrates both localization and activity recognition modules that have been implemented. Section 4 describes how commonsense reasoning can be used to augment localization with user activities. Section 5 details experimental results under different configurations. Finally, Section 6 concludes the paper.

2   Related Work

The spreading of location-based applications for mobile phones made localization an exciting research topic during the last decade. Since early 2000s, due to its high energy requirements and poor accuracy in indoor and dense urban areas, GPS localization has been augmented with WiFi and/or GSM data [17,7].

During the same years, the conceptual switch from "positions" to "places" was discussed. The idea has been initially proposed in [10], while later works realized probabilistic engines to identify visited places on the basis of temporal patterns [13,4].

Considering "places" instead of "positions" quickly grounded embryonic ideas about context-aware localization; that is, augmenting localization with contextual information gathered from alternative sensors. In 2004, Bao and Intille showed how to detect 9 everyday activities using a couple of biaxial accelerometers that could have been easily embedded in a mobile phone [3]. After that, numerous localization techniques using contextual data have been developed. For example, [1,2] discussed the use of light and sound sensors and delineated the concept of ambient fingerprinting; while [16,11] illustrated how to embed information coming from cameras and accelerometers. However, integrating alternative sensors within the localization process posed the problem of extracting relations between different domains (e.g., accelerations and geographical coordinates). The majority of existing works solved this problem by searching relations within training data. This approach, showed to be prone to over-fitting, is sensitive to application domain and requires more data to initialize the system [8].

Recently, few attempts have been made to overcome these problems. In particular, instead of extracting relations among different domains from the data itself, some authors tried to use pre-existing, external, commonsense knowledge bases. In [15], for example, Mamei et al. used Cyc to improve automatic place identification considering historical data about the user.

3   Sensor Setup

To develop our activity-aided localization system, a GPS-based localization sensor and an accelerometer-based activity sensor have been implemented. While the former has been designed to natively run on Symbian smart phones, the second requires dedicated hardware (i.e. SunSpot nodes). However, our results abstract from specific implementation details and could be reproduced with alternative systems with a comparable accuracy. Both sensors are described below in this section.

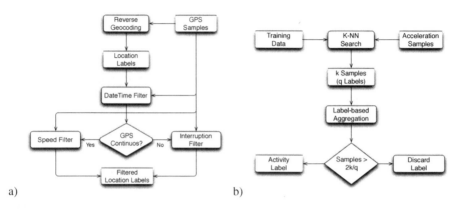

a)   b)

Fig. 1. (a) *Location classification process*; reverse geocoded labels are filtered on the basis of time, date, speed and eventual interruptions. (b) *Activity classification process*; for each sample, k nearest neighbors (associated to q classes, $k = 64$, $q <= k$) are identified. The sample is then associated to all the classes (at most 3) associated to al least $k/2q$ training samples.

3.1   Location Recognition

To classify user's location we implemented a tool [15,9] for Symbian OS. It samples GPS coordinates and classifies user's location by querying Google Maps. Specifically, Google Maps takes in input a couple of geographic coordinates and a radius, returning a list of locations of interest associated with a label coming from a predefine set (i.e., road, square, park, shop, cinema, mall, restaurant, gym). Unfortunately several practical drawbacks affect this process:

1. Smart phones are not equipped with high-precision GPS receivers. Under normal operating conditions this error is smaller than 100m [15], however the error can reach 200m.
2. Google Maps database is not perfect. Although we do not have accurate statistics, we noticed that a portion of locations is still missing and coordinates might be unprecise. Furthermore, Google Maps does not provide information about locations' geometry. Due to this, especially with large-sized instances (e.g., parks, squares) locations can be misclassified.

To mitigate these problems and avoid false negatives, the system has been setup to use a search radius of 250m. Clearly, the number of reverse geo-coded locations is proportional to the search radius. The bigger the radius, the more the returned location labels. Because of this, especially in densely populated areas, the system might produce numerous false positives. To reduce them, we implemented three filters acting on different dimensions of the GPS signal (see Figure 1(a)).

DateTime filter acts on the assumption that each label is more likely to be visited during defined portions of the week. For example, banks are closed during the night, while cinemas are unlikely to be visited during the morning. Thus, we associated to each label a probability distribution (i.e., 24-7) describing how likely that category of places is going to be visited.

Speed filter works on continuous GPS signals (suggesting an outdoor location). A common misclassification happens when a user moving on a street is associated to all the locations she goes by. To avoid this, the filter analyzes user's speed. If the user is moving, only *road*, *park* and *square* are allowed.

Finally, Interruption filter works on discontinuous GPS signals indicating, with high probability, an indoor location. It works on the assumption that each category of places is fairly characterized by the duration of the visit. Thus, we defined for each category a probability distribution of durations.

3.2 Activity Recognition

To classify user's activities we made use of the system detailed in [5]. Here we provide only an informal introduction. It collects data from 3-axis accelerometers, sampling at 10Hz, positioned in 3 body locations (i.e., wrist, hip, ankle) and classifies activities using instance-based algorithms. To initialize the system, each user is required to collect a certain amount (i.e., 250-500) of training samples for each activity. Furthermore, considering that human activities have a minimum duration, it aggregates classification results over a sliding window and performs majority voting on that window. Each window is associated with the most frequent label. For the sake of experimentation, we modified this module in two ways:

1. First, we implemented both training and classification modules on Sun Spot nodes. Instance-based algorithm perfectly suit this need in that they support on-line classification and training and can be implemented on resource-constrained devices. Client nodes send their samplings to a master node which classifies them and stores the result. This way, it is possible to discard raw samplings and store only high-level activity labels, allowing the execution of 4+ hours experiments without using heavy and obtrusive equipment.

2. Second, we modified it to deal with uncertainties. Instead of producing a single label for each sensor sampling, we implemented a mechanism to produce multiple labels associated with a degree of confidence. Specifically, for each sample to be classified, k nearest neighbors (associated to q classes, $k = 64$, $q <= k$) are identified. The sample is then associated to all the classes (at most 3) associated to al least $k/2q$ training samples.

The architecture of this classification process has been summarized in Figure 1(b).

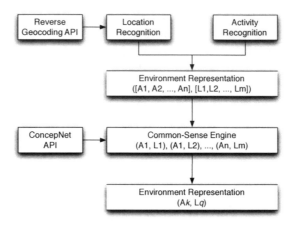

Fig. 2. Location and activity labels concur to define a representation of the environment. Each and every couple *(location, activity)* is ranked on a commonsense basis using ConceptNet assertions.

4   Augmenting Localization

The two sensors described in Section 3, periodically output classification labels. Specifically, the localization sensor outputs a tuple of candidate locations (i.e., road, square) , while the activity sensor outputs a tuple of candidate activities (i.e., walk, read).

Our approach for augmenting mobile localization is based on the assumption that locations and activities are semantically tied and commonsense knowledge can be used to measure proximity among them. The more an activity and a location are proximate, the more it is likely they have been recognized within the same situation. In other words, given a set of possible locations and activities, our goal is to rank each and every couple *(location, activity)* on a commonsense basis (see Figure 2).

To measure the commonsense proximity between locations and activities there is the need for *(i)* a knowledge base containing relations between locations and activities have to be selected; and *(ii)* a method for computing proximity among these concepts.

4.1   ConceptNet

First, since we are dealing with a situation recognition problem, the ideal knowledge base should: *(i)* include a vocabulary covering a wide scope of topics, and *(ii)* incorporate tricky relations hard to be discovered in an automatic way. ConceptNet best suits these requirement. It is a semantic network designed for commonsense reasoning. It has been built from a collection of 700,000 sentences provided by thousands of people. It is organized as a massive directed and labelled graph made of about 0.3 million nodes and 1.6 million edges, corresponding to concepts and relations between them, respectively. Most nodes represent common activities or chores given as phrases (e.g., "drive a car" or "buy food"). Its structure is uneven, with a group of highly connected nodes, and "person" being the most connected, having in- degree of about 30,000 and out- degree of over 50,000. There are over 86,000 leaf nodes and approximately 25,000 root nodes. The average degree of the network is approximately 4.7.

4.2   Measuring Semantic Proximity

A preliminary round of experiments with ConceptNet led us to identify the following principles:

1. Proximity increases with the number of unique paths. However, this is not a reliable indicator given that even completely unrelated concepts might be connected through long paths or highly connected nodes.
2. Proximity decreases with the length of the shortest path; nodes connected directly or through some niche edges are in a short distance, hence they are proximate;
3. Connections going through highly connected nodes increase ambiguity, therefore proximity should be inversely proportional to the degrees of visited nodes;
4. ConceptNet has been created from natural-language assertions. Thus, errors are frequent and algorithms have to be noise-tolerant;

Majewski et al. recently proposed an interesting algorithm for commonsense text categorization inspired to similar observations [14]. Despite it has been conceived for a different problem, it can be applied to localization as well. The algorithm is based on the assumption that proximity among concepts (i.e., in our case locations and activities) is proportional the to amount of some substance s that reaches the destination node v as a result of injection to node u. The procedure has been built around two key biological paradigms such as *diffusion* and *evaporation* and works as follow:

1. a given amount of substance s is injected to a node u;
2. at every node, a fraction α of the substance evaporates and leaves the node;
3. at every node, the substance diffuses into smaller flows proportional to the out degree of the node;
4. nodes never overflow. If multiple paths visit the same node, the previous amount of substance s can be incremented;
5. target nodes are ranked according with the amount of substance s received.

Figure 3 exemplifyies the algorithm in action. A certain amount (i.e., 128) of substance s is injected into a node representing a candidate activity (i.e., *Run*). Then, the substance diffuses over the graph and halves by evaporation at each node it visits. The overall amounts of s that reach nodes *Park* and *Road* respectively are 36 and 16. *Park* is considered more proximate than *Road* to *Run*.

Finally, it is interesting to note how this bio-inspired algorithm matches with the principles we deduced from our preliminary studies on ConceptNet. In fact: *(i)* the evaporation process assures that short paths imply high proximity; while *(ii)* the diffusion process takes into account the total amount of connections among two concepts while diminishing the relevance of highly-connected paths.

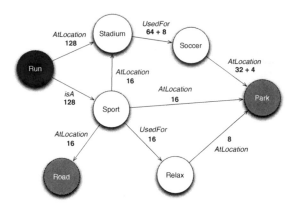

Fig. 3. An example of the proposed algorithm in action. Nodes and edges are associated with their respective weights.

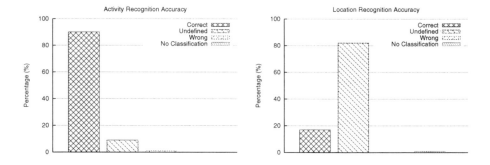

Fig. 4. Experimental results of the Activity Recognition and Location Recognition module stand alone respectively. While the Activity Recognition (a) provides reliable classifications, the Location Recognition (b) can rarely provide a correct classification.

5 Experimental Results

In this section we discuss the experimental results obtained. A volunteer equipped with the sensing system collected data while going about his normal life and manually annotating ground truth data.

The activity recognition module has been trained to recognize 8 activities (i.e., climb, use stairs, drive, walk, read, run, use computer, stand still, drink). For each class, 300 training samples have been collected. The location recognition module, instead, has been run on a Nokia N95 smartphone. GPS traces has been collected using a sampling period of 30 seconds and has been associated with a label coming a predefined set (i.e., road, square, park, shop, cinema, mall, restaurant, gym).

Experimental results have been analyzed considering to the following four categories: *Correct Classification* for the situations in which both modules provide a single and correct result that can be easily put together; *Undefined Classification* for accounting situations in which one or both the module provide more than one result, in this case there is the need for an additional mechanism to choose the most proper activity and/or location; *Wrong Classification* for situations in which either a classifier or both of them provided a wrong classification; *Missing Data* for accounting situations in which the GPS or the accelerometers didn't provide data to be classified.

We first discuss the results obtained independently by activity recognition and the location recognition systems. The activity recognition produce reliable classifications (see Figure 4 (a)) . Indeed around 90% of the samples are correctly classified, while 9% are undefined (undefined results may occur for actions that generate alike patterns of accelerations) and only the remaining 1% classifications are wrong.

On the other hand, the location recognition module doesn't exhibit a comparable level of reliability. The results of this experiment are reported in Figure 4 (b), and they actually show that in the majority of cases (82,4%), the algorithm provides an undefined classification because many locations are ranked equally likely. Analyzing undefined data points, it emerges that the the module can filter out few categories.

The combined classifier uses these data and combines them with the use of ConceptNet in order to improve the classification accuracy. It classifies data collected and processed from acceleration sensors and GPS off-line and works with two separate files that must be synchronized and streamed in parallel in order to get corresponding feature vectors and places in a given time window. Four situations can occur: *(i)* both data about the action and the place are available for the given time slot; *(ii)* only the data about the action is available for the given time slot; *(iii)* only the data about the place is available for the given time slot; *(iv)* no data available for the given time slot.

The first situation make use of ConceptNet to combine data coming from sensors and improve the context recognition result with the common sense exploitation. In both the second and the third situation only a data source is available. In these cases the common sense can be used to identify a possible place or action respectively in order to complete the action-place couple. Finally in the last situation, no data is available and different processing based on predictions can be performed. In the reported experiments we focus on the first situation, that is the most common ones.

Figure 5 (c,d) shows the results of the combined classifier and compares them with a basic system composed by the action recognition and the location recognition modules but without the Common Sense glue. In the basic system (see Figure 5 (c)) the majority of results are in the Unclassified category, mainly due to the location recognition module's output. This proves that the is there is the need for a mechanism to effectively put together data coming from diverse classifiers. The combined system (see Figure 5 (d)), instead, shows a significant improvement with 75% of data correctly classified and 25% of wrong classifications. It is worth noticing that the Undefined Classification category is lowered to zero meaning that ConceptNet is always capable of providing a ranking of action-place couples. Also the Missing data category is lowered to zero, in fact one of the advantage of the use of ConceptNet is to provide missing data. Please note that in our experiment we never experienced the concurrent lack of both sensorial data, that should have called for different strategies similar to activity and location prediction, such as bayesian networks [4]. Overall, these preliminary experiments prove that:

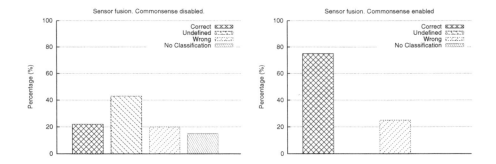

Fig. 5. Experimental results combining the Activity Recognition and Location Recognition systems. In particular, (c) shows that there is the need for some intelligent mechanism to combine the data, and (d) proves that CommonSense can be effectively used in this application.

1. Common Sense can provide an effective basis to combine contextual data coming from different classifiers
2. Common Sense is useful in a number of likely to happen situations, such as either when classifiers outputs more than a classification label or when a label is missing
3. The better the accuracy of the classifications module combined together through common sense reasoning, the better the overall results.

6   Conclusions

Although pervasive services require to perceive (i.e., classify streams of data) their operating environment, current classifiers are still inaccurate and unreliable. In this paper we presented a novel approach that combines well established classifiers using the ConceptNet knowledge base. User's activities and their relations with locations have been used to improve localization accuracy. The approach has been discussed through a realistic case study and encouraging results have been presented.

Acknowledgment. Work supported by the ASCENS project (EU FP7-FET, Contract No. 257414).

References

1. Azizyan, M., Choudhury, R.R.: Surroundsense: mobile phone localization using ambient sound and light. SIGMOBILE Mob. Comput. Commun. Rev. 13, 69–72 (2009)
2. Azizyan, M., Constandache, I., Roy Choudhury, R.: Surroundsense: mobile phone localization via ambience fingerprinting. In: Proceedings of the 15th Annual International Conference on Mobile Computing and Networking, MobiCom 2009, pp. 261–272. ACM, New York (2009)
3. Bao, L., Intille, S.S.: Activity recognition from user-annotated acceleration data, pp. 1–17. Springer, Heidelberg (2004)

4. Bicocchi, N., Castelli, G., Mamei, M., Rosi, A., Zambonelli, F.: Supporting location-aware services for mobile users with the whereabouts diary. In: Proceedings of the 1st International Conference on MOBILe Wireless MiddleWARE, Operating Systems, and Applications, MOBILWARE 2008, pp. 6:1–6:6. ICST, Brussels (2008)
5. Bicocchi, N., Mamei, M., Zambonelli, F.: Detecting activities from body-worn accelerometers via instance-based algorithms. Pervasive and Mobile Computing 6(4), 482–495 (2010)
6. Brush, A.B., Karlson, A.K., Scott, J., Sarin, R., Jacobs, A., Bond, B., Murillo, O., Hunt, G., Sinclair, M., Hammil, K., Levi, S.: User experiences with activity-based navigation on mobile devices. In: Proceedings of the 12th International Conference on Human Computer Interaction with Mobile Devices and Services, MobileHCI 2010, pp. 73–82. ACM, New York (2010)
7. Chung Cheng, Y., Chawathe, Y., Lamarca, A., Krumm, J.: Accuracy characterization for metropolitan-scale wi-fi localization. In: Proceedings of Mobisys 2005, pp. 233–245 (2005)
8. Duong, T., Phung, D., Bui, H., Venkatesh, S.: Efficient duration and hierarchical modeling for human activity recognition. Artificial Intelligence 173, 830–856 (2009)
9. Ferrari, L., Mamei, M.: Discovering daily routines from google latitude with topic models. In: IEEE International Conference on Pervasive Computing and Communications, Workshop on Context Modeling and Reasoning. IEEE Computer Society, Washington, DC, USA (2011)
10. Hightower, J.: From position to place. In: Proceedings of The 2003 Workshop on Location-Aware Computing, pp. 10–12 (October 2003)
11. Jung, D., Teixeira, T., Savvides, A.: Towards cooperative localization of wearable sensors using accelerometers and cameras. In: Proceedings of the 29th Conference on Information Communications, INFOCOM 2010, pp. 2330–2338. IEEE Press, Piscataway (2010)
12. Krumm, J.: Ubiquitous Advertising: The Killer Application for the 21st Century. IEEE Pervasive Computing 10(1), 66–73 (2011)
13. Liao, L., Fox, D., Kautz, H.: Extracting places and activities from gps traces using hierarchical conditional random fields. Int. J. Rob. Res. 26, 119–134 (2007)
14. Majewski, P., Szymański, J.: Text Categorization with Semantic Commonsense Knowledge: First Results. In: Neural Information Processing, pp. 769–778. Springer, Heidelberg (2008)
15. Mamei, M.: Applying commonsense reasoning to place identification. IJHCR 1(2), 36–53 (2010)
16. Ofstad, A., Nicholas, E., Szcodronski, R., Choudhury, R.R.: Aampl: accelerometer augmented mobile phone localization. In: Proceedings of the first ACM International Workshop on Mobile Entity Localization and Tracking in GPS-Less Environments, MELT 2008, pp. 13–18. ACM, New York (2008)
17. LaMarca, A., Chawathe, Y., Consolvo, S., Hightower, J., Smith, I., Scott, J., Sohn, T., Howard, J., Hughes, J., Potter, F., Tabert, J., Powledge, P., Borriello, G., Schilit, B.: Place Lab: Device Positioning Using Radio Beacons in the Wild. In: Gellersen, H.-W., Want, R., Schmidt, A. (eds.) PERVASIVE 2005. LNCS, vol. 3468, pp. 116–133. Springer, Heidelberg (2005)
18. Zheng, Y., Zhang, L., Ma, Z., Xie, X., Ma, W.-Y.: Recommending friends and locations based on individual location history. ACM Trans. Web 5, 5:1–5:44 (2011)

Hierarchical Activity Recognition
Using Automatically Clustered Actions

Tim L.M. van Kasteren[1], Gwenn Englebienne[2], and Ben J.A. Kröse[2]

[1] Department of Computer Engineering
Boğaziçi University, Istanbul, Turkey
[2] Intelligent Systems Lab Amsterdam
University of Amsterdam, The Netherlands
tim0306@gmail.com

Abstract. The automatic recognition of human activities such as cooking, showering and sleeping allows many potential applications in the area of ambient intelligence. In this paper we show that using a hierarchical structure to model the activities from sensor data can be very beneficial for the recognition performance of the model. We present a two-layer hierarchical model in which activities consist of a sequence of actions. During training, sensor data is automatically clustered into clusters of actions that best fit to the data, so that sensor data only has to be labeled with activities, not actions. Our proposed model is evaluated on three real world datasets and compared to two non-hierarchical temporal probabilistic models. The hierarchical model outperforms the non-hierarchical models in all datasets and does so significantly in two of the three datasets.

Keywords: Hierarchical Models, Activity Recognition, Sensor Networks.

1 Introduction

The automatic recognition of human activities such as cooking, showering and sleeping allows many potential applications in the area of ambient intelligence [10]. In recent years, temporal probabilistic models have been shown to give a good performance in recognizing activities from sensor data [3,9]. However, many of these models assume a direct correlation between activities and the sensor data. Because activities contain a rich hierarchical structure, modeling this hierarchy explicitly might be beneficial for the recognition performance of the model.

In this paper, we use a hierarchy in which we assume that each activity consists of a number of actions. For example, the activity cooking might consist of an action 'cutting vegetables and meats' and an action 'frying them in a pan'. We present a two-layer hierarchical model for activity recognition in which the top layer of the model corresponds to activities and the bottom layer corresponds to actions. Although it is possible to train such a model using data which is annotated with labels of both activities and actions, in this paper, we train

D. Keyson et al. (Eds.): AmI 2011, LNCS 7040, pp. 82–91, 2011.
© Springer-Verlag Berlin Heidelberg 2011

the model using only labels for the activities. There are two advantages to this approach: 1) Annotating the data becomes significantly less involved when only the activities have to be annotated, 2) We do not force any structure upon the model with respect to the actions, but rather let the model find this structure in the data automatically. The automatic allocation of structure can be considered as a clustering task. The clusters found in the data do not necessarily have to be meaningful clusters that correspond to actual actions that are intuitive to humans. We therefore distinguish between the term 'action clusters' to refer to the actions found through clustering and 'actions' to refer to the actions intuitive to humans. We evaluate our approach by comparing the recognition performance of our hierarchical model to the recognition performance of two non-hierarchical temporal probabilistic models and we do so using three real world datasets.

The remainder of this paper is organized as follows. In Section 2, we compare our approach to related work. Section 3 provides the details of our hierarchical model and its learning and inference algorithms. Section 4 presents the experiments and results and in Section 5 we discuss these results. Finally, in Section 6, we sum up the conclusions.

2   Related Work

In previous work hierarchical models have mainly been applied to video data to recognize activities such as entering and leaving a store [6]. Nguyen et al. compare the performance of a learned hierarchical hidden Markov model (HHMM), a hand-coded HHMM and a conventional hidden Markov model (HMM), the learned HHMM gives the best performance [8]. Duong et al. compare the performance of the HHMM and the hidden semi-Markov model (HSMM). In their work, the HHMM gives very poor performance in the recognition task which, according to the authors, is caused by a poorly estimated transition matrix. They do not explain why the hierarchical model is unable to learn the transition matrix, while the semi-Markov model is able to learn this matrix accurately [2]. In work by Luhr et al., hierarchical models consisting of several layers are hand crafted by closely inspecting the sequence of actions performed by the subject. Their results show that these models perform well in recognizing several cooking related activities [5].

Overall these works confirm the potential of using hierarchical models for activity recognition, however, none of these works involve the recognition of activities from a wireless sensor network data. Our paper contributes by providing experimental results on several real world datasets, consisting of several weeks of data and involving a large number of activities. We provide a systematic comparison between our HHMM and the HMM and HSMM, showing that the use of a hierarchy results in an increase in performance. Furthermore, we compare two ways of modeling observations in a hierarchical model and show which approach is most effective in modeling activities. Finally, our work demonstrates that the automatic clustering of actions leads to accurate activity recognition with a limited need for annotation.

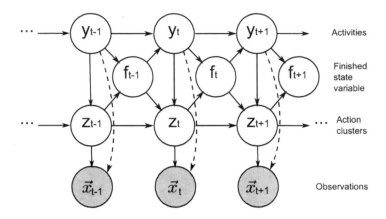

Fig. 1. The graphical representation of a two-layer HHMM. Shaded nodes represent observable variables, the white nodes represent hidden states. The dashed line is an optional dependency relation; we can choose to model the observation probability as $p(\boldsymbol{x}_t \mid y_t, z_t)$ or as $p(\boldsymbol{x}_t \mid z_t)$.

3 Hierarchical Hidden Markov Model

We assume a house in which we perform activity recognition is equipped with a sensor network of binary sensors. The data obtained from the sensors is discretized into T timeslices of length Δt. A single feature value is denoted as x_t^i, indicating the value of feature i at timeslice t, with $x_t^i \in \{0, 1\}$. In a house with N installed sensors, we define a binary observation vector $\boldsymbol{x}_t = (x_t^1, x_t^2, \ldots, x_t^N)^T$. The activity at timeslice t, is denoted with $y_t \in \{1, \ldots, Q\}$ for Q possible states. We use an HHMM to form a mapping between a sequence of observations $\mathbf{x}_{1:T} = \{\boldsymbol{x}_1, \boldsymbol{x}_2, \ldots, \boldsymbol{x}_T\}$ and a sequence of activities $\mathbf{y}_{1:T} = \{y_1, y_2, \ldots, y_T\}$ for a total of T timeslices.

In this section, we discuss the details of a two-layer hierarchical model for activity recognition and explain the inference and learning algorithms.

3.1 Model Definition

We consider a two-layer hierarchical model for activity recognition. The top layer state variables y_t represent the activities and the bottom layer variables z_t represent the action clusters (Fig. 1). Each activity consists of a sequence of action clusters and the temporal ordering of the action clusters in a sequence can vary between different executions of an activity. Of particular interest to us is the last action cluster that is performed at the end of an activity, because this action cluster signifies the end of a sequence and announces the start of a new sequence of action clusters. We therefore introduce a third variable, the finished state variable f_t, which is used as a binary indicator to indicate the bottom layer has finished its sequence.

We further explain the details of this model by going over all the factors of the joint probability distribution of hidden states and observations given by:

$$p(\mathbf{y}_{1:T}, \mathbf{z}_{1:T}, \mathbf{f}_{1:T}, \mathbf{x}_{1:T}) = \prod_{t=1}^{T} p(x_t \mid y_t, z_t) p(y_t \mid y_{t-1}, f_{t-1})$$
$$p(z_t \mid z_{t-1}, y_t, f_{t-1}) p(f_t \mid z_t, y_t)$$

where we have defined $p(y_1 \mid y_0, f_0) = p(y_1)$ and $p(z_1 \mid z_0, y_1, f_0) = p(z_1 \mid y_1)$ for the sake of notational simplicity. The entire model consists of a set of parameters $\theta = \{\pi_0, \pi_{1:Q}, A_0, A_{1:Q}, B, \phi\}$. The initial state parameters π and transition parameters A exist for both the top layer and bottom layer states. To distinguish between these two types of parameters, we include a 0 in the subscript to indicate that a parameter is of the top layer and an index of 1 to Q for each of the bottom layer parameters. The distributions of the bottom layer states depend on which top layer state the model is in and so there is a separate set of bottom layer state parameters for each possible top layer state, with Q being the number of top layer states. For example, if the model at one point is in the top state $y_t = k$, then the transition parameter A_k is used for the bottom layer state transitions. We now provide a detailed explanation of each of the factors that make up the joint probability and how they are parameterized.

At the first timeslice, the initial state distribution of the top layer states is represented by a multinomial distribution which is parameterized as $p(y_1 = j) = \pi_0(j)$. This top layer state generates a bottom layer state, also represented by a multinomial distribution and parameterized as $p(z_1 = j \mid y_1 = k) = \pi_k(j)$.

The factor $p(z_t = j \mid z_{t-1} = i, y_t = k, f_{t-1} = f)$ represents the transition probabilities of the bottom layer state variable. These transitions allow us to incorporate the probability of a particular temporal order of action clusters with respect to a given activity. A transition into a new state z_t, depends on the previous bottom layer variable z_{t-1}, the current top layer state variable y_t and the finished state variable f_{t-1}. Two distributions make up this factor, depending on the value of the finished state variable f_{t-1}. Either a new sequence of bottom layer states starts $(f_{t-1} = 1)$, or a transition within an existing sequence takes place $(f_{t-1} = 0)$.

These two cases can be compactly formulated as:

$$p(z_t = j \mid z_{t-1} = i, y_t = k, f_{t-1} = f) = \begin{cases} A_k(i,j) & \text{if } f = 0 \\ \pi_k(j) & \text{if } f = 1 \end{cases} \qquad (1)$$

Transitions of the top layer state variables are represented by the factor $p(y_t = j \mid y_{t-1} = i, f_{t-1} = f)$. Depending on the finished state variable f_{t-1}, the model either transitions into a new state $(f_{t-1} = 1)$ or remains in the same state $(f_{t-1} = 0)$. These two cases can be compactly formulated as:

$$p(y_t = j \mid y_{t-1} = i, f_{t-1} = f) = \begin{cases} \delta(i,j) & \text{if } f = 0 \\ A_0(i,j) & \text{if } f = 1 \end{cases} \qquad (2)$$

where $\delta(i, j)$ is the Kronecker delta function, giving 1 if $i = j$ and 0 otherwise.

The probability of a bottom layer state sequence finishing is represented by the factor $p(f_t = f \mid y_t = j, z_t = l)$. This factor depends on both the bottom layer state z_t and the top layer state y_t. Even though the variable f_t indicates whether z_t is a finishing state, it is important that the distribution is also conditioned on the top layer state y_t. This is because the probability of a particular action cluster being the last action cluster for that activity can differ among activities. The factor is represented using a binomial distribution, parameterized as $p(f_t = f \mid y_t = j, z_t = l) = \phi_f(j, l)$.

Two possible observation models. In the graphical representation of our hierarchical model, shown in Figure 1, there is a dashed line between the top layer state variables y_t and the observation variables $\boldsymbol{x}_t$. This line represents an optional dependency relationship, because we wish to experiment with two types of observation models. If we do take the dependence relation into account, our observation model is represented by the factor $p(\boldsymbol{x}_t \mid y_t, z_t)$. In this model, each combination of top and bottom state values gets its own set of parameters. Alternatively, if we do not include the dependence relation, our observation model is represented by the factor $p(\boldsymbol{x}_t \mid z_t)$. In this case, the observation model is independent of the top layer state variable. Note that in the transition probabilities of the bottom layer state variable described above, there still exists a dependency on the top layer state, regardless of which observation model is used. The same holds for the finished state probability distribution.

Observations are modeled as independent Bernoulli distributions, with each sensor corresponding to one Bernoulli distributions. In case of model 1 the observation probability factorizes as $p(\boldsymbol{x}_t \mid y_t, z_t) = \prod_{n=1}^{N} p(x_n \mid y_t, z_t)$, with $p(x_n \mid y_t = j, z_t = k) = \mu_{jkn}^{x_n}(1 - \mu_{jkn})^{(1-x_n)}$. For model 2 we get $p(\boldsymbol{x}_t \mid z_t) = \prod_{n=1}^{N} p(x_n \mid z_t)$ with $p(x_n \mid z_t = k) = \mu_{kn}^{x_n}(1 - \mu_{kn})^{(1-x_n)}$, where N is the number of sensors used. Model 1 requires Q times more parameters than Model 2, because of the additional dependency on the top layer states, with Q being the number of top layer state values. The observation parameters are collectively represented by a variable $B = \{\mu_{jkn}\}$ for Model 1 and $B = \{\mu_{kn}\}$ for Model 2.

3.2   Inference and Learning Using a Flattened Implementation

Inference in our proposed HHMM can be done by using the Viterbi algorithm for HMMs [7]. We can flatten our HHMM to a HMM by creating a HMM state for every possible combination of states in the HHMM. Because our model structure is not fully connected some parameters will be shared between states, this means the same set of parameters is used for different states. The use of a flattened implementation allows us to perform inference in linear time.

Parameters are learned iteratively using the Expectation Maximization (EM) algorithm [1]. The E-step consists of using the forward-backward algorithm to calculate the probability distribution $p(\mathbf{y}_{1:T}, \mathbf{z}_{1:T}, \mathbf{f}_{1:T} \mid \mathbf{x}_{1:T}, \theta)$ given a set of parameters θ. From this distribution, we can calculate the expectation and reestimate the parameters in the M-step. Because no labels are available for the action clusters, we start with a set of randomly initialized parameters. The procedure of calculating the forward-backward probabilities and reestimating the parameters is repeated until the parameter values converge, indicating a local maximum has been reached.

4 Experiments

Our experiments are aimed at answering three questions: 1) What number of action clusters is needed for modeling activities? 2) Which observation model gives the best performance? 3) How does the performance of our hierarchical model compare to the performance of the HMM and the HSMM, two commonly used models for activity recognition? Our first experiment compares the performance of the hierarchical model using Observation Model 1 to the performance of the HMM and the HSMM. The second experiment makes the same comparison, but uses Observation Model 2. In both experiments, results are given for various number of action clusters. In the remainder of this section we present the details of our experimental setup, we describe the experiments and their results and finally discuss the outcomes.

4.1 Experimental Setup

We used three publicly available datasets and Matlab code used in previous work for the HMM and HSMM [3]. A summary of the relevant details for each dataset can be found in Table 1. The datasets were recorded using wireless sensor networks consisting of simple binary sensors such as reed switches to measure whether doors and cupboards are open or closed; pressure mats to measure sitting on a couch or lying in bed; mercury contacts to detect the movement of objects (e.g. drawers); passive infrared (PIR) to detect motion in a specific area; float sensors to measure the toilet being flushed. The observed sensor data is ambiguous with respect to which activity is taking place. For example, the sensors can observe that the refrigerator is opened, but cannot observed which item is taken from the refrigerator. This makes the recognition task especially challenging.

The datasets include annotation of activities, but do not include annotation of actions. Since we do not have any ground truth for the actions and because we are only interested in using action clusters for modeling purposes, our evaluation is based solely on the inferred activities. We used the F-measure metric for evaluation, which is a combination of the average precision and recall per activity. This metric considers the recognition of each activity as equally important and provides a reliable way for evaluating activity recognition methods [3].

Data obtained from the sensors is discretized in timeslices of length $\Delta t = 60$ seconds and transformed to the changepoint representation, which has been shown to consistently gives a good performance in activity recognition [3]. We split our data into a test and training set using a 'leave one day out' cross validation. In this approach, one full day of sensor readings is used for testing and the remaining days are used for training, we cycle over all the days in the

Table 1. Information about the datasets used in the experiments

	House A	House B	House C
Activities	10	14	16
Sensors	14	23	21
Days of data	25 days	13 days	18 days

dataset and present the average performance over all test days. In the case of the HHMM, we repeat the experiment five times and present the average over those five runs. This is done because the EM algorithm requires a random initialization of the parameters.

4.2 Experiment 1: Observation Model 1

In this experiment, we use Observation Model 1 ($p(\boldsymbol{x}_t \mid y_t, z_t)$). We compare the performance of our HHMM to the performance of the HMM and HSMM. Furthermore, we experiment with various number of action clusters. The average F-measure performance over five runs for various number of action clusters is given in Figure 2 for all three houses.

We see that the performance of the HHMM is equal to the HMM when a single action cluster per activity is used. Using a single action cluster for each activity is equivalent to using an HMM and therefore results in the same performance.

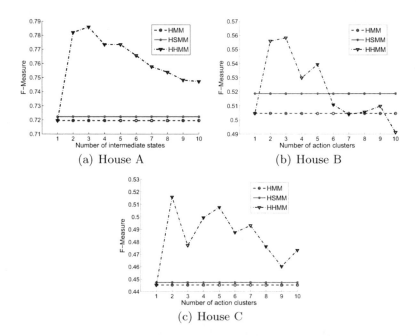

(a) House A   (b) House B

(c) House C

Fig. 2. Experiment 1: Plot of the F-measure performance of the HMM, HSMM and HHMM using Observation Model 1. The number of action clusters signifies the number of state values that are used for the bottom layer state variable of the HHMM.

Generally the best performance for the HHMM is obtained when using two or three action clusters, the performance decreases as more action clusters are considered. To determine the significance of our results we used a one-tail student t-test with matching paired days. The increase in F-measure performance of the HHMM, taken over an average of five runs, compared to the F-measure performance of the HMM and the HSMM is significant for houses A and C, at a confidence interval of 95%.

4.3 Experiment 2: Observation Model 2

In experiment 2 Observation Model 2 ($p(\boldsymbol{x}_t \mid z_t)$) is used. The experimental setup is similar to experiment 1 and the average F-measure performance over five runs for various number of action clusters is given in Figure 3 for all three houses.

We see that in Houses A and B, the HHMM does not manage to perform better than the HMM or the HSMM. In House C, we see a slight improvement in performance over the HMM and the HSMM, when 15 action clusters are used, but this increase in not significant. Overall, the best performance is obtained when using 10 or 15 action clusters. Using more or less action clusters than that quickly results in a significant decrease in performance.

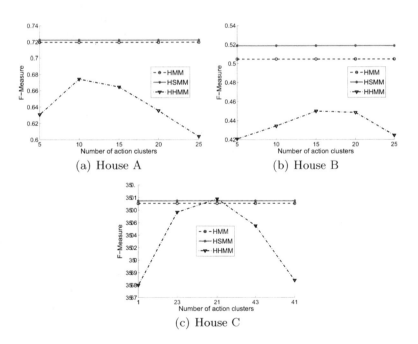

Fig. 3. Experiment 2: Plot of the F-measure performance of the HMM, HSMM and HHMM using Observation Model 2. The number of action clusters signifies the number of state values that are used for the bottom layer state variable of the HHMM.

5   Discussion

The results from our experiments show that observation model 1 (separate set of actions) gives significantly better performance than Observation Model 2 (shared set of actions). Observation model 1 includes a dependency on the activity, which means action clusters are allocated separately for each activity. In observation model 2 action clusters are found independent of the activities, as a result the clusters found might not be ideal for distinguishing activities, which results in a lower performance.

The use of two or three action clusters gives the best performance, when using a separate set of action clusters for each activity. Too few action clusters does not provide the model with enough expressive power, while too many action clusters results in too many parameters for which there is too little data to estimate them accurately.

Our proposed HHMM significantly outperformed the HMM and the HSMM in two of the three houses. This increase in performance is mainly due to differences in the observation model and the modeling of transition probabilities of the bottom layer state variable. The inclusion of action clusters allows the model to divide activities into separate stages, based on the actions that are performed. By modeling the transition probabilities between consecutive action clusters, we are able to calculate the probability of a particular temporal ordering of action clusters within an activity.

The presented results assume recognition is performed in an offline fashion on a daily basis. Such an approach is useful in applications such as long term health monitoring in which the activity behavior of a patient is studied over long periods of time (several months). Recognition can also be done in an online fashion, which means the recognized activity can be made available in realtime. Using online recognition will result in a decrease in performance, since only the sensor data up to the point of recognition can be used during inference. A comparison of online and offline recognition in the case of the HMM can be found in one of our previous works [4].

6   Conclusion

We presented a two layer hierarchical hidden Markov model for activity recognition in which one of the layers corresponds to action clusters and one layer corresponds to the activities. Two observation models were proposed and experiments on three real world datasets revealed that using a separate set of action clusters for each activity works best. Using a shared set of action clusters does not necessarily result in meaningful clusters and therefore using that observation model gives a significantly lower performance.

Our proposed hierarchical model outperforms the HMM and the HSMM in all datasets and does so significantly in two of the three datasets, with an increase of 7 percentage points in F-measure performance for both datasets. The gain in performance shows that our proposed hierarchy allows a more accurate modeling of the activities recorded in the datasets. This is primarily caused by the ability of the model to take into account the temporal order of both activities and action clusters.

References

1. Bilmes, J.: A gentle tutorial of the EM algorithm and its application to parameter estimation for Gaussian mixture and hidden Markov models. Technical Report TR-97-021, International Computer Science Institute (1997)
2. Duong, T.V., Bui, H.H., Phung, D.Q., Venkatesh, S.: Activity recognition and abnormality detection with the switching hidden semi-markov model. In: Proceedings of the International Conference on Computer Vision and Pattern Recognition, CVPR, pp. 838–845. IEEE Computer Society, Washington, DC, USA (2005)
3. van Kasteren, T.L.M., Englebienne, G., Kröse, B.J.A.: Activity Recognition in Pervasive Intelligent Environments. In: Human Activity Recognition from Wireless Sensor Network Data: Benchmark and Software, ch. 8, pp. 165–186. Atlantis Press (2011)
4. van Kasteren, T.L.M., Noulas, A., Englebienne, G., Kröse, B.J.A.: Accurate activity recognition in a home setting. In: Proceedings of the 10th International Conference on Ubiquitous Computing, Ubicomp, pp. 1–9. ACM, New York (2008)
5. Lühr, S., Bui, H.H., Venkatesh, S., West, G.A.W.: Recognition of human activity through hierarchical stochastic learning. In: Proceedings of the 1st International Conference on Pervasive Computing and Communications, PerCom, pp. 416–422. IEEE Computer Society, Washington, DC, USA (2003)
6. Muncaster, J., Ma, Y.: Hierarchical model-based activity recognition with automatic low-level state discovery. Journal of Multimedia 2(5), 66 (2007)
7. Murphy, K., Paskin, M.: Linear time inference in hierarchical hmms. In: Advances in Neural Information Processing Systems 14, NIPS (2001)
8. Nguyen, N.T., Phung, D.Q., Venkatesh, S., Bui, H.: Learning and detecting activities from movement trajectories using the hierarchical hidden markov models. In: Proceedings of the International Conference on Computer Vision and Pattern Recognition, CVPR, pp. 955–960. IEEE Computer Society, Washington, DC, USA (2005)
9. Patterson, D.J., Fox, D., Kautz, H.A., Philipose, M.: Fine-grained activity recognition by aggregating abstract object usage. In: Proceedings of the 9th International Symposium on Wearable Computers, ISWC, pp. 44–51. IEEE Computer Society (2005)
10. Turaga, P., Chellappa, R., Subrahmanian, V., Udrea, O.: Machine recognition of human activities: A survey. IEEE Trans. on Circuits and Systems for Video Technology 18(11), 1473–1488 (2008)

Real-Time Analysis of Localization Data Streams for Ambient Intelligence Environments

Dimokritos Stamatakis, Dimitris Grammenos, and Kostas Magoutis[*]

Institute of Computer Science (ICS)
Foundation for Research and Technology Hellas (FORTH)
Heraklion GR-70013, Greece
{dstamat,gramenos,magoutis}@ics.forth.gr

Abstract. In this paper we describe a novel methodology for performing real-time analysis of localization data streams produced by sensors embedded in ambient intelligence (AmI) environments. The methodology aims to handle different types of real-time events, detect interesting behavior in sequences of such events, and calculate statistical information using a scalable stream-processing engine (SPE) that executes continuous queries expressed in a stream-oriented query language. Key contributions of our approach are the integration of the Borealis SPE into a large-scale interactive museum exhibit system that tracks visitor positions through a number of cameras; the extension and customization of Borealis to support the types of real-time analysis useful in the context of the museum exhibit as well as in other AmI applications; and the integration with a visualization component responsible for rendering events received by the SPE in a variety of human readable forms.

Keywords: Scalable stream processing, location-tracking via cameras.

1   Introduction

Ambient Intelligence (AmI) environments require the ability to sense physical locations in space (e.g., human visitors in a museum exhibit) and to interact with them in a context-specific manner. It is important in such environments to have the ability to detect interesting events (e.g., a visitor approaching a specific spot), interesting behavior within sequences of events (e.g., visitor is following a specific path), and provide easy access to statistical information (e.g., popularity of certain exhibit over a specific time window in the past) in real-time. There are several ways to sense presence and location (using cameras, ultrasound, or magnetic field sensors) and transmit it to an AmI application in the form of localization data streams. However, performing complex processing of those streams is currently done in an ad-hoc manner, constraining the ability of AmI deployments to evolve and scale over time. In this paper we propose a novel methodology to process localization data streams using a new class of

---

[*] We thankfully acknowledge the support of the European FP7-ICT program through the SCALEWORKS (MC IEF 237677) and CUMULONIMBO (STREP 257993) projects.

D. Keyson et al. (Eds.): AmI 2011, LNCS 7040, pp. 92–97, 2011.

data processing systems called continuous stream-processing engines [2]. The advantages of our approach include the ability to express interesting events and behavior in terms of continuous-queries expressed in a structured stream-oriented query language. Besides the extensibility that this allows, our approach offers the ability to scale the stream-processing engine as the volume of events increases [3] and to tolerate failures in the underlying infrastructure [4]. In this paper we improve on the state of the art by presenting a proof-of-concept prototype that integrates an open-source SPE (Borealis [2]) with an interactive museum exhibit within which a computer vision system [1] uses cameras to track the position of visitors; describing our extensions to the Borealis SPE for expressing the different types of events, behavior, and statistics that are useful in the museum exhibit and more generally in AmI applications; and finally, describing our novel visualization component in terms of both its interaction with the SPE as well as its feature-rich user interface.

2   The Stream-Processing Engine

Stream processing engines (SPEs) support the execution of continuous queries expressed in stream processing languages. The data operated on (often referred to as *tuples*) are associated with a monotonically increasing timestamp, forming a time series. An example of a tuple typical in localization data streams consists of the fields <visitor ID, x, y, epoch>, meaning a specific visitor was observed in "box" (x, y) within a specific epoch. A continuous stream processing query is composed of one or more interconnected operators, each computing a function (such as sum, average, max – in general any aggregation function) over sets (also known as *windows*) of tuples. A window selects all tuples that satisfy a certain predicate on one or more of the tuple fields, also referred to as the *group-by fields* (e.g., group-by (x, y) selects all tuples carrying the same (x, y) values). Standard SPEs such as Borealis close a window either when a certain number of tuples have entered that window (count-based) or a timeout has been reached (time-based) and produce an output tuple at the closing of a window. We have extended Borealis to support the production of an output tuple either at the opening of a window, or periodically while the window is open, or (the default) at closing time. Additionally, we allow closing of a window w_i either when a *correlated* window w_j opens (where correlated is defined by w_i, w_j sharing a value at a certain field or satisfying some other predicate on their field values) or when the window is not updated during one or more tuple epochs (where epoch is defined based on a specific tuple field). Our SPE currently supports a range of event-processing queries used in the interactive museum exhibit described in Section 3:

Popularity of a box (x, y): At the core of this query is an aggregate operator grouping tuples by "box" (x, y) and counting visitor ID observations within each box. The operator produces output tuples periodically and windows remain open indefinitely.

Time visitor spent in the room: This query is similar to the previous one except that the aggregate operator groups tuples by visitor ID.

Trajectory of a visitor: This query uses an aggregate operator grouping tuples by (x, y, visitor ID) and produces an output tuple only when a window opens. A window (x, y, visitor ID) closes when a correlated window (x′, y′, visitor ID) opens.

Reduce flicker/noise in the localization stream: This query uses an aggregate operator grouping tuples by (x, y, visitor ID) and producing an output tuple when a window opens. In this query we use a different definition of correlation: A window w_i = (x, y, visitor ID) closes when a window (x′, y′, visitor ID) opens whose distance to w_i exceeds a certain radius R. Since a number of windows can be within R, a window opening can cause the closure of several windows. This query avoids producing unnecessary outputs when a visitor flickers (goes back and forth) between neighboring boxes. This query can also detect the case when a visitor travels over long distances rapidly by checking for window distance exceeding a large constant R′.

Visitor appears or disappears: This query uses an aggregate operator grouping tuples by visitor ID and producing an output tuple when a window opens, identifying a new visitor and its location (x, y). The window state is always the last position seen of a given visitor ID and its associated epoch. Windows must be updated at each epoch unless cameras can no longer locate the visitor. This query identifies internally whether a window misses an epoch update and if so, closes the window, producing a tuple with the location of the lost visitor. A subsequent operator checks whether the event took place at a valid (e.g., a door) or invalid (e.g., middle of the room) location.

Fig. 1. (left) Overview of the museum exhibit; (right) zone map

3   Application Example: Interactive Museum Room

The extended SPE system described in Section 2 was integrated into a large-scale interactive museum exhibit that takes up a whole room ($6x6x2.5m^3$). In this room a computer vision subsystem (for more details see [1]) with 8 cameras tracks the position of visitors. On one wall a dual-projector back-projection screen is installed. Localization of persons is performed at 10Hz and has an accuracy of ~2cm. In our demo installation (Fig. 1 - left), the projection screen presents a wall painting. Visitors enter the room from an entrance opposite the display. The vision system assigns a unique ID number to each person entering the room. The room is conceptually split in

5 zones of interest, delimited by different themes presented on the wall painting. These zones cut the room in 5 vertical slices. The room is also split in 4 horizontal zones that run parallel to the wall painting, which are delimited by their distance from it. Thus, a 5x4 grid is created, comprising 20 interaction slots (Fig. 1 - right). When a visitor is located over a slot, the respective wall painting part changes and, depending on the slot's distance from the wall, visitors can see a sketch, a restored version or a detail of the wall part, accompanied by related information. All information is presented in the user's preferred language.

A schematic representation of the full system setup is illustrated in Fig. 2: The computer vision subsystem emits localization events (comprising user IDs and their position in space) which are picked up by the interactive application that is responsible for: (a) updating the visual information presented on the projection screen; and (b) providing the SPE subsystem with both low-level (e.g., position) and semantic (e.g., interaction slot that the user is on, user language) localization data. The SPE analyzes and stores this data on-the-fly and feeds a visualization component which presents quantitative and qualitative information about the exhibit's visitors.

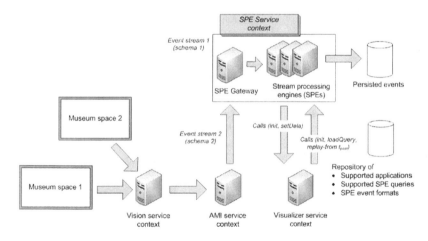

Fig. 2. System setup for the museum exhibit application

More specifically, the SPE propagates: User position; Accumulated time spent by visitors in specific positions; Total time spent by each visitor in the exhibit, average time for all users; "interesting" or "abnormal" patterns, such as: (i) too long distance between consecutive user positions; (ii) too short / long user stays in the room; (iii) incomplete user visits (where a user appears or disappears in locations other than entries/exits). The visualization component interacts with the SPE to set parameters such as type of data it is "interested" in and how to analyze and interpret them (e.g., how long should the distance between user observations be to be considered "abnormal").

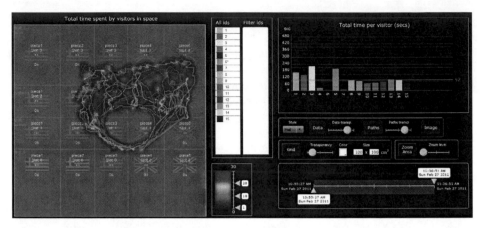

Fig. 3. User interface of the visualization component

The main part of the visualization component's user interface (Fig. 3) comprises a top-down view of the room and its interactive slots (as in Fig. 1 right). On this view user paths are presented (using a different color for each distinct user). "Abnormal" (i.e., too long) path sections are presented using thicker lines. Additionally, accumulated user time spent on a specific area is illustrated in the form of a heat map. Users can get quantitative information about each point of the heat map by positioning the mouse pointer over it. Additionally, they can modify several parameters of this view, for example changing the transparency level of the paths or the heat map, hiding the background image, overlaying a grid and changing the coloring scheme of the heat map. Furthermore, they can zoom in any part of the view at different levels.

The interface also hosts a list which contains all detected user IDs. This list has a multifunctional role, since it: (i) works as a legend for correlating path colors to user IDs; (ii) highlights user IDs related to identified patterns (e.g., an asterisk '*' is appended to IDs related to long path sections, a minus '-' to IDs with incomplete paths); and (iii) can be used to filter out data by selecting a subset of IDs (simply by clicking on them). Next to the IDs list, there is a graph presenting the total time spent by each visitor in the room and the average time for all visitors. Finally, there is an interactive control for setting a time period of interest that can be used for filtering data according to the time of their creation. The visualization component can be used to work with both real-time and stored data.

4   Conclusions and Future Work

In this paper we presented a novel approach to extensive and scalable real-time analysis of sensor data in AmI Environments. Currently, the presented solution has been installed and tested in a laboratory space at ICS-FORTH containing a fully working version of the aforementioned museum exhibit. Since this exhibit is also installed in a permanent exhibition of a major museum in Greece, our next steps include testing our proposed solution under real conditions.

References

1. Zabulis, X., Grammenos, D., Sarmis, T., Tzevanidis, K., Argyros, A.A.: Exploration of Large-scale Museum Artifacts through Non-instrumented, Location-based, Multi-user Interaction. In: Proc. of VAST 2010, Paris, France, September 21-24 (2010)
2. Carney, D., et al.: Monitoring Streams: A New Class of Data Management Applications. In: Proc. of the 28th VLDB, Hong Kong, China (August 2002)
3. Ahmad, Y., et al.: Distributed Operation in the Borealis Stream Processing Engine. In: Proc. of the 2005 SIGMOD, Baltimore, MD (June 2005)
4. Sebepou, Z., Magoutis, K.: CEC: Continuous Eventual Checkpointing for Data Stream Processing Operators. In: Proc. of 41st IEEE/IFIP DSN, Hong Kong, China (June 2011)

The Autonomic Computing Paradigm in Adaptive Building / Ambient Intelligence Systems

Aliaksei Andrushevich, Stephan Tomek, and Alexander Klapproth

CEESAR-iHomeLab, Lucerne University of Applied Sciences and Arts, Technikumstr. 21,
6048 Horw, Switzerland
{aliaksei.andrushevich,stephan.tomek,
alexander.klapproth}@hslu.ch

Abstract. This work is devoted to the classification and adaptation of current ambient intelligence (AmI) research activities from the viewpoint of the autonomic computing paradigm. Special attention is given to the implementation of AmI's user-centric focus in autonomic computing.

Keywords: Ambient Intelligence, Autonomic Computing, self-adaptive system, user-centric requirements, human-centered design.

1 Introduction and Motivation

AmI systems are typically based on the adaptation of artificial intelligence (AI) techniques on low-power, low-cost, heterogeneous and physically distributed pervasive / ubiquitous computing infrastructure. The main aim of AmI systems is however in supporting the end-user's daily activities in an unobtrusive and easy way through user-centric architecture and human-centered design.

Building Intelligence (BI) is a type of AmI implemented on underlying technical architecture and infrastructure of buildings, homes and other construction objects. Considering constantly changing user-needs different building automation applications may have partially contradictory control strategies for commonly shared resources. Moreover, many building automation applications pursuing energy efficiency, comfort, user safety and security or ambient assistance are only widely accepted as a part of an AmI system if the configuration and maintenance efforts will be kept to a minimum. Considering constantly changing user requirements during the whole lifecycle of AmI applications, self-adaptive system properties quickly become inevitable for AmI adoption.

In order to make the system self-adaptive IBM introduced in 2001 the paradigm of autonomic computing (AC) [1] that systemizes and formalizes the necessary properties and functional components of *self-managing* system architecture. An extensive amount of focused research [2] has resulted in usage of AC paradigm in different applications areas including power management in wireless sensor networks (WSN), dynamic resource management and administration in GRID computing systems, and

D. Keyson et al. (Eds.): AmI 2011, LNCS 7040, pp. 98–104, 2011.

pervasive/ubiquitous computing vision aiming at building intelligent environments by usage of heterogeneous sensing-computing-actuating devices [3].

2   Autonomic Computing

The high-level core self-management properties of the AC paradigm include self-configuration, self-optimization, self-healing and self-protection. The intuitive sense of the autonomic system is in reflexing of the current environmental context or in reflecting dynamism in the system [2].

Generally, the implementation of AC paradigm is defined in the IBM's reference model for autonomic control loops and called MAPE-K loop - Monitoring, Analysis, Planning, Execution, and gathered Knowledge.

Five AC Adoption Model Levels were also introduced by IBM in 2003 to be able to measure the systems on their way to autonomicity. These levels include 1 - Basic, 2 - Managed, 3 - Predictive, 4 - Adaptive and 5 - Autonomic. A recent AC-focused survey [2] on self-managing systems (those of AC Levels 4 and 5) suggests to classify the ongoing AC research through the following four key autonomicity elements:

- Support – when improving the complete system performance by focusing on one aspect or component;
- Core – when end-to-end self-management solution drives the core application without heading higher-level human based goals;
- Autonomous – when full end-to-end self-management typically agent-based solution self-adapts to the environment but not measuring own performance;
- Autonomic – when full architecture is reflecting its own performance and adapting itself considering higher-level human based goals.

3   AmI Research in Components of AC Architecture

Figure 1 shows our understanding about the way different works of current AmI research can contribute to the implementation of intelligent self-managing and adaptive to the user building management system (BMS).

The state-of-the-art in context-aware ubiquitous computing middleware [4, 5] looks promising in terms of performing the data acquisition from different sensors and implementing data fusion mechanisms in the *monitoring* functional block of the AC control loop architecture.

The introduction of context, the usage of context-modeling as well as context deriving procedures based on consistent previously prepared sensor data can be used for implementations of the *analyzing* component of the MAPE-K loop.

Following the AC paradigm and mainly focusing on monitoring and analyzing, the AutoHome project [6] is a successful example on creation of the context-aware BMS.

The algorithmic know-how, gathered by AmI researchers offers a number of AI approaches meant for generation of correction action schedules or *plans* for adaptive systems. Useful for AmI techniques mainly address pattern recognition, unsupervised machine learning and scheduling. Some of these AI methods are included in [7]:

- Event-Condition-Action (ECA) rules with first order logic or fuzzy logic;
- Artificial neural networks (ANN) perform well but unable to explain output;
- Classification techniques based on decision trees, ECA-rules or ANNs;
- Probabilistic Bayesian networks;
- Sequence discovery techniques based on Markov models or temporal logic;
- Instance based learning using Case-Based Reasoning;
- Evolutional/genetic algorithms requiring the cost function for optimization;
- Reinforcement learning allowing run-time adaptation of recognized patterns.

Our approach to implement the AC *Planning* component is to apply multiple scheduling algorithms, listed above, possibly encapsulated in multi-agent intelligence unit(s). Every intelligence unit agent would generate its own correction action schedule based on the same data and context model delivered from the *Analysis* component of MAPE-K.

The *Execution* component is actually responsible for the best effort selection mechanism for the next action from multiple schedules. To enable action selection each generated *Planning* schedule will be associated with Quality of Schedule meta-information containing qualitative characteristics of the generating algorithm. Several characteristic examples can be algorithm convergence speed, uniqueness of schedule, sensitivity to computation errors, schedule correctness confidence level, etc.

One possible architectural integration approach of multi-algorithmic set for achieving the optimal trade-off between competing application domains can be taken from the hierarchical concept of Semantic Buildings [8]. Different definitions for the optimum have to be considered. As a result, the proposed self-adaptive management system framework will allow choosing the most appropriate for the user and building action planning intelligence approach at runtime of BMS. Technically we plan to integrate the algorithms from the AI libraries like WEKA.

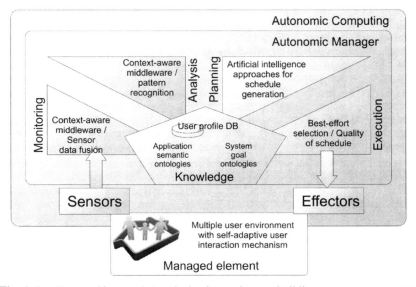

Fig. 1. Intelligent self-managing and adaptive to the user building management system

The simplest form of a *Knowledge* component in AC is rule-based. The main difficulty of the rule-based approach however is in ensuring consistency between all the rules. The more structured way of storing the application knowledge is nowadays implemented through dedicated ontologies, each containing the interconnected data between application terms and their relations. We suggest the following structuring into ontologies for the Building Intelligence Knowledge [8]: higher-level human based BMS semantic goals, application domain activity knowledge (Energy Efficiency, Ambient Assisted Living, Comfort), user type characters, system states, service functionalities, device classification, building space plans and activity time schedules. One of the drawbacks of the ontologies-based approach is the typical need to construct them manually. However, several research activities have been recently devoted to the automatic construction of ontologies [9].

4   Embedding the User-Centric Focus in AC Paradigm

Since the human activity [10] and building performance parameters [11] (BPPs) can be recognized [12] using a unified system of sensors, we suggest that the end-users and buildings are seen as one entity of „Managed Element". From the AC viewpoint this approach will allow considering building's user behavior in the MAPE-K loop without the need to introduce an additional architectural component. The *interaction* between human and building going through standard information input/output devices will be recognized as *logical* sensors and effectors input/output in the AC architecture. Here logical sensors and effectors conform to their definition in context-aware middleware [4, 5] and consist of physical and software sensors and effectors.

Since some parameters of the building cannot be directly influenced by the user, the sensitivity analysis of BPPs to dynamic user behavior [11] has to recognize the sensitive BPPs that may lead to conflicts between BMS decisions and user wishes.

The simulations of indoor user behavior combined with context-modeling and 3D visualization allow finding out the optimal configuration parameters for the control algorithms used by building management systems. Possible solution is given in [11].

The important topic of interaction with user in building automation and control is placed under the research area of human-building interaction (HBI) Current research [13] distinguishes between explicit and implicit human computer interaction (HCI).

The main argument in favor of implicit HCI is in possibility for the user to focus on the task itself and not on dealing with the user interfaces as in case of traditional explicit HCIs like ones with keyboard/mouse [13]. Since the user does not always perceive as s/he interacts with a system, the implicit HCIs are also called disappearing or transparent. As a price for its advantages, the trade-off between invisibility and added value of implicit HCIs has to be considered to ensure the user acceptance.

To ensure the personalized adaptive property of HBI, the system has to rely on the current user context. One implementation challenge in regard of context-sharing between users, applications and user interfaces (UI) is in the choice between context-push and context-pull architecture. In practice however mixed architectures are used to combine the advantages from both approaches in performance and required communication bandwidth. One more challenge of using context as an input is possible problems with predictability of the UI. Generally, the trade-off between stability and adaptation of the UI has to be always found [13].

The other aspect in adaptive HCI is using the current user context for run-time filtering and/or mediating the communication in cases like switching the privacy level upon the arrival of persons without access rights to the previously shown content [13].The promising approach for adaptive user interaction with separating the applications from its user interaction is used by open distributed framework of the EU IST project PERSONA [14]. Using this framework the applications can be developed completely independent from the input / output devices physically available in the smart environment. The framework is also responsible for the personalized adaptive property of HBI by implementing the modality adaptation including modality fusion for input and modality fission for output. The content adaptation by for instance privacy level or location change is also implemented by the framework.

From the AC viewpoint the adaptive user interaction implementation in PERSONA has all the components of the MAPE-K control loop as well.

5   Conclusion, Discussion and Future Work

We proposed an AC-based self-adaptive ambient intelligence framework that could provide increased adaptability in control strategies in building and home automation. This allows achieving better trade-off between constantly changing user needs, building assistive functionality and resource usage. A promising from the AC viewpoint implementation for adaptive user interaction in AmI has been recognized.

We have also identified the research potential in implementation of *Planning* and *Execution* components of AC paradigm in regard of BI / AmI applications. It is clear so far that no AI approach can fully satisfy the AmI requirements on self-adaptability to the constantly changing user needs. Moreover, no *united* run-time AmI simulation tool possibly similar to Building Controls Virtual Test Bed (BCVTB) [15] but integrated with some available context-aware ubiquitous / pervasive computing middleware with the following features together was found:

- Multiple users' involvement by run-time behavior simulation in 3D-space
- Integration of different AI algorithms worth to apply in control strategies
- Integration of self-adaptive user interaction mechanisms

According to the identified gap we suggest the following future research steps:

1. An overview of environments for simulating and modeling of different BI / AmI components like context-aware middleware, AI-algorithms libraries, building information modeling, user behavior models and HBI frameworks;
2. Careful selection, integration and partial development of the BI binding platform like BCVTB [15] based on the results from the first step;
3. Integrating run-time multiple-user behavior in selected BI/AmI environment;
4. Integration of the state-of-the-art adaptive user interaction mechanisms;

5. Unified Integration of the existing AI simulation libraries/tools in order to create the basis for the interoperability of the I/O data between several AI-algorithms from adjacent tasks. The goal is to learn from the user behavior, to generate correcting action plans and control strategies in BMS;

6. Scientifically-proven definition of the performance criteria set of the AI-algorithms from the previous steps. This criteria set can contain for example the convergence speed, accuracy or sensitivity to computational errors and will serve as a ground of BI's action plan selection mechanism. Quality of Schedules generated by every AI algorithm can be introduced;

7. Explore the "best-effort" strategy for action selection based for example on voting, wave propagation or probability mechanisms. As a result we are going to implement this strategy in the BI / AmI action selection algorithm;

8. Defining the 3-4 application benchmarks (for energy efficiency, comfort, safety, security, AAL) within selected BI / AmI environment;

9. Performance evaluation and optimization for our "best effort" selection strategy / algorithm has to be created through simulation framework using application benchmarks. The visualization through performance plots for every application domain and for the whole action selection strategy / algorithm will help to recognize the optimization opportunities;

References

1. Kephart, J.O., Chess, D.M.: The Vision of Autonomic Computing. ACM Computer 36(1), 41–50 (2003)
2. Huebscher, M.C., McCann, J.A.: A Survey of Autonomic Computing\—Degrees, Models, and Applications. ACM Computing Survey 40(3), article 7 (2008)
3. Weiser, M.: The Computer for the 21st Century. ACM SIGMOBILE Mobile Computing and Communications 3(3), 3–11 (1999)
4. Baldlauf, M., Schahram, D., Rosenberg, F.: A survey on context-aware systems. Journal of Ad Hoc and Ubiquitous Computing 2(4) (June 2007)
5. Kjaer, K.E.: A survey of context-aware middleware. In: Proceedings of the 25th Conference on IASTED International Multi-Conference: Software Engineering. ACTA Press (2007)
6. Bourcier, J., Diaconescu, A., Lalanda, P., McCann, J.A.: AutoHome: an Autonomic Management Framework for Pervasive Home Applications. ACM Trans. Auton. Adapt. Syst. 6(1), article 8, 1(212), 1–9 (2011)
7. Aztina, A., Izaguirre, A., Augusto, J.C.: Learning Patterns in Ambient Intelligence Environments: a Survey. Artificial Intelligence Review 34(1), 35–51 (2010)
8. Andrushevich, A., Staub, M., Kistler, R., Klapproth, A.: Towards semantic buildings: Goal-driven approach for building automation service allocation and control. In: Proceedings of IEEE Conference on Emerging Technologies and Factory Automation, pp. 1–6 (September 2010)
9. Drumond, L., Girardi, R.: A Survey of Ontology Learning Procedures. In: Proceedings of the 3rd Workshop on Ontologies and Their Applications, SBIA, Brazil (2008)
10. Kim, E., Helal, S., Cook, D.: Human activity recognition and pattern discovery. IEEE Pervasive Computing 9(1), 48–53 (2010)

11. Hoes, P., Hensen, J.L.M., Loomans, M.G.L.C., de Vries, B., Bourgeois, D.: User behavior in whole building simulation. Energy and Buildings 41(3), 295–302 (2009)
12. Rashidi, P., Cook, D., Holder, L., Schmitter-Edgecombe, M.: Discovering activities to recognize and track in a smart environment. IEEE Transactions on Knowledge and Data Engineering 23(4), 527–539 (2011)
13. Riva, G., Vatalaro, F., Davide, F., Alcañiz, M.: Interactive Context-Aware Systems Interacting with Ambient Intelligence. In: Schmidt, A. (ed.) IOS Press (2005)
14. Tazari, M.-R.: Open Distributed Framework for Adaptive User Interaction in Ambient Intelligence. In: de Ruyter, B., Wichert, R., Keyson, D.V., Markopoulos, P., Streitz, N., Divitini, M., Georgantas, N., Mana Gomez, A. (eds.) AmI 2010. LNCS, vol. 6439, pp. 227–238. Springer, Heidelberg (2010)
15. Wetter, M., Haves, P., Building Controls Virtual Test Bed,
    https://gaia.lbl.gov/bcvtb

Using Active Learning to Allow Activity Recognition on a Large Scale

Hande Alemdar, Tim L.M. van Kasteren, and Cem Ersoy

Boğaziçi University, Department of Computer Engineering, NETLAB,
Istanbul, Turkey
hande.ozgur@boun.edu.tr
http://www.netlab.boun.edu.tr

Abstract. Automated activity recognition systems that use probabilistic models require labeled data sets in training phase for learning the model parameters. The parameters are different for every person and every environment. Therefore, for every person or environment, training is needed to be performed from scratch. Obtaining labeled data requires much effort therefore poses challenges on the large scale deployment of activity recognition systems. Active learning can be a solution to this problem. It is a machine learning technique that allows the algorithm to choose the most informative data points to be annotated. Because the algorithm selects the most informative data points, the amount of the labeled data needed for training the model is reduced. In this study, we propose using active learning methods for activity recognition. We use three different informativeness measures for selecting the most informative data points and evaluate their performances using three real world data sets recorded in a home setting. We show through experiments that the required number of data points is reduced by 80% in House A, 73% in House B, and 66% in House C with active learning.

1   Introduction

Recognizing human activities in an automated manner is essential in many ambient intelligence applications such as smart homes, health monitoring and assistance applications, emergency services, and transportation assistance services [7,3]. There are already several activity recognition systems that are designed for in-home settings [12,4] and also there are systems for outdoor settings [11]. It is foreseen that in the near future, activity recognition systems will be deployed on a large scale and become a part of future daily life. Probabilistic models for human activity recognition have been shown to work well [21,9,6]. However, these models require labeled training data to learn the model parameters. Moreover, because the model parameters are different across different people and environments (e.g. houses), a labeled data set is needed for each person and each house. Therefore, scalability problems arise.

We can record and annotate data sets for training the system from scratch for every house and every person but this will be extremely costly. Instead, we

D. Keyson et al. (Eds.): AmI 2011, LNCS 7040, pp. 105–114, 2011.
© Springer-Verlag Berlin Heidelberg 2011

can use a machine learning technique called active learning to select the most informative data points for annotation. By requesting annotation only for the most informative data points, we reduce the amount of training data needed and minimize the annotation effort. In this paper, we propose a framework for active learning that can be used with any probabilistic model. We assess the performance of our method by conducting experiments on the multiple real world data sets.

The paper is organized as follows. In Section 2, we give a brief literature review on active learning applications to activity recognition. In Section 3, we provide the details of the model and active learning methods we used. Section 4 gives the details of our experiments with real data. Finally, we conclude with Section 5.

2   Related Work

Activity recognition systems proposed so far in the literature generally make use of miniature sensors. Sensors used can be both ambient [21] or wearable [1]. Ambient sensors include tiny wireless sensors that can measure several properties of the environment such as humidity, temperature, light and sound levels. They can also determine whether there is a motion in the environment or certain objects are being used by using passive infrared sensors or RFID sensors [5]. Ambient sensors are generally used for in-home settings. Wearable sensors can also be used for outdoors as well as indoor settings [13,8]. Some systems make use of both types of sensors [12]. Also, there are systems that make use of cellphones for activity recognition [14].

Although proposed systems employ various sensing modalities and try to recognize different types of activities in different settings, the common point in all types of systems is that they all use pattern recognition methods for inferring the activities. Probabilistic models are used often and they work well for activity recognition. Especially, HMMs are widely used to model the human activity recognition since they are well suited for sequential nature of human activities [21,9,6].

Active learning is a technique for selecting the most informative data points for annotation and it has been generally used in part of speech tagging problems in natural language processing [18,2]. The use of active learning in activity recognition systems is studied by a few other researchers. In [16], Liu et al. use active learning with in a decision tree model to classify the activities collected by a group of wearable sensors. In [19], a similar study is presented using classifiers like decision tree, joint boosting and Naive Bayes. In both studies, uncertainty based active learning methods are employed and active learning has been showed to work well. These earlier studies use classifiers that do not take the sequential nature of the data into account. In this study, we propose a method to use active learning with a model that considers the temporal nature of human activities.

In [10], the authors propose to use active learning for adapting to the changes in the layout of the living place. They use an entropy based measure to select the

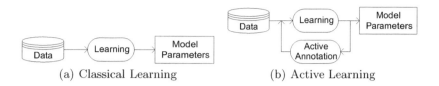

Fig. 1. Learning Frameworks

most informative instances and they evaluate the performance under laboratory conditions making two different controlled changes in the sensor deployment. Reported results indicate 20% decrease in the amount of training data required to retrain the system. In this study, we evaluate our work on three large real world data sets and show that the required number of data points is reduced by 80% in House A, 73% in House B, and 66% in House C with active learning.

3   Active Learning

In this section, we first provide brief information about existing machine learning techniques that do not use active learning. After that, we describe our proposed active learning framework and state how it differs from the classic learning approach. Finally, we describe three measures that can be used in active learning for selecting the most informative data points.

In order to use a probabilistic model a set of model parameters have to be learned. In Figure 1(a), the classical learning framework is depicted. The model parameters which we denote by θ, can be learned using a supervised method which only uses the data whose labels are obtained through annotation.

In our framework, we use only the labeled data points for obtaining the model parameters and the unlabeled data is disregarded. As depicted in Figure 1(b), the active learning algorithm iteratively

1. Learns new parameters using supervised learning
2. Selects the most informative data points according to the current model parameters and obtain their labels

The iterations continue until convergence. More formally, we define $x = \{x_1, x_2, ...x_T\}$ as the set of data points (i.e. data collected from the sensors), $y = \{y_1, y_2, .., y_T\}$ as the set of true labels (i.e. activity performed by the user). The *labeled data set* is $\mathcal{L} = \{x_i, y_i \mid x_i \in x, \quad y_i \in y, \quad 1 \leq i \leq T\}$. The *unlabeled data set* is $\mathcal{U} = \{x_i \mid x_i \notin \mathcal{L}, \quad 1 \leq i \leq N\}$. Typically we have a lot more unlabeled data than labeled data, $N \gg T$. We define the union of these data sets as $\mathcal{D} = \{\mathcal{L} \bigcup \mathcal{U}\}$ and the size of $\mathcal{D}$ is fixed.

At each iteration, we transfer the data points from $\mathcal{U}$ to $\mathcal{L}$ by performing annotation. The size of $\mathcal{L}$, denoted by T, increases while the size of $\mathcal{U}$, denoted by N, decreases. The data points that will be transferred from $\mathcal{U}$ to $\mathcal{L}$ are selected by the active learning method according to some informativeness measure. We use uncertainty for assessing the most informative data points [15]. Probabilistic models need to calculate the probability distribution of the activities at each data point to perform inference. For many probabilistic models there exist efficient algorithms to calculate these quantities, for example the forward-backward algorithm is used for HMMs [17]. The forward-backward algorithm gives the probabilities for each activity at each time slice. While performing the inference, the model selects the activity that has the highest probability value for that time slice. We use the forward-backward algorithm to obtain the probabilities of each activity at each time slice according to the current model parameters θ, which we denote with P_θ. After that, to select the most informative data point, x^*, we use three different methods.

1. *Least Confident Method* considers only the most probable class label and selects the instances having the lowest probability for the most likely label.

$$x^* = \arg\max_x(1 - P_\theta(\hat{y} \mid x)) \tag{1}$$

where $\hat{y} = \arg\max_y P_\theta(y \mid x)$ is the class label with the highest probability according to the current model parameters θ.

2. *Margin Sampling* selects the instances that the difference between the most and the second most probable labels is minimum.

$$x^* = \arg\min_x(P_\theta(\hat{y_1} \mid x) - P_\theta(\hat{y_2} \mid x)) \tag{2}$$

where $\hat{y_1}$ and $\hat{y_2}$ are the two most probable classes.

3. *Entropy based* method selects the instances that have the highest entropy values among all probable classifications.

$$x^* = \arg\max_x -\sum_i (P_\theta(\hat{y_i} \mid x) log P_\theta(\hat{y_i} \mid x)) \tag{3}$$

4   Experiments

We search for the effect of active learning for reducing the annotation effort in activity recognition. That is, we want to recognize the activities as accurate as possible while using the minimum amount of labeled data. Also, we do not want to disturb the user for a label that he possibly does not remember. Asking about the label of the activity that had been performed a month ago is not realistic. In this study, we propose a daily querying approach and evaluate its performance on real world data sets.

4.1   Experimental Setup

For the experiments, we use an openly accessible data set collected from three houses having different layouts and different number of sensors. The activities performed at each house is different from each other. Data are collected using binary sensors such as reed switches to determine open-close states of doors and cupboards; pressure mats to identify sitting on a couch or lying in bed; mercury contacts to detect the movements of objects like drawers; passive infrared (PIR) sensors to detect motion in a specific area; float sensors to measure the toilet being flushed. The recorded activities include leaving the house, toilet use, showering, brushing teeth, sleeping, having breakfast, dinner, snacking, and other. The data sets are continuous and the activities are not presegmented. Detailed information about the data sets are given in [21].

Sensor data is discretized in 60 seconds intervals. After that, it is represented using change point feature representation since it has been shown to give good performance in activity recognition [21]. In change point representation, if the sensor value changes the feature value for that sensor becomes 1, and is 0 otherwise. To simulate the real world situation in our experiments, we assumed that we do not have any labels at the beginning. For obtaining the labels, we assumed an annotator that can give the true label of any time slice whenever it is asked.

We use a hidden Markov model (HMM) for activity recognition model for all experiments with the following joint probability distribution [21,9].

$$p(y_{1:T}, x_{1:T}) = p(y_1) \prod_{t=1}^{T} p(x_t \mid y_t) \prod_{t=2}^{T} p(y_t \mid y_{t-1}) \tag{4}$$

The hidden states correspond to the activities performed and the observations correspond to the sensor readings. There are three factors in the distribution: the initial state distribution $p(y_1)$ is represented as a multinomial distribution parameterized by π; the observation distribution $p(x_t \mid y_t)$ is a combination of independent Bernoulli distributions (i.e. one for each feature), parameterized by B, and the transition distribution $p(y_t \mid y_{t-1})$ is represented as a collection of multinomial distributions (i.e. one for each activity), parameterized by A. The entire model is therefore parameterized by a set of three parameters $\theta = \{\pi, A, B\}$. For learning the model parameters, we use a supervised approach using only the labeled data.

We use leave-one-day-out cross validation in our experiments. We use one full day of data for testing and the remaining days for training. We use training days in a sequential manner, that is, after we process a day's data, we move to the following day and do not use the previous day's data for obtaining labels. As stated previously, we iteratively learn new model parameters and select the most informative points to be annotated. In the learning phase, we use all the data points whose labels we already obtained. However, we do not select data points for annotation except from the current day. In other words, in each iteration we learn model parameters with all the data that we obtained thus far. After that, according to the newly learned parameters, we select the data points to be annotated from only the current day. We cycle over days for testing and use every day once for testing. We report the average of the performance measure.

For measuring the performance, we use F-measure, which is the harmonic mean of precision and recall values. It is a common metric to evaluate the performance [22]. For a multi-class classification problem

$$Precision = 1/Q \sum_{i=1}^{Q}(TP_i/(TP_i + FP_i)),$$

$$Recall = 1/Q \sum_{i=1}^{Q}(TP_i/(TP_i + FN_i)), \text{ and}$$

$$F - measure = (2.Precision.Recall)/(Precision + Recall)$$

where Q is the number of classes, TP_i is the number of true positive classifications for class i, FP_i is the number of false positive classifications for class i, and FN_i is the number of false negative classifications for class i.

4.2   Active Learning vs. Random Selection

We compare the performance of three different informativeness measures to random selection with two different selection sizes. We start with uniformly initialized parameters since we have no information about the model parameters at the beginning. At each iteration, we select just one data point to be labeled from each day using the current model parameters according to three different informativeness measures and also we select a point randomly from each day for comparison. Based on these single points obtained at each day, we update the model parameters and proceed to the following day. Figure 2 shows the results for all three houses. The results show the better performance of active learning methods over random selection even with the model parameters obtained out of a single point. Since we use very very little amount of data, the recognition performance is very low.

The results also show the effect of the quality of the model parameters on the selection performance. With more accurate parameters we select more informative points. This, in turn, leads to more accurate parameters in the next iterations. For House A, the difference between active learning and random selection is prominent from the beginning. For House B, the random selection seems to outperform the active learning methods at the first iterations, however, random selection converges quickly and upwards trend for active learning methods can be clearly seen at the last iterations. The same thing is observed for House C. Since the data sets come from three different houses, they include different number of days and different activities.

In Figure 3, we show the results of a selection size of 10 points instead of a single point. The upper bound that can be achieved with fully annotated data, that is the labeled data for the full day of data, is also depicted in the figure. The recognition performance is higher than the previous experiment because we use more points at each iteration to learn the new model parameters. Again, for all three houses, the active learning methods work better than the random selection.

4.3   Discussion

In the experiments, we showed active learning to work well for an activity recognition application. With the active learning framework, the activity recognition

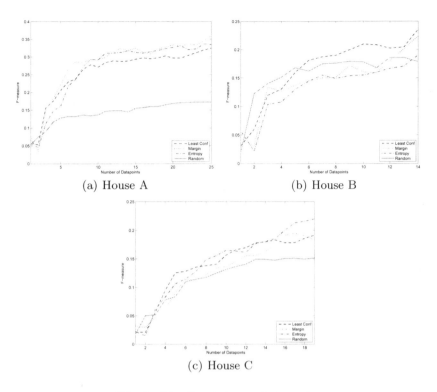

(a) House A

(b) House B

(c) House C

Fig. 2. Selecting 1 data point per day

system selects the most informative points. Then, the system is trained iteratively, using only the most informative points' labels. In our experiments, we
selected the points that needed to be annotated on a daily basis. At the end
of each day, the system asks the user what he has been doing during the time
slices that are chosen to be the most informative. In our scenario, the user is
disturbed only once a day, possibly before going to bed, by the system and asked
about some activities he performed during that day. The active learning framework we propose allows different number of data points to be selected from each
day. Having more data points is always better but the number can vary from
one to up to all data points. This also allows the user to determine the number
of data points to be annotated himself each day. In Figure 3, we used 10 data
points to be annotated for each day in 10 iterations. The model parameters are
recalculated after each obtained label since each labeled point is of significant
importance to obtain accurate model parameters. Since we use a supervised approach, recalculating the parameters is very fast and the user does not have to
wait to be asked about the following label. We iteratively select points and update the model parameters, therefore, bias on selection do not propagate. Also,
since we always obtain the true labels for the selected points, bias on learning
the model parameters is very unlikely to occur.

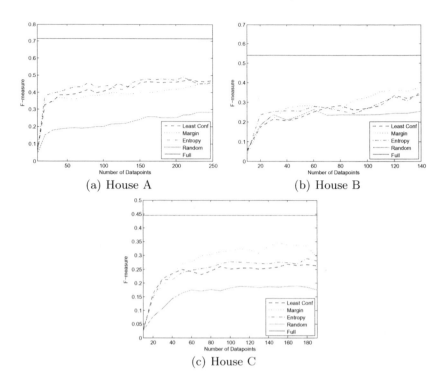

(a) House A   (b) House B

(c) House C

Fig. 3. Selecting 10 data points per day

In all cases, random selection performs worse than active learning methods. We run experiments on the data to obtain the same level of performance with random selection. The results reveal that, with random selection, we need 5 times more number of data points in House A, 3.7 times more in House B, and 3 times more in House C for the same level of performance. Therefore, the required number of data points is reduced by 80% in House A, 73% in House B, and 66% in House C.

Achieving high performance in activity recognition systems using probabilistic models depends on model parameters that are learned using the labeled data. With active learning, we aim to reach the most accurate model parameters iteratively using the parameters obtained from previous iterations for selecting the most informative data points. In the first iterations, the parameters are based on few number of data points, therefore, not accurately estimated. This leads to a poor estimate of the informativeness of data points at the first iterations. We can see from the results that even with a small amount of training data obtained after a few iterations, the selection gets better quickly. Instead of randomly initializing our parameters in the first iteration, we can use a method called transfer learning which allows the use of model parameters that have been learned previously to be used in another setting [20]. Using transfer learning together with active learning methods can lead to better estimates of the parameters even at the first iterations. In the future, we plan to extend our experiments using transfer learning together with active learning.

5   Conclusion

In this study, we addressed the scalability problems of automated human activity recognition systems since they require labeled data sets for adapting themselves to different users and environments. Collecting the data, annotation and retraining the systems from scratch for every person or every house is too costly. Therefore, redeploying these systems in different settings should be accomplished in a cost effective and user friendly way. For this purpose, we propose active learning methods which reduce the annotation effort by selecting only the most informative data points to be annotated. In our framework, we also consider the user friendliness. We showed that by disturbing the user only once a day for obtaining the minimum amount of labels, we can still learn accurate model parameters.

We used three different measures of uncertainty for selecting the most informative data points and evaluated their performance by using real world data sets. We used HMM as the probabilistic model for all experiments. Experiments showed that all three proposed method works well for the activity recognition system. We showed through experiments on real world data sets that, by using the active learning instead of random selection, the required number of data points is reduced by 80% in House A, 73% in House B, and 66% in House C.

Acknowledgement. This research is supported by Bogazici University Research Fund (BAP) under the grant number 6056.

References

1. Altun, K., Barshan, B., Tunc, O.: Comparative study on classifying human activities with miniature inertial and magnetic sensors. Pattern Recognition 43, 3605–3620 (2010)
2. Anderson, B., Siddiqi, S., Moore, A.: Sequence selection for active learning (2006)
3. Atallah, L., Lo, B., Ali, R., King, R., Yang, G.Z.: Real-time activity classification using ambient and wearable sensors. IEEE Transactions on Information Technology in Biomedicine 13(6), 1031–1039 (2009)
4. Biswas, J., Tolstikov, A., Jayachandran, M., Foo, V., Aung, A., Wai, P., Phua, C., Huang, W., Shue, L.: Health and wellness monitoring through wearable and ambient sensors: exemplars from home-based care of elderly with mild dementia. Annals of Telecommunications 65, 505–521 (2010)
5. Buettner, M., Prasad, R., Philipose, M., Wetherall, D.: Recognizing daily activities with RFID-based sensors. In: 11th International Conference on Ubiquitous Computing, pp. 51–60. ACM (2009)
6. Cheng, B.C., Tsai, Y.A., Liao, G.T., Byeon, E.S.: HMM machine learning and inference for Activities of Daily Living recognition. The Journal of Supercomputing 54, 29–42 (2010)

7. Cook, D.J., Augusto, J.C., Jakkula, V.R.: Ambient intelligence: Technologies, applications, and opportunities. Pervasive and Mobile Computing 5(4), 277–298 (2009)
8. Fletcher, R.R., Dobson, K., Goodwin, M.S., Eydgahi, H., Wilder-Smith, O., Fernholz, D., Kuboyama, Y., Hedman, E.B., Poh, M.Z., Picard, R.W.: iCalm: wearable sensor and network architecture for wirelessly communicating and logging autonomic activity. IEEE Transactions on Information Technology in Biomedicine 14(2), 215–223 (2010)
9. He, J., Li, H., Tan, J.: Real-time daily activity classification with wireless sensor networks using Hidden Markov Model. In: International Conference of the IEEE Engineering in Medicine and Biology Society 2007, pp. 3192–3195 (2007)
10. Ho, Y., Lu, C., Chen, I., Huang, S., Wang, C., Fu, L.: Active-learning assisted self-reconfigurable activity recognition in a dynamic environment. In: IEEE International Conference on Robotics and Automation, pp. 813–818 (2009)
11. Hong, Y.J., Kim, I.J., Ahn, S.C., Kim, H.G.: Mobile health monitoring system based on activity recognition using accelerometer. Simulation Modelling Practice and Theory 18(4), 446–455 (2010)
12. Ince, N.F., Min, C.H., Tewfik, A., Vanderpool, D.: Detection of Early Morning Daily Activities with Static Home and Wearable Wireless Sensors. EURASIP Journal on Advances in Signal Processing 2008, 1–12 (2008)
13. Kao, T.P., Lin, C.W., Wang, J.S.: Development of a portable activity detector for daily activity recognition. In: IEEE International Symposium on Industrial Electronics, pp. 115–120 (2009)
14. Kwapisz, J.R., Weiss, G.M., Moore, S.A.: Activity Recognition using Cell Phone Accelerometers. In: 4th International Workshop on Knowledge Discovery from Sensor Data, pp. 10–18 (2010)
15. Lewis, D.D., Catlett, J.: Heterogeneous uncertainty sampling for supervised learning. In: 11th International Conference on Machine Learning, pp. 148–156 (1994)
16. Liu, R., Chen, T., Huang, L.: Research on human activity recognition based on active learning. In: International Conference on Machine Learning and Cybernetics (ICMLC), vol. 1, pp. 285–290 (2010)
17. Rabiner, L.R.: A Tutorial on Hidden Markov Models and Selected Applications in Speech Recognition. Proceedings of the IEEE 77(2), 257–286 (1989)
18. Settles, B., Craven, M.: An analysis of active learning strategies for sequence labeling tasks. In: Conference on Empirical Methods in Natural Language Processing - EMNLP 2008 (2008)
19. Stikic, M., van Laerhoven, K., Schiele, B.: Exploring semi-supervised and active learning for activity recognition. In: 12th IEEE International Symposium on Wearable Computers (ISWC 2008), pp. 81–88 (2008)
20. van Kasteren, T.L.M., Englebienne, G., Kröse, B.J.A.: Transferring Knowledge of Activity Recognition across Sensor Networks. In: Floréen, P., Krüger, A., Spasojevic, M. (eds.) Pervasive Computing. LNCS, vol. 6030, pp. 283–300. Springer, Heidelberg (2010)
21. van Kasteren, T.L.M., Noulas, A., Englebienne, G., Kröse, B.J.A.: Accurate activity recognition in a home setting. In: 10th International Conference on Ubiquitous Computing - UbiComp 2008 (2008)
22. Van Rijsbergen, C.J.: Information Retrieval. Butterworth–Heinemann (1979)

Tagging Space from Information Extraction and Popularity of Points of Interest

Ana O. Alves[1,2], Filipe Rodrigues[1], and Francisco C. Pereira[1]

[1] CISUC, University of Coimbra, Portugal
{ana,camara}@dei.uc.pt, fmpr@student.dei.uc.pt
[2] ISEC, Coimbra Institute of Engineering, Portugal
aalves@isec.pt

Abstract. This paper is about automatic tagging of urban areas considering its constituent Points of Interest. First, our approach geographically clusters places that offer similar services in the same generic category (e.g. Food & Dining; Entertainment & Arts) in order to identify specialized *zones* in the urban context. Then, these places are analysed and tagged from available information sources on the Web using KUSCO [2,3] and finally the most relevant tags are chosen considering not only the place itself but also its popularity in social networks. We present some experiments in the greater metropolitan area of Boston.

Keywords: Context-Awareness, Semantic Enrichment, Web Mining.

1 Introduction

Understanding local context has been a recurrent challenge in Pervasive Computing. Besides information from sensors (e.g. latitude/longitude, wifi, cell-id, bluetooth, etc.), some functional or semantic properties can be collected that inform the overall context. Progress has been done in identifying such information for individual POIs [3]. However, besides just knowing about the exact place where we are (e.g. a specific Point of Interest), which per se can be more than enough to support many location based services, identifying the "big picture" of the area can bring this context to another level. Aided by social network popularity indicators (e.g. Gowalla[1] check-ins), we can even ground ourselves on what are, according to these communities, the most relevant spots to consider.

Ideally, the spatial resolution of this local context can vary from the point of interest to the entire city, depending on the application. A user might want enriched information about a specific place or about an entire region. In any case, for our research, the smallest entity is indeed the POI (Point-of-Interest). We consider a POI to be a touristic place (e.g. Boston Common) or a space with a given functionality (e.g. a post office agency).

These POIs are nowadays available from commercial or public POI sources (e.g. Manta[2] and Yahoo!Local[3]) and they generally refer to *buildings* rather

---

[1] http://www.gowalla.com
[2] http://www.manta.com
[3] http://local.yahoo.com

D. Keyson et al. (Eds.): AmI 2011, LNCS 7040, pp. 115–125, 2011.

than other kinds of places, like: parts inside buildings, regions, junctions, and others[9].

We propose an approach to visualize the urban space through tags taking in account available online information (more static knowledge) and popularity (more dynamic) about places in the social Web. This aim is accomplished by following some steps for a given city: First, POIs are massively extracted from public POI sources. These POIs are then grouped by Machine Learning techniques as clusters of related services considering generic categories (e.g. Recreation & Sporting Goods; Government & Community) that are geographically close. In parallel, tags are associated to each POI using Web Mining and Natural Language processing to extract relevant concepts which best describe the given place. And finally, a social network (Gowalla) is used to infer the popularity of places in order to compute the social significance of a given area considering this community and to select a tag that best represents it. Hence, the main contribution described in this paper is to extend KUSCO's tag ranking. KUSCO previously has considered all POIs in the city of equal importance, but the approach here proposed adds another dimension to the selection of most representative tags, the popularity of POIs.

The remaining of this paper is organized as the following: in the next section we present the related work. In section 3, the methods to obtain the POI data and group it in clusters are described. The process of information retrieving, extracting and computing the relevance of tags is detailed in section 4. Some experiments and validation are summed up in section 6. And finally, in section 7 we presents the conclusions and discuss future work.

2   Related Work

Context is any information that can be used to characterize the situation of an entity at a given time. An entity is a person, place, or object that is considered relevant to the interaction between a user and an application, including the user and applications themselves. Context generally refers to all types of information pertaining to a service and/or the user of the service[1]. Knowledge typically refers to more general information, of which context is a specific type. Knowledge would typically include information about users and their preferences, and also information that can be inferred from other sources. A system is context aware if it observes, reacts and changes accordingly to the context. Context information can be gathered from several sources including sensors, devices, data repositories and information services. Context data can be used to make inferences.

The key aspects of context are: location, agent or person, time and activity. These elements are used to answer basic questions related to a user, place or object which is target of context representation: *Where, Who, When, Why*. The main focus of this research is to represent *Where* in a more meaningful way with semantic tags.

The possibility to automatically associate labels has been investigated in the literature [4,7,10,14,11]. These approaches either use additional information, such as time of day and point-of-interest databases, to determine the type of building, or attempt to assign labels by comparing places across users. Some works use machine learning algorithms to induce these labels based also in other variables (time of day, weekday, etc.). These labels are limited to generic and personal ones like: work, home, friend and other. But our approach is not centered in the user, instead in the *Place* itself. And this representation should include public aspects and the functionality of places, not being of great importance the relation between some individual and the place itself. We think that a richer representation of Place with more meaningful common-sense concepts associated will help works like these described above.

From these works the most related is that proposed by Rattenbury et al. [14]. They identify place and event from tags that are assigned to photos on Flickr. They exploit the regularities on tags in which regards to time and space at several scales, so when "bursts" (sudden high intensities of a given tag in space or time) are found, they become an indicator of event of meaningful place. Then, the reverse process is possible, that of search for the tag clouds that correlate with that specific time and space. They do not, however, make use of any enrichment from external sources, which could add more objective information and their approach is limited to the specific scenarios of Web 2.0 platforms that carry significant geographical reference information. And the main difference to our approach is that we automatically *generate* tags not depending on contribution given by users.

Regarding the use of Gowalla, its potential and the potential of other similar location-based services like Foursquare[4] and Facebook Places[5] has already been demonstrated in recent work and it is being increasingly exploited as the dimensions of such services grow. Cheng et al. [6] provide an assessment of human mobility patterns by analyzing the spatial, temporal, social, and textual aspects associated with the hundreds of millions of user-driven footprints (i.e., "check-ins") that people leave with these services. Anastasios et al. [13] provide a similar study but they also analyze activity and place transitions. Both of these studies are very interesting and motivating for a further exploitation of this kind of services. For example, in [5] the authors exploit the use of Gowalla to develop a Recommender System for places in location-based Online Social Network services (OSN) based on the check-ins of the entire user base.

3   POI Mining

POI Mining refers to the processes of extraction, pre-processing and pattern recognition (namely clustering) in POI data that are the basis of the approaches that will be later presented in this paper.

---

[4] https://foursquare.com/
[5] http://www.facebook.com/places/

3.1   POI Extraction

The growing number of smartphones and social networks during the latest years has been producing a vast amount of geo-referenced information on the Web. Capture devices such as camera-phones and GPS-enabled cameras can automatically associate geographic data with images, which is significantly increasing the number of geo-referenced photos available online. Social networks also have an important role. They are a great medium where users can share information they collect with their mobile devices. As a consequence, the amount of online descriptive information about places has reached reasonable dimensions for many cities in the world.

In spite of their importance, the production of POIs is scattered across a myriad of different websites, systems and devices, thus making it extremely difficult to obtain an exhaustive database of such a wealthy information. There are thousands of POI directories in the Web, with POIs for places all over the World. These are in fact great sources of information. However, each one uses its own format to represent the POIs and its own taxonomy to classify them. Also, the Web servers that provide POI information (e.g., Yahoo!, Manta, Yellow Pages, CitySearch, Upcoming) are mere repositories, and therefore, they don't take advantage of the full potential of such information.

Despite the fact that our approach could be applied to any POI source and that for the sake of completeness multiple POI sources should be used, doing so would require a careful process of POI matching and integration, therefore, for just a matter of simplicity, in this paper we focus only on POI data extensively extracted from Yahoo! through its public API for the Boston Metropolitan Area.

3.2   Clustering

Clustering allows the identification of groups of data instances that are similar in some sense. In this context, clustering allows us to identify groups of nearby POIs in the city according to the geographic distance between their coordinates.

The subgroup of density-based clustering algorithms are devised to discover clusters of arbitrary shapes where each is regarded as a region in which the density of data instances exceeds a threshold, making them perfect for the identification of "hotspots" of POIs in the city (i.e. places with high concentrations of POIs). In this paper we use DBSCAN [8] to identify such "hotspots" that would be the basis of the Semantic Enrichment (Section 4) and Visualization (Section 6) processes.

In order to take the categories in consideration in the clustering process, we adopted a two-level clustering approach. In the first level, we group together POIs that are closer to each other according to their proximity in the Yahoo! taxonomy, and in the second we apply DBSCAN over these groupings, thus producing clusters of geographically nearby POIs that also have a similar set of categories. This approach will give us a different perspective of the POI data.

4   Semantic Enrichment of POIs

An approach that is able to extract relevant semantics from places can be useful for any context-aware system that behaves according to position. The level of information considered in this work brings another layer to add to other sensors (GPS, accelerometer, compass, communications, etc.), eventually pushing forward the potential for intelligent behavior. This section presents an approach to such a system and its implementation, resulting in an architecture called KUSCO a system which tags POIs using available sources of information (perspectives) on the Web. We briefly summarize this system for completeness of this paper, but redirect the reader to any of earlier publications for further details and evaluation of this approach[2,3].

Beyond the data available from commercial and community based POI sources, enrichment with public information is desired. Initially, the entire Web was used to retrieve such information but the great level of noise obtained led us to constrain our enrichment source to Wikipedia[6]. It is on this database that we apply two different methods, the "red and yellow perspectives" of place.

Low-detail labeling: the red wiki perspective

In the red wiki perspective, we extract the Wikipedia page corresponding to the identified category of a POI. Local POI directories are normally structured in a hierarchical tree of categories. This taxonomy may be created by the company itself or be collaboratively built by suggestion of users who feed the system with new POIs.

Since no API is currently available from Yahoo! to extract the entire taxonomy of POI categories, we have created a wrapper based on regular expressions in order to automatically extract it. Yahoo! only presents categories through menu navigation along its web site.

Each POI is only associated to leaf categories (more specific ones) instead of generic categories. These categories, in the middle and top of the taxonomy, are completely hidden from API when retrieving POIs. Curiously, a dynamic property of this POI source is also observed in the fact that this taxonomy is different depending on which city we are virtually visiting. Namely, Yahoo builds dynamically their menus, thus presenting proper taxonomies to distinct cities. Through time, this taxonomy grows with new types of services and places.

To contextualize each category in the corresponding Wikipedia article we base ourselves on string similarity between the category name and article title. We have opted for a top-down approach, from main categories to taxonomy leaves. To increase the confidence of this process, we disambiguate manually the main categories to start with and make sure that at least a more generic category will be connected to the Wikipages of its hypernym. When a POI has many categories, we obtain the articles for each one and consider the union of all the resulting articles as the source of analysis. Since there are many different combinations of categories, we can guarantee that each POI gets its own specific flavor of category analysis. For instance, consider the POI *Boston University* which is

---

[6] http://www.wikipedia.org/

classified under the Yahoo! categories: (1) Colleges & Universities; (2) High Schools; (3) School Districts. These categories are automatically mapped by KUSCO to the respective Wikipedia articles: (1) http://en.wikipedia.org/wiki/ Universities & http://en.wikipedia.org/wiki/Colleges; (2) http://en.wikipedia. org/wiki/High_schools; (3) http://en.wikipedia.org/wiki/School_districts.

Medium-detail labeling: the yellow wiki perspective

While the previous approach is centered on place category, here we focus our attention on Place name. We use string similarity to match Place name to Wikipage title in order to find the Wikipedia description for a given place. On a first glance, this method is efficient in mapping compound and rare place names such as 'Beth Israel Deaconess Medical Center' or 'Institute of Real State Management', however it can naively induce some wrong mappings for those places with very common names (e.g., Highway - a clothing accessories store in New York, Registry - a recruitment company in Boston, Energy Source - a batteries store in New York). We approach this problem by determining the specificity of place names, and only considering those with high Information Content (IC)[15]. The Information Content of a concept is defined as the negative log likelihood, -logp(c), where p(c) is the probability of encountering such concept. For example, 'money' has less information content than 'nickel' as the probability of encountering the concept, p(Money), is larger than encountering the probability of p(Nickel) in a given corpus. For those names present in Wordnet (e.g. Highway, Registry), IC is already calculated [12], while for those not present in Wordnet, we heuristically assume that they are only considered by our approach if they are not a node in Wikipedia taxonomy, i.e., a Wikipage representing a Wikipedia category (case of Energy Source), but being only a Wikipedia article.

Having a set of textual descriptions as input, KUSCO extracts a ranked list of concepts. This ranking is based solely on TF-IDF [16] (Term Frequency × Inverse Document Frequency) value in order to extract the most relevant terms that will represent a given place.

5   Tag Relevance Computing Based on Popularity

Beyond the traditional TF-IDF computed for individual POIs against other indexes in the POI database, we also use Gowalla to infer a popularity-based TF-IDF for the terms of a POI p in a given cluster c using the POI check-ins. The idea is that concepts associated with POIs that are very popular should be weighted favorably. Equation 1 shows how the popularity-based TF-IDF is calculated for each concept i in a given cluster c based on the POIs p that belong to that cluster.

$$Popularity\text{-}based \ TF\text{-}IDF_{i,c} = \frac{1}{|c|} \sum_{p \in c} TF\text{-}IDF_{i,p} * check\text{-}ins_p \qquad (1)$$

6   Experiments

Using as a test scenario the greater metropolitan area of Boston, we extracted 156364 POIs from the Yahoo! public API. Each POI has an average of 2 categories and the Yahoo! taxonomy is spread across three different levels of specificity, where the top level has 15 distinct categories and the lower level has a total of 1003 categories[7]. Table 1 shows the distribution of the extracted POIs over the top categories.

Table 1. POI distribution over the different Yahoo! categories for the different perspectives

Yahoo! Category	Total number of POIs	# POIs with RedWiki	# POIs withi YellowWiki
Automotive	8109	1698 (20.9%)	377 (4.6%)
Business to Business	37321	9488 (25.4%)	1034 (2.8%)
Computers & Electronics	3767	652 (17.3%)	100 (2.7%)
Education	3822	1277 (33.4%)	213 (5.6%)
Entertainment &Arts	4327	1611 (37.2%)	250 (5.8%)
Food & Dining	10383	1734 (16.7%)	433 (4.2%)
Government & Community	10646	2640 (24.8%)	186 (1.7%)
Health & Beauty	17100	4344 (25.4%)	317 (1.9%)
Home & Garden	22577	5127 (22.7%)	153 (0.7%)
Legal Financial Services	10727	1823 (17.0%)	188 (1.8%)
Professional Services	11658	3270 (28.0%)	436 (3.7%)
Real Estate	7059	1066 (15.1%)	50 (0.7%)
Recreation & Sporting Goods	3029	1051 (34.7%)	77 (2.5%)
Retail Shopping	9021	1663 (18.4%)	324 (3.6%)
Travel Lodging	3944	1599 (40.5%)	111 (2.8%)

In the clustering phase we grouped together POIs that shared the same top-level category, and then for each top-level category we applied DBSCAN using the POI coordinates. The parameters of the DBSCAN we manually tuned by running the clustering algorithm many times with different parameter setting and visually validating the results in a map. The goal was to choose a set of parameters that produced a balanced number of clusters that covered most of the different areas of the city. Figure 1 depicts the centroids of a possible clustering solution. We can see that the dominance of some categories over the others is also reflected in the clustering.

Table 1 shows for each Yahoo! top category the number of POIs extracted as the number of POIs enriched for both perspectives by KUSCO. We can observe the greater coverage of Red Wiki perspective as opposite to Yellow Perspective. This can be explained by the fact that almost every POI is categorized under at least one category in Yahoo!, and each category is mapped to at least one Wikipedia article (except in the case where there are more than one mapping

---

[7] These numbers refer only to the data we collected.

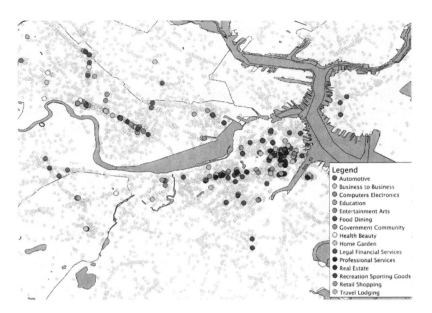

Fig. 1. Centroids of the clusters identified using the POI data enriched with the Red-Wiki perspective and the correspondent Yahoo! categories

to Wikipedia, e.g. Computers & Electronics). While in the Yellow Perspective, KUSCO searches for more specific information on Wikipedia: the POI article, when it exists. The enrichment process was validated earlier in previous studies [3] and we obtained a precision over than 60% ($\sigma = 20\%$) using a survey to 30 visitors or inhabitants of Boston.

In order to visualize and understand the whole process, consider the top 5 most popular categories in Gowalla (and the respective Yahoo! category) [8] for the greater metropolitan area in Boston. They are: Food (Food & Dining), Shopping & Services (Retail Shopping), Architecture & Buildings (Real State), Nightlife (Entertainment & Arts), College & Education (Education). From the first view of the city (Figure 2), we can observe a great predominance of common concepts as the system is dealing with generic information associated to the POI categories (perspective Red Wiki). The more relevant is a tag, the greater its font size. For instance, the term *health services* comes from POIs belonging to a not so popular category regarding Gowalla: Health & Beauty. But the concentration of very similar POIs related to the health services is so high [9], that this specialized zone is identified and the most relevant tag in all these related subcategories of Health top category is chosen (no matter the popularity of its POIs).

Another interesting example that helps us understand how the popularity is crucial to determine the most relevant tag, is the cluster identified by *secondary*

---

[8] Data extracted from Gowalla in May, 2011.
[9] e.g. MT Auburn Pulmonary Service, Cambridge Urological Association, Associated Surgeons, Cambridge Gastroenterology.

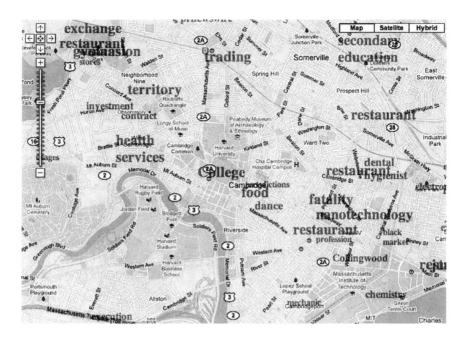

Fig. 2. Most relevant tags from the RedWiki perspective using DBSCAN (epsilon=0.0005, minPoints=15) to cluster POIs

education. In this cluster, different types of POIs we grouped, in this case in a not a so specialized *zone* [10], but as the most popular POI among them is a High School with a lot of checkins associated, this fact biased the weight of chosen tag.

Considering a different region of the city (Figure 3), by the Yellow Wiki perspective we find more specific tags as we are dealing with the proper Wikipedia article to each POI (when it exists). In the Yellow perspective, as we only have extracted information about each POI itself, we opted for displaying only the most popular POIs. In this figure, we can see interesting POI-tag relationships: Cambridge Innovation Center - *business incubator*; Boston Common - *Central Burying Ground*; Massachusetts General Hospital- *Harvard Cancer Center*; Boston University - *Colleges*; Louisburg Square-*Beacon Hill*; Best Buy-*forbes*; California Pizza Kitchen-*Richard*. The last two examples reflect some difficulties that we have faced in the present methodology: the company 'Best Buy' related to the concept Forbes (a magazine). This is not so relevant to understand the POI since this fact [11] is only referred in the summary of Wikipedia article since the second paragraph. This could be used to decrease the weight of extracted concepts: how long they are from the first paragraph.

---

[10] e.g. Somerville High School, GC Vocal Studio, Dexter Painting and Carpentry, FISH Magical Enterprises.

[11] Best Buy has won Forbes prizes in two consecutive years.

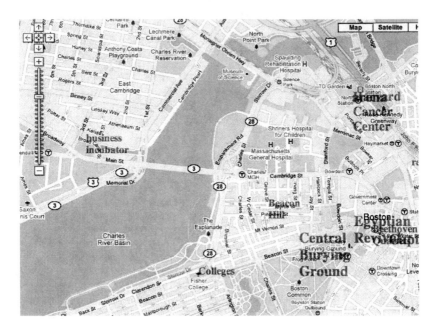

Fig. 3. Most relevant tags from the YellowWiki perspective using most popular POIs according to Gowalla (no clustering)

Considering the last pair POI-tag showed before, it is relatively straight-forward to verify that Richard Rosenfield is a co-founder of California Pizza Kitchen. In this sense if we knew more about this POI, namely the semantic behind it, regarding DBpedia*http://dbpedia.org/page/California_Pizza_Kitchen* it would be possible to infer their relationship: founder(California_Pizza_Kitchen, Richard Rosenfield).

7   Conclusions and Further Work

We presented a methodology for extracting semantic information about arbitrary sized areas, depending on the availability of Points of Interest. The nature of this process is ultimately subjective since all information is extracted automatically from crowd sourced resources. However we rely ourselves in techniques that favor statistical relevance, specificity and popularity to select the words (or tags) that should represent better the context according to "how people understand that space". Furthermore, the concept of "perspectives" explicitly models the unavoidable ambiguity in this problem. We took two approaches to Wikipedia as two ways to understand the same space. Others could be included (e.g. using twitter, facebook, eventful, etc.).

The use of popularity, from Gowalla, helps understanding the social dimension of space. From a purely democratic point of view, the more people that enters a place (and happily reports it), the more it is relevant for the community.

Of course, this raises questions itself on how representative is the population that uses Gowalla, and how they actually report the places they visit (e.g. don't they check in more often when waiting in a fast food queue than when having fun?). The work here presented will become more representative as such communities grow. As a further improvement of our approach, we plan to also use the POI radius available from Gowalla as a feature to consider in the cluster algorithm, since very wide POIs (e.g. MIT), at this time, have the same weight of the small POIs (Starbucks).

References

1. Abowd, G.D., Dey, A.K., Brown, P.J., Davies, N., Smith, M., Steggles, P.: Towards a Better Understanding of Context and Context-Awareness. In: Gellersen, H.-W. (ed.) HUC 1999. LNCS, vol. 1707, pp. 304–307. Springer, Heidelberg (1999)
2. Alves, A.O., Pereira, F.C., Biderman, A., Ratti, C.: Place Enrichment by Mining the Web. In: Tscheligi, M., de Ruyter, B., Markopoulus, P., Wichert, R., Mirlacher, T., Meschterjakov, A., Reitberger, W. (eds.) AmI 2009. LNCS, vol. 5859, pp. 66–77. Springer, Heidelberg (2009)
3. Alves, A.O., Pereira, F.C., Rodrigues, F., Oliveirinha, J.a.: Place in perspective: extracting online information about points of interest. In: Proc. of AmI 2011 (2011)
4. Amitay, E., Har'El, N., Sivan, R., Soffer, A.: Web-a-where: geotagging web content. In: SIGIR 2004, pp. 273–280. ACM, New York (2004)
5. Berjani, B., Strufe, T.: A Recommendation System for Spots in Location-Based Online Social Networks. In: Proc. of Eurosys Works on Social Network Systems (2011)
6. Cheng, Z., Caverlee, J., Lee, K., Sui, D.Z.: Exploring Millions of Footprints in Location Sharing Services. In: ICWSM 2011, Barcelona, Spain (2011)
7. Dubinko, M., Kumar, R., Magnani, J., Novak, J., Raghavan, P., Tomkins, A.: Visualizing tags over time. In: WWW 2006, pp. 193–202. ACM, New York (2006)
8. Ester, M., Kriegel, H.P., Sander, J., Xu, X.: A density-based algorithm for discovering clusters in large spatial databases with noise. In: KDD, pp. 226–231 (1996)
9. Falko Schmid, C.K.: In-situ communication and labeling of places. In: 6th International Symposium on LBS & TeleCartography. Springer, Heidelberg (September 2009)
10. Jaffe, A., Naaman, M., Tassa, T., Davis, M.: Generating summaries and visualization for large collections of geo-referenced photographs. In: MIR 2006, pp. 89–98 (2006)
11. Lemmens, R., Deng, D.: Web 2.0 and semantic web: Clarifying the meaning of spatial features. In: Semantic Web meets Geopatial Applications, AGILE 2008 (2008)
12. Mihalcea, R.: Semcor semantically tagged corpus. Tech. rep., University of North Texas (1998), http://citeseer.ist.psu.edu/250575.html
13. Noulas, A., Scellato, S., Mascolo, C., Pontil, M.: An Empirical Study of Geographic User Activity Patterns in Foursquare. In: ICWSM 2011, Barcelona, Spain (2011)
14. Rattenbury, T., Good, N., Naaman, M.: Towards automatic extraction of event and place semantics from flickr tags. In: SIGIR 2007, pp. 103–110 (2007)
15. Resnik, P.: Using information content to evaluate semantic similarity in a taxonomy. In: IJCAI, pp. 448–453 (1995)
16. Salton, G., Buckley, C.: Term-weighting approaches in automatic text retrieval. Information Processing and Management 24(5), 513–523 (1988)

Context-Aware Integration of Smart Environments in Legacy Applications

Philipp Lehsten, Alexander Gladisch, and Djamshid Tavangarian

University of Rostock, Graduate School MuSAMA
{firstname.lastname}@uni-rostock.de
http://www.musama.de

Abstract. As opposed to conventional applications, smart environments are designed to offer transparent user assistance by decoupling users from devices. Apart from the lack of realised systems there are numerous applications that are strongly interwoven with the users' workflow and hard to replace, commonly called legacy applications. Instead of creating new applications, our approach is the loose integration of these both, the smart environment and the legacy application. In our work, we propose a generic architecture that is applicable to various kinds of environments and applications. The architecture comprises an intermediate layer that enables a loose coupling between smart environment and legacy application. Furthermore, we introduce a workflow to refine the generic architecture to fit the requirements of specific use cases. For our use case, we apply the vision of a pervasive university. Here, we integrate functionalities of smart lecture rooms into a learning management system that is commonly used in German universities and therefore hard to replace.

Keywords: smart environment, legacy application, pervasive computing, service-oriented architecture.

1 Introduction

Since pervasive computing was envisioned by Weiser [1], developing Smart Environments (SEs) is a major objective for researchers of various disciplines. SEs are designed to offer "anytime and anywhere computing" and moreover transparent user assistance by decoupling users from computing devices.

Assisting the user in his workflow is only partially realized by today's applications. However, workflows may comprise not only computing tasks, which can be facilitated by applications, but also interactions with the physical environment that can be improved by assistance of these SEs. Therefore, the consequence is the need to integrate smart capabilities in existing applications that already assist the user in his workflow in general and especially for applications that cannot be easily replaced, e.g. legacy applications.

Decoupling users from computing devices implies unobtrusiveness by hiding the complexity from the user. For that purpose, in the first visions on SEs, complete proactive user assistance was discussed [2]. However, undesired situations

D. Keyson et al. (Eds.): AmI 2011, LNCS 7040, pp. 126–135, 2011.

may occur because of error-prone intention recognition mechanisms. Moreover, if an explicit user interface is missing, the user is not able to adapt a new configuration. For these reasons, the users need options to interact, without getting overburdened by complexity of the SE.

To achieve these goals, we propose a generic architecture, which is applicable to various kinds of SEs and applications. The architecture comprises an intermediate layer between both systems and therefore enables the integration of the smart capabilities into an existing application. The layer includes an explicit but also context-aware user interface, which provides further assistance, e.g. by providing preset configurations. Thereby, the user can interact directly with the environment without being aware of the complexity. Furthermore, we describe a general workflow to analyse specific environments and applications. Based on the analysis results, the generic architecture can be refined to fit a specific use case. Finally, we present an enriched learning management system in the context of a pervasive university as implemented use case.

The rest of the paper is organized as follows: preliminary considerations are taken in section 2 to foster our approach. Section 3 introduces related work. Section 4 defines the generic architecture with the intermediate layer, while section 5 presents our workflow to refine our generic architecture for a specific use case. Then we present a use case according to the vision of a pervasive university in section 6. Here, we integrate functionalities of smart lecture rooms in a learning management system that is commonly used in German universities. Finally, we present our conclusion in section 7.

2   Preliminary Considerations

In general, SEs are considered as systems to support the users to achieve their goals. For this purpose, user intentions need to be recognized, e.g. by evaluating information that relates to users current situation. Such information is considered as context [3]. Additionally, devices and services, which are integrated into the environment, need to be configured and controlled in order to assist the users. Depending on the capabilities and available facilities of the environment, this task can be very complex.

SEs are applied for various fields of applications, smart meeting rooms [4], smart homes [5], smart university campus [6] or smart transportation systems (known as intelligent transportation systems) [7] are common examples. Accordingly, requirements on the infrastructure and therefore the context information differ significantly, not only in pure availability but also in granularity. For example smart homes for people, who suffer from dementia, have to recognize fine-grained subtasks to prevent injuries or to continue assistance after interruptions of users workflow. Therefore, user position and other fine-grained context data, as well as sensors to gather this information, is needed. On the other hand, assistance in smart lecture rooms can be realized by collecting coarse-grained context, such as: "Which person is giving a lecture at what time?". Here, among others identification and authorization of the user are necessary tasks of the workflow and can be realised utilising global repositories.

By now, workflows for simple tasks are often facilitated by single applications where workflows for complex tasks are mostly encouraged by compound enterprise applications. These kinds of applications are often legacy applications and therefore replacement is laborious as well as time consuming. However, up to now, both kinds of application do not integrate assistance provided by SEs, whereas the integration of assisting capabilities into the user workflow is promising.

Despite the problems caused by heterogeneity and complexity of the SEs and existing applications, the coupling offers also multiple benefits. Legacy applications are often used as storage for large amounts of context information (e.g. resource management of rooms, time schedules or personal information) and they provide a graphical user interface as well as identification and authorization mechanisms. Therefore they are able to provide some information needed to evaluate the user context without using installed hardware sensors. Furthermore, they offer an interface, which the user is already used to and which is already mapped to the workflows. Using these applications as interface can help to accustom users to newly installed technologies. Therefore, we advocate the integration of an interface to the SE into the user interface of legacy applications. The generic architecture, we propose, comprises an intermediate layer that includes such an interface and allows a loose coupling of the legacy system with the SE. This allows among others a fast adoption to new interfaces and the support of a multitude of SEs.

3 Related Work

When examining user interfaces (UI) for SEs, physical UIs are highlighted in many cases. In [8], a toolkit for physical UIs for ubiquitous computing environments was developed. The focus of this work was on the integration of different I/O devices and their software proxies. In [9], Smartphones were considered as the default physical UI for ubiquitous computing applications. In their work, the authors examined and evaluated several interaction techniques where the capabilities of smartphones were used.

In [10] three different physical interfaces (PC, media terminal and smartphone) to control smart home environments were analysed. In their work the authors highlighted that users might not be ready to interact with their familiar environment by using new interaction techniques. Furthermore, they did a user study to evaluate the considered UIs. Here, the smartphone was also the most frequently used UI. Beyond the interfaces itself, various types of interactions with the UIs of SEs were identified in [10], among others speech, gesture and graphical UI (explicit UIs) as well as automatic interaction (implicit UIs). The subjects of the user study ranked automated interaction as the most relevant technique but they also highlighted that a full automation is undesirable due to missing possibilities of human intervention. The subjects wanted chains of functions (preset configurations) they could set up themselves.

In contrast to that, in [11] the authors postulate that (learning) activities are neither bound to a specific environment nor prestructured. For that reason, the users (learners) should be able to create their own learning environment by configuring the available resources of the environment in ways they find most comfortable. Due to the multitude of available resources and functionalities in a SE, we doubt that this is possible for the user. Therefore, we want to support in our work the user by providing preset configurations, where the user is able to choose the environmental components, which fit best to his requirements.

4   Generic Architecture

Despite the heterogeneity of possible SEs and applications, we define a generic architecture, which is theoretically applicable to various combinations of SEs and applications. Afterwards, we introduce in section 5 a workflow, which allows the customization of the generic architecture for specific use cases. The proposed architecture comprises a transparent intermediate layer, which couples the SE and the legacy application. From the application point of view, the layer provides an extension of the UI to integrate additional functionalities. This requires a plug-in functionality or at least some kind of access to the source code of the application interface. From the other point of view, it provides commands to control the SE. Here again some kind of interface access is needed, like web services that can be used to control the SE. Thus, the intermediate layer allows a loose coupling without losing independent functionality of the SE and the application. Furthermore, the interfaces of the proposed intermediate layer can be exchanged to integrate other applications or SEs.

The intermediate layer consists of three components as shown in figure 1: (1) adaptive GUI, (2) rules engine and (3) context storage with importers. The core

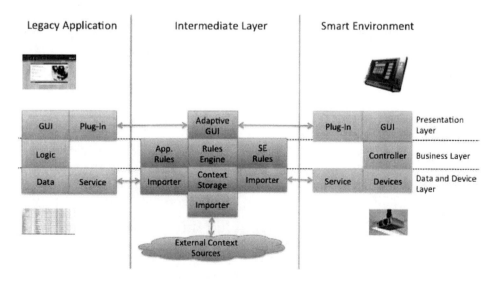

Fig. 1. Proposed architecture with intermediate layer to interconnect smart environment and legacy application

of the intermediate layer is the rules engine, which does the context processing. This engine integrates the logic of intended assistance functionalities into the system by providing and executing rules. The rules are based on context information, which is provided by a context storage. The context storage receives context information from the importers, stores and manages it and aggregates the context information if needed. To realize the rules engine, e.g. a knowledge-based system can be applied. The output of the rules engine are context-based preset configurations for the adaptive GUI, which allow to configure and to control assistance of the SE easily. Therefore, the complexity of the configuration remains widely hidden from the user. Moreover, on basis of the context, only preset configurations, which are most properly applicable to assist the user in his current situation, are produced by the rules engine. Thus, the interaction of the user with the SE is further simplified. The set of possible preset configurations is filtered and therefore the (manual) choice of the preset configurations, which fulfil the users demands best, is less complex for the user.

The context information itself is gathered by the importers. Every importer consists of a data converter and a communication handler. The data converter allows the conversion of gathered context information into a target format, which can be used by the rules engine. The context information is gathered by the communication handlers, which encapsulate the communication with the context information source. Therefore, they act as gateway between intermediate layer and SE or legacy application respectively. The realisation of these components can be done with web services or agents.

The preset configurations are provided to the user via (explicit) UI. The UI is customized to the presentation layer of the application. Here, it is possible to generate add-ons for a GUI (e.g. an additional website for an web interface) or any other kind of UI if needed. Due to the interconnection to the adaptive GUI, the UI receives the generated preset configurations. The manual choice of a specific preset configuration is easy for the user. The context-aware generation of preset configuration limits the number of options that are presented to the user. Therefore, complexity of the systems remains mostly hidden to the user. The interconnection of the user interface to the SE enables the direct application and execution of preset configurations. Thus, the SE is configured according to the preset chosen by the user and assists the user as desired.

The entire architecture is developed as modular as possible to allow extensions in any direction easily. An extension of the architecture allows the seamless integration of various SEs into various applications while using the same rules engine and context repository.

5   Workflow for Pervasive Service Integration

Due to heterogeneity of SEs and legacy applications, we propose a workflow to refine our generic architecture to fit the requirements of specific use cases. The workflow consists of three phases: (1) analysis phase to identify possible interactions and interfaces between both as well as available context data; (2)

concept phase to refine the generic architecture for the specific use case on basis of the gathered data in analysis phase; (3) implementation phase which includes, in addition to implementation, basic functional tests.

5.1 Analysis Phase

In this phase, the SE as well as the legacy application need to be examined. The analysis consists of two parts: (1) technical analysis and (2) logical analysis. Table 1 provides an overview on examined attributes.

In the technical analysis, technical possible integration points for interfaces (to establish a connection and to integrate the UI) and available functionalities need to be identified. Thus, the infrastructure of the environment as well as the software architecture need to be unveiled. Furthermore, used technologies (e. g. web services) need to be examined. While using information that was gathered in this part of the analysis, it is possible to design the technical integration.

Table 1. Analysis phase: Overview on examined attributes

Analysis	Smart Environment	Legacy Application
Technical	- Accessible services	- Software architecture
	- Software interfaces	- Software technology
	- User interfaces	- Interfaces (plug-ins, UI)
Logical	- User assistance	- Use case
	- AAA	- AAA
	- Context data	- Context data
	- Rules and decision models	

In the logical analysis, we examine the overall context and possible use cases of user assistance. Thus, factors such as use case of the application, assistance functionalities provided by the SE, AAA (authentication, authorization, accounting), and available context data need to be examined. Additionally, the users workflow needs to be examined to identify concrete actions that can be supported. A user workflow consists of actions the user executes on application and/or environment to perform a task. Here, we include tasks that are achieved by using the application (such as navigating, authenticating or downloading of files) as well as manual tasks (such as interconnecting or adjusting devices). Thus, the logical analysis allows the identification of integration points on a semantic level.

5.2 Concept Phase

In this phase, a concept to refine the generic architecture on basis of the gathered data in analysis phase will be developed. The phase is divided into three parts: (1) process definition; (2) definition of context data flow; (3) integration of data converters.

In the process definition, the potential user workflows are identified, which can be assisted by applying capabilities of the SE. Therefore, the workflows are reproduced, including the tasks that can be supported by the SE. The workflows with high benefits are chosen while those where the added functionality is only marginal can be neglected. This ensures, that the support by SE is integrated only into relevant workflows, which reduces the work and maintenance effort.

The next step identifies the required context data and sources. The processing of this information is done by applying rules stored in the rules engine. To design these rules, every action of the SE in the workflow is enriched with conditions, which need to be met. These rules are evaluated by a rules engine, which checks the facts of the conditions in the background. Facts are provided by importers which are specific for every context source and therefore every context source needs an importer. Now the context information and rules are added as well as possible interfaces to local and global information sources. This ensures that the system can access every information, which is necessary to meet the requirements in the workflow as well as possible security considerations.

In the last part the converters for the importers are defined. This makes sure that the data provided by the importers match the format used by the rules engine. Additionally, the rules are refined to be as precise as possible to handle every possible condition. At this point, the developed workflow should be as fine grained as possible. If there are no inconsistencies left, then the last phase with the implementation can be approached.

5.3   Implementation Phase

The implementation phase is divided into realisation of the refined architecture and following functional tests. The implementation is processed according to results of the first and second phase. To execute functional tests is possibly complex, especially due to context-awareness of the system. Here, in addition to the functionality of the specified processes also the influences of different context information needs to be taken into account.

6   Use Case

For our use case, we apply the vision of a pervasive university [6]. Especially for the deployment and test of SEs, a university campus is a good environment. Usually, it is well equipped with communication and service infrastructure. In addition, there are many young people with a high grade of affinity to new technologies available within a university. Thus, several proposals that apply the ubiquitous and pervasive computing paradigm for campus environments can be found in literature [12], [13], [14], [15], [6] and reflect this advantages.

To implement the proposed architecture and to evaluate the practicability of our workflow, we decided to enrich the Stud.IP [16] learning management system (LMS) by integrating functionalities of a smart lecture room, which is available in our university. Stud.IP can be considered as a legacy application, which is used by numerous German universities and educational institutions. It provides an all-purpose web 2.0 platform to support students in their studies, lecturers

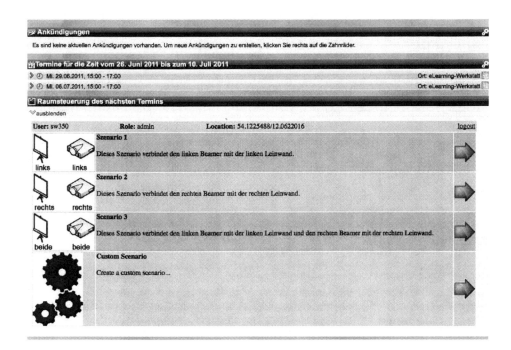

Fig. 2. Screenshot of the presented use case

in giving lectures and administration as well as campus management tasks. The smart lecture room provides several sensors (e.g. SensFloor) and other integrated devices (multiple digital projectors, monitors, cameras, microphones, visualizer, smartboard, etc.) to assist the lecturer. Currently, the room is controlled by an AMX Board with proprietary software. By implementing our architecture for this scenario, we want to achieve two goals: (1) the simplification of configuration and control of the smart lecture room as well as (2) a loose coupling of smart lecture room and LMS with a familiar UI for the lecturer. Furthermore, we want the ability to exchange the smart learning environment easily. Following the proposed workflow, our analysis revealed results as shown in table 2.

On basis of the analysis we decided to realize the UI for the integration of smart lecture room functionalities as an extension of the Stud.IP web page, which is available for every lecture course and which is accessible only by lecturers. The importer for the Stud.IP was realized using a web service, which interconnects the Stud.IP DB via MySQL. The importer for the smart lecture room is realized by using the available web services. To interconnect the university LDAP a web service is used as importer as well. The knowledge gathered by the web services is transferred via message bus to a knowledge-based system, which was implemented using JBoss Drools. Here, predefined rules are applied on the gathered knowledge; preset configurations are generated and provided to the GUI. Thus, suitable preset configurations are displayed as web page, which is embedded in Stud.IP as shown in fig. 2.

Table 2. Analysis results of Stud.IP LMS and smart lecture room

Analysis	Smart lecture room	Stud.IP LMS
Technical	- Device control - Web services - GUI (via AMX-Board)	- 3-tier web application - PHP, Java Script, MySQL - Web services, plugins, DB, GUI
Logical	- Presentation assistance - Only physical access restriction - Indoor position via SensFloor - Predefined preset configurations	- Lecture management, course schedules, lecture supporting media files - University LDAP, Stud.IP user groups - (Web 2.0) user profiles, time and room schedules, university calendar

7   Conclusions

In this paper, we introduced a generic architecture to integrate SEs into existing, especially legacy, applications. The architecture acts as intermediate layer
between SE and application and allows the loose coupling of both independent
systems. For that purpose, we introduced a workflow which includes analysis of
current situation, refinement of the proposed architecture and implementation.
On basis of our concept, we implemented a use case referred to the vision of the
pervasive university. Here, we integrated functionalities of a smart lecture room
into the learning management system Stud.IP.

Acknowledgements. Philipp Lehsten's and Alexander Gladisch's work are
both supported by the German National Research Foundation (DFG), Graduate
School 1424 MuSAMA. The authors would also like to thank Martin Hölzel and
Stefan Wendt for implementing the system.

References

1. Weiser, M.: The Computer for the 21st Century. Scientific American, (Communications, Computers, and Network) (September 1991)
2. Satyanarayanan, M.: Pervasive computing: vision and challenges. IEEE Personal
Communications 8(4), 10–17 (2001)
3. Abowd, G.D., Dey, A.K., Brown, P.J., Davies, N., Smith, M., Steggles, P.: Towards
a Better Understanding of Context and Context-Awareness. In: Gellersen, H.-W.
(ed.) HUC 1999. LNCS, vol. 1707, pp. 304–307. Springer, Heidelberg (1999)
4. Giersich, M., Heider, T., Kirste, T.: Ai methods for smart environments: A case
study on team assistance in smart meeting rooms. In: Proceedings of Scientific
Workshop 1: Artificial Intelligence Methods for Ambient Intelligence on European
Conference on Ambient Intelligence (AmI 2007), Darmstadt, Germany (November
2007)
5. Orpwood, R., Adlam, T., Evans, N., Chadd, J., Self, D.: Evaluation of an assisted-
living smart home for someone with dementia. Journal of Assistive Technologies 2,
13–21 (2008)

6. Lucke, U., Tavangarian, D.: Eine Service- und Kontext-basierte Infrastruktur für die Pervasive University. In: GI Jahrestagung, pp. 1935–1949 (2009)

7. Wang, F.-Y., Zeng, D., Yang, L.: Smart cars on smart roads: An IEEE intelligent transportation systems society update. IEEE Pervasive Computing 5(4), 68–69 (2006)

8. Ballagas, R., Ringel, M., Stone, M., Borchers, J.: Istuff: a physical user interface toolkit for ubiquitous computing environments. In: Proceedings of the SIGCHI Conference on Human Factors in Computing Systems, CHI 2003, pp. 537–544. ACM, New York (2003)

9. Ballagas, R., Borchers, J., Rohs, M., Sheridan, J.G.: The smart phone: a ubiquitous input device. IEEE Pervasive Computing 5(1), 70–77 (2006)

10. Koskela, T., Väänänen-Vainio-Mattila, K.: Evolution towards smart home environments: empirical evaluation of three user interfaces. Personal and Ubiquitous Computing 8, 234–240 (2004), doi:10.1007/s00779-004-0283-x

11. Syvanen, A., Beale, R., Sharples, M., Ahonen, M., Lonsdale, P.: Supporting pervasive learning environments: adaptability and context awareness in mobile learning. In: IEEE International Workshop on Wireless and Mobile Technologies in Education, WMTE 2005, page 3 (November 2005)

12. Weiser, M.: The future of ubiquitous computing on campus. Commun. ACM 41(1), 41–42 (1998)

13. Griswold, W.G., Shanahan, P., Brown, S.W., Boyer, R., Ratto, M., Shapiro, R.B., Truong, T.M.: Activecampus: experiments in community-oriented ubiquitous computing. Computer 37(10), 73–81 (2004)

14. Barkhuus, L., Dourish, P.: Everyday Encounters with Context-Aware Computing in a Campus Environment. In: Davies, N., Mynatt, E.D., Siio, I. (eds.) UbiComp 2004. LNCS, vol. 3205, pp. 232–249. Springer, Heidelberg (2004)

15. Al Takrouri, B., Canonico, A., Gongora, L., Janiszewski, M., Toader, C., Schrader, A.: Eyejot - a ubiquitous context-aware campus information system. In: 2nd International Conference on Pervasive Computing and Applications, ICPCA 2007, pp. 122–127 (2007)

16. Stud.IP developer group. Stud.ip - Studienbegleitender Internetsupport von Praesenzlehre, http://www.studip.de/home/ (last access: May 2011)

A Lightweight Service Registry
for Unstable Ad-Hoc Networks

Paulo Ricca[1], Kostas Stathis[1], and Nick Peach[2]

[1] Royal Holloway, University of London, UK
[2] PB Partnership, UK
{paulo.ricca,kostas.stathis}@cs.rhul.ac.uk,
nick.peach@pbpartnership.com

Abstract. We present a distributed systems framework for sharing knowledge and capabilities in ad-hoc networks of devices where network bandwidth, network connectivity and device computing power are severely limited. We develop a distributed registry to store knowledge of device capabilities and their invocation, implement it and show how it can be deployed in a set of network nodes to exemplify its usefulness. The ideas are exemplified with an ambient intelligence scenario known as autonomous road trains.

Keywords: distributed service registry, unstable ad-hoc networks.

1 Introduction

Ambient Intelligence (AmI) is a vision of the future where people interact with networks of computing devices, often in the form of everyday objects within a physical environment, to better carry out their everyday activities [1]. According to how objects or their capabilities are used, networks of devices enable user applications that may acquire environment knowledge via sensors, intelligently process this acquired knowledge and share it with other devices, and possibly change the environment's state using actuators.

In many AmI applications persistent connectivity, software homogeneity and unlimited computational power of devices cannot be taken for granted. As a result, how to share knowledge and capabilities between devices within an application is an important consideration. More specifically, a centralized approach is less tolerant and averse to scaling [3], while a simple custom and ad-hoc solution is not always reusable in similar applications, especially when application devices are heterogenous and their connectivity is both unreliable and dynamically formed.

We develop a distributed registry to store knowledge of device capabilities and their invocation, implement it and show how it can be deployed in a set of network nodes to exemplify its usefulness. Our contribution lies in the integration of selective distributed systems technologies combined with peer-to-peer techniques and a service-oriented approach targeted to low-powered devices. We allow nodes to register themselves or others to receive notifications when data that is applied

D. Keyson et al. (Eds.): AmI 2011, LNCS 7040, pp. 136–140, 2011.

to certain filters is created, modified or removed, inside the registry (making it easy to construct simple reactive applications as well). In addition, we support data independently of its description languages to better accommodate heterogeneous systems. The end result mixes the usefulness of a directory service, the flexibility of a distributed database and the ease of use of a data-driven query and storage mechanism, into a very lightweight peer-to-peer platform which is suitable for AmI environments.

2 Scenario

As shown in Fig. 1, we consider the operation of an Autonomous Road Train (ART), a changing set of vehicles driving in a platoon formation under autonomous control in order to reduce fuel consumption, improve safety and increase driver convenience in motorways (for more information on ARTs see [2]). When a vehicle enters a motorway where ART's are allowed, it should try to discover ARTs (step 1) through SR's and query them (step 2) in order to find out which of them would be the most useful for the vehicle's trip e.g. in terms of direction and speed. The queried SRs return data related to the state of an ART The state schema describes data relative to an ART, such as location, speed, direction, train size and position on the train sequence (slot). After choosing an ART to join, the vehicle's decision mechanism registers the synchronization and triggering mechanism (step 3) for the piece of data received by the ART (making it part of the data replication and triggering loop). Next, the car's decision module fills the ART data inserting a reference to itself on an empty slot and changing this slot's state (step 4). The synchronization mechanism ensures that all the cars in the ART are informed of this change. The vehicle can now position itself in the ART. When the vehicle reaches its destination, it changes its internal state to leave the ART (step 5), informing others of its intentions, so that the other vehicles can distance themselves (step 6) so that the car can exit the ART (step 7).

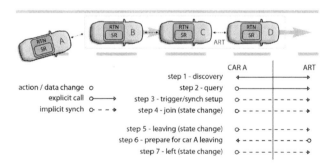

Fig. 1. Cars as Road Train Nodes (RTNs) with Service Registries (SRs)

3   Service Registry Prototype

One of the requirements within an ART is how to coordinate heterogenous nodes that are dynamically added to, removed from or moved about the network. Traditional co-ordination mechanisms are often achieved using a central controller that has been made robust against failure. However, using a remote radio data link to a distant central point is inherently dangerous, due to data link dropouts, therefore local connections within the ART are essential with peer-to-peer computing principles replacing the central controller system.

The Service Registry that we propose is a module of a larger end-to-end system prototype which aims at creating a highly decentralized, structured and flexible approach to orchestrate behaviour in the form of workflows. The objective is to create a visual designer tool and a run-time node to connect and coordinate low-powered and heterogenous devices on unreliable networks similar to the one discussed in [5]. In this context, the Service Registry is designed to be a custom lightweight and modular directory service structure composed of four main components depicted in Fig. 2. The Interface allows applications/devices to interact with the Service Registry. The Registry stores, searches and modifies schemas and data entities. The Query Interpreter processes requests (described on one particular protocol and data format) communicated via the Interface and interacts with the Registry accordingly. The Trigger Manager registers the interest of external components in registry events related to specific data, and notifies them accordingly when these take place. The Synchronizer performs synchronization between different service registries and, finally, the External Interface represents the Interface module of a neighbour registry.

To develop the registry we have chosen Rest [8] as a lightweight mechanism for remote and embedded local communication, Json [7] for data type and schema representation. Data is stored in a database-driven registry supported by Apache Derby, a lightweight database management system based storing and querying module. Each schema creates one main database table and one secondary table for each complex (objects or arrays) schema field, recursively for there may be other complex fields inside these, when it is registered. Below is an example of schema, Json data, internal database data and triggers used in the ART scenario.

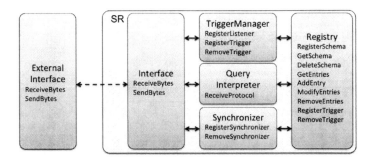

Fig. 2. Overview Implementation Architecture of the Service Registry with the description of each module's basic methods

ARTState Json schema:

{type:"object", properties:{slot:{type:"number"}, carId:{type:"string"},
    state:{type:"string"}, acks:{type:"array", items: {type:"string"}}}}

ARTState Json data:
{slot:0, carId:"Car A", state:"Occupied", acks:["Car A", "Car B"],
slot:1, carId:"Car B, state:"Occupied", acks:["Car B", "Car A"]}

ARTState internal data:
```
database table ARTSTATE:
ID; SLOT; CARID; STATE; ACKS
32; 0; "Car A"; "Occupied", 51
33; 1; "Car B"; "Occupied", 52


database table COMPLEX_ARTSTATE_ACKS:
ID;  ACKS
51; "Car A"
51; "Car B"
52; "Car B"
52; "Car A"
```

Trigger:
```
ID; GRABBERID; SCHEMA; EVENTTYPE; FILTERFIELD; FILTERVALUE
80; "Car A"; "ARTState"; MODIFY; STATE; "Occupied"
```

We use an implementation of the observer pattern to implement triggers[1]. For the above example, when the ARTState schema is registered, the registry stores the schema and creates two tables: ARTSTATE and COMPLEX_ART-STATE_ACKS as the acknowledgements represented in a complex array. The Registry checks the data against the schema and adds the appropriate fields to the two tables created before. The trigger described above states that the entity identified by "Car A" should be notified when data related to the "ARTState" schema is modified, and the "STATE" field contains the string "Occupied". In this way, triggers allow the decision-making module of nodes to be notified of changes on the network. In our ART scenario triggers allow a car letting other cars know of its intentions to leave the ART, so that they can act accordingly, leaving enough space for it to leave securely.

4   Conclusions, Related and Future Work

We have presented a distributed systems framework for sharing knowledge and capabilities in ad-hoc networks of devices where network bandwidth, network connectivity and device computing power are severely limited. We have developed a distributed registry to store knowledge of device capabilities and their invocation, implement it and show how it can be deployed in a set of network nodes to exemplify its usefulness. We believe that such a registry is a sweet spot

---

[1] http://www.research.ibm.com/designpatterns/example.htm

for AmI, Internet of Things and any heterogenous distributed systems which may lack a stable network connection.

Directory Services offer a good way of storing, querying and sharing bits of structured information but they lack the lightweightness that is needed for Ambient Intelligence environments as in our case study. Lightweight Database Management Systems such as SQLLite, HyperSQL or Apache Derby provide the previously referred lightweightness required but used alone, they lack some useful features such as device notification of data update, smart synchronization between devices, data-format independence and allowing clients to use their own data formats on the registry. Data-Driven querying solutions such as OrientX [4], XPath or JsonPath allow clients to keep using their current data-formats but lack all the flexibility of directory services or common database management systems. The ad-UDDI [6] project suggest an active and distributed service registry which optimizes and extends the usage of UDDI mainly for service discovery. Although this solution offers an interesting and proven approach for active service discovery, it does not cover the issue of working on unstable networks, and as it's primarily focused on service description, it does not offer a generic solution for sharing information in such scenarios.

As part of our future work we plan to complete the synchronization mechanism provided, introduce a security layer, provide a global (ldap²-like) syntax for interacting with the registry and offer an accurate method for measuring results and comparing to other solutions.

References

1. Aarts, E., Harwig, R., Schuurmans, M.: Ambient Intelligence. In: The Invisible Future: The Seamless Integration of Technology into Everyday Life. McGraw-Hill Professional (2001)
2. Bergenhem, C., Huang, Q., Benmimoun, A., Robinson, T.: Challenges of Platooning on Public Motorways. In: 17th World Congress on Intelligent Transport Systems, Busan, Korea (2010)
3. Cai, M., Frank, M.: A Scalable Distributed RDF Repository based on A Structured Peer-to-Peer Network. In: WWW 2004 (2004)
4. Meng, X., et al.: OrientX: A Schema-based Native XML Database System. In: Proceedings of the VLDB, pp. 1057–1060 (2003)
5. Peach, N.: Decentralized operating procedures for orchestrating data and behavior across distributed military systems and assets. In: Interoperability II. SPIE 8047, 80470B, Orlando (2011)
6. Du, Z., Huai, J., Liu, Y.: Ad-UDDI: An Active and Distributed Service Registry. In: Bussler, C., Shan, M.-C. (eds.) TES 2005. LNCS, vol. 3811, pp. 58–71. Springer, Heidelberg (2006)
7. Crockford, D.: The application/json Media Type for JavaScript Object Notation (JSON). Internet informational RFC 4627 (2006)
8. Fielding, R.: Architectural Styles and the Design of Network-based Software Architectures. PhD thesis, University of California, Irvine, Irvine, California (2000)

---

² http://www.openldap.org/

Hall Effect Sensing Input and Like Polarity Haptic Feedback in the Liquid Interface System

Kasun Karunanayaka, Jeffrey Tzu Kwan Valino Koh,
Eishem Bilal Naik, and Adrian David Cheok

Keio-NUS CUTE Center, NGS, National University of Singapore
{kasun,jeffrey,adriancheok}@mixedrealitylab.org
http://mixedrealitylab.org

Abstract. Liquid Interface is an organic user interface that utilizes ferrofluid as an output display and input button embodiment. Using a matrix of Hall effect sensors, magnetic fields generated by rare-earth magnets worn on the fingertips are measured and are then converted into signals that provide input capability. This input actuates an array of electromagnets. Both Hall effect sensors and electromagnets are contained beneath the surface of the ferrofluid. By matching like polarities between the electromagnets and the rare-earth magnets, haptic force feedback by means of magnetic field repulsion can be achieved.

Keywords: Organic User Interface, Ferrofluid, Magnetic, Hall Effect.

1 Introduction

Building on the idea of previous ferrofluid artworks [2], and adhering to the characteristics of organic user interfaces (OUI) [1], Liquid Interface (LI) provides an input/output solution based on ferrofluid.

The system is composed of a pool of ferromagnetic liquid combined with a sensing and actuation mechanism. The sensing is achieved through the use of an array of Hall effect sensors. Actuation is produced by an array of electromagnets. Users can interact with the system by wearing magnetic rings. The magnetic ring position is detected by the array of Hall effect sensors, which in turn actuates the electromagnets and the audio server. The magnetic field of the active electromagnets morphs the ferrofluid to create "buttons". When a button is pressed the system generates a sound. The electromagnetic fields produced by the array repel the rare-earth magnets worn on the fingertips, giving the user a haptic response. Our previous work includes a detailed system description as well as describes a series of experiments to measure spike height versus current, distance of two adjacent spikes, transient state of the system and the static linearity of the system [4].

In order to discern the parameters in which Hall effect sensing would be most effective, a new series of experiments were conducted. These include experiments for understanding the vertical distance of rare-earth magnets from the surface embedded with Hall effect sensors, the horizontal sensing effectiveness

D. Keyson et al. (Eds.): AmI 2011, LNCS 7040, pp. 141–145, 2011.

to understand the quality of precision for cartesian coordination, and finally an experiment to characterize the effectiveness of the Hall effect sensors employed under the influence of multiple magnetic fields.

2   Experiments and Results

2.1   Experiment 1: Hall Effect Sensor Reading versus Vertical Distance

This experiment has been conducted using a Hall effect sensor and an electro-magnet that generates an average flux density on the surface from 450 to 1950 Gauss for the range of 6V to 24V with 1.9 to 7.5A of electrical current. In the experiment we kept the power of the electromagnet at a constant voltage of 10V and a driven current of 2.44A, with the sensor on the vertical axis on top of the electromagnet. The sensor reading is measured versus the distance to the elec-tromagnet. The value of the sensor output voltage taken is the mean value in one second. This plot shows that the sensor is most sensitive with respect to the vertical distance from 0cm to 3cm. When the distance is greater than 3cm, the change in output is much smaller. At larger distances, for example the values of 6cm and 7cm, the difference in voltage is only 0.011 volts. However such a small voltage difference is not detected by the micro-controller used for this iteration of the system.

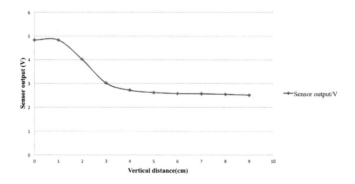

Fig. 1. Sensor output versus vertical distance

2.2   Experiment 2: Hall Effect Sensor Reading versus Horizontal Distance

Once more keeping the power of the electromagnet constant, the sensor is placed on the vertical axis of the electromagnet, at 2cm, since at this distance the sensor is most sensitive, registering the largest change in values with respect to distance moved. The plot shows that the sensor voltage is very close to 2.5 volt (zero field voltage) after 3.5cm displacement. Experiment 1 shows that the

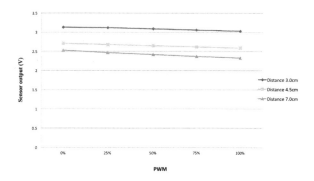

Fig. 2. Sensor output versus horizontal displacement

resolution of the system cannot distinguish any smaller change that within 0.02 volts, the magnetic field at 3.5cm and beyond are too small to cause a change in the microprocessor. This experiment shows that the magnetic field out of the horizontal area of the magnet is too small to be detected at the optimal vertical distance.

2.3 Experiment 3: Characterization of Hall Effect Sensor Readings under the Influence of Multiple Magnetic Fields

In this experiment the readings of the Hall effect sensor are measured to determine the influence of the magnetic fields generated by the electromagnets and neodymium magnets. The goal of this experiment is to determine which combinations of the two magnetic fields (electromagnet and neodymium) cancel one another.

The sensor is supplied the rated of 5V and is positioned such that it is in level with the top of the electromagnet and directly next to it. Its output is connected to an oscilloscope. A non-magnetic material at varying heights directly above the

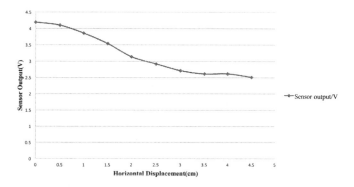

Fig. 3. Sensor reading values obtained for different distances versus PWM

sensor holds the neodymium magnet. Its pole direction is fixed, with the South Pole facing downwards. The reading of the steady-state output voltage of the sensor is recorded using the oscilloscope, while varying the height and direction of the neodymium magnet and the PWM input to the electromagnet.

First the default sensor value is taken without the neodymium magnet or electromagnet influence. Next, with the neodymium magnet pole at South Pole (facing down), the PWM values and distances are measured. Here the strength of the electromagnets field serves to decrease the reading of the sensor, whereas the position of the neodymium magnet field serves to increase the reading of the sensor. This results in a case in which the value of the sensor is unable to detect the presence of the neodymium magnet due to the electromagnet's field.

From the data we gathered, this occurs in the case when the distance of the neodymium magnet is 7.0cm. If the electromagnet is off, the reading is 2.53V, but if the electromagnet is turned on, the reading falls below the 2.50V neutral value. To circumvent this problem, we use like poles instead of unlike poles. This approach has the peripheral advantages of preventing the two magnets from attracting each other and preventing the neodymium magnet from picking up the ferrofluid as well as add haptic feedback.

3   Discussion

By using the results obtained in these three experiments, we were able devise an algorithm that performs accurate sensing of nearby magnetic fields for the Liquid Interface system. It is possible to track magnets worn on finger tips precisely as each sensor needs only to be able to detect a given magnet directly above it and will not be affected or disturbed by other magnets nearby. The sensitivity of our sensor is very effective in detecting movement within the 3cm range. It is able to detect even very subtle movements. The sensors are placed directly on top of each electromagnet while the user's fingertips carry strong neodymium magnets with like poles of each magnet/electromagnet pair facing one another. When the electromagnet is turned on, the sensor's output becomes fully saturated. If a neodymium magnet of the same pole is brought near to it, the sensor's output drops. This is detected as the presence of the user's hands.

The micro-controller firmware handles the sensing input, actuation output and communication with the server to produce music. Upon system initialization, the system first performs a calibration. This process takes up to 20 seconds. During the calibration each electromagnet is turned on to maximum power in order to find the offset value of the sensor. This offset value is then used in determining if a neodymium magnet (user's hand) is nearby when the value varies from the offset. To handle the sensing input, the micro-controller continuously polls the analog-to-digital converter modules at a frequency of once every 200 milliseconds. This is accomplished using a timer module and is to ensure that each analog-to-digital conversion is given sufficient time to complete. Complex gestures are handled by constantly storing interactions from the previous 2 seconds in the program memory. The stored interactions can then be interpreted as necessary to produce any gestures other than simple activation. To handle actuation output the micro-controller sets the PWM duty cycle for each output if necessary. Each time an interaction is recorded, the micro-controller sends a unique character to the server via an RS-232 connection. This is interpreted by the server for use in music production.

4 Conclusion

We outlined in this paper, three new experiments that enabled us to develop an input sensing mechanism based on the Hall effect. These include findings reveal the relationship between perpendicular and horizontal distances of the Hall effect sensor and the magnetic field generated by the electromagnetic array, the characterization of the magnetic Hall effect sensor readings under the influence of multiple magnetic fields, and the relationship of distance from the sensor versus PWM.

We also discussed the addition of haptic feedback facilitated by the repelling force of rare-earth magnets placed on the fingertips with like polarities matched to the electromagnets, thus providing an additional modality of feedback. This input accessory provides a means for users to interact with the LI system without the need to touch the ferrofluid, and still provides instantaneous tactile response.

Acknowledgement. This research is carried out under CUTE Project No. WBS R- 7050000-100-279 partially funded by a grant from the National Research Foundation (NRF) administered by the Media Development Authority (MDA) of Singapore.

References

1. Holman, D., Vertegaal, R.: Organic user interfaces: designing computers in any way, shape, or form. Communications of the ACM 51, 48–55 (2008)
2. Kodama, S.: Dynamic ferrofluid sculpture. Communications of the ACM 51, 79 (2008)
3. Koh, J.T.K.V., Karunanayaka, K., Sepulveda, R., Tharakan, M.J., Krishnan, M., Cheok, A.D.: Liquid interface: a malleable, transient, direct-touch interface. In: Proceedings of the 7th International Conference on Advances in Computer Entertainment Technology (ACE 2010), pp. 45–48. ACM, New York (2010)

Self-configuration of "Home Abstraction Layer" via Sensor-Actuator Network

Zheng Hu[1,2], Gilles Privat[1],
Stéphane Frenot[2], and Bernard Tourancheau[2]

[1] Orange Labs, 28 Chemin du Vieux Chêne 38240 Meylan, France
{firstname.lastname}@orange-ftgroup.com
[2] CITI/INRIA INSA de Lyon, 6 Av. des Arts 69621 Villeurbanne, France
{firstname.lastname}@inria.fr

Abstract. We propose a mechanism and system for the identification, self-configuration, monitoring and control of non-networked home devices through a shared backplane of networked sensors and actuators. The resulting generic home abstraction layer interfaces to all kinds of physical entities of the home through a software proxy, as if they were state-of-the-art networked devices. The matching of the entities being discovered in the home/building environment to known semi-generic models is performed by iterative approximation. The architecture and OSGi-based implementation of this system is described. Examples are provided for typical home appliances and other subsystems of the home/building that may be dealt with in a similar way.

Keywords: Home as Smart Environment, Home device management, OSGi, Sensor, Actuator.

1 Introduction

Home automation systems have a decades-long track record, but they have yet to move beyond specialized applications tied to their own dedicated infrastructure. Sharing a multipurpose backplane of sensors, actuators, networks and local server/gateway devices to support a broad portfolio of home/building applications should make it possible to amortize the cost of this infrastructure across the board and to jumpstart the take-up of a home automation service portfolio that has, so far, proved vexingly elusive.

Among these applications, energy management has appeared as a new pacesetter, spurred on by the rising cost of energy and the requirement to shrink the carbon footprint of buildings, potentially warranting the investment in such a shareable open ICT infrastructure for the building. Home energy management services, offerings have so far been mostly limited to energy monitoring or simple load shedding/shifting. The next stage in home energy management systems will be towards the integration of all energy-relevant devices, appliances and components of the building in a comprehensive monitoring and control system relying on a shared infrastructure for this.

D. Keyson et al. (Eds.): AmI 2011, LNCS 7040, pp. 146–150, 2011.

The ReActivHome[1] project aims at designing and prototyping such a comprehensive home energy management system. This system is intended to manage and optimize at the home level the balance between energy consumption, generation and storage according to both local and global criteria. This system relies on the monitoring and actuation of the energy-consuming, -storing or -generating components, devices and legacy appliances of the home through a complete shared infrastructure of sensors and actuators. A key issue is then how to integrate all these entities in the perimeter of such a system, knowing that most of them do not have any kind of digital interface to a data network, neither for monitoring nor for control. Crucially, the economic viability of such a system mandates that setting it up should not be made conditional upon an all-out upgrade of the building and its appliances, and should not require a complex and costly manual configuration.

The solution we propose draws inspiration from networked-device configuration mechanisms such as UPnP or DPWS, applying similar concepts to non-networked legacy physical entities for which available sensors and actuators play the role of network interfaces. Addressing as target entities both devices and subsets of the home such as rooms, our approach conjoins two separate strands of research that had been pursued under the ambient intelligence research agenda[3], smart devices and smart environments.

2   Principle of the Home Abstraction Layer

The Home Abstraction Layer (HAL) we propose is an analogue of Hardware Abstraction Layers used by operating systems : it hides the specifics of the home hardware beneath a set of generic models and interfaces, acting as a generic informational interface to the home as a physical system. Within the HAL, Subsystem Identification Monitoring and Control (SIMC) modules act as proxies for each individual physical entity/subsystem of the home, using associated sensors and actuators, which can be shared among them (e.g. an infrared camera and a microphone could be used to monitor all appliances of a room).

2.1   SIMC Life-Cycle

The SIMC relies on a simple hybrid model of each target subsystem as a finite state machine, with associated continuous attributes. These models are not meant to be exact, they are supposed to be sufficiently generic to represent categories of subsystems. Figure 1 presents the finite-state machine model used by a room SIMC. Similar models can be used for usual home appliances.

The SIMC can be in either of two main modes: configuration or runtime. The configuration phase is used to identify the Runtime State Machine(RSM), the state machine model that best matches the entity, and associating sensors and actuators. There are three predefined states. The initialization state is active when the existence of a physical entity (such as an appliance) has just been

---

[1] ANR ReActivhome : https://reactivhome.rd.francetelecom.com

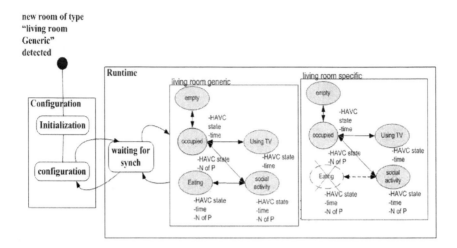

Fig. 1. Example SIMC life-cycle

discovered from a set of sensors. The configuring state is active when a dedicated SIMC instance is associated with real sensors/actuators and its RSM.The runtime mode maintains as persistent variables the current states of the SIMC while the physical entity works. In runtime mode the SIMC component may always go to the waiting for synch state when an error occurs, or when the state is unknown.Configuration is dynamic and may occur at anytime, following changes in the home environment.

2.2   SIMC Identification

The SIMC classification engine chooses one among several predefined prototype outputs from aggregate sensor inputs. and is used for the identification of the target physical entity model, the runtime identification of current states, and the state sequence conformance checking.

A "root" SIMC contains a classifcation engine and a RSM. Its role is to monitor the global context. When new entities are detected, the "root" SIMC tries to identify them and spawns a new generic SIMC. Those "generic" SIMCs follow their own life-cycle and each can finally reach a specific SIMC by iterative approximation. Note that the "root" SIMC, "Generic" SIMCs and "specific" SIMCs all have the same architecture.

The SIMC management system and architecture are independent of the particular classification algorithm used inside the classification engine. In our first prototype we use an Artificial Neural Network engine.

3 HAL Implementation with OSGi

3.1 SIMC Architecture in OSGi Framework

Our purpose in choosing OSGi[2] is to enable application reconfiguration at run-time. So, each SIMC functional module is modelled as a bundle[1], and its application functions are packaged in the bundle as services.

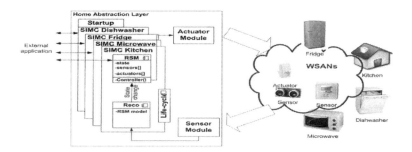

Fig. 2. SIMC architecture based upon the OSGi framework

To achieve the full functionality described in section 2, we model the architecture of the SIMC management system as shown in figure 2. Three bundles are initially started:

The Sensor Module bundle communicates with all the sensors in the HAL environment. Each piece of sensor data is transferred by the sensor module which achieves the following tasks: 1) Physical interface for heterogeneous sensor management[2]; 2)Identification and authentication of data source; 3)Cartography of the observed environment; 4)Dynamic integration of sensors according to their own protocol, for which we mostly (not exclusively)use Zigbee[4].

The Actuator Module, counterpart of the Sensor Module, takes in high-level commands expressed as state changes of target physical entities and fans them out as specific controls to the associated actuators.

The StartUp bundle waits for the activation of the Sensor Module and Actuator Module, in order to start the first "root" SIMC. SIMC is made up of these operating services:1)The Life-cycle service is the core of SIMC, it is capable of starting or stopping SIMCs. It is invoked by the "root" SIMC, and requests the creation of a defined type of device corresponding to a set of sensed data;2)Classification is based on a model which produces a unique output from various sensor inputs of sensed data in a single classifier. This output can be transferred to RSM;3)RSM service maintains the current state by receiving notification from the recognition engine. It can communicate with the application layer to provide the physical entity information as well as to receive commands for the physical entity.

---

[2] OSGi Alliance:http://www.osgi.org

3.2 Prototyping

As a proof of concept, we developed a prototype whose goal is to show how to handle sensor data, build an SIMC and notify client applications when the corresponding state changes. The prototype performs state identification on simple home appliances.

The physical characteristics that can be sensed are sound, vibration and temperature, together with electrical current. The first three were captured with a wireless sensor mote comprising of a microphone, a 2-axis accelerometer, a temperature sensor and a light sensor. For our test system, a single PC hosts the HAL running a SUN JDK 1.6 with the Apache Felix OSGi implementation. And the specific sensors setup that we use is a MEMSIC[3] MICAz wireless sensor mote and an MTS310 sensor board.

4 Conclusion and Future Work

The conceptual model described here has wide-ranging potential applications, which we have barely touched on. Limiting ourselves to the home environment for the time being, the aim is to validate this concept as a common foundational software layer that interfaces all kinds of legacy home entities for all kinds of ambient intelligence applications such as energy management, home automation, ambient assisted living, jointly broadening the scope of AmI and IoT research to non-networked entities that become interfaced through this common layer.

We have yet to validate the system with a broad set of target entities, appliances and rooms and corresponding models, monitored under varied operating conditions with a wide spectrum of shared sensors.

We will investigate more closely the potential improvement of the system from operating as a closed loop control system, where actuators come into play not only for the runtime control of the target home entities, but also for the self-configuration of the HAL system itself.

References

1. Bottaro, A., Simon, E., Seyvoz, S., Gérodolle, A.: Dynamic Web Services on a Home Service Platform. In: 22nd International Conference on Advanced Information Networking and Applications, pp. 378–385. IEEE (2008)
2. Gurgen, L., Roncancio, C., Olive, V., Labbé, C., Bottaro, A.: SStreaMWare: a Service Oriented Middleware for Heterogeneous Sensor Data Management. In: Proceedings of the 5th International Conference on Pervasive Services, pp. 121–130 (2008)
3. Streitz, N., Privat, G.: Ambient Intelligence. In: Stephanidis, C. (ed.) The Usniversal Access Handbook, pp. 1–60. CRC Press, Taylor & Francis Group (2009)
4. Ha, Y.-G.: Dynamic Integration of Zigbee Home Networks into Home Gateways Using OSGi Service Registry. IEEE Transactions on Consumer Electronics 55(2), 470–476 (2009)

---

[3] Crossbow/Berkeley sensor motes: http://www.memsic.com

Predicting Sleeping Behaviors in Long-Term Studies with Wrist-Worn Sensor Data

Marko Borazio and Kristof Van Laerhoven

TU-Darmstadt, Germany
http://www.ess.tu-darmstadt.de

Abstract. This paper conducts a preliminary study in which sleeping behavior is predicted using long-term activity data from a wearable sensor. For this purpose, two scenarios are scrutinized: The first predicts sleeping behavior using a day-of-the-week model. In a second scenario typical sleep patterns for either working or weekend days are modeled. In a continuous experiment over 141 days (6 months), sleeping behavior is characterized by four main features: the amount of motion detected by the sensor during sleep, the duration of sleep, and the falling asleep and waking up times. Prediction of these values can be used in behavioral sleep analysis and beyond, as a component in healthcare systems.

Keywords: sleep behavior, wearable computer, long-term studies.

1 Introduction

Approximately a third of our life is spent sleeping. With sleep researchers steadily discovering new ways in which sleep impacts quality of life, sleep is considered to be equally important to life as nutrition [3], while contributing significantly to regeneration and healing [1][6]. Scientists also analyze sleep to assess its quality and to discover potential irregularities [5]. While the significance of sleep was identified as an important factor in the medical field, it also attracted interest from psychology due to its impact on daytime behavior, and from an increasing group of consumers who want to keep track of their sleeping behavior. Different commercial products are available that estimate the quality of past nights. The Zeo [7], for example, uses a headband for recording brain waves and showing users how well they slept by assigning a sleep score to the data.

This paper contributes with a behavioral sleep model based on actigraphy-like motion data from a wrist-worn sensor collected in a long-term and continuous dataset of 141 days. From the original 100Hz sensor samples, user-specific data from nights is categorized into four different features, which built up the behavioral model. These features are: *amount of motion, duration of sleep, sleep start time* and *sleep stop time*. In this preliminary study, our model is capable of capturing regularities from working days, weekends, as well as from individual days of the week, enabling it to predict likely future sleeping behavior by observation of past nights, and discover irregularities that deviate from prior observations.

D. Keyson et al. (Eds.): AmI 2011, LNCS 7040, pp. 151–156, 2011.

In section 2 the sleeping features are first described, before focusing in section 3 on the method used to obtain the dataset for this study and performing a first evaluation, while explaining our preliminary results. We conclude this paper in the final section 4, giving an outlook on the tasks that still have to be performed.

2   Sleep Behavior

After multiple discussions with sleep experts in the medical field, we identified several characteristic features based on inertial-only measurements for characterizing sleeping behaviors. We will first describe these features and then discuss their value for current behavioral research.

Sleep Duration. Observing a person's hours slept gives an insight to the usual habits as well as to irregularities whenever a person is not reaching the usual amount of sleeping hours. Health care systems benefit from such information. Although there are different theories on how much a person should sleep, a deviation in the daily routine makes irregularities immediately visible.

Start and Stop Time of Sleep. The second and third descriptors of sleep are the falling asleep and waking up times. Persons tend to have regular habits, especially during working days, and therefore this feature is an important characteristic in a person's sleep behavior. People tend to go to bed earlier on working days in contrast to weekends.

Motion. Movement during the night is an indicator for sleep quality: increased movement is considered as a sign for a qualitatively bad night. Sleep scientists for example assign the amount of posture changes to a normal (15-20 posture changes) or abnormal night (over 30) [4]. Here, motion not only appears while changing postures, but also during spontaneous movements in the same posture. In order to describe a person's night, we use the amount of motion detected between non-motion segments.

Discussion. Sleep quality estimation is an interplay of the previously mentioned features. Extracting these features from long-term and especially continuous motion data is therefore important in such assessments. This work focuses on prediction of sleeping behaviors based on previous nights for following nights.

In interviews with sleeping specialists from the local sleeping lab, the value of the chosen features was discussed. Since sleep is usually investigated in sleeping labs, long-term studies are only conducted to assess a patient's circadian rhythm, which is simply the self-regulation of one's 24-hour cycle, including sleeping behaviors. Sleeping disorders like *Delayed Sleep Phase Syndrome* are usually immediately visible in such long-term observational studies. Although we focus in this work on sleeping behavior for night prediction, the importance in further studies is apparent and strengthens the selection of our features.

3   Night Time Prediction

The main reason for building a sleep model based on past behavior is to first predict a user's upcoming night to discover regularities as well as irregularities and evaluate a person's sleep on a long-term basis. We will illustrate how data is collected and further processed, resulting in a preliminary evaluation on night prediction.

3.1   Method and Dataset

The dataset used for this purpose was obtained from a healthy 30 year old male. An actigraph-like sensor was worn on the non-dominant wrist, recording inertial data at 100Hz from a 3D accelerometer, which resulted in an almost continuous dataset of 141 days. In the beginning of the recordings minor problems were experienced in the hardware, leading to a few gaps in the dataset. The last 105 days were then continuously recorded 24/7.

The data was further processed by extracting night segments with a threshold-based algorithm inspired by [2], which uses motion, light intensity and sleep time for classifying potential night segments. Ground truth is provided by a time diary maintained by the test subject. The resulting night segments are used to calculate the sleep duration given by start and stop time of sleep.

The amount of motion segments are identified as follows: over a window of $2sec$ the variance of the acceleration is calculated. Whenever the variance exceeds a threshold $vthresh$ of 1, a motion segment is being detected, until the variance is above $vthresh$. We experimentally estimated $vtresh$ by video observation.

3.2   Evaluation

The obtained features were used in two different scenarios. The first depicts how well the features describe usual sleep habits in the weekend (Friday and Saturday night) and during working days (Sunday to Thursday night). The second scenario displays what sleep habits the same weekdays exhibit.

Weekend vs. Working Days. We state that there is a significant difference between a person's sleeping behavior on weekends and that on working days. The weekends are defined by Friday and Saturday, due to the fact that the person is not working the next day.

In Figure 1, all examined nights (gray = working days, red = weekends) are displayed with the average falling asleep and waking up times depicted as black lines. By visual inspection, differences between weekends and working days are already visible, showing different patterns in both environments.

The features extracted for this scenario are displayed in Table 1. The difference in all features depicts the deviation between both, showing almost none in sleep duration and amount of movements, but a significant one in falling asleep and wake up times. As expected, the person falls asleep later on weekends, exhibiting a completely different pattern in contrast to working days. Interestingly, the user shows an average sleep duration of approximately 430 minutes for both environments, strengthening the theory that a person uses a typical amount of sleep. We conclude that it is possible to detect differences in sleeping behaviors on weekends and working days. In the next section a more fine-grained approach is performed by comparing same weekdays to each other.

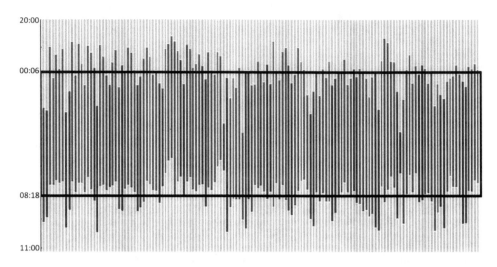

Fig. 1. All 141 nights (gray = working days, red = weekends) are displayed with portions of day data (blue) prior and after sleep. The black lines describes the average falling asleep and waking up times calculated on the whole dataset.

Table 1. Average sleep duration, falling asleep time, waking up time, and amount of movement for all nights, observed during week- and weekend days. The differences in the last row show for this data especially stark differences in the start and stop times.

	sleep duration	start	end	#movements
weekends	428 min	01:55	08:02	61
working days	434 min	23:47	07:01	59
diff	**6 min**	**2hrs 8min**	**1hr 1min**	**2**

Same Weekdays. Only a dataset of about six months makes it possible to gather a sufficient amount of data to observe which sleeping behavior exists on same weekdays. On average we obtained for each weekday 20 days to build the model. In order to examine the features for these days, we performed a leave-one-out cross-validation, by calculating for all other features the average and comparing the results to the day that was left out. For this, we used a threshold for all features, which displays how well the model fits to the night. The thresholds are: duration of sleep (+/-) 45 minutes, wake-up or falling asleep time each (+/-) 45 minutes and amount of motion-detections (+/-) 15.

The results are displayed in Table 2. Due to the limited space, only the final results are listed. The table shows how allocation of the same weekday to the model of the other same weekdays performed. Overall, we can state that crucial parameters for similar nights are *falling asleep* and *waking up times*. These are regular during all scrutinized nights, which strengthens the assumption that a person tends to follow a time-critical sleep habit. Although the sleep duration and the amount of movements vary a lot on same weekdays, these features need

Table 2. Accuracy results for the leave-one-out cross-validation over all weekdays (Sunday, Monday, ..., Saturday). The last row lists how well the four features were captured overall by the prediction model. As the start and stop times of sleep were important in this dataset, it is not surprising that their accuracies are also well predicted.

accuracy for...	sleep duration	start sleep	end sleep	#movements
Sundays	79%	95%	89%	79%
Mondays	62%	86%	90%	76%
Tuesdays	71%	76%	86%	76%
Wednesdays	76%	76%	100%	67%
Thursdays	53%	79%	63%	68%
Fridays	62%	81%	76%	52%
Saturdays	53%	89%	89%	42%
total	65%	83%	85%	66%

more individual analysis in the context of sleep quality. As stated in section 2, movement is an indicator for sleep quality, as well as sleep duration.

4 Conclusion

This paper illustrates how sleep data features can be used to describe sleep trends, on a continuous dataset of 141 days from a 30 year old healthy (not suffering from sleep disorders) male. We designed a model that, with the use of four features, characterizes trends such as weekdays, weekends and individual days. Furthermore, we could assess the test subject's night by our prediction model as a prior, using new nights as input to the model and categorizing them to regular and irregular nights.

We illustrated that our technique is feasible on this particular data set, modeling his normal nights, which can be put into contrast to a model of an irregular night. Further experiments are underway in a sleeping lab, monitoring multiple patients over a 6-month timespan – with nights in and outside a sleep lab, where all information of a patients sleep is gathered and analyzed by sleep scientists.

References

1. Adam, K., Oswald, I.: Sleep helps healing. British Medical Journal (Clinical research ed.) 289(6456), 1400 (1984)
2. Borazio, M., Van Laerhoven, K.: Combining Wearable and Environmental Sensing into an Unobtrusive Tool for Long-Term Sleep Studies. In: 2nd ACM SIGHIT International Health Informatics Symposium (IHI 2012), Miami, Florida, USA (in Press, 2012)
3. Everson, C.A., Bergmann, M., Rechtschaffen, A.: Sleep Deprivation in the Rat: III. Total Sleep Deprivation. Sleep 12(1), 13–21 (1989)
4. Gordon, S.J., Grimmer, K.A., Trott, P.: Self reported versus recorded sleep position: an observational study. Internet Journal of Allied Health Sciences and Practice 2(1) (2004)

5. Gregory, J.M., Xie, X., Mengel, S.A.: SLEEP (sleep loss effects on everyday performance) model. Aviation, Space, and Environmental Medicine 74, A125– A133 (2004)
6. Krachmann, S.L., Criner, G.J., D'Alonzo, G.E.: Sleep in the intensive care unit. Chest 107(6), 1713 (1995)
7. Zeo Inc., http://www.myzeo.com/

FORE-Watch – The Clock That Tells You When to Use: Persuading Users to Align Their Energy Consumption with Green Power Availability

Johann Schrammel[1], Cornelia Gerdenitsch[1], Astrid Weiss[2], Patricia M. Kluckner[2], and Manfred Tscheligi[1,2]

[1] CURE - Center for Usability Research & Engineering
{schrammel,gerdenitsch,tscheligi}@cure.at
[2] HCI & Usability Unit, ICT&S Center, University of Salzburg
{astrid.weiss,patricia.kluckner}@sbg.ac.at

Abstract. Besides saving energy, using it at the right time (i.e. when there is a supply surplus, and the power is produced by sustainable power sources such as hydroelectricity or wind) is an important possibility to achieve positive effects for the environment. To enable the user to align their behavior with the dynamics of the energy generation they need to be informed about the current status of power supply and grid capacity. Furthermore, to be able to plan their behavior and possibly delay or advance consumption activities to more proper moments they also need to have access to high-quality forecasts about the future status of green energy supply. In this paper we present an ambient display design solution based on a common watch that is optimized for providing this information in an unobtrusive, ambient and persuasive way. We present and discuss requirements identified by use of literature analysis, focus groups and end-user questionnaires, outline approaches to calculate basic power generation forecasts based on weather forecast data and present an ambient interface concept designed to meet the identified requirements. We conclude that the developed approach has high potential to support desired behavior changes, and that achieving acceptable accuracy levels for the generation forecast is feasible with relatively little effort.

Keywords: ambient display, persuasion, eco-feedback, user-centered design.

1 Introduction and Motivation

Ecological issues related to energy generation and consumption become more and more pressing, and new ways to address the arising challenges are needed urgently. Different means to help users in engaging in positive behavior have been developed, and ambient displays have been identified as very suitable means to communicate this information to the end-user. Recent work mainly focused on providing ambient feedback on the current energy consumption [e.g. 5, 6, 21]. Our work addresses the aspect of supporting people to plan their near future consumption behavior with the goal to align it with the availability of green energy (i.e. energy produced by sustainable means) thereby achieving positive ecological effects. This interest on

D. Keyson et al. (Eds.): AmI 2011, LNCS 7040, pp. 157–166, 2011.

developing methods and ambient interfaces for shifting consumption times rather than reducing consumption is generated by needs from smart grids and from user requirements.

An approach that received considerable attention in the past years is smart grids. The main idea here is to shift energy loads from peak demand times to times of less demand. Additionally, balancing of generation and consumption levels should take place at a local level as far as possible to avoid transportation losses and the need for high transportation capacities. Further details regarding power supply dynamics are discussed in section 1.1.

Recently different approaches have been developed to influence consumption behavior of users. Section 1.2 provides a detailed discussion of selected solutions and their advantages and disadvantages. One major conclusion of this analysis is that available solutions so far mainly provide feedback on energy consumption, and that there is a strong need for interfaces that support the users in planning their behavior according to ecological needs.

To successfully apply the concept in real life conditions we based the design of the ambient display on detailed user requirements collected by different means. Section 2 describes the process, methods and resulting requirements.

In Section 3 we then present our design solution – the FORE-Watch (**F**orecast **O**f **R**enewable Energy - **Watch**) – and discuss it in the context of related work.

1.1 Power Supply and Smart Grids

Energy is generated by different means, and each country – depending on its natural possibilities and historic political decisions – has its own typical mix of energy sources. In the paper we focus on the example of Austria, but the basic dynamics are similar in different countries, and the general approach and methods can be applied with minor adaptations. In the case of Austria – due to its location in the Alps and the political decision to not use nuclear power – the typical energy mix is dominated by hydroelectric power (43.3% run-of-river plants and 19% reservoir power stations) followed by thermal power stations (33.9%) and wind (2.8%). Also, additional electricity needs to be imported to meet the demands [4].

Availability and production rate of green energy sources (mainly hydroelectric and wind power in the case of Austria) is highly depending on external factors most of which are related to different aspects of weather conditions. Another aspect that has to be considered in this context is the status and transportation capacity of the energy grid. The situation might arise that there is enough energy available, but not at the right place, and that the power grid is not able to transport the needed amount of energy.

Green electricity in Austria typically originates from three different sources: wind, hydroelectric generation and – to a much smaller extend – photovoltaic cells. All of these production modes are related in some way to the current or recent weather conditions. Also biomass is used in thermal power plants, however we do not further discuss this power source in this paper as generation of power by this means can be controlled by careful management and therefore is not of prior relevance with regard to inducing load shifts by consumers.

Possible output of a wind park is directly related to the wind speed. Based on knowledge of placement of major wind parks, their nominal capacity as well as localized forecasts of wind speeds it is relatively easy to develop a forecast of wind power production that is sufficiently accurate. For example, detailed forecast models are developed by the project *WindFX* at the University of Innsbruck [22].

The output of photovoltaic installations is directly related to the sunshine intensity and duration. Again, provided the location and characteristics and amount of installed photovoltaic elements are known, it is relatively easy to model and forecast the power generation of the photovoltaic cells.

The third relevant source of green energy in Austria is hydroelectric power. The power output of a hydroelectric power station is mainly related to the flow rate of water, which itself depends on the current and past weather conditions. As it takes time for water to drain off and collect in creeks and rivers, forecast of hydroelectric power generation is much more complex than in the prior cases. Fortunately, this is an active area of research, e.g. [8], and models of related areas especially flood prediction can be reused to develop accurate forecasts.

The typical temporal dynamics for these production means naturally possess different characteristics. Whereas production of wind power can change rather fast, the changes in the production of run-of-river power plants are much slower. These differences in the characteristics naturally need to be considered for the design of the persuasive ambient display, especially with regard to providing the users with actionable feedback – see section 3 for more details.

Besides these influences related to power production also the status of the grid and its power transportation capability needs to be considered for example to be able to estimate if the produced green energy actually can be distributed to the customers. Basically, the management of energy grid networks is based on the balance of demand and supply. To be able to do so already now different planning and forecast methods are used to be able to better match the supply with the demand [12], and these information can also be used as input for the calculation of recommendations for the users.

1.2 Persuasive Technology and Energy Feedback for Influencing Energy Consumption Patterns

Within the recent years the utilization of different approaches and (persuasive) technologies for influencing the energy consumption patterns of the end users have been developed [7]. Existing methods to manage (i.e. reduce or temporarily shift) power consumption could be clustered into three main approaches.

First, paper-based efforts try to make energy consumption more visible by increasing the frequency of the traditional paper-based bill. People receive their energy bill more frequently e.g. every month compared to once a year.

Second, dedicated software programs visualizing the present and previous energy consumption across time were developed. Thereby users can compare e.g. their monthly consumption. Example systems for this approach are the *PowerMeter* by Google [10], *Hohm* by Microsoft [18], and *GreenPocket* [11]. *Hohm* and *PowerMeter* are accessible through web, whereas *GreenPocket* is available as smartphone app.

Third, dedicated ambient devices within the user's home are used to provide information for the consumer. Ambient devices are characterized by a high stimulating nature and therefore have the possibility to attract the users' attention, make consumption visible in real time and support behavioral change. *Wattson* [21] for example provides real-time information about the actual energy use in kilowatt hours (kWh) as well as monetary values. Additionally it glows in different colors depending on the amount of used energy. This feature is also used by the *Power-Aware Cord* [13], which represents energy consumption through glowing pulses, color, and intensity of light. Another system that guides energy consumption is called *Energy Orb* [6]. This orb provides visual feedback whether at the present moment it is relatively good or bad to consume energy. The *Energy AWARE Clock* [5] provides feedback on the past energy consumption on the clock-face thereby enabling the users to develop a good overview and understanding on their past consumption patterns.

1.3   Effectiveness of Energy Feedback/Management Methods

The general goal of the described methods is to make energy consumption more transparent to the individuals and thereby initiate a behavioral change towards a more pro-environmental management of energy. Consequently, there is high interest in evaluating and quantifying the achievable effects, to compare the effectiveness of different approaches, and to study which effects the introduction of different methods has on the everyday life of people.

Darby [2] provides a comprehensive meta-analysis of numerous empirical evaluations on the effectiveness of different types of energy feedback. Feedback which is provided in real-time from a display monitor is labeled *direct feedback* by her. A typical example for this kind of feedback is the above-mentioned *Wattson* system. Achievable savings using this approach are between 5 and 15%. Besides this direct feedback effectiveness of indirect feedback was analyzed. Information that is provided through *indirect feedback* has been processed before reaching the energy consumer and does not use real-time data. Typical examples are paper-based bills or the above-mentioned Google *PowerMeter* and Microsoft *Hohm*. Identified effects on savings for indirect feedback reach from 0-10%. Darby argues that this wide range of effects is described through the quality of information that is prepared for the end-users. To describe how best cases of feedback are designed, Fischer (2008) has reviewed 29 published studies. According to her, computerized feedback with interactive elements works best.

2   Identifying Design Requirements

Starting point for the design work was our goal to design an ambient device that allows users to align their energy consumption with requirements from production and distribution within the grid as described above. The design process was based on input from different sources, both theoretical and user-based.

2.1 Requirements Identified in Related Work

Energy-consumption-related information is traditionally provided through websites, smartphone applications, home displays, ambient devices but also paper-based efforts. Several scientific research studies and analyses describe how users interact with those technologies and how they process this data e.g. [2, 7, 15, 16]. In the following we focus on four main requirements from a user perspective, which we incorporated for our work.

First, there is the question about how to present the information about energy consuming behavior to motivate a long-term change. Studies showed that kilowatt hours or CO_2 units are hard to understand for the traditional users [2], which leads to the fact that people prefer monetary units in energy-related displays [15]. However, financial savings are not a long-term motivator for a behavioral change [15, 20]. Jaccuci et al. [16] suggest that the main energy feedback should address knowledge and action synergically, and that it should be combined with energy conservation tips to increase the impact of the feedback.

Second, feedback is traditionally provided based on past or present energy consumption (e.g. information about the total consumption of the previous day/week/month, or also real-time information). There is no possibility to change this amount of energy consumption any more, and for the future there is also the question about how to change consumption. Consequently there is the need to instruct consumers about how to behave in the future. Tailored suggestions and energy-saving tips are therefore highly important to guide the users for the future [7].

As a *third* main aspect we want to mention is comfort. Energy consumption is highly associated with comfort. Gerdenitsch et al. [9] for example studied behavioral barriers that prevent energy-savings within the domestic context. Results showed that besides a lack of attention (e.g. forgetting), comfort is a major barrier. According to this study it is important to allow people to satisfy their needs of comfort, but at the same time to also inform them about potential savings.

Finally there is the requirement of tailoring the feedback. Some kind of personalization of energy-related information on the specific socio-demographic, behavioral and also contextual variables is recommended by several authors [1, 7, 16]. Midden et al. [19] also pointed out that tailored feedback is more effective than comparative feedback. Also results of a literature review by Fischer [7] suggest tailoring the information given to the motives and also norms of the specific target group.

2.2 Requirements Identified in a User Interface Workshop

As a follow-up on previous work and studies, we conducted a co-design workshop based on the inspiration card technique [14], which was already successfully used in other research projects that focused on sustainability [3]. The purpose of the requirements and design workshop was to collect and identify requirements and ideas for the design of ambient interfaces with the goal to persuade people to save energy. 52 inspiration cards were prepared and used as basis material for the workshop. The cards focused on the following areas: visualization, electricity devices, state-of-the-art ambient displays, motivation slogans, household areas/rooms, state-of-the-art energy saving interfaces, different granularities of information (overview vs. detail), different types of information (money saved, energy tips, energy saved compared to other, etc.), and timing aspects (energy saved today, last month, last year, etc.). The 6 participants were split up into 3 groups of 2 with the task to combine the inspiration cards into the ideal ambient persuasion interface for energy information. The results were discussed and analyzed both together with the participants and post-hoc by the researchers, and the following main requirements could be identified:

Placement. Two main spots could be identified as good placement opportunities for ambient energy displays: First the kitchen, as that's the place where people come together. Second, the antechamber, as that's the place where one notices a display before leaving or when coming home.

Information. Participants wanted a simple presentation of energy saving potential for the current situation of their specific household as well as a suggestion of several options how to save energy. General and unspecific tips (such as e.g. switch of the lights when not used) or household changing tips (e.g. buy energy saving devices or don't use a game console) were not appreciated.

Timing. The information should be visible the whole day and the user can decide when to take action. Also users would like to have timely feedback to see that a behavior modification actually changed their energy consumption.

Attractiveness. Participants did not want a novel "electric device" (such as the *Energy Orb* or *Wattson*), but something attractive or something they can hide, e.g. inside of a kitchen cupboard.

Social Rewards. Participants did not want to have a direct social comparison in energy saving behaviors between household members or neighborhood.

Reduction. Participants only wanted very reduced information, with the focus on when and how one could save energy in the household to be „in the green" (independently of how green is defined, money, nature, etc.).

2.3   Requirements Identified in Online Survey

To further inform design we were also interested in learning which energy-consuming everyday activities such as cooking, washing and ironing consumers are willing to shift or delay, and how big the temporal window for this actions were. An online questionnaire was used to collect data from volunteers regarding these questions. The questionnaire listed ten common activities and users where required to answer whether they are willing to postpone or shift this activity and in case of yes, for what amount of time in the maximum.

Additionally, participants were asked the same question with regard to recharging electro-vehicles. This is not yet a common activity, however recharging vehicles is expected to have great impact and opportunities for the smart grid and shifting demand loads.

A total of 66 users (23 male, 43 female, average age 31.2 ± 8.93 years) filled in the questionnaire. As we suggest the housing situation as a main mediator variable we asked participants about their actual status. Most of the participants (60.6%) resided together with one other person, 24.2% of participants lived alone, and 15.2% lived with three to five people in the same household. Table 1 summarizes the main results from the questionnaire.

Table 1. Results from online questionnaire regarding willingness to shift activities according to ecological needs

	Number of valid answers	Mean	Median	Minimum	Maximum
Cooking	65	1h:34m	1h:30m	0h:00m	3h:00m
Dish washing	65	12h:44m	6h:00m	0h:00m	48h:00m
Washing machine	64	21h:25m	24h:00m	0h:00m	48h:00m
Entertainment electronics	61	3h:38m	0h:00m	0h:00m	48h:00m
Showering/bathing	63	2h:17m	1h:30m	0h:00m	24h:00m
Vacuuming	62	25h:54m	24h:00m	0h:00m	48h:00m
Ironing	50	26h:23m	24h:00m	0h:00m	48h:00m
Blow-drying & shaving	62	4h:55m	0h:10m	0h:00m	48h:00m
Cleaning	63	24h:26m	24h:00m	0h:00m	48h:00m
Gardening	49	29h:25m	48h:00m	0h:00m	48h:00m
Charging electro-vehicle	31	9h:44m	2h:00m	0h:00m	48h:00m

Analyzing the results from the questionnaire, we can identify two distinct planning horizons for the end users. A first set of activities is directly related to personal needs (e.g. cooking, personal hygiene), and users are only willing to shift actions in a very narrow time window, typically 10 to 30 minutes. A second set of actions is related to different housekeeping activities (e.g. cleaning, washing, and vacuuming). Here the time window for shifting actions is much bigger, and typically users are willing to delay actions for one day (24h). Therefore, the ambient display should be able to communicate the action guidelines for two different time horizons.

Short term planning. First, the ambient display should be able to communicate the green energy forecast for the next 12 hours very precisely. Additionally, the display needs to provide a sufficiently detailed temporal resolution to allow people to plan short-term activities.

Medium term planning. Second, the display should support the planning of activities with regard to a medium term perspective (i.e. one day). In contrast to the short term planning no detailed temporal resolution should be displayed, as the forecast information will be not very adequate, but an overall recommendation (whether to delay activities for one day or not) should be provided.

3   Design Solution: The FORE-Watch

Based on the identified design requirements and also influenced and inspired by related work (especially the energy aware clock [5]) we developed a design solution we call the *FORE-Watch*. The central design element of the solution is a common and fully functional clock. The clock is enhanced with three additional items: the outer ring, the inside gauge and the history view (see Figure 1).

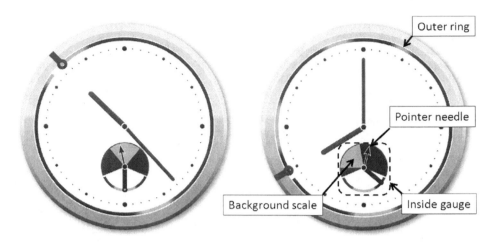

Fig. 1. The FORE-watch design shown in two different situations

The outer ring. The main function of the outer ring is to display the forecasted availability of green energy for the next twelve hours. Availability is displayed coded in the three traffic light colors: green indicates there is plenty of green energy available, yellow that there is some green energy available and red, that it is expected that there will be a lack of green energy. This display allows the users to immediately perceive the forecast for the next hours, and to also see this directly in context of time. Therefore it supports the users to make decisions whether they use energy for required tasks immediately or whether they want to shift the activity to another time slot. For example a user might delay starting the dish washer until after having been gone jogging, in case the outer ring shows that green electricity probably will become available only one hour later.

The semantic color-coding of the forecast (i.e. whether the outer ring shows green, yellow or red) is calculated relatively on basis of the forecast for the next twelve hours, not absolute. Individual forecast values for the next 12 hours are calculated, and moments with values in the top third of this period are shown green, the middle third yellow and the lower third red. This is done to always provide meaningful possibilities to act more sustainable for users within this time frame. This is especially important because of the temporal characteristics of hydroelectric power generation. Generation here changes very slowly, and using absolute or long term instead of relative and short term calculation methods would result in an undifferentiated display (e.g. only showing red for the next 12 hours) that doesn't allow users to adapt their behavior within their limited temporal horizon for planning activities (compare section 2.3).

The inside gauge. The inside gauge consists of two main elements. The pointer needle and the background scale. The pointer needle shows the current amount of energy consumption of the household which is provided by a smart meter.

The rotatable background scale provides a semantic indication (again using the three traffic light colors) whether the current consumption is low (pointer needle in front of green segment on background scale), average (yellow) or high (red). In contrast to other design solutions the semantic definition of what is 'good' or 'bad' is not static but influenced by the current status of availability of green energy. In the interface this is indicated by the rotatability of the background scale, which is adapted in real time. To communicate the link between the status of the availability of green energy (indicated by the position of the short hand on outer ring) and the degree of rotation of the background scale the background scale is equipped with a handle that moves over an arc which shows a color gradient from green through yellow to red. The similar indicator symbols at the short clock hand and the handle of the background scale are designed to communicate this connection to the users.

History overview. A third functionality that is provided by the clock is that it allows viewing a historical record of one's own behavior. To not annoy the users with too much visual clutter, this overview is only visible at explicit request by tapping anywhere on the clock face. The display automatically disappears after a short activation time of 5 seconds. In contrast to most existing approaches the clock however shows a weighted consumption history. The view shows the cumulated time the user spend with their pointer needle over the red, green and yellow area of the background scale.

Tomorrows Forecast. Together with the history overview the user also activated the display of the forecast for the next day. The feedback contains an overall estimation whether delaying consumption options is a recommended alternative or not based on the current forecasts.

4 Future Work

The next step in the development of the *FORE-Watch* is the long-term evaluation of its effectiveness in real conditions. Within the PEEM project (http://peem.cure.at) *FORE-Watches* will be installed in 30 households and be running there for at least 9 months. Electric power consumption will be measured and recorded in real time. Effects of the *FORE-Watch* will be evaluated both, quantitatively and qualitatively. We'll compare the power consumption patterns with the predictions and analyze whether significant effects in consumption shift can be found. Qualitative data from interviews with household members will further help to understand the dynamics of the *FORE-Watch* on consumption behavior.

Besides the evaluation of the approach we will look into applying the concepts and design solution to similar areas. We are especially looking into the areas of solar energy plants, traffic density, local production of energy, and price development.

References

1. Abrahamse, W., Wokje, A., Steg, L., Vlek, C., Rothengatter, T.: A review of intervention studies aimed at household energy conservation. Journal of Environmental Psychology 25(3), 273–291 (2005)

2. Darby, S.: The effectiveness of feedback on energy consumption. A review for DEFRA of the literature on metering, billing and direct displays. Environmental Change Institute, University of Oxford (2006)
3. Davis, J.: Participatory design for sustainable campus living. In: Proceedings CHI Extended Abstracts, pp. 3877–3882. ACM, New York (2010)
4. E-Control: Ökostrombericht (2009)
5. Energy AWARE Clock, http://www.tii.se/node/5984
6. Energy Orb, http://www.ambientdevices.com/cat/orb/PGE.html
7. Fischer, C.: Feedback on household electricity consumption: a tool for saving energy? Energy Efficiency 1, 79–104 (2008)
8. Garc, M.B., Dubus, L.: Forecasting precipitation for hydroelectric power management: how to exploit GCM ' s seasonal ensemble forecasts. International Journal of Climatology 1705, 1691–1705 (2007)
9. Gerdenitsch, C., Schrammel, J., Döbelt, S., Tscheligi, M.: Creating Persuasive Technologies for Sustainability – Identifying Barriers Limiting the Target Behavior. Persuasive (2011)
10. Google PowerMeter, http://www.google.com/powermeter/about/
11. GreenPocket, http://www.greenpocket.de/
12. Gross, G., Galiana, F.D.: Short-term load forecasting. Proceedings of the IEEE 75(12) (1987)
13. Gustafsson, A., Gyllenswärd, M.: The Power-Aware Cord: Energy Awareness through Ambient Information Display. In: Proceedings CHI 2005. ACM, NY (2005)
14. Halskov, K., Dalsgard, P.: Inspiration card workshops. In: Proceedings of the 6th Conference on Designing Interactive Systems (DIS 2006), pp. 2–11. ACM, New York (2006)
15. Hargreaves, T., Nye, A., Burges, J.: Making energy visible: A qualitative field study of how householders interact with feedback from smart energy monitors. Energy Policy 38, 6111–6119 (2010)
16. Jacucci, G., Spagnolli, A., Gamberini, L., Chalambalakis, A., Björksog, C., Bertoncini, M., Torstensson, C., Monti, P.: Designing Effective feedback of Electricity Consumption for Mobile User Interfaces. PsychNology Journal 7(3), 265–289 (2009)
17. Kollmuss, A., Agyeman, J.: Mind the Gap: why do people act environmentally and what are the barriers to. Environmental Education 8(3), 239–260 (2002)
18. Microsoft Hohm, http://www.microsoft-hohm.com/
19. Midden, C.J.H., Meter, J.F., Weenig, M.W.H., Zieverink, H.J.A.: Using feedback, reinforcement and information to reduce energy consumption in households: A field-experiment. Journal of Economic Psychology 3(1), 65–86 (1983)
20. Neuman, K.: Personal values and commitment to energy conservation. Environment and Behavior 18(1), 53–74 (1986)
21. Wattson, http://www.diykyoto.com/uk
22. WindFX, University of Innsbruck, http://imgi.uibk.ac.at/dynamics/windfx

Flexible, Non-emissive Textile Display

Roshan Lalintha Peiris, Owen Noel Newton Fernando,
and Adrian David Cheok

Keio-NUS CUTE Center,
NUS Graduate School for Integrative Sciences and Engineering
National University of Singapore
{roshan,newtonfernando,adriancheok}@mixedrealitylab.org,
ambikraf.mixedrealitylab.org

Abstract. This paper describes current progress in the implementation of flexible ubiquitous textile display. We use thermochromic inks and miniature peltier semiconductor elements to create a non-emissive textile display. Here we present some of the initial work into the use of custom made miniature peltier elements. We describe some of the early works into the integration of this technology into the fabric to present a flexible non-emissive display.

Keywords: thermochromic, peltier, thermoelectric, textile, fabric, display.

1   Introduction

Fabrics are a common form of material we interact with daily. Since its recorded uses from prehistoric times fabrics have become an integral part of our daily lives in the form of our clothes, home furnishing, architecture and other numerous range of uses. Besides its common use as a fashion statement nowadays, such uses of fabrics have become a medium for expression allowing arts and crafts to find its way into fabrics.

With the advancement of technology and the introduction of new concepts and smart materials, researchers are able to embed more and more electronics into our fabrics paving way for a new era of fabric displays. With this development, researchers have been looking into various forms of fabric displays that are mainly emissive, such as embedding LEDs, electroluminscent sheets and wires, complete LCD displays, etc. The unnatural and non subtle nature of these technologies present a rather obtrusive emissive displays, preventing their application in fabrics and traditional arts.

With this paper, we present the current progress in the implementation of a, non-emissive fabric display with fast color change allowing us to present novel animations on fabrics. This technology uses an integration of thermochromic ink and peltier semiconductor elements to achieve these properties. Our previous work AmbiKraf [4] which uses this technology has some major limitations such as high power consumption, inflexibility, and the requirement to use heatsinks

D. Keyson et al. (Eds.): AmI 2011, LNCS 7040, pp. 167–171, 2011.

for the display. Here, in the next version of AmbiKraf, we try to overcome these limitations using our latest customized technologies. This paper describes this attempt and some initial results of the system.

2   Related Works

To focus on a more ambient approach for fabric displays researchers have focused many works on non-emissive fabric displays [5]. A more commonly used ink in these works are thermochromic inks. Thermochromic inks change color based on temperature. In 'SMOKS' [2], a wearable display uses a shoulder pad made of thermochromic inks which when touched turns the color by means of the body temperature. Shimmering Flower [1] uses thermochromic inks which are actuated by conductive yarn that is woven into the fabric. When powered up, the conductive yarn heats up and in turn actuates the thermochromic inks to change the color. In 'Mosaic Textiles' [5], authors use liquid crystal inks which work on the same principle as thermochromic inks, actuated by conductive yarn. Almost all of the above non-emissive displays have been used in an omni-directional manner. That is, these works only use a heating source such as body heat or conductive yarn without any cooling method. Due to this reason the absolute controllability thus the ability to animate the display is not profound.

Hence, our approach is to use thermochromic inks due to its non-emissivity and peltier semiconductor elements due to their ability to rapidly heat and cool the fabric allowing it to animate. In addition the use of customzed miniature Peltier semiconductor modules allow the technology to be seamlessly integrated into the fabric compared to our previous version of AmbiKraf.

2.1   Technology

The core components of this technology are thermochromic inks and peltier semiconductor elements. The overall system is shown in Figure 1.

Thermochromic inks work on the principle that when they are heated beyond their 'actuation temperature' they become colorless and reappear when cooled below this actuation temperature. Their actuation temperatures can be customized based on the requirement.

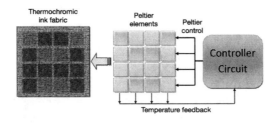

Fig. 1. Overall System

As the thermochromic inks are thermally actuated, we use peltier semiconductor elements since hey have the capability to heat and cool on the same surface by simply reversing the voltage polarity. However, in this newest version of our project we use miniature peltier elements that can be eaisly embedded on to the fabric (Figure 2(a)).

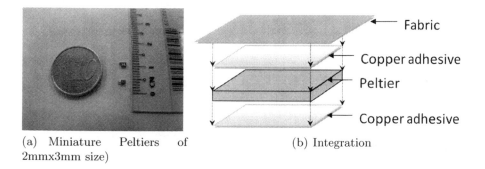

(a) Miniature   Peltiers   of 2mmx3mm size)

(b) Integration

Fig. 2. Main technologies and the integration of the system

The fabric display is made out of few pixels, with each pixel being a peltier element. A feedback control system with a fine tuned PI (Proportional-Integral) controller circuit accurately controls the temperature of each peltier element thus in turn triggering the color change of each pixel.

To have a feedback control system, temperature of each pixel should be fed back to the temperature controller. As we use miniature peltier elements, placing individual temperature sensors, on each pixel is unfeasible as it would reduce the heat transfer surface between the peltier and fabric and also require more wiring thus reducing the flexibility of the fabric. Hence, we are investigating the use of the seebeck effect [3], the reverse operation of peltier elements. I.e., as the peltiers change the temperature they produce a voltage proportional to the temperature. This voltage is fedback to the controller completing the feedback loop. Thus, the repeating actuating and sensing cycle, allows us to actuate the pixel while controlling its temperature accurately.

2.2   Integration

Integration of these peltier pixels on to the textile is a crucial step in implementing this color changing textile. Hence, as a first proof-of-concept attempt in this version of the system, we use thermally conductive adhesives to attach the peltier elements on to the fabric. This first step was an attempt in trying to recognize the optimal arrangement of the pixels in terms of the space in between the textile, and the flexibility of the fabric. Thus, the integration is as in Figure 2(b).

3   Results

The current system uses thermochromic inks that actuate at 32^0C. Thus the transient response of the system, 1.6s for color change, is shown in Figure 3(a). The steadystate error of maximum 2 is depicted in Figure 3(b). Currently, the system depicts acceptable controllability. However, in our further investigations, we hope to fine tune the controller more to increase the response time further thus speeding up the display.

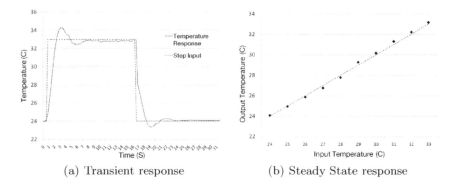

(a) Transient response   (b) Steady State response

Fig. 3. Temperature controllability results of the system

The first prototype is a 4x4 matrix display as shown in the Figure 4(a). Figure 4(b) shows basic animations of two letters. As seen in Figure 5, with the use of miniature peltiers have resulted in the textile becoming more flexible. In addition, due to low power and higher efficiency of these peltiers, the requirement of heatsinks as in the previous versions of our work was not required.

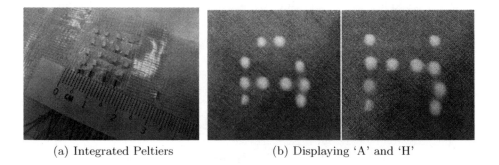

(a) Integrated Peltiers   (b) Displaying 'A' and 'H'

Fig. 4. Results

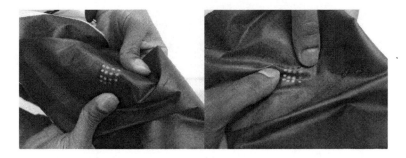

Fig. 5. Flexibility with the integrated system

4   Discussion and Future Work

This paper describes our work in progress towards implementing a flexible textile display. The use of miniature peltier elements compared to the previous version has greatly improved the flexibility of the textile. However, still there are some key areas that we are working on as discussed below.

Currently the peltiers are simply attached to the fabric using thermally conductive adhesives. Instead, our main goal is to completely embed these peltiers right into the fabric. For this we are investigating a few techniques including weaving the peltiers using conductive yarns directly into the textile.

Acknowledgements. This research is carried out under CUTE Project No. WBS R- 7050000-100-279 partially funded by a grant from the National Research Foundation (NRF) administered by the Media Development Authority (MDA) of Singapore.

References

1. Berzowska, J.: SIGGRAPH 2004: ACM SIGGRAPH 2004 Sketches, New York, NY, USA (2004)
2. Berzowska, J., Coelho, M.: Smoks: the memory suits. In: CHI 2006: Extended Abstracts on Human Factors in Computing Systems, pp. 538–543. ACM, New York (2006)
3. Odhner, L., Asada, H.: Sensorless temperature estimation and control of shape memory alloy actuators using thermoelectric devices. IEEE/ASME Transactions on Mechatronics 11(2), 139–144 (2006)
4. Peiris, R.L., Cheok, A.D., Teh, J.K.S., Fernando, O.N.N., Yingqian, W., Lim, A., Yi, P., Polydorou, D., Ong, K.P., Tharakan, M.: Ambikraf: an embedded non-emissive and fast changing wearable display. In: ACM SIGGRAPH 2009 Emerging Technologies, SIGGRAPH 2009, pp. 1:1–1:1. ACM (2009)
5. Wakita, A., Shibutani, M.: Mosaic textile: wearable ambient display with non-emissive color-changing modules. In: ACE 2006: Proceedings of the 2006 ACM SIGCHI International Conference on Advances in Computer Entertainment Technology, p. 48. ACM, New York (2006)

Voice Control in Smart Homes Using Distant Microphones: A VoiceXML-Based Approach

Gloria López, Victor Peláez, Roberto González, and Vanesa Lobato

Fundación CTIC, c/Ada Byron, 39, Edificio Centros Tecnológicos,
Parque Científico y Tecnológico Gijón, Asturias, 33203, Spain
{gloria.lopez,victor.pelaez,roberto.gonzalez,
vanesa.lobato}@fundacionctic.org

Abstract. This paper proposes the design of a voice control module for intelligent environments, primarily oriented to home environments. An intelligent environment is understood to be a ubiquitous space equipped with embedded devices. This solution is based on the main standards in the field of speech technologies (VoiceXML, MRCP, SRGS and SISR), dynamically adaptable to structural changes in the home automation system and scalable to the number of rooms and devices in the home. The final solution has been validated in a real home automation installation, using distant speech recognition and a keyword detection approach (keyword spotting, KWS). KWS works as an input filter for the dialogue system, making it more robust against noise. Test results have shown the technical feasibility of the solution and promising user acceptance.

Keywords: smart home, ambient intelligence (AmI), voice control, distant speech recognition, keyword spotting (KWS).

1 Introduction

In a world in which the home is a space composed of a growing number of increasingly complicated digital devices, the concept of ambient intelligence takes on new importance. In this context, it is particularly necessary to facilitate human interactions through natural and intuitive interfaces embedded in objects which form a part of the environment, and voice and multimodal interfaces play a key role [1]. The aim of these interaction types is to use the natural modes of human communication, such as language and behaviour, by applying different recognition technologies, such as those based on voice or gestures.

In the field of speech interfaces, there are many studies focused on natural interaction [2][3] with limited success. Therefore, limitations of natural speech interaction have led to usability being questioned even within the scientific community [4]. There are also less ambitious alternatives to natural interaction in terms of language restriction, but more suited to commercial applications in terms of effectiveness. These alternatives are based on the use of language models restricted to specific domains and speech recognition grammars [5].

Apart from the type of interaction, there are other two key factors when designing voice control solutions for home environments: the standardization of speech

D. Keyson et al. (Eds.): AmI 2011, LNCS 7040, pp. 172–181, 2011.

technologies and the evaluation of the voice control solution. VoiceXML is the most relevant standard for dialogue management with high commercial acceptance. However, although there is a wide range of VoiceXML products on the market, their use in the digital home is limited to remote voice control via telephone [6]. Other often overlooked aspect of voice control in ambient intelligence is the necessity of using pre-installed or embedded microphones, also known as distant microphones. These microphones are not intrusive but are more sensitive to the high degree of variability in the speech signal than close-talk microphones [7], resulting in an increase in the percentage of speech recognition errors. The improvement of robustness against noise in smart environments has been addressed from various perspectives, such as the use of microphone arrays [8] or keyword spotting approaches [9]. However, it is not usually addressed in evaluations of real installations [10][11].

The basis of this work is to develop a voice control solution for digital homes, without the restriction of a specific user group, based on the use of generic hardware and, as far as possible, based on the most widely used speech technology standards. It also includes the evaluation of the proposed system by real users in a home automation environment equipped with built-in microphones. As a continuously enabled speech recognition system is more sensitive to noise, a keyword spotting technique is used. In this way, the KWS approach can be evaluated using live audio, a type of test rarely documented in scientific literature although such techniques are widely accepted in smart home solutions.

2   System Overview

2.1   General Overview

Two aspects of the proposed solution are related to speech technology standardization. Firstly, the core of the software architecture is a VoiceXML platform with MRCP protocol support. The use of the MRCP protocol for communication with the speech synthesis (TTS) and speech recognition (ASR) technology offers several advantages. It guarantees the interoperability of these technologies with any other product with similar features on the market, and simplifies the distribution of the elements over the network. Secondly, taking into account that natural interaction is one of the remaining challenges of speech technology [4], restricted grammars are used to increase efficiency although the size of these grammars is large enough to ensure an adequate degree of naturalness in communication. These grammars fulfil the Speech Recognition Grammar Specification (SRGS) and also include semantic interpretation (SISR).

Dynamic adaptability to changes in the home automation installation is mainly related to the way in which the initialization of the context information is addressed. In this work, this information consists of an XML configuration file for each type of device in the installation. This file defines the actions supported by each type of device and any other relevant information regarding these actions, such as configuration parameters and correspondence with actions in the automation middleware.

Focusing on the specific logic of the dialogue manager, a frame-based approach [12] is used. The slots of these frames are generated dynamically based on the state of the dialogue and the context information handled by the dialogue system. In a home automation installation, each device belongs to a class shared with other devices of similar functionality. Each device also has a unique name which distinguishes it from other devices of the same type. With this device identification and given that actions can have a variable number of parameters, each frame is composed of four elements: action, type of device, device name and list of action parameters (optional).

As the design and evaluation of the system uses distant microphones, the proposed architecture includes the use of a keyword spotting technique, which activates and deactivates the dialogue system.

The proposed hardware solution is based on common computers, one for each voice-enabled room, and other generic audio devices such as speakers, microphones and optional microphone preamplifiers. This feature facilitates the scalability of the solution in terms of the number of rooms that can be controlled. In addition, the solution is independent of the specific hardware in the home automation installation.

2.2 Software Architecture

Fig. 1 shows the proposed software architecture based on a distributed model with two blocks: a specific module for the speech, called the voice control module; and a second block, called the hardware controller, which handles the communication with the hardware devices to be controlled. The integration of these two independent blocks is based on two aspects. Firstly, the inclusion of the information related to the translation of each action into tasks on the home automation installation in the XML configuration files. Secondly, the integration of the dialogue manager and the alert generator as two new services of the service architecture used by the hardware controller module.

The dialogue manager has been implemented as a web application, and is responsible for controlling dialogue flow and turning dialogue actions into hardware controller tasks. The flow of the dialogue depends on the previous dialogue turns and other contextual information obtained from the automation hardware controller. The output of the dialogue manager is based on a set of predefined templates which will be completed dynamically, depending on the state of the dialogue.

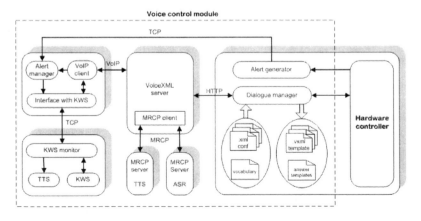

Fig. 1. System software architecture

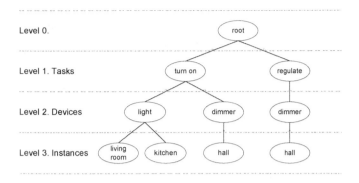

Fig. 2. Intermediate tree-shaped representation

For the internal structure of the dialogue manager, we propose the use of an intermediate tree-shaped representation which allows the storage of environment information. This tree-shaped representation facilitates the access and processing of environment information during the dialogue as in [13]. This intermediate representation is generated during the start up of the dialogue manager, using a sequential scan over all the home automation devices managed by the automation hardware controller. The evaluation of each device instance for which the Visitor design pattern is essential involves the processing of the XML file for that particular type of device, as well as the processing of the linguistic information associated with that file. In addition, if there is some specific information about the device itself (e.g. its name), that information will also be loaded at this point. As a result, the representation shown in Fig. 2 is obtained. Each level contains the following information:

- Level 1 (tasks): all actions that can be performed on the devices via voice
- Level 2 (devices): the types of devices that are related to each action
- Level 3 (instances): the instances or specific devices identified by their name

With this representation, each dialogue turn is translated into an in-depth search over the described tree to determine the type and content of the response according to the current state of the dialogue. Each type of response will be associated with a VoiceXML template (e.g. question, answer, confirmation, etc.) and also with other templates that contain the guidelines for generating the answer sentences.

The voice control module has two additional software components (see the left-hand section of Fig. 1). The first one includes a VoIP client, which is responsible for contacting the dialogue system through the VoiceXML platform. The second component implements the keyword spotting module and also has a local TTS system, whose function within the architecture is essentially limited to the voice conversion of the alerts that come from the home automation hardware. The keyword spotting technique detects a specific keyword and triggers an alert addressed to the VoIP client indicating the need to start a new connection with the dialogue system.

Focusing on keyword spotting approaches, and taking into account that there are several alternatives, some of the most common HMM-based approaches (Hidden

Markov Models) have been developed and evaluated. Three keywords (habitación - room-, apartamento -apartment- and casa -house-) were selected because of their relevance in the context of this work and their high frequency in the training corpus. The KWS approaches evaluated were the filler models based on triphones, filler models based on phonemes, a large vocabulary continuous speech recognition / LVCSR system, and a hybrid system in which the approach based on LVCSR and the approach based on triphones run in parallel.

3 Evaluation and Results

A completely functional prototype of the system was developed using a commercial VoiceXML platform and some specific tools (ATK and Flite) for the KWS module in order to evaluate the proposed design. The prototype was deployed in a laboratory equipped with a home automation network.

3.1 Evaluation Methodology

Testing was carried out in two phases. Firstly, various KWS approaches were evaluated using the Figure of Merit metric [14]. The performance of these techniques was compared and some of their configuration parameters were adjusted.

The second part of the test was the validation of the complete voice solution. Although the PARADISE methodology [15] is the most popular initiative in the evaluation of dialogue systems, there is still no single standard criterion for evaluating, comparing and predicting the performance and usability of such systems. Therefore, in the absence of a standard evaluation methodology and considering the possible limitations of PARADISE, such as excessive coupling between usability and user satisfaction [16] or a very limited predictive capacity [17], qualitative and quantitative measurements are addressed separately in this work. Later, the relations between both types of measurements are statistically analyzed.

Some of the most common quantitative measurements, also known as interaction parameters, are presented in [18][19][20]. After studying these parameters and the characteristics of the proposed system, the following parameters were considered:

1. Number of dialogues (ND).
2. Dialogue duration (DD). Average duration of a dialogue in seconds.
3. System-turn duration (STD) and user turn duration (UTD). Average duration of a system/user turn in seconds.
4. System response delay (SRD). Average delay of a system response in seconds.
5. User response delay (URD). Average delay of a user response in seconds.
6. Number of turns (NT). Average number of turns uttered in a dialogue.
7. Number of system turns (NST). Average number of system turns in a dialogue.
8. Number of user turns (NUT). Average number of user turns in a dialogue.
9. Number of helps (NH). Average number of user-help requests in a dialogue.
10. Number of ASR rejections (NAR). Average number of ASR rejections in a dialogue (the system was unable to "hear" or to "understand" the user).
11. Number of ASR errors (NAE). Average number of ASR errors (the system understood incorrectly the user prompt).

12. Task success (TS). Average number of tasks completed successfully.
13. Incomplete dialogues (ID). Average number of incomplete dialogues.
14. Number of KWS rejections (NKR). Average number of times the user has to repeat a keyword until the system detects it.
15. Voicexml response delay (VRD). Average time delay between the KWS system calling the VoiceXML platform and the user receiving the prompt response.

The subjective evaluation of spoken dialogue systems is usually done with user questionnaires. Some of the most common questionnaires in the evaluation of spoken dialogue systems are not specifically designed for voice, such as AttrackDiff [21] or SUMI [22]. However, users often have preconceived ideas of what the interaction should be, closely linked to the characteristics of conversation between humans. The naturalness, intuitiveness and ability are particularly important in the evaluation of spoken dialogue systems but are not covered in sufficient detail in the general questionnaires [23]. Some of the most common voice-specific questionnaires are: SASSI [23], SERVQUAL [24], the questionnaire for telephone services based in dialogue systems proposed in [17] or the questionnaire proposed in [18]. For the reason described above, the SASSI questionnaire was used in this test. In addition, questions relating to user antecedents and to general opinions about the overall system proposed in [17] were given to each user at the beginning and end of the test session.

3.2 Test Set-Up

To perform the KWS test, three men and three women reported a set of utterances, some of which contain keywords and other not. These utterances were recorded using a headset and a distant microphone placed 1.80 meters and 3 meters from the speaker.

Eleven men and six women between 23 and 40 years of age (mean=28) participated in the second part of the test. Users were cited individually in the testing room where they received a sheet containing brief instructions as well as a map of the testing room. The map showed the locations and the names of the voice-enabled devices and a summary of the supported actions.

During the tests users were required to control the status of the lights in the room. There were several lights with adjustable intensity and several lights with only on/off function. The option of requesting contextualized help or of cancelling the ongoing dialogue was also continuously available. The users filled out a SASSI questionnaire after completing each scenario. The following scenarios were used:

1. Turn on / off two lights, with or without adjustable intensity.
2. Set the intensity of two lights at a level between 0 and 100%.
3. Ask for help and exit the system.

The interaction parameters will be calculated for each dialogue and averaged later for the three scenarios described.

3.3 Results

In the first part of the test, the KWS technique that best suited the test conditions was the filler models method, based on triphones.

In the second part of the test, 169 dialogues (Turn on/off: 94, Regulate: 48, Help/Exit: 27) were obtained. Thus, the results commented in this section are based on the analysis of 169 samples of the interaction parameters, 54 SASSI questionnaires (3 per user) and 18 ITU-T questionnaires (1 per user).

Table 1 shows the results obtained for the questionnaires which in both cases have a 7-point Likert scale. Before analyzing their results, a value of 7 was assigned to the most positive category of the scale and a value of 1 to the most negative category. A value of 4 represents a neutral judgment.

SASSI results for each task are logical given the estimated level of complexity of the three tasks. The SASSI overall satisfaction has been calculated as the average of the values obtained for the three individual tasks, resulting in a low standard deviation. In general, per task or per system, the SASSI results show that users valued positively the questions about system response accuracy, likeability, habitability and speed categories. In addition, a neutral-low score in the most negative categories (cognitive demand and annoyance) can be interpreted as a positive user opinion about the system. The first question of the ITU-T questionnaire refers specifically to the overall impression or satisfaction, classifying it as extremely bad (value=1), bad, poor, fair, good, excellent or ideal (value=7). Most of the users responded that their overall impression was good (mean=4,78 and mode=5, with 80% of responses equal to 5 and 6), giving the worst score to the question related to the help expected from the system. The help provided by the system is an aspect to be improved in the future along with a study of the users' suggestions collected at the end of the ITU-T questionnaire.

Table 1. Summary of SASSI and ITU-T questionnaires results

		Tasks			Overall Satisfaction
		Turn on/off	Regulate intensity	Help / Exit	
SASSI Categories	System Response Accuracy	4,94 (σ =1,50)	4,60 (σ =1,77)	5,53 (σ =1,91)	5,02 (σ =0,47)
	Likeability	5,59 (σ =1,18)	5,36 (σ =1,29)	5,79 (σ =1,46)	5,58 (σ =0,22)
	Cognitive Demand	3,20 (σ =1,36)	3,30 (σ =1,37)	2,60 (σ =1,44)	3,03 (σ =0,38)
	Annoyance	3,70 (σ =1,76)	4,24 (σ =1,60)	3,02 (σ =1,76)	3,66 (σ =0,61)
	Habitability	4,31 (σ =1,57)	4,28 (σ =1,55)	4,58 (σ =1,87)	4,39 (σ =0,17)
	Speed	4,58 (σ =1,50)	5,06 (σ =1,24)	5,44 (σ =1,42)	5,03 (σ =0,43)
ITU-T (question 1)		----	----	----	4,78 (σ =1,48)

In the same way as the PARADISE philosophy, multiple linear regression (MLR) was used to determine the relationship between user satisfaction (dependent variable) and the values obtained for the interaction parameters (independent variables). Before doing the regression, the correlation between the parameters was studied. Thus, the parameters highly correlated (coefficient greater than 0.7) and less statistically significant (with greater p values) to the dependent variable were removed. In addition, the standard Z-score normalization function was applied to the dataset.

Table 2. Multivariate Linear Regression Models

Dependent Variable	Significant Predictors			Coefficient of determination R2
User Satisfaction (SASSI Likeability Score)	+ 0.798 * TS (sig 0,010)			0.401 (sig 0.024)
TS	- 0.657 * NAR (sig 1,949E-08)	- 0.601 * NAE (sig 2,0629E-06)	- 0.384 * ID (sig 0.0008)	0.847 (sig 1,0428E-11)

Table 2 shows the regression results. In the first model, user satisfaction was used as a dependent variable and was calculated as the sum of the responses corresponding to the Likeability category of the SASSI questionnaire. Only the percentage of tasks completed successfully (TS) proved to be a significant predictor, explaining 40% of the variance of the dependent variable.

User satisfaction was removed in the second regression model and task success was used as the dependent variable. The second regression model shows that the number of ASR rejections (NAR), the number of ASR errors (NAE) and the number of incomplete dialogues (ID) are, in this order, the parameters that have the most influence on the task success. In the second model, the significance and the coefficient of determination are higher than in the previous approximation.

Among the parameters that have the most direct influence on task success, and therefore indirectly on user satisfaction, only the number of incomplete dialogues (ID) is related to the combination of a VoiceXML platform with a KWS technique, the main peculiarity of the proposed solution. The number of incomplete dialogues alludes to communication errors between the VoIP client and the VoiceXML server and could probably be minimized by using a different VoiceXML platform.

The other parameters closely related to the type of solution proposed in this work were the VoiceXML response delay (VRD) and the number of KWS rejections (NKR). Although none of these parameters appeared as a predictor factor in the regression models, it is worth commenting the results obtained in both cases. One of the doubts cleared during the tests is whether the VRD remains constant during tests (mean=1,74, standard deviation=0,82, 90th percentile=1,76). The NKR mean was 1,73 and the NKR value was less than 2 in the 78,11% of every cases. Although this seems a positive result, it is true that the standard deviation in this case was 2,87 which justifies that many users complain about difficulty in accessing the system due to the high number of rejections.

4   Conclusions and Future Work

This work proposes a voice control solution for the devices installed in houses using main voice standards. It uses technology available in the market and facilitates the integration of new voice products such as speech recognition engines or VoiceXML platforms. The solution is independent of the devices to be controlled and it is also able to adapt dynamically to changes in these devices. The proposal has been implemented and then validated with user tests characterized by the control of real devices and the use of distant speech recognition.

Test results have shown the technical feasibility of the solution and promising user acceptance. The most important factor to maximize user satisfaction was the task success, which is mainly related with the number of ASR rejections, ASR errors and incomplete dialogues due to unexpected system errors. In addition, user answers to the last questionnaire report that the number of KWS rejections was high.

As future work, it is important to minimize the ASR rejections, ASR errors, unexpected system errors and the number of KWS rejections to improve user acceptance. In addition, it would be interesting to perform a second evaluation study by installing the solution in a real house and collecting data over an extended period of time. Finally it would be advisable to design new mechanisms to improve the dialogue and facilitate the correction of errors by users.

References

1. López-Cózar, R., Calleja, Z.: Multimodal dialogue for ambient intelligence and smart environments. In: Nakashima, H., Aghajan, H., Augusto, J.C. (eds.) Handbook of Ambient Intelligence and Smart Environments, pp. 559–579. Springer US, Boston (2010)
2. Florencio, E., Amores, G., Manchón, P., Pérez, G.: Aggregation in the In–Home domain. Procesamiento del Lenguaje Natural (40), 17–26 (2008) ISSN 1135-5948
3. Yates, A., Etzioni, O., Weld, D.: A reliable natural language interface to household appliances. In: Proc. 8th International Conference on Intelligent User Interfaces, pp. 189–196. ACM Press (2003)
4. Edlund, J., Gustafson, J., Heldner, M., Hjalmarsson, A.: Towards human-like spoken dialogue systems. Speech Communication 50(8-9), 630–645 (2008)
5. Montoro, G., Alamán, X., Haya, P.A.: Spoken interaction in intelligent environments: a working system. In: Ferscha, A., Hoertner, H., Kotsis, G. (eds.) Advances in Pervasive Computing, pp. 217–222. Austrian Computer Society, OCG (2004)
6. Dimopulos, T., Albayrak, S., Engelbrecht, K., Lehmann, G., Moller, S.: Enhancing the Flexibility of a Multimodal Smart Home Environment. In: Proc. Int. Conf. on Acoustics (DAGA), Stuttgart, Germany, pp. 639–640 (2007)
7. McTear, M.: Spoken dialogue technology: Enabling the conversational user interface. ACM Computing Surveys 34(1), 90–169 (2002)
8. Coelho, G.E., Serralheiro, A.J., Neto, J.: Microphone array front-end interface for home automation. In: Proc. Hands-free Speech Communication and Microphone Arrays (HSCMA), Trento, Italy, pp. 184–187 (2008)
9. Potamitis, I., Georgila, K., Fakotakis, N., Kokkinakis, G.: An integrated system for smart-home control of appliances based on remote speech interaction. In: Proc. 8th European Conference on Speech Communication and Technology, Geneva, Switzerland, pp. 2197–2200 (2003)
10. Möller, S., Krebber, J., Raake, A., Smeele, P., Rajman, M., Melichar, M., Pallotta, V., Tsakou, G., Kladis, B., Vovos, A., Hoonhout, J., Schuchardt, D., Fakotakis, N., Ganchev, T., Potamitis, I.: INSPIRE: Evaluation of a smart-home system for infotainment management and device control. In: Proc. 4th International Conference on Language Resources and Evaluation (LREC), Lisbon, pp. 1603–1606 (2004)
11. Gárate, A., Herrasti, N., López, A.: GENIO: an ambient intelligence application in home automation and entertainment environment. In: Proc. Joint Conference on Smart Objects and Ambient Intelligence, pp. 241–256 (2005)

12. Neto, J.P., Mamede, N.J., Cassaca, R., Oliveira, L.C.: The Development of a Multi-purpose Spoken Dialogue System. In: Proc. Eurospeech 2003, Genéve, Switzerland (2003)
13. Haya, P.A., Montoro, G., Alamán, X.: A Prototype of a Context-Based Architecture for Intelligent Home Environments. In: Meersman, R. (ed.) OTM 2004. LNCS, vol. 3290, pp. 477–491. Springer, Heidelberg (2004)
14. Rohlicek, J.R., Russell, W., Roukos, S., Gish, H.: Continuous hidden Markov modeling for speaker-independent word spotting. In: Proc. of IEEE International Conference on Acoustics, Speech and Signal Processing (ICASSP), vol. 1, pp. 627–630 (1989)
15. Walker, M.A., Litman, D., Kamm, C., Abella, A.: PARADISE: a general framework for evaluating spoken dialogue agents. In: Proc. of the 35th Annual General Meeting of the Association for Computational Linguistics, ACL/EACL, pp. 271–280. ACL, Madrid (1997)
16. Dybkjaer, L., Bernsen, N., Minker, W.: Evaluation and usability of multimodal spoken language dialogue systems. Speech Communication 43, 33–54 (2004)
17. ITU-T Rec. P.851, Subjective Quality Evaluation of Telephone Services Based on Spoken Dialogue Systems. International Telecommunication Union, Geneva (2003)
18. Walker, M.A., Kamm, C.A., Litman, D.J.: Towards developing general models of usability with PARADISE. Natural Language Engineering: Special Issue on Best Practice in Spoken Dialogue Systems (2000)
19. Möller, S., Smeele, P., Boland, H., Krebber, J.: Evaluating Spoken Dialog Systems According to De-facto Standards: A Case Study. Computer Speech and Language 21(1), 26–53 (2007)
20. ITU P series Rec, Parameters Describing the Interaction with Spoken Dialogue Systems, ITU, Geneva (2005)
21. Hassenzahl, M., Burmester, M., Koller, F.: AttrakDiff: Ein Fragebogen zur Messung wahrgenommener hedonischer und pragmatischer Qualität. In: Ziegler, J., Szwillus, G. (eds.) Mensch & Computer 2003. Interaktion in Bewegung, pp. 187–196 (2003)
22. Kirakowski, J., Corbett, M.: SUMI: The software usability measurement inventory. British Journal of Educational Technology 24(3), 210–212 (1993)
23. Hone, K., Graham, R.: Towards a tool for the Subjective Assessment of Speech System Interfaces (SASSI). Natural Language Engineering 6(3-4), 287–303 (2000)
24. Hartikainen, M., Salonen, E., Turunen, M.: Subjective evaluation of spoken dialogue systems using SERQUAL method. In: Proc. of International Conference on Spoken Language Processing (ICSLP) (2004)

Design and Analysis of Interactions with Museum Exhibits

Takashi Kiriyama[1] and Masahiko Sato

[1]Tokyo University of the Arts, Yokohama 231-0001, Japan

Abstract. The Definition of Self is a museum exhibition at 21_21 DE-SIGN SIGHT in 2010, intended to speculate our attributes in the contemporary world. This paper discusses design and interaction of two exhibits created for The Definition of Self. Pool of Fingerprints presents a new way of looking at fingerprints by using fingerprint matching technology. The visitor feels emotional attachment to his/her fingerprint. The Nominal Divide let the visitor experience how he or she is seen by computer vision.

1 Introduction

In our everyday life, we are asked for presenting various kinds of attributes. Security systems use biometric sensors for personal identification. International travelers are scanned fingerprints at immigration. A face recognition system may be profiling customers by gender and age. Fingerprints, iris patterns, blood vessel patterns, walking patterns, handwriting features, voice profiles, and ultimately DNA information are all in the growing list of attributes that we are dealing with in the modern society.

"The Definition of Self" [1] was a museum exhibition held from July 16 to November 3, 2010 at 21_21 DESIGN SIGHT in Tokyo (Figure 1). In the four-months period, a total of 59,152 visitors experienced the exhibition. It was conceived as an exhibition to speculate our attributes in the contemporary world. The exhibition presented 22 works, most of which are newly created for this exhibition. The works can be categorized in four groups, i.e., physical attributes, social attributes, behavioral attributes, and cognitive attributes.

Works in physical attributes demonstrate what biometric technologies made possible. Works in social attributes present attributes that are imposed by the society. "Pool of Fingerprints" and "The Nominal Divide" that we discuss later fall into these two categories, respectively. Works in behavioral attributes show various attributes that are found in behaviors. In "Write a Letter to Mr. Masahiko Sato", the visitor writes a letter to the Exhibition Director Masahiko Sato. At the exit of exhibition, the visitor receives a reply letter, which is written in the visitors own handwriting. When the visitor wrote the letter, his/her handwriting is captured by a digital pen. OCR recognizes hiragana characters in the handwriting image, which is then used to compose a reply letter. The visitor feels that their ownership of handwriting is lost.

D. Keyson et al. (Eds.): AmI 2011, LNCS 7040, pp. 182–189, 2011.

Works in cognitive attributes is a collection of exhibits demonstrating that recognizing attributes are subject to the mental state. In "You < Goldfish", the visitor stands in front of a fake mirror that reflects everything but the visitor. Contrary to the missing image of the visitor, there is a goldfish in the mirror but not in the room. Most visitors notice that there is a goldfish in the mirror, but fail to recognize that they are missing in the mirror. It means we are sensitive to the presence of others but not to the absence of our own presence.

In the rest of this paper, we present "Pool of Fingerprints" and "The Nominal Divide", the two symbolic exhibits of The Definition of Self. We discuss their design and the behavior of visitors, followed by a related study on the analysis of human behaviors in "Arithmetik Garden", an earlier exhibit of us.

Fig. 1. Entrance to the exhibition

2   Pool of Fingerprints

2.1   Exhibit with Fingerprint Identification

"Pool of Fingerprints" is intended to provide a new way of looking at the fingerprint. The installation, as shown in Figure 2, consists of a large horizontal display surface and a fingerprint scanner. The display is an inter-connected 3 by 3 array of 46-inch HD monitors. The surface is populated with fingerprints swimming like a school of fish (Figure 3). As shown in a sketch in Figure 4, the visitor can release his/her own fingerprint and watch it swim with others.

When a visitor places his/her finger on the scanner, a scanned image of the fingerprint appears in the display. A moment later, the fingerprint starts to swim away to join other fingerprints. Later on, when the visitor comes back and scans the same finger, the one released earlier will respond and come back in front of the visitor. The fingerprint gradually disappears as if it merges into the fingertip (Figure 5).

For fingerprint identification, we used NEC's SecureFinger [2]. The system extracts feature points in a fingerprint, including branches and ends. It then creates a template containing information about feature points and the number

Fig. 2. Pool of Fingerprints

of lines between them. "Pool of Fingerprints" holds the latest 800 fingerprints and matches the new one against them. Visitors may release fingerprints before viewing other exhibits and come back some time later to retrieve them when they leave the museum.

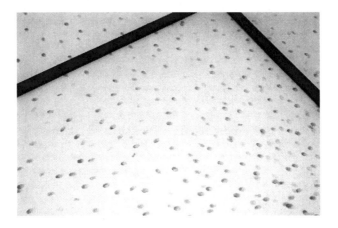

Fig. 3. Swimming Fingerprints

2.2 Emotional Attachment

We usually do not care about fingerprints, nor have any emotion to it. At the Pool of Fingerprints, some visitors said that they felt emotional attachment to their fingerprints for the first time. In fact, most visitors tried to scan twice to see if their fingerprints can recognize the owners. Animating separation and reunion with fingerprints certainly reinforced the emotional attachment to them.

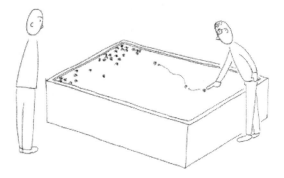

Fig. 4. Early sketch for Pool of Fingerprints

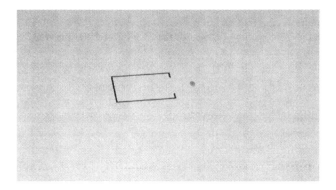

Fig. 5. A fingerprint returning to the owner

The surface area of "Pool of Fingerprints" measures 3.1 m x 1.8 m. A floor area of 10m by 6m was reserved for this installation, so that visitors could watch fingerprints by surrounding the display (Figure 6). Since the influence from other visitors are part of the interaction, the space around the installation plays an essential role in reinforcing the experience.

3   The Nominal Divide

3.1   Exhibit with Face Recognition

"The Nominal Divide" is an installation to discover how we are recognized by computer vision. The installation, shown in Figure 7, consists of three pairs of gates, namely the male gate and the female gate in the first row, the under 29 gate and the over 30 gate in the second row, and the smile gate and the blank gate in the third row. There are cameras in front of each gate to capture the face of visitor, as depicted in Figure 8.

Fig. 6. Installation space

At the first row, the visitor stands in front of the male gate or the female gate, depending on which the visitor believes to belongs to. The system decides gender by analyzing the facial image. The visitor must go through the gate opened by the system, regardless of the actual gender. At the second row, the visitor chooses between under 29 or over 30. The system recognizes the age of visitor and opens the gate, accordingly. At the third row, the visitor chooses between the smile gate or the blank gate. If a smile of 20% is sustained for two seconds before five seconds of timeout, the smile gate opens, otherwise the blank gate does instead.

The system uses Segmentation Sensor and Smile Sensor of OMRON Corporation. The segmentation sensor detects a face in a live video feed and produces gender or age information. The smile sensor measures the level of smile in a scale of 0 to 100%. Both sensors parameterize facial features including eyes, nose, mouth, and forehead. It tracks the position and orientation of face by comparing with a 3D model.

The nominal divide is built in a long, narrow space. We built tall walls to partition both sides of the space. The row of gates gives a challenging feeling to the visitor. People waiting for their turn can see other visitors going through the gates. The approach leading to the exhibit serves as an observation area.

3.2   Observing Behavior

We collected data of which gates visitors chose in The Nominal Divide. The data still need detailed analysis, but an initial look indicates that the visitor is emotionally influenced by the system positively or negatively, depending on whether the system agrees with the choice of visitor. For instance, if a visitor chooses the under 29 gate and the system indeed opens it, the visitor feels as if he she is approved by the system. It seems to cause a faster movement to the next gate. We are statistically verifying correlation between agreement and positive emotions. Figure 9 depicts a screenshot of analysis tool. For each visitor and each row of gate, the tool visualizes the one chosen by the visitor and the one the system opened, along with a time stamp of opening. We can also see the movement of visitor in a video that synchronizes with the analysis tool.

Fig. 7. The Nominal Divide

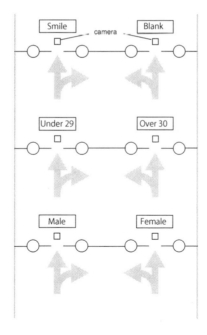

Fig. 8. Layout of The Nominal Divide

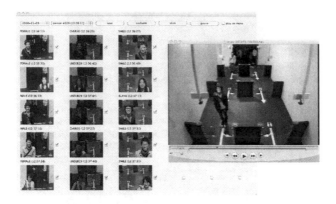

Fig. 9. Analysis of The Nominal Divide

Fig. 10. Arithmetik Garden

4   Related Work

Prior to Definition of Self, the authors created another museum installation called "Arithmetik Garden", shown in Figure 10. In Arithmetik Garden, starting from an initial number -8, -1, 2, 4, 5, 7, 8, 36, 87, or 91, the visitor tries to make the number equal to 73 by going through six arithmetic gates of $+5$, $+8$, $\times 3$, $\times 7$, 4, and $\div 2$. For instance, if the visitor starts with 2 and goes through the $\times 7$ gate, the current number will become $2 \times 7 = 14$. One can walk along a path such as $(2 \times 7 + 8) \div 2 \times 7 - 4 = 73$.

In the exhibition of Arithmetik Garden, we stored paths taken by visitors. By analyzing the data, we found that people started to run near the end of the path when they became confident about how to make the goal [3,4]. It found in the data that the intervals from a gate to the next became shorter near the end of path. We located such changes of intervals in data and reviewed the video of that moment. The video recording indicated that people were indeed excited at discovering how to reach the goal. Similar to the case of Arithmetik Garden, we believe that we are able to detect emotional change in the records of The Nominal Gate.

5 Conclusions

By observing visitors, we believe that Pool of Fingerprints made visitors feel emotional attachment to their fingerprints. Animation of fingerprints help develop this emotion. In The Nominal Divide, the visitor feels approved when their choice of gate agrees with the result of face recognition. The change of emotion influences the movement of visitor from a gate to the next one. We will confirm the influence in data collected during the exhibition. By designing interactions with museum exhibits, we can explore new relationship with the environment and thus accumulate knowledge for deploying ambient intelligence.

Acknowledgments. The authors are thankful to NEC Corporation, Samsung Japan, Omron Corporation, Toshiba Corporation, and Security Gate Japan for supporting the exhibits presented in this paper. The authors are also thankful to Miyuki Tanaka, curator of The Definition of Self.

References

1. 21_21 DESIGN SIGHT, Exhibition The Definition of Self (2010),
   http://www.2121designsight.jp/en/program/id/
2. Mizoguchi, M., Hara, M.: Fingerprint/Palmprint Matching Identification Technology. NEC Technical Journal 5(3), 18–22 (2010)
3. Kiriyama, T., Sato, M.: Observing Human Behaviors in an Interactive Art Installation. In: Desmet, P.M.A., Tzvetanova, S.A., Hekkert, P., Justice, L. (eds.) Proceedings from the 6th Conference on Design & Emotion (2008)
4. Kiriyama, T., Sato, M.: Analyzing Human Behaviors in an Interactive Art Installation. In: Jacko, J.A. (ed.) HCII 2009, Part IV. LNCS, vol. 5613, pp. 345–352. Springer, Heidelberg (2009)

Cut and Paste: Ambient Interaction Using Annotated Cut-Outs

Geert Vanderhulst and Lieven Trappeniers

Alcatel-Lucent Bell Labs
Copernicuslaan 50, 2018 Antwerpen, Belgium
{geert.vanderhulst,lieven.trappeniers}@alcatel-lucent.com

Abstract. We present a novel way of interacting with an ambient environment through semantic cut-out images. These images represent resources that appear on a regular image shot by a camera – people, buildings, anything of interest – which are cut out of the original image and pasted into a new image with transparent background. Hence these images can be placed in a different context such as a background that tells more about a resource's current state. By annotating cut-outs and incorporating them in user interfaces for ambient environments, we show how the interaction experience within such environments can be made more personal, visually appealing and intuitive. To this end, we first transform a series of images and their cut-outs into a visual knowledge base.

1 Introduction

An image often says more than a thousand words. Images help us map resources represented in the digital world on physical resources in the real world and vice versa. While the role of an image in an ambient environment is typically limited to simplify human object recognition, some works [3,4] also suggested the use of images as an interactive instrument to operate the environment. In their approach, an interactive dialog related to a selected resource pops up in overlay on an image that depicts the resource. We witness a similar trend in augmented reality applications where interactive layers are projected on top of live camera stills. These layers help us navigate through the environment or reveal things we cannot perceive in the real world such as the name of buildings and their history.

To improve the effectiveness of image-driven ambient interaction, we propose the use of *annotated cut-outs*. These are images that represent a resource that is cut out of another image and which are enriched with semantics. Ambient applications can benefit from semantic cut-outs in several ways. First, by highlighting cut-outs on the image they originate from, the selection of resources on an image becomes more intuitive (cfr. highlighting buttons on a website). Second, by annotating cut-outs and their relations to other cut-outs, images become part of a visual knowledge base. In addition to tags that describe the context of an image superficially, resources that appear on the image can be described in more detail. Third, by placing cut-outs in a different background, we can visually assign meaning to

D. Keyson et al. (Eds.): AmI 2011, LNCS 7040, pp. 190–194, 2011.

resources. A background or graphical effect can express the state of an resource or result in a more appealing presentation of the resource in a user interface. In this paper, we show how (cut-out) images are transformed into a visual knowledge and explain how the latter was used to build two prototype applications.

2 Images Inside Images

To make an image interactive, its contents should be annotated such that an application can translate input events on the image into actions (e.g. navigation, showing a user interface, etc). A major step in the annotation process is the selection of the interactive parts of the image. Using Flickr Notes[1], StippleIt[2] and Facebook[3], objects and people can be marked on an image, albeit only rudimentary by indicating a spot or rectangular area on the photo. More accurate selections are obtained using the LabelMe application [2], which features a polygonal selection tool allowing for detailed selections using only a mouse as input device. Besides, free form selections are naturally supported via pen-based input devices such as Wacom tablets.

Assisted by such easy to use selection tools, we support ordinary users in carefully marking the interactive parts of an image such that the resources they represent can be separated from their background. Cut-outs can then be placed in a different context, as illustrated in figure 1. In this example, the Statue of Liberty is marked as an interactive part on an image. The figure depicts how the current weather conditions in New York are visualized by embedding the cut-out of the statue in a background rendered by a weather application. By jumping back and forth from image to image, one can navigate through the environment and access related applications. In the next section, we explain how extra metadata enriches the navigation experience and facilitates searching for resources.

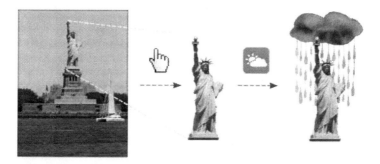

Fig. 1. Cut-outs enable precise interaction with resources on an image and can be integrated in context-aware visualizations

3   Towards a Visual Knowledge Base

To classify images in a visual knowledge base, we identify tagging opportunities at three levels: i) annotation of source images; ii) annotation of cut-out images; and iii) annotation of relations between (cut-out) images. We transparently support these different stages by organizing images in a 'tag tree'. This approach is inspired by Tagstore[4] where a tree of tags is used to manage files and folders instead of a file system's conventional hierarchy. This allows users to navigate to a file in several ways; there is no longer a strict destination folder. Likewise, we embed images in (multiple) virtual folders which are composed of tags and which describe the external context of the image. Moreover, tags attached to (cut-out) images or links between images describe the internal context of an image. Figure 2 shows an example of a visual knowledge base that is constructed from holiday photos. A virtual root folder with tags 'California' and 'Summer 2010' denotes when and where the vacation took place. As several images originate from the San Francisco region, we classified them in a subfolder tagged 'San Francisco'. In one of the images, the cut-out of a person was annotated as well as the shirt he is wearing. The shirt was bought in a shop near Fisherman's Warf which is indicated by a tagged link between the shirt and a photo of the Warf area. Similar, cut-outs that represent the same resource can be defined equivalent using a predefined 'same as' relation.

Fig. 2. Tags are used to classify an image in a hierarchy (external context) and to describe the objects and people that appear on the image (internal context)

To efficiently navigate through a visual knowledge base that can grow large, additional meta-data is needed that helps a computing system better understand the meaning of keywords. A faceted classification approach has been proven a successful way to provide access to image collections [5]. By adding category labels to a tag – e.g. 'place' to a 'San Francisco' tag and 'person' to a 'Michael' tag – facets are created that describe the characteristics of an image or a resource on the image. These facets enable users to navigate along conceptual dimensions of an image and hence help to narrow down search results. Extra

---

[4] http://tagstore.ist.tugraz.at/

meaning is provided by mapping data contained in tags on a taxonomy or controlled vocabulary such as the WordNet [1] lexicon, which is used in LabelMe [2] to unambiguously identify the meaning of keywords. We include cut-out representations of resources in search results such that users can browse a visual knowledge base both in a top-down fashion (starting from an image or facet) and bottom-up way (starting from a resource).

4 Application Prototypes

We built two application prototypes that illustrate the practical use and possibilities of annotated cut-out images, presented in figure 3.

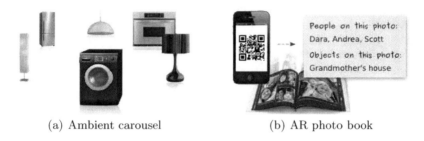

(a) Ambient carousel   (b) AR photo book

Fig. 3. The first prototype (a) shows how interactive real-world resources that are cut out of an image are lined up in a 3D carousel. The second prototype (b) augments physical photos with a digital layer that includes information about people and objects that appear in an highlighted region on the image.

4.1 Ambient Carousel

The ambient carousel is a menu composed of cut-out images. It lines up smart resources that meet provided search criteria in an interactive carousel as illustrated in figure 3(a). When an item is selected, it pops out of the carousel and graphical effects are applied to visualize the current state of the corresponding resource. Examples of such effects include the weather visualization shown in figure 1, a yellow glow around a light that is on, music notes dancing around a loudspeaker and so on. Using the ambient carousel, people obtain a personalized interaction experience as they are presented with their own real-world resources instead of predefined representations. This way, it also becomes easier to distinguish between similar resources such as a table light and a ceiling lamp.

4.2 AR Photo Book

In the AR photo book, printed photos are accompanied by a QR code referring to their interactive digital counterpart. By scanning the code with a mobile device, the digital version appears on the screen. Here, users get to see additional information about who/what is on the photo and when/where it was taken. This information is generated from annotations that were added to the image using the approach discussed in sections 2 and 3. For each tag that adds up to the photo book's visual knowledge base, we require the user to indicate whether it concerns a place or time related tag or if it refers to a person or object.

5   Conclusions

We propose easy to use selection tools that enable ordinary users to create annotated cut-outs. These cut-outs are parts of an image depicting a particular resource and give rise to interactive images. By annotating images and their cut-outs, we build up a visual knowledge base that can be exploited in an ambient environment. For instance, it enables users to identify resources and locate them in the environment using visual representations of a resource and its surroundings. Moreover, we illustrate how ambient applications can act on cut-outs to visualize context information in an attractive way.

We also aim to incorporate mobile devices in the creation process. Mobile phones and tablets are popular camera devices and an annotation tool for mobile platforms would be useful to make a photo interactive right after shooting it.

References

1. Fellbaum, C. (ed.): WordNet: An Electronic Lexical Database (Language, Speech, and Communication). MIT Press (1998)
2. Russell, B., Torralba, A., Murphy, K., Freeman, W.: LabelMe: A Database and Web-Based Tool for Image Annotation. International Journal of Computer Vision 77(1), 157–173 (2008)
3. Suzuki, G., Aoki, S., Iwamoto, T., Maruyama, D., Koda, T., Kohtake, N., Takashio, K., Tokuda, H.: u-Photo: Interacting with Pervasive Services Using Digital Still Images. In: Gellersen, H.-W., Want, R., Schmidt, A. (eds.) PERVASIVE 2005. LNCS, vol. 3468, pp. 190–207. Springer, Heidelberg (2005)
4. Vanderhulst, G., Luyten, K., Coninx, K.: Pervasive Maps: Explore and Interact with Pervasive Environments. In: 8th International Conference on Pervasive Computing and Communications (PERCOM 2010), pp. 227–234 (2010)
5. Yee, K.P., Swearingen, K., Li, K., Hearst, M.: Faceted Metadata for Image Search and Browsing. In: International Conference on Human Factors in Computing Systems (CHI 2003), pp. 401–408 (2003)

A Dynamic AR Marker for a Paper Based Temperature Sensor

Roshan Lalintha Peiris, Owen Noel Newton Fernando,
and Adrian David Cheok

Keio-NUS CUTE Center,
NUS Graduate School for Integrative Sciences and Engineering
National University of Singapore
{roshan,newtonfernando,adriancheok}@mixedrealitylab.org
www.mixedrealitylab.org

Abstract. This paper presents a proof of concept technology for a novel concept of dynamic markers for Augmented Reality. Here, by dynamic we mean markers that can change on external stimuli. Thus, the paper describes the use of ambient dynamic Augmented Reality Markers as temperature sensors. To achieve this technology we print patterns on an AR marker using thermochromic inks of various actuation temperatures. Thus, as the temperature gradually changes, the marker morphs into new marker for each temperature range. Thus here we present our preliminary results for three temperature ranges and discuss this work can be extended and applied in the future.

Keywords: thermochromic, sensor, temperature, paper based, paper.

1 Introduction

Augmented Reality (AR), 2D Barcode, etc are becoming powerful technologies that surround us in the world today. Many such technologies are used in various fields to present more information, enhance interactivity, experience, etc. One common feature that most such technologies have is the use of a marker/tag which is recognized through the use of a camera. Technologies for such recognition and processing of these markers have become more and more powerful and even moving onto mobile devices such as smartphones [4]. As these devices get smaller but more powerful, users today are able to install these complex programs and carry them around making the Augmented Reality technologies move towards ubiquity [3].

Using this move as an advantage, this paper focuses on a new type of markers for AR technologies. One main characteristic of Augmented Reality markers are that they are static. Thus, this work tries to address this characteristic by introducing another dynamic characteristic to the marker. We use thermochromic inks to achieve this dynamic characteristic. Thermochromic inks are inks that become colorless when you heat them beyond their actuation temperature and reappear when it cools below this actuation temperature. Thus, by printing

D. Keyson et al. (Eds.): AmI 2011, LNCS 7040, pp. 195–199, 2011.

squares of different actuation temperature themrochromic inks, we intend to explore the dyanamicity of this marker.

As a proof of concept, this paper presents the initial work, the development of a paper based temperature sensor using dynamic AR markers. For situations where a device temperature needs to be measured through a computer, we envision an application where we use this dynamic marker as a temperature sensor. Thus, in most cases, this method will replace complex temperature sensing circuitry with a simple paper based sensor and a camera. In addition, it could also be a simple piece of paper that you could carry in your wallet or bag as a mobile temperature sensor by simply reading it with your smart phone.

One of the closely related works to this work is the use of thermal markers used in a medical related application [2]. This work uses the difference between the body temperature and reflective marker read by a thermal camera to identify persons. However, in this paper we focus more on the change of the marker due to the temperature. Thus we present this paper based temperature sensor.

2   Method

As our initial prototype, we printed a modified ARToolkit [1] marker as a temperature sensor as in Figure 1(a). In this case, as shown in the example Figures 1, inks with different actuation temperatures are printed in the form of a AR marker with each pixel being a different temperature inks (or groups of pixels strategically placed being same ink). As the temperature increases each pixel would become colorless as seen in Figures 1(b),(c),(d). With more pixels with different actuation temperatures, we could achieve a higher resolution for the temperature.

Once this tag is placed on the device we require to measure the temperature, the relevant pixels will disappear and the tag will reveal the current temperature of the device. Then a simple web camera with an AR application could read the temperature off the AR maker.

For this initial version, in addition to a simple OpenCV AR algorithm for the marker detection, we implemented a basic AR application for the temperature

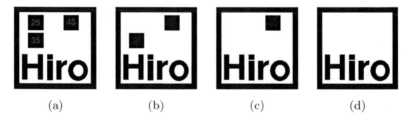

    (a)   (b)   (c)   (d)

Fig. 1. Example AR marker for temperature sensing (Red marking are the actuation temperatures of each pixel and would not appear in the marker) (a) Marker at temperatures below 25^0C, (b)Marker at temperatures between 25^0C and 35^0C, (C)Marker at temperatures between 35^0C and 45^0C, (d) Marker at temperatures above 45^0C

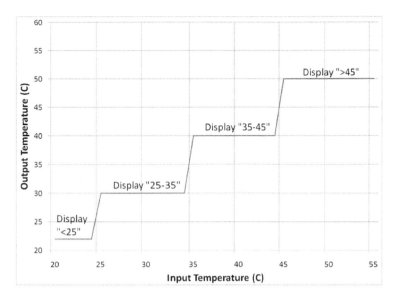

Fig. 2. Measuring and displaying the temperatures

detection. Thus upon detection of the marker, the application displays the range of the temperature on to the display (Figure 2).

3   Results

Example application is as in Figure 3 and Figure 4. Here, we attached the marker to a 3D printer during its idle time. Currently the detection shows the temperature to be between 35^0C to 45^0C (Actual temperature was 37^0C). In the second application we attached the marker to a server machine which displays the temperature as 20^0C to 35^0C. These readings can be improved further by adding more pixels with thermochromic inks of different actuation temperature.

Fig. 3. Measuring the temperature of a 3D printer

Fig. 4. Measuring the temperature of a server

As the results indicate, as the inks have a gradual change over about 2^0C, the reading is not accurate during the margins of the ink actuation temperatures. However, as mentioned before the use of inks with customized actuation temperatures would increase this accuracy.

4   Discussion

As observed, this temperature sensor gives fairly easy reading of the temperature. However, the current implementation is limited in its range and resolution due to the use of off the shelf thermochromic inks. The actuation temperature of thermochromic inks are customizable. Hence, based on the application, this temperature sensor can be extended in its range and resolution to get a more accurate temperature reading. Thus, this marker has the potential to be applied anywhere in a very ambient manner.

However, there are some key limitations to this technology. First is, as this technology uses, AR methods, lighting, and clear vision should be available for proper reading of the marker. In addition, in some occasions, if the temperature is such that, some of the pixels are only slightly actuated, it may result in incorrect readings. For this purpose, the actuation temperatures must be fine tuned.

4.1   Potential Applications

The simplicity and the ease of use this temperature sensor holds a key possibility to apply this technology to many fields of application. One of the earliest possible uses is the personal uses, where as mentioned earlier, the users can carry this temperature sensor in their wallets or bags just as a piece of paper. Thus upon requirement the temperature can be easily read using a smart phone instantly.

In addition, similar to QR codes on various products, the marker can be also integrated on to temperature sensitive products. Thus by simply placing the marker on the product, the users can read the temperature of the marker. To increase the robustness of this application on products, we are exploring the use of QR codes instead of AR markers for this purpose. In addition, this would help the use of widely available third party applications to read the dynamic QR codes.

The ability to use this temperature sensor as an inexpensive 'wireless' sensor could be useful in various industrial applications. In particular cases where the use of isolation chambers, etc. are required, such a sensor can easily replace messy or expensive wiring and temperature sensing equipment to simply use this sensor with a web-camera. Thus in similar applications, this type of paper based sensor could be useful as an inexpensive and simpler alternative.

5   Future Works

This is our initial work into the exploration of dynamic markers for Augmented Reality. As a proof of concept this paper presents some initial results of the development of a paper based temperature sensor.

As one of the major areas we are researching with this technology is dynamically 'actuating' this marker. I.e., we are exploring the possibility to change the marker based on various external stimuli. For this purpose, we are investigating the use of peltier elements as the thermal actuator. Peltier elements have the capability to heat and cool its surface just by reversing the supply voltage polarity. Thus once attached to the marker in a pixelated format, they can dynamically heat and cool different pixels, allowing the marker to morph into another marker. Hence, this would radically open up a new area of AR marker technology, adding a time variance dimension.

Acknowledgements. This research is carried out under CUTE Project No. WBS R- 7050000-100-279 partially funded by a grant from the National Research Foundation (NRF) administered by the Media Development Authority (MDA) of Singapore.

References

1. Artoolkit, http://www.hitl.washington.edu/artoolkit/
2. Bluteau, J., Kitahara, I., Kameda, Y., Noma, H., Kogure, K., Ohta, Y.: Visual support for medical communication by using projector-based augmented reality and thermal markers. In: Proceedings of the 2005 International Conference on Augmented Tele-Existence, ICAT 2005, pp. 98–105. ACM, New York (2005)
3. Höllerer, T.H., Feiner, S.K.: Telegeoinformatics: Location-Based Computing and Services. In: Mobile Augmented Reality, ch. 9. CRC Press (March 2004)
4. Papagiannakis, G., Singh, G., Magnenat-Thalmann, N.: A survey of mobile and wireless technologies for augmented reality systems. Comput. Animat. Virtual Worlds 19, 3–22 (2008)

On Developing a Platform for Mobile Outdoor Gaming for Children

Iris Soute, Herman Aartsen, and Chet Bangaru

Department of Industrial Design
Eindhoven University of Technology
Den Dolech 2, 5612 AZ Eindhoven, the Netherlands
{i.a.c.soute,h.j.aartsen,c.bangaru}@tue.nl

Abstract. In this paper we describe the development of a platform for creating Head Up Games. Nowadays, technology is becoming more and more ubiquitous, but in the field of pervasive gaming it seems that development is mostly centered on smart phones. We argue that for outdoor games for children this might not be the best medium; and we propose the design of our platform that is designed to better support outdoor, active games.

1   Introduction

The concept of Head Up Games (HUGs) was proposed by Soute and Markopoulos (10), as a new pervasive play experience for children that stimulates physical activity en encourages social interaction. Head Up Games are games that combine play-elements of 'traditional games' (e.g., tag, hide-and-seek) with technologies of pervasive games, to create new, fun, children's games.

So far, we have developed several games, e.g. Camelot (12), Stop the Bomb (7), and HeartBeat (8). For each game dedicated hardware was developed from the ground up. Now, with the experience of developing these games and the corresponding hardware, we are building a generic platform to be able to more rapidly develop outdoor, pervasive games for children. In this paper we describe the process of developing the first prototypes of this platform.

2   Related Research

Research in pervasive gaming is growing, and several games have been developed. Most games have been developed using GPS-enabled PDAs or smart phones as a platform, e.g. *Feeding Yoshi* (4) and *Interference* (6). Children's pervasive games are less common, two notable examples are *Savannah* (5) and *Ambient Woods* (9). Although not games per se, interactive objects for open ended play (3) aim to achieve similar play behaviors as HUGs.

Development of platforms for pervasive games seems mostly focussed on developing middleware (software) for game deployment on smart phones (e.g., (11)), though Akribopoulos et al. (1) have developed both hardware and software for a platform for developing pervasive applications and interactive installations.

D. Keyson et al. (Eds.): AmI 2011, LNCS 7040, pp. 200–204, 2011.
© Springer-Verlag Berlin Heidelberg 2011

3 The Head Up Games Platform

From our previous experiences of designing HUGs, we learned what kind of interaction mechanisms and what corresponding technologies are useful for these the type of games, and we argue that smart phones are not the ideal medium to play these games with. In our opinion, the affordance of a screen on a smart phone directs, during design, the game designer towards screen-based interactions and distracts, during play, the player from interacting with other players. Thus, we aim to create a platform that offers other types of interactions besides screen-based interactions.

Another requirement for the platform is that the devices need to be small, portable and robust, as they are intended for children in an outdoor environment.

Furthermore, our aim is that game designers and developers can quickly adopt the platform, without needing a thorough understanding of the embedded electronics or software. Finally, our budget is fixed to approx. €5000, which we aimed to develop around 10 devices with.

3.1 Technology

The following list presents the most important components that were integrated in the device:

- Battery
- Arduino ATMega processor
- RFID reader
- XBee Module
- Accelerometer
- Sound chip and speaker
- SD card reader
- Microphone
- Real time clock
- Rotation encoder
- Touch area
- Push button
- 4 RGB LEDs and 3 white LEDs
- Mini USB socket
- Extra headers

All components are integrated on a dedicated printed circuit board (PCB), to keep the size as small as possible , see Figure 1. The PCB's size is now approximately 15cm by 4cm, which is just small enough to be portable for children. Of course, smaller is technically possible, but would not have fit our budget.

Especially the battery was carefully chosen to fit our requirements, as it needs to be small, portable and powerful at the same time. Also, it must be easy to recharge and be protected against deep discharging. Charging of the battery is done through the USB connection, which is also used to upload new software to the device.

Next, the heart of the device is the processor. We selected to base the device on the Arduino Mega (2), as this processor offers many input/output channels. Also, this platform is often used within our department, and on the internet an active user community exists that exchanges experiences. The Arduino can be programmed in C/C++ and we provide designers with small examples of code for each component.

Fig. 1. Printed Circuit Board (PCB) with some of the components

What might seem striking is that we decided not to incorporate a GPS receiver and/or a WiFi module. Both components are very often used in pervasive gaming applications. However, we argue that within the Head Up Games concept it is not absolutely necessary to have exact location information available. In contrast to adults, who might play games that are played on a large geographical area, children play co-located games; meaning that they are relatively close together within the same area. For the HUG games we have designed so far, we have only needed relative location information, i.e. information on how far players are apart. This can be achieved by using for example the signal strength measured from the xbee modules. Admittedly this information is not as precise as information from a GPS receiver, but it is sufficient. Finally, children often play in areas where there is no WiFi covering, and since we aim the devices to be take-up-and-play-anywhere, adding a WiFi module is superfluous.

3.2   Casing

While developing the electronics of the devices, we simultaneously started designing the casing, as choices that concern the electronics components influence the exterior design - and vice versa. We decided to develop hardware and casing in such a way, that they can be easily separated. So, if a developer wants to create a casing specifically for his game, he can easily do so.

In Figure 2 the first prototype of the casing is shown. Clearly visible is the wheel, which can be turned unlimited in both directions, backlit by 4 RGB LEDs. The light of the LEDs is visible both in the wheel as well as at the sides of the device. Not yet visible in this prototype is that there will be a speaker below the wheel. Furthermore, means for attaching the device to a key-cord will be added.

Fig. 2. First prototype of the exterior design

4 Conclusion

The very first prototype has been tested for its functionality, and we are now in the process of making minor changes to the PCB; subsequently ten PCBs will be produced and assembled. Also, the design of the casing will be completed. Then we can start developping games based on the prototypes and evaluate them with children.

References

[1] Akribopoulos, O., Logaras, M., Vasilakis, N., Kokkinos, P., Mylonas, G., Chatzigiannakis, I., Spirakis, P.: Developing multiplayer pervasive games and networked interactive installations using ad hoc mobile sensor nets. In: Proceedings of the International Conference on Advances in Computer Enterntainment Technology, ACE 2009, pp. 174–181. ACM, Athens (2009) ACM ID: 1690418, http://doi.acm.org.janus.libr.tue.nl/10.1145/1690388.1690418

[2] Arduino: Arduino mega, http://arduino.cc/en/Main/ArduinoBoardMega

[3] Bekker, T., Hopma, E., Sturm, J.: Creating opportunities for play: the influence of multimodal feedback on open-ended play. International Journal of Arts and Technology 3(4), 325–340 (2010)

[4] Bell, M., Chalmers, M., Barkhuus, L., Hall, M., Sherwood, S., Tennent, P., Brown, B., Rowland, D., Benford, S.: Interweaving mobile games with everyday life. In: Proceedings of the SIGCHI Conference on Human Factors in Computing Systems, pp. 417–426. ACM, Montréal (2006),
http://portal.acm.org/citation.cfm?id=1124835&dl=GUIDE&coll=Portal&CFID=19743253&CFTOKEN=75667873

[5] Benford, S., Rowland, D., Flintham, M., Drozd, A., Hull, R., Reid, J., Morrison, J., Facer, K.: Life on the edge: supporting collaboration in location-based experiences. In: Proc. of CHI 2005, pp. 721–730. ACM, Portland (2005),
http://portal.acm.org/citation.cfm?id=1055072&dl=GUIDE&coll=Portal&CFID=19743253&CFTOKEN=75667873

[6] Bichard, J., Waern, A.: Pervasive play, immersion and story. In: Proceedings of the 3rd International Conference on Digital Interactive Media in Entertainment and Arts - DIMEA 2008, Athens, Greece, p. 10 (2008), http://portal.acm.org/citation.cfm?doid=1413634.1413642

[7] Hendrix, K., Yang, G., van de Mortel, D., Tijs, T., Markopoulos, P.: Designing a Head-Up game for children. In: Proceedings of the HCI 2008 Conference on People and Computers XXII, vol. 1, pp. 45–53 (2008), http://www.bcs.org/upload/pdf/ewic_hc08_v1_paper5.pdf

[8] Magielse, R., Markopoulos, P.: HeartBeat: an outdoor pervasive game for children. In: Proceedings of the 27th International Conference on Human Factors in Computing Systems, pp. 2181–2184. ACM, Boston (2009), http://portal.acm.org/citation.cfm?id=1518701.1519033&coll= Portal&dl=GUIDE&CFID=19743253&CFTOKEN=75667873

[9] Rogers, Y., Price, S., Fitzpatrick, G., Fleck, R., Harris, E., Smith, H., Randell, C., Muller, H., O'Malley, C., Stanton, D., Thompson, M., Weal, M.: Ambient wood: designing new forms of digital augmentation for learning outdoors. In: Proc. of IDC 2004, pp. 3–10. ACM, Maryland (2004), http://portal.acm.org/citation.cfm?doid=1017833.1017834

[10] Soute, I., Markopoulos, P., Magielse, R.: Head up games: combining the best of both worlds by merging traditional and digital play. Personal and Ubiquitous Computing 14(5), 435–444 (2009), http://dx.doi.org/10.1007/s00779-009-0265-0

[11] Trinta, F., Ferraz, C., Ramalho, G.: Middleware services for pervasive multiplatform networked games. In: Proceedings of 5th ACM SIGCOMM Workshop on Network and System Support for Games. NetGames 2006. ACM, Singapore (2006) ACM ID: 1230049, http://doi.acm.org.janus.libr.tue.nl/10.1145/1230040.1230049

[12] Verhaegh, J., Soute, I., Kessels, A., Markopoulos, P.: On the design of camelot, an outdoor game for children. In: Proceedings of the 2006 Conference on Interaction Design and Children, pp. 9–16. ACM, Tampere (2006), http://portal.acm.org/citation.cfm?id=1139073.1139082&coll= Portal&dl=GUIDE&CFID=19743253&CFTOKEN=75667873

Personalized Persuasion in Ambient Intelligence: The APStairs System

Ryo Sakai[1], Sarah Van Peteghem[1], Leoni van de Sande[1], Peter Banach[1], and Maurits Kaptein[2]

[1] Eindhoven University of Technology, Eindhoven, Netherlands
{r.sakai,s.v.peteghem,l.v.d.sande,p.j.banach}@tue.nl
[2] Eindhoven University of Technology / Philips Research
maurits@mauritskaptein.com

Abstract. Can ubiquitous technologies intended to change people's behavior benefit from personalization? This paper addresses the development of an *adaptive persuasive system* intended to increase stair climbing at work: APStairs. Based on their *persuasion profile*, individuals are distinguished by their susceptibility to different social influence strategies. This paper contributes a first application of persuasion profiling in the domain of ambient intelligence; it reports the deployment of the APStairs system in a real life setting for a period of five weeks involving 34 participants. Although a longer deployment period is needed to statistically validate the system, this first deployment of the system has shown the feasibility of adaptive persuasion.

Keywords: Persuasive Technology, Adaptive Persuasive Systems.

1 Introduction

Ambient technologies open up the possibility of influencing human behavior by providing persuasive content, sensitive to human activity and its context. This has been pointed out early on by Fogg [4], who emphasized the importance of delivering persuasive messages at the right place and at the right time to increase compliance. The field of ubiquitous technologies needs theoretical and methodological guidance for the design of persuasive systems. Such guidance has been traditionally imported from social sciences; see [5], but also [3] for some alternative perspectives on design strategies.

In this paper, we focus on the application of social influence strategies in ambient intelligence. Social influence strategies are extensively researched in the field of social psychology and compose different means to reach a pre-defined end. We explore the ways in which ambient systems can adapt their approach(es) to influence user behavior based on the behavioral responses of the user.

In our design, we adopted three of the six social influence strategies identified by Cialdini [2]: *Authority* (when a request or statement is made by a legitimate authority, people are more inclined to comply), *Commitment and Consistency* (people do as they said they would), and *Consensus (*people do as other people do). Each of these strategies can be utilized to increase compliance, irrespective of the target behavior of the persuasive attempt.

D. Keyson et al. (Eds.): AmI 2011, LNCS 7040, pp. 205–209, 2011.

The effectiveness of these influence strategies has been shown at an *average* level (i.e., over groups of people). However, when studied in more detail, there appear to be large differences in the responses of *individuals* to implementations of these social influence strategies [1]. Besides, Kaptein et al. [5] and [6] have shown that people have preferences for *distinct* influence strategies, and using the *wrong* strategy for a specific user can have a negative effect at individual level, even when the average compliance of this strategy is positive. This suggests that to increase the effectiveness of persuasive applications, influence strategies should be adapted to individual users.

An *adaptive* persuasive system, one that is responsive to the presence of users and automatically adapts the way in which a behavior is promoted on individual basis, has not yet been implemented, and automated adaptation at the level of influence strategy usage has not yet been explored in a real life setting. We define adaptive persuasive systems as *systems that select the appropriate influence strategy to use for a specific user based on its estimated success.* We identify three key functional requirements such systems should embrace: (1) *identification*: identify individuals, (2) *representation*: represent one end goal through various social influence strategies, and (3) *measurement*: measure the persuasive attempts' outcomes to adapt to individuals.

2 The APStairs System

APStairs is an adaptive persuasive system, designed to encourage people to take the stairs rather than the elevator. To unobtrusively *identify* unique users, Bluetooth inquiry-based scanning was used. Globally unique Bluetooth addresses of discovered Bluetooth-enabled mobile phones, together with their timestamps were stored.

Messages that aimed at persuading people entering the building to take the stairs instead of the elevator were *represented* on a large screen in the hallway of an office building. Per social influence strategy, three messages were created (see Table 1).

Table 1. Messages shown to users of the APStairs system: Each message implements one of the three social influence strategies to increase compliance

Persuasion strategy	Message
Authority	1. "You get a good exercise by taking the stairs instead of the elevator." – Bert Clarenbeek, gym instructor
	2. Doctors recommend taking the stairs.
	3. "Taking the stairs helps you shape up your buttocks." – Jessica de Groot, zumba instructor
Commitment and Consistency	4. Planned to become healthier? Start by taking the stairs!
	5. Committed to get in shape? Start by taking the stairs!
	6. Promised yourself to be more physically active? Take the stairs!
Consensus	7. 70% of the people in this building already take the stairs. What about you?
	8. The majority of the people in this building takes the stairs. Join them now!
	9. Follow many other people; take the stairs!

Given our context, we defined a message to be successful for an individual if after the message was shown, he or she took the stairs. To *measure* the success of different messages, scanners were installed on every floor of a five-story office building. Each scanner independently scanned for nearby Bluetooth-enabled mobile phones and uploaded its results to a central server. Figure 1 schematically shows APStairs.

A simple adaptation method was implemented to select the messages. We modeled the probability of success of a message as binomial random variable, $B(n,p)$, where n denotes the number of times a message that implemented a specific strategy (e.g., *Authority*) was shown to a user, and p denotes the probability of success (i.e., the user took the stairs). Given M different influence strategies – three in our setup – one can compute for each individual i, for each strategy m, the probability $p_{mi} = k_{mi} / n_{mi}$, where k_{mi} is the number of observed successes after representation of strategy m, n_{mi} times to a specific user i.

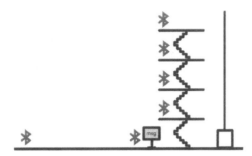

Fig. 1. Overview of the APStairs system: Users entering the office building are recognized by the first bluetooth scanner (left). Next, they are presented a message encouraging them to take the stairs. Finally, scanners in the stairway measure the success of the message.

We then used a Beta-Binomial model to track the estimated effectiveness of a single strategy over time points for a single user. Messages for users entering the lobby were selected not just based on the expected value of the distribution, but also based on that estimate's certainty. New users of the APStairs system were not by default shown a *Commitment and Consistency* implementation (highest estimated probability of success based on a pretest of the developed messages), but rather a random message was selected if the *80%* confidence intervals of the estimates of strategy effectiveness overlapped. This *80%* bound was used early in the deployment of the system to get information about each of the strategies from each user (*explore* period). After running the system live for three weeks, this uncertainty bound was decreased (to *20%*) to *exploit* the knowledge gained about individual users. The collection of estimates of the success of different social influence strategies for a specific user is called a *persuasion profile*.

3   System Evaluation

To evaluate the APStairs system, we employed it for five weeks in an office building. Users – people entering the building whose mobile phone's Bluetooth key was scanned – were randomly assigned to one of two conditions: (1) the *adaptive condition*, where the system chose a random message belonging to the persuasion strategy with the highest probability of success for the identified user, and (2) the *non-adaptive condition*, where the system chose a random message. Each user was presented messages that were selected based on their condition. For users in the *adaptive* condition, a persuasion profile was used to select the most appropriate social influence strategy. Subsequently, the behavioral response was recorded and the persuasion profile was updated.

3.1   Preliminary Results

To see whether there was a difference in compliance to persuasive messages between the two conditions, the proportions of stair taking were calculated for each user. Even though the estimated success-rates of the two systems seemed to diverge according to our expectations – with the adaptive version of the system being more successful – this trend was not statistically significant; the results suggest the need for a longer term deployment of the system that involves a larger number of participants.

However, to illustrate how APStairs functions for users in the adaptive condition, the history of one of our participants, 'user 94', is presented in Figure 2.

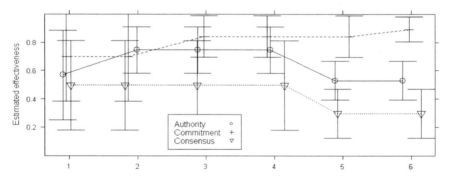

Fig. 2. Estimates of the effectiveness of the different strategies for user 94. It is clear that the commitment and consistency strategy is most effective for this user.

For user *94*, the first message that was presented implemented the *Authority* strategy, which was successful and thus raised the estimated success of this message. During the second visit, a message implementing the *Commitment and Consistency* strategy was shown, which was also successful, increasing the estimated success for this message. Next, the user received an implementation of the *Consensus* strategy, which was unsuccessful. On his or her last visit an implementation of the *Commitment and Consistency* strategy was shown. As expected, this last message was successful.

After the quantitative evaluation a total of *12* (possible) users (i.e., office workers entering the building at the day the system was dismantled) were interviewed. Overall, users commented that the messages were delivered clear in sight and precisely at the moment when the decision to use either the stairs or the elevator was taken. Moreover, the timing and duration of the messages was found to be adequate, and the content indeed triggered people's consciousness about stair taking behavior.

4 Discussion

We deployed an adaptive persuasive system created to increase stair usage amongst office workers in a real life setting for several weeks. This first deployment of the system has shown the feasibility of adaptive persuasion, illustrating how different strategies can be implemented and selected in accordance to the user's behavior. Our field test showed that for a good number of individuals, the system converged to their personal most successful strategy. We hope that this demonstration and description of the implementation of our adaptive persuasive system encourage designers of persuasive technologies to use personalization at the level of social influence strategies to increase the effectiveness of their systems.

While we succeeded in building the first adaptive persuasive system that personalized its influence strategies – as opposed to the end goals – to responses by users, it should also be noted that our setup and evaluation have limitations. Most importantly, we suffered from an insufficient number of observations to successfully evaluate the system. Although the number of users entering the building was rather large, the technology excluded around 90% of the potential users: those who did not have Bluetooth enabled phones. Furthermore, the duration of the deployment was too short to fully explore users' susceptibility to different influence strategies and *exploit* them in full to create valid comparisons between the two conditions in the evaluation.

While promising, persuasion profiles and their use in adaptive persuasive systems should be looked at with caution. There are obvious ethical considerations (especially when systems are used for less socially accepted goals), and the unobtrusive tracking processes pose serious privacy concerns that should guide future research efforts.

This paper presented our first steps in the exploration of adaptive persuasive systems. We hope to be able to deploy the APStair system for a longer period of time. This will lead to *(a)* a statistically valid comparison of the performance of an adaptive system to a random system, and *(b)* a better insight into the effects of different influence strategies over time.

References

1. Cacioppo, J.T., Petty, R.E., Kao, C.F., Rodriguez, R.: Central and Peripheral Routes to Persuasion: An Individual Difference Perspective. Journal of Personality and Social Psychology 51, 1032–1043 (1986)
2. Cialdini, R.: Influence, Science and Practice. Allyn & Bacon, Boston (2001)
3. Consolvo, S., McDonald, D.W., Landay, J.A.: Theory-driven Design Strategies for Technologies that Support Behavior Change in Everyday Life. In: Proceedings of the 27th International Conference on Human Factors in Computing Systems, pp. 405–414. ACM, New York (2009)
4. Fogg, B.J.: Persuasive Technology: Using Computers to Change What We Think and Do. Morgan Kaufmann, San Francisco (2002)
5. Kaptein, M., Lacroix, J., Saini, P.: Individual Differences in Persuadability in the Health Promotion Domain. In: Ploug, T., Hasle, P., Oinas-Kukkonen, H. (eds.) PERSUASIVE 2010. LNCS, vol. 6137, pp. 94–105. Springer, Heidelberg (2010)
6. Kaptein, M., Markopoulos, P., de Ruyter, B., Aarts, E.: Can You Be Persuaded? Individual Differences in Susceptibility to Persuasion. In: Gross, T., Gulliksen, J., Kotzé, P., Oestreicher, L., Palanque, P., Prates, R.O., Winckler, M. (eds.) INTERACT 2009. LNCS, vol. 5726, pp. 115–118. Springer, Heidelberg (2009)

Motivate: Context Aware Mobile Application for Activity Recommendation

Yuzhong Lin, Joran Jessurun, Bauke de Vries, and Harry Timmermans

Eindhoven University of Technology
Eindhoven, The Netherlands
y.lin1@tue.nl

Abstract. This paper presents the design, implementation and evaluation of a context-aware recommendation system that promotes the adoption of a healthy and active lifestyle. A Smartphone application that provides personalized and contextualized advice based on geo information, weather, user location and agenda was developed and evaluated by a user study. The results show the potential of this mobile application in triggering behavior change by suggesting simple daily activities.

Keywords: context-aware, mobile application, healthy living, recommendation system.

1 Introduction

According to WHO by 2015, approximately 2.3 billion adults will be overweight and more than 700 million will be obese [1]. Overweight and obesity can lead to many serious health problems. It is a challenge to stay motivated to maintain a sufficient amount of physical activity. Nowadays with the development of mobile technologies, mobile device may act as powerful persuaders because they can intervene in the right context and a convenient way in order to prompt users into behavior change [2]. The mobile device tracks context and prompts users to take action, as Fogg's description of one persuasive role of mobile phones - "coach" [3]. Ubiquitous computing and context-aware persuasive technologies [3] offer a new healthcare opportunity to promote health behavior by presenting "just-in-time information" [4]. The newest trend of using Smartphone and location-based technologies makes the just-in-time information presented at a right location and time feasible.

In this paper, we present a Smartphone application "Motivate" that provides users with personalized and contextualized advice on possible physical activities to do. We introduce the design, implementation and an evaluation test of the "Motivate" system. The main focus of the design is to motivate people to behave more physically active by providing recommendations fitting their daily life. The reason is that lifestyle interventions can yield positive and long-term effects in terms of increasing the levels of moderately intense physical activity [5].

D. Keyson et al. (Eds.): AmI 2011, LNCS 7040, pp. 210–214, 2011.

2   Motivate Design and Implementation

Motivate system consists of Motivate service, Motivate web application and Mobile API which communicates with Motivate mobile application. The Motivate mobile application is compatible with Android phone version 2.0. It sends the phone location detected by either GPS or GSM localization to Motivate service which generates advice. Users get advice on the phone application and send their responses back to the Motivate Service. The Motivate web application is developed for users to edit user personal information and for system administration. The Motivate Service consists of services including Advisor, Location, Agenda, Weather, Profile, Time and Event.

2.1   Advice Generation

The Advisor Service sends a query to one or more of the Services and acquires their analysis results. It calculates for each advice in the advice database its suitability for the given situation. Each advice consists of a process and a template. The If-Then rules defined in the "process" specify which constraints must be met for each advice. If any good advice is found, the Advisor Service creates a message to send to the mobile UI and then store it in the Message Database. There were in total 34 pieces of advice including 20 kinds of activities with different constraints. The constraints are:

- Location: suggested activity location must be within a certain distance or travel time. The geo information of green places such as parks, lakes, forests from OpenStreetMap [6] is added in the geo database. Shopping centers, markets, cinemas, users' significant locations, namely home and work place, etc were implemented in the geo database.
- Agenda: it is used to determine the timing of each advice, e.g., a lunch walk advice being sent during lunch time. Users can add activities such as "Go to work", "Work", "Lunch", "Go home", "Dinner" and "Busy" with the starting and ending time of that activity by using Motivate web applicaiton. It is a weekly schedule and can be adapted for each week
- Weather: outdoor activity advice requires good or fair weather conditions. The weather history data is retrieved from the website of Weather Underground [7] and stored in whether cache. The Weather Service updates the database and picks up the weather record with the time closest to the query time.
- Profile: users edit their profile such as gender, age, family status, transportation, home, work place address, etc. advice such as cycling to work requires users' possession of bike.
- Time: suggested activity is applicable for a certain specified time period (e.g., Saturday morning to go to the market)
- Event: the detailed information of events of every weekend in the city was added to the database and sent to users 2-3 days before the events.

If all the constraints are met, the advice becomes a candidate to be randomly chosen. One example of a "Lunch walk advice" contains the following constrains: the day of week is a weekday; a user's agenda activity "Lunch" starts within twenty minutes; a user's agenda is free for one hour; the current weather is fair; there is a green place within walking time (within 300m for a short walk). The field "template" of the chosen advice can dynamically compile the text of the message to be sent. In this example the template is "It's pretty good weather outside, how about a short walk to < the name of suggested the green place in the geo database> during lunch break?" To avoid repetition we keep track of the sent messages and categorize them into different types. They are configured that the same type of advice won't occur within a certain time, e.g., at most 1 taking stairs advice per day or 1 walking to supermarket advice in 3 days.

2.2 Motivate Mobile User Interface

The application is developed using the Android Software Development Kit. If there is a message found, a notification is sent to a user. A message is shown on the screen (see Fig. 1, upper left). By clicking the map icon, a user can view the suggested place on Google map and where he or she is at that moment (see Fig. 1, lower left). The 4 possible responses are as follows for users to choose:

- *"Yes, I will do it now"* (referred as Yes)
- *"Yes, I will do it later"* (referred as Yes Later)
- *"Yes, because I am already doing or have planned something similar"* (referred as Yes Already)
- *"No, I will not do it"* (referred as No)

Fig. 1. Motivate mobile application screenshots

If a user chooses "No, I will not do it" he is asked to choose from a list of reasons (details in the results section) or give their own reasons. All the received messages were listed in the main interface of the application. The left thumb up or thumb down icon indicates the response of users indicating if they have any intention of behavior change. In order to measure whether there is any actual behavior change, we ask users to report if they have followed the advice later by "validation". By clicking the icon to the right of each message indicates they can validate their choice by choosing green check for "Yes, I did it" or red circle for "No, I didn't do it". The pink background indicates that the message has not been validated yet. This validation process is designed to record if there's any actual behavior change based on users' self report (see Fig.1, right).

3 Evaluation User Study

25 Android phone users were recruited for the user test through our Motivate website. They (8 females and 17 males) aged from 21 till 54 years old with average age of 34 years old. They all went to work at least 4 days per week. According to BMI calculation 7 of them were overweight while 18 of them are with normal weight. Each participant was required to use Motivate for 5 weeks in total. In the first week, we collected user location data and added their home and work location into the database. After this assessment period participants started to receive messages for another 4 weeks. The Motivate application is running in the background continuously and communicates with the server every 15 minutes. Users get a notification when they receive a message.

3.1 Results and Discussions

In total 3556 messages were sent to participants, which is on average 3-4 messages per day. This number varied for individual participant from 1.4 to 5.5. 2854 (80.3%) out of all the messages were given responses. 47.8% of the messages were given positive response (24.5% for "Yes", 12.5% for "Yes Later", 10.8% for "Yes Already"). 52.2% of the messages were given negative response. The mostly chosen reasons for not following the advice were: "I already have other plans" (29.6%) and "I am busy and have no time" (23.3%), which indicates the lack of detailed information of Agenda service is one major cause for negative responses. The other reasons were "I don't feel like doing it" (22.3%), "Not feasible to follow" (10.3%), "unsuitable weather" (3.6%, mostly duo to problems with the data of Weather Underground [7]), "unsuitable location" (2.0%) and other reasons (6.1%, e.g., "I am sick").

There were 2352 (82.4%) out of the answered 2854 messages that were validated. 85.5% of messages were validated consistently which means their behavior matched their earlier responses of their intention. In overall 46.8% of the messages were given "Yes, I did it" while 53.2% of them were reported as "No, I didn't do it."

The messages were categorized into different types in Table 1. The more frequently sent messages were suggesting outdoor activities and taking a small break. For the advice of taking a break, taking stairs and doing some housework were given positive responses more than the other types. These activities required fewer efforts compared with the activities such as planning a cycling trip or going to an event. Although these small activities do not increase the physical activity dramatically in turns of calorie burning, they do help users to adopt a healthy lifestyle by changing habits. This is in line with the reason that we only include simple daily activities in the advice database [5].

Table 1. Messages and responses

Messages	Example	Positive responses
Outdoor activity (35.7%)	A small walk during lunch; cycle to green places	28.7%
Break (28.3%)	Walk to the coffee corner, stretch, workout at home	64.7%
Weekend activity (9.7%)	Go to movie, events in the city	25.5%
Shopping (7.9%)	Supermarket, market; weekend shopping	33.7%
Take stairs (7.1%)	Take stairs during work	49.5%
Transportation (6.4%)	Walk/cycle to work for a change; detour home	15.8%
Housework (5.0%)	Mopping, washing dishes, gardening	47.1%

4 Conclusions

This paper has presented the design and user evaluation of Motivate mobile application. We made personalized and contextualized recommendation available for the user's mobile device at any time. The integration of various inputs such as geo information, weather, user agenda, and city events is shown to be efficient for generating various advices. The results show that almost half of the responses to messages were positive and the validation suggested certain consistency between intention and actual behavior. The simple-to-do activities that required fewer efforts could trigger more behavior change. The application is believed to be beneficial for people who want to pursue a healthy lifestyle, especially for those who have a regular job and participate insufficient in physical activity. The "Motivate" can be a gentle push and reminder for simple daily activities, as well as offering innovative activity ideas for their free time. Further analysis of possible influence in different context such as location and time on user feedbacks will be performed in the future.

References

1. WHO Media Centre, Obesity and Overweight (2011), http://www.who.int/mediacentre/factsheets/fs311/en/
2. Fogg, B.J.: Persuasive Technology: Using Computers to Change What We Think and Do. Morgan Kaufmann, San Francisco (2003)
3. Fogg, B.J., Eckles, D.: Mobile Persuasion: 20 Perspectives on the Future of Behavior Change. Stanford Captology Media, California (2007)
4. Intille, S.S.: Ubiquitous Computing Technology for Just-in-Time Motivation of Behavior Change. MedInfo. 107, 1434–1437 (2004)
5. Frank, L., Engelke, P., Schimid, T.: Health and Community Design: the Impact of the Built Environment on Physical Activity. Island Press, Washington, DC (2003)
6. OpenStreetMap data (2011), http://download.geofabrik.de/osm/europe/
7. Weather Undergrond (2011), http://www.wunderground.com/

AULURA: Engaging Users with Ambient Persuasive Technology

Jabe Piter Faber[1], Panos Markopoulos[1], Pavan Dadlani[2], and Aart van Halteren[2]

[1] Department of Industrial Design, Eindhoven University of Technology,
Den Dolech 2, 5600 MB Eindhoven, The Netherlands
jabe@jpfdesign.nl, p.markopoulos@tue.nl
[2] Philips Research, High Tech Campus 34, 5656 AE Eindhoven, The Netherlands
{pavan.dadlani,aart.van.halteren}@philips.com

Abstract. This paper describes the design and preliminary evaluation of Aulura, a system designed for motivating people to increase their physical activity. Aulura is an ambient information display that aims to 'lure' users to interact with it, to review their progress and set personal goals. We present the design of 'ambient cues' added to a picture frame with the aim to increase user interaction with the device and engagement with a physical activity promotion service. Empirical evaluation in a home simulation laboratory provided positive feedback relating to its potential to further engage participants in an online lifestyle management service.

Keywords: Persuasive technology, ambient information displays, calm computing, wellbeing, activity monitoring, engagement.

1 Introduction

Although the benefits of a healthy lifestyle and sufficient physical activity are well known, most people find it difficult to make lasting changes to the sedentary lifestyle that is prevalent in Western societies. This has prompted research into persuasive technologies that encourage people to be more active. Consolvo et al. [1] put forward four main requirements for such technologies: (1) give users proper credit for activities, (2) provide personal awareness of activity level, (3) support social influence, and (4) consider the practical constraints of a users' lifestyle.

The first requirement pertains especially to the quality of the sensing and processing of data collected regarding the user's activity. The second requirement is addressed by several dedicated devices and related applications available to date, like the Nike+iPod[TM] and Nintendo Walk with me![TM] as they provide feedback on a personal device and access to personal history of activity on related online services. In this paper we examine how to address the latter two requirements. More specifically, we examine how extending a mobile persuasive technology for activity monitoring and its related personalized web-based service with a dedicated domestic appliance can motivate people to be more active.

D. Keyson et al. (Eds.): AmI 2011, LNCS 7040, pp. 215–221, 2011.

2 Related Work

Persuasive technologies are often explored and implemented to support healthy living and lifestyle change. Studies such as [4,6,7] indicate a growing interest in motivating people to be physically active at both home and work settings. Many approaches to stimulate motivation have been explored, e.g. [7] shows that visual and auditory feedback can lead to increased physical activity. Studies like [2,8,9] show that digital picture frames are an acceptable medium for integrating technology within the home environment and the lifestyle of users. Obermain et al. [9] argue that *"ambient intelligence allows surrounding the user with persuasive technology in their everyday life, giving the possibility for persuasive interventions just at the right time and at the right place"*. Their *perFrames* concept is a good example of how a picture frame can move from the periphery of the users' attention to their full attention, where subtle changes reflect updates of information and persuade users to change their sitting behavior. Another example is that of the ambient display for exercise awareness [4], where persuasive technology is implemented into a mirror. The study of Lin et al. [6] describes the *Fish 'n Steps* concept that stimulates behavioral change through an online game linked to the physical activity of users on a monitor within their working environment.

Multiple benefits of using digital picture frames as devices that deliver persuasive content to users have been reported. However, in most of these studies feedback is only given in response to users' initiative and/or the performance of certain actions. Here we examine how such a device can engage users in interaction in a more pro-active way as they go about in their daily domestic activities.

Rozendaal et al. [11] indicate that interaction richness and control can be extended to enhance engagement with an electronic device. Successful examples of using engagement to stimulate behavioral change are the Power Agent project [5] where users' energy consumption patterns are implemented into a game to decrease the energy level, and the Neat-O-Race [3] which stimulates physical activity with a pervasive game on cell phones. These examples of changing context and control over data have been shown to have a positive impact on user behavior. We argue that augmenting digital picture frames with similar interactive behavior can further impact the users' health and wellbeing.

We report the design and preliminary evaluation of an ambient picture frame which stimulates the physical activity of users by involving them in a more pro-active way. This device extends an existing online activity monitoring program enhancing the role of social influence as a persuasion strategy and targeting the domestic context.

3 A Web Service for Physical Activity Promotion

The design challenge described above was addressed in the context of a commercial web service[1] that helps users on a journey towards a healthy physical activity level. It tries to do so by monitoring and coaching the user throughout a personalized activity plan. The service consists of three parts: (1) a small device carried by users,

---

[1] DirectLife: http://www.directlife.philips.com

monitoring their level of physical activity over time, (2) an online service where users can monitor their own and other users' progress, and (3) a coaching service that gives useful online feedback on their achievements. The service is quite successful in motivating people to change a sedentary lifestyle into a lifestyle with sufficient physical activity, in particular for participants that frequently engage with the coaching service.

4 Aulura

The developed domestic application entitled Aulura is seen as an extension to the current online coaching service where we focus on how users can be triggered within their home environment and compare their progress with family members. The moments of reviewing activity data are important for the motivation of the user and are those that can instigate effective behavioral change. During private time, people have more freedom to choose what they do, so it is then that showing the progress on their physical activity plan is most likely to lead to a change in behavior.

Aulura is an ambient display [10] that can be placed at a visible location at home, e.g., the kitchen or living room. Users' physical activity is displayed with a light-based progress indicator embedded on the frame of the device, where color is used to identify a user. Detailed information is displayed on the screen. The identity and number of users in the vicinity determines the activity information displayed. The distance between users and Aulura determines the interaction mode – separating the space in different interaction zones (see Figure 1), where progressively more detail and interactivity are offered in different modalities as users approach the device.

Fig. 1. Five different zones of interaction, corresponding to: off mode, blend mode, displaying ambient information, detailed information, and manipulating the information

When the user is in the *Blend area* the device displays a slideshow of personally uploaded pictures. As the user approaches the device and enters the *Ambient Information area*, physical activity is visualized by gradually 'filling' the frame from one of the four corners. The amount of light occupying the frame indicates the level of achievement. For example, if the light occupies the full frame, the user's daily target has been reached. When a user enters the *Detailed Information area*, the onscreen slideshow fades out and a startup screen displays detailed information about the day's achievements such as the user's pictogram, achieved percentage of targeted physical activity level, calories burned and time spent walking and running on that day (see Figure 2). Around the user's data other pictograms of friends or family are displayed. These can be selected by the user to show a comparison of respective physical activity levels. When a user engages in full interaction in the *Manipulation area*, more detailed information can be browsed by touching the pictograms, allowing users to easily compare their data with that of peers and to check their activity history.

Fig. 2. Aulura's interface with user activity level presented on both screen and frame. Clickable pictograms of friends and family are located around the user's pictogram.

5   Evaluation

A first evaluation of the use and aesthetics of Aulura was performed within a laboratory that simulates a home environment. The test evaluated the interactivity described above relating to engaging users proactively, which we refer to below for brevity as 'ambient cues'.

Nine male and seven female users, within the age groups of 20-40 (N=10) and 40-60 (N=6), of the current activity monitoring service participated in the evaluation. This ensured that data was available and actual through the online service. The only change was accessing the online service through Aulura. Participants received a replacement activity monitor which was able to communicate wirelessly with Aulura and which had to be carried during the complete day prior to the lab-test. Participants were asked to choose a color to identify them and provide five personal pictures that they would like to display on Aulura. Tests lasted 90 minutes; participants carried out two conditions: with and without ambient cues on Aulura. In both conditions, participants were asked to perform some domestic tasks, e.g., to make a cup of coffee, or read some pages of a magazine, so that the interaction with Aulura would be secondary (see Figure 3). In the case where Aulura was actively attempting to attract the participant's attention, ambient cues were shown at the five different zones of interaction. Furthermore, in the condition with ambient cues they were asked to estimate the amount of activity for the last day based only on the ambient information, i.e., the coloring of the LED lights on the frame. In both conditions participants were expected to review their activity data regarding aspects of their own and others' activity progress displayed on Aulura.

Besides observation, qualitative data was collected at the end of each session through an interview focused on the differences in usability, aesthetics and persuasiveness of both conditions in relationship with users' experience of the current activity monitoring service. Questions included whether users noticed and understood the ambient cues; whether the different areas of interaction were luring them towards the frame and motivating them to explore more data; and whether they would share this information with family and friends. The interviews were analyzed through an affinity diagram where key results give a first impression of how users experience the interaction model and aesthetics of Aulura.

Fig. 3. User interacting with Aulura during the lab-test

6   Results and Discussion

6.1   Persuasiveness

Post-test interviews indicated that almost every participant (N=13) noticed and understood the ambient cues. In comparison to the current service, participants indicated to be more motivated to check on their progress because of the availability and efficiency of the data given and stated that the ambient cues initiated by Aulura raised the awareness of their physical activity. Although observation showed that multiple participants (N=9) reacted on the ambient cues given while performing the tasks in the home setting (looking or walking towards the device), almost half (N=7) reported that they did not experience the ambient cues as an added value to their activity progress in comparison with the picture frame without ambient cues. Probably because of the brevity of the user test and because it was still not part of actual daily routines, we did not find an increase in the persuasiveness of the device that can be attributed to the cues. However, the interviews indicated that more than half (N=9) of the participants experienced the use of light as pleasurable and clear.

Two participants would not use such a device in their home, indicating that it was too obtrusive.

6.2 Social Influence

Sharing activity data with family and friends was considered as more motivating (N=7) than showing a large amount of users with whom they have no emotional relation. Participants indicated that the abstract way of showing activity progress through the frame resulted into a more pleasant interaction, mostly because of the different levels of information that are presented. Privacy was considered an issue by some (N=6), who indicated that they would not share their detailed activity data with people outside the family. However, they were still positive about using the device at home if they would have control with respect to turning the ambient cues on and off, e.g., when visitors are present.

7   Implications

Overall, during this first evaluation Aulura was experienced positively. Although the level of obtrusiveness and behavioral change have to be determined over a longer period of time, first qualitative results indicate that the 'luring' behavior was not experienced as annoying and has potential for further engaging participants with an online coaching service within the home environment. The use of light as a persuasive cue was experienced as pleasant though its aesthetics could be further refined, as respondents indicated several other ways to display their activity level on the frame. The functionality of the light was considered efficient, clear and usable. The use of distance and/or position of the user in relationship with the device to determine the information flow were experienced as desirable. The availability and efficiency of activity data in a digital frame for the home environment was considered to stimulate the engagement and ease of use.

The results presented are encouraging regarding the design and use of ambient home displays, especially regarding their potential for lifestyle change. However, we still are not in a position to evaluate its impact regarding the effectiveness of such displays in changing people's behavior, and this needs to be evaluated in a longitudinal field study.

References

1. Consolvo, S., Everitt, K., Smith, I., Landay, J.A.: Design requirements for technologies that encourage physical activity. In: Proc. of CHI 2006, pp. 457–466. ACM Press (2006)
2. Dadlani, P., Markopoulos, P., Sinitsyn, A., Aarts, E.: Supporting Peace of Mind and Independent Living with the Aurama Awareness System. Journal of Ambient Intelligence and Smart Environments 3, 37–50 (2011)
3. Fujiki, Y., Kazakos, K., Puri, C., Buddharaju, P., Pavlidia, I., Levine, J.: NEAT-o-games: blending physical activity and fun in the daily routine. ACM Comput. Entertain. 6(1), article 21 (2008)

4. Fujinami, K., Riekki, J.: A Case Study on an Ambient Display as a Persuasive Mediu for Exercise Awareness. In: Proc. of PERSUASIVE 2008, pp. 266–269. ACM Press (2008)
5. Gustafsson, A., Bang, M.: Evaluation of a pervasive game for domestic energy engagement among teenagers. In: Proc. of ACE 2008, pp. 232–239. ACM Press (2008)
6. Lin, J.J., Mamykina, L., Lindtner, S., Delajoux, G., Strub, H.B.: Fish'n'Steps: Encouraging Physical Activity with an Interactive Computer Game. In: Dourish, P., Friday, A. (eds.) UbiComp 2006. LNCS, vol. 4206, pp. 261–278. Springer, Heidelberg (2006)
7. Maitland, J., Sherwood, S., Barkhuus, L., Anderson, I., Hall, M., Brown, B., Chalmers, M., Muller, H.: Increasing the Awareness of Daily Activity Levels with Pervasive Computing. In: Proc. of Pervasive Health 2006, pp. 1–9. IEEE (2006)
8. Mynatt, E., Rowan, J., Jacobs, A., Craighill, S.: Digital Family Portraits: Supporting Peace of Mind for Extended Family Members. In: Proc. of CHI, pp. 333–340. ACM Press (2001)
9. Obermain, C., Reitberger, W., Meschtscherjakov, A., Lankes, M., Tscheligi, M.: Perframes: Persuasive Picture Frames for Proper Posture. In: Proc. of PERSUASIVE 2008, pp. 128–139. ACM Press (2008)
10. Pousman, Z., Stasko, J.: A taxonomy of ambient information systems: four patterns of design. In: Proc. of AVI 2006, pp. 67–74. ACM Press (2006)
11. Rozendaal, M.C., Keyson, D.V., de Ridder, H.: Product behavior and appearance effects on experienced engagement during experiential and goal-directed tasks. In: Proc. of DPPI 2007, pp. 181–193. ACM Press (2007)

Human Behavior Analysis in Ubiquitous Environments for Energy Efficiency Improvement[*]

Ovidiu Aritoni[1,2] and Viorel Negru[1,2]

[1] Research Institute E-Austria
[2] West University of Timişoara,
Timişoara, Romania
{oaritoni,vnegru}@info.uvt.ro

Abstract. The goal of this paper is to discover human habits using the received sensors data-streams, in order to improve the energy efficiency. We propose a multi-agent architecture and a formalism to describe scenarios in ubiquitous environments based on a wireless sensors network. We have used sensor data and simulations about a four person family, to validate our prototype.

Keywords: sensors network, ubiquitos environment, scenario recognition, multi-agent system, pattern recognition, energy efficiency.

1 Introduction

Ubiquitos spaces are intelligent systems which use sensors networks to understand the environment [8]. Based on the gathered sensor data, intelligent systems take some decisions in order to improve one or several aspects of the ubuiquitos space. We use in our study as a ubiquitos environment a house. The goal is to discover the people habits and the correlation between these habits and the energy consumption. Using wireless sensor networks, we can obtain data-streams, which describe different aspects of the environment and the interactions between the people and devices/appliances or other objects.

First, we must understand what happens in the house. To achieve this goal we have defined a formalism to describe all the actions and the events, the Human Behavior Scenario Description Language (HBSDL). An intelligent agent analyses the sensors' data-stream and builds scenarios. Other approaches for activity recognition use image recognition [6], neural networks [5], Hidden Markov Model [7] and others data mining [3] or statistical techniques. Our model is based on decision-trees and a set of constraints. Second, we discover patterns in the behavior of house residents. A pattern recognition agent is used in order to process and analyse the HBSDL scenarios. We analyse the habits which have associated a significant energy consumption.

In the next section of the paper we present our approach to scenarios formalisation and the activities recognition process. After we outline the pattern recognition process over scenarios time-series and the system multi-agent architecture. We conclude the paper with discussions about the results and with the important fields of the future work.

---

[*] This work was partially supported by the Romanian project PNII nr.12-122/2008 ASISTSYS and nr. 12-118/2008 SCIPA.

D. Keyson et al. (Eds.): AmI 2011, LNCS 7040, pp. 222–227, 2011.

2   System Architecture and Principles

Human Behavior Scenarios Description Language. The purpose is to describe the human behavior over large periods of time and for that, we use scenarios (a list of actions linked together). The goal is to describe the human interactions with devices and appliances. There are three categories of actions:

   (i) Instant-actions (the person spent less than one minute to perform that action), such as: wake up, goes to bed, turns on, etc.
  (ii) Long time exclusive actions (the person can perform at a certain moment only one action, with a significant time interval), such as: uses toilet, uses sink, etc.
 (iii) Long time non-exclusive actions (the person can perform at a certain moment that action and also others action), such as: watching TV, uses washing-machine, etc.

In the scenario's description we defined and used a special language, HBSDL (Human Behavior Scenarios Description Language), with a syntax and a vocabulary similar with the English language. To assure that scenarios are accurate, we have defined a HBSDL compiler. We store the scenario for each house resident, in a different file:

```
Alice _wakes _up _in _0#Bedroom _at _08:30:20
Alice _turns _on _light _at _08:30:25
Alice _turns _on _television _at _08:31:00
Alice _enters _2#Bathroom _at _08:50:00
. . . . . . . . . . . . . . . . . . . . . . . . . . . . . . . . . . .
Alice _goes _to _bed _at _22:10:00
```

The activities recognition process means to have an intuition about the actions and the objectives of one or more people, using an observations set, about the person actions and the environment. Our approach uses a bidrectional process: we analyse the sensors data-streams and we analyse the context in the same time.

A flexible definition about the context takes in account: user location, his identity and preferences, the identity of other people which share the same location, the interacting objects (especially appliances), the weather, the time-moment, the temperature, etc [4]. We use a subject-centric approach of the context, based on the use of RFID [1] sensors. In this way, we know for each person where they are, at each moment.

To **represent the context** we use a matrix, with three dimensions: who, where and when. The household profile describes the household structure and the house residents: preferences, weekly schedule, sex, age, etc [1]. Using the data about house resident we can build a set of constraints. For example, if at a certain time the subject and the place is "a man in the kitchen", and we have on the same time a woman in the kitchen, using the man preferences, we build the following constraint: "the man is not cooking". We have obtained data about the household residents using a questionnaire. A large study using more than 800 households and more than 2000 people, from Romanian region of Banat, was developed in order to build a set of household profiles.

For a person p, from the room r at the moment t the context matrix element *context(p,r,t)* contains:

---

[1] Each person has a RFID label and in each room we have a RFID sensor which detects the identity of all the subject from that location.

(i) A scenario which describes the last actions from the moment 00:00 AM to the moment $t - 1$.

(ii) A set of constraints about the actions with small probabilities to occur.

(iii) The temperature, the lightening and the movement level.

(iv) The number and the identity of other people from the same room r.

The analysis of sensors data-streams is used only for the sensors related with the domestic ressources consumption: electricity, gas, water. The current-cost sensor data-stream analysis provides us information about the running devices. The gas/water consumption is used to understand the cooking type or the washing type. We have defined a set of models which we use to analyse the current-cost, gas-consumption and water-consumption sensors data-streams. For each device, the model contains the average/the minimum/the maximum consumption. Also, we define the minimum/average/maximum consumption for each washing-type. The results of sensors data-streams analysis are inserted in the system knowledge base. A rule-based engine uses as input this results and the context matrix elements and provides as output the activity type as HBSDL instruction.

Human Behavior Patterns. Pattern recognition means examining input data and recognize patterns based on a priori knowledge or on statistical information extracted from the patterns. To discover patterns in scenarios (user habits) we must to "translate" the scenario from HSBDL in a numerical time-series, **the scenario time-series**. For the long time non-exclusive actions, we insert in the time-series the start-action time and the end-time action. In order to improve the energy efficiency we are interested to obtain patterns related to the long time actions. We consider a pattern in the scenario time-series, a subsequence of more than three elements. Our pattern recognition agent discovers in the scenario time-series subsequences and calculates for each subsequence the frequence and the average start-time. The context validation agent is used to check all the constraints over all the contextual data.

Multi-Agent Architecture. Our software prototype is a multi-agent system based on a blackboard architecture, using the JADE[2] platform. Our system uses an agent to build the context from the household profile and the RFID sensor data-stream. An ontology which describes the household is developed using the household profile. A parser analyses the XML file, which describes the household profile, and based on this data we generate as output the ontology. The communication between the agents is based on this ontology. For each current-cost/gas/water sensor data-stream, we have developed an agent which analyses it in order to recognize the model (e.g washing model, cooking model, energy-consumption model,etc). The scenarios recognition is based on a rules database which was developed in JESS (Java Expert System Shell Language) and embedded in an agent. The blackboard contains the context, the computed models, the sensor data, the scenarios and information about the household. An agent parses the scenario to discover some patterns. As a future work, we want to develop agents which compute statistics and association rules about the scenario actions.

---

[2] http://jade.tilab.com/

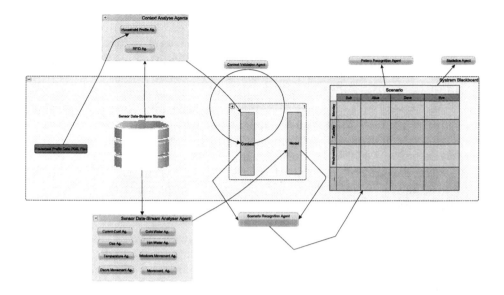

Fig. 1. The Multi-Agent Architecture

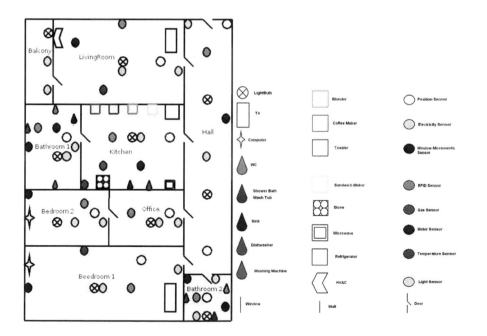

Fig. 2. House Description

3   Results and Discussions

In this section we will present an example: a family composed by four persons (Alice, Bob, Dave and Eve) which live in the house described in the figure 2 . The scenario which describes this family behavior for seven days contains 624 sentences (actions). Bob scenario's summary can be view in the figure 3. The Bob scenario is described using 164 sentences, and for each sentence the main attributes are the action, the start-time and end-time. For each action we associate a colour: dark blue for "wakes up", red for "goes", blue for "turn on / uses *an appliance*", gray for "washes", pink for "turns off", light green for "exit", yellow for "comes", purple for "goes to bed", etc. For each day of the week you can see a column which describes what actions are performed in that day. Table 1 explains the results of the scenario recognition and patterns discovering process over the scenario time-series. The recognition rate represents the similarity measure between the original scenario time-series and the recognized scenario time-series. We use the Dynamic Time Warping metric to calculate the similarity between these two time-series [2]. In our case, due to the recognition rate the original and the "recognized" time-series can have different lengths and for this reason we use this metric. From the structural point of view Monday, Tuesday, Wednesday and Friday Bob's schedules are

Table 1. Results of habits recognition process

Scenarios	Recognition Rate	Identified Patterns	Minimum Patterns Length	Maximum Patterns Length	Total Energy Consumption
Monday.sce	0.95	4	3	5	10.003 Kwh
Tuesday.sce	0.95	4	3	5	10.340 Kwh
Wednesday.sce	0.96	5	4	5	11.152 Kwh
Thursday.sce	0.94	3	3	4	8.1100 Kwh
Friday.sce	0.92	5	3	5	10.420 Kwh
Saturday.sce	0.87	4	5	8	9.0010 Kwh
Sunday.sce	0.95	4	3	4	8.1430 Kwh

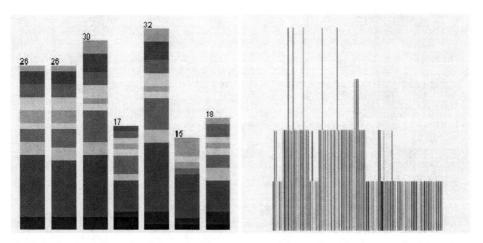

Fig. 3. Left - Bob Scenario: the seven days summary. Right- Bob Scenario: start time for all the actions.

very similar. The same patterns are discovered for all these days. The washing activities are concentrated on Saturday. On weekend the most activities are started on morning. Also, on weekends there are few activities, from the numerical point of view, but longer comparing with the other days.

4   Conclusions and Future Works

We are developing a multi-agent recommendation system for energy efficiency improvement (MARSEEI) [1]. The software prototype presented in this paper is integrated in the MARSEEI system, which is a work-in-progress. The first level of abstraction is the scenario recognition process, based on a bidirectional approach. The HBSDL language is used in order to formalise the human behavior. A second level of abstraction is developed in order to extract the user habits, from the household residents scenarios. A research about the influence of human behavior on energy consumption will be developed, for providing recommendations using these observations. We will define a **contextual model** which it will take into consideration patterns from the received data. The minimum sensor network dimension which it can be used to obtain relevant data about the household resident behavior is another important research future direction.

References

1. Aritoni, O., Negru, V.: A Multi-Agent Recommendation System for Energy Efficiency Improvement. In: Yonazi, J.J., Sedoyeka, E., Ariwa, E., El-Qawasmeh, E. (eds.) ICeND 2011. CCIS, vol. 171, pp. 156–170. Springer, Heidelberg (2011)
2. Berndt, D.J., Clifford, J.: Finding Patterns in Time Series: A Dynamic Programming Approach. In: Advances in Knowledge Discovery and Data Mining, pp. 229–248. American Association for Artificial Intelligence (1996)
3. Chen, C., Das, B., Cook, D.J.: A data mining framework for activity recognition in smart environments. In: Proc. of Sixth Int. Conf. on Intelligent Environments, IE 2010, pp. 80–83. IEEE Computer Society (2010)
4. Dey, A.K., Abowd, G.D., Salber, D.: A conceptual framework and a toolkit for supporting the rapid prototyping of context-aware applications. Hum.-Comput. Interact. 16, 97–166 (2001)
5. Györbíró, N., Fábián, Á., Hományi, G.: An activity recognition system for mobile phones. Mob. Netw. Appl. 14, 82–91 (2009)
6. Lymberopoulos, D., Bamis, A., Teixeira, T., Savvides, A.: Behaviorscope: Real-time remote human monitoring using sensor networks. In: Proc. of Int. Conf. on Information Processing in Sensor Networks, IPSN 2008, pp. 533–534. IEEE Computer Society (2008)
7. van Kasteren, T., Noulas, A., Englebienne, G., Kröse, B.: Accurate activity recognition in a home setting. In: Proc. of 10th Int. Conf. on Ubiquitous computing, UbiComp 2008, pp. 1–9. ACM (2008)
8. Weiser, M.: The computer for the 21st century. SIGMOBILE Mob. Comput. Commun. Rev. 3, 3–11 (1991)

Friend or Foe? Relationship-Based Adaptation on Public Displays

Ekaterina Kurdyukova, Karin Bee, and Elisabeth André

University of Augsburg, Universitaetsstrasse 6a,
86159 Augsburg, Germany
{kurdyukova,karin.bee,andre}@hcm-lab.de

Abstract. Personalization of content on public displays is likely to cause the disclosure of user's private data. In order to protect the user's privacy, different protection strategies are used, e.g. the private data is hidden, occluded or blurred. Existing systems usually follow a uniform protection strategy, applying it every time a spectator is detected in the display proximity. However, the necessity in privacy protection often depends on the personal relationships between the user and the spectator. This work investigates how the relationship context influences user preferences in adaptation strategies. Additionally, we study how privacy level of data and the presence of a mobile device influence this preference. The obtained results can guide adaptation designers in creation of more flexible privacy protection mechanisms.

Keywords: Public displays, Adaptation, Privacy Protection.

1 Introduction

Modern public displays utilize various strategies to protect private data, e.g. occluding, removing, or blurring the private content. As a rule, these techniques are uniformly applied every time a spectator is detected near the display [1, 2]. However, user willingness to expose or hide private content usually depends on the relationship with the spectator. Thus, people may want to demonstrate the content to their close friends, but protect it from the eyes of a stranger.

Different protection strategies can be applied to different relationships. Similarly to the trusted groups in social networks (such as Facebook), spectators can be classified into groups. Each group is assigned a specific adaptation strategy, providing stronger or weaker data protection.

This paper aims to investigate how relationship context impacts user preferences in adaptation strategies. Using two example applications, designed for community public displays, we analyze user attitudes towards protection necessity in different scenarios. Besides the relationship context, we take a look at additional context sources such as privacy level of content and the presence of a mobile device in the setting.

After an overview of the existing privacy protection techniques, we motivate the need for relationship-based adaptation. Then, we describe the experiment, comment on the obtained results, and discuss their application in adaptive public displays.

D. Keyson et al. (Eds.): AmI 2011, LNCS 7040, pp. 228–237, 2011.

2 Privacy Protection on Public Displays

Adaptation aimed at the personalization of content is widely utilized on public displays. For example, it facilitates the selection of relevant news [3], gives the audience more details about the speaker [4], or reminds the user on important information [1, 2, 5].

Besides evident benefits, the personalization brings the risk of privacy disclosure [4]. In order to avoid the disclosure, public displays can adapt to the presence of spectators using various protection strategies. The protection power of these strategies may vary from strong, such as a complete removal of private data from the display, to very low, e.g. doing nothing or just minimizing the size of the private content. All in all, the display reaction aimed at privacy protection can be classified into the following groups, ordered by ascending protection power:

1. *Do Nothing*: the display is insensitive to the presence of spectators. All private data remains on the screen [4].

2. *Minimize*: private content is minimized in size, or changes its transparency [2] or sharpness. Spectators can still view the private data, though the visual access to the data is hampered. The user can continue interaction with the data.

3. *Mask*: private content on the display is occluded with blinders [6], pixelized [7], or covered with some neutral display elements [6]. Spectators can clearly see that some content is hidden; however, they cannot view the content itself. Since the private data is protected, users need to interrupt the interaction.

4. *Remove Private Part*: if the personalized content is partially neutral (e.g. selected news) and partially private (e.g. user's name), protection mechanism removes only the private part from the display. Spectators cannot notice that some content is hidden or missing [8]. Users have to interrupt the interaction.

5. *Remove All*: All personalized content is removed from the public screen. Spectators cannot notice that the content is hidden; user interrupts the interaction.

Existing adaptive displays usually follow a uniform protection strategy independently on the personality of the spectator. Such a uniform privacy protection brings certain inflexibility into the system, since the concept of privacy depends on the relationship with the spectator [9, 10]. People's need to differentiate between trusted groups can be clearly seen on the example of social networks [11]. In online network communities, users specify unique policies for the groups of friends, family, colleagues, etc. and thus control the access to their private data [12]. The need in such relationship-based trusted groups also holds for public displays. The system should be able to determine the group of the current spectators and perform the adaptation according to the group's policy. Such relationship-based adaptation will not only increase the comfort of interaction, but also will increase user trust [13].

Although modern researchers often emphasize the need for a flexible relationship-based adaptation [9, 10, 11], there is no research in the domain of public displays that studies this question in greater details.

Besides the relationship context, other factors influence the necessity in data protection: for example, privacy level of content [1] and the current technical setting [14]. Modern research proposes diverse technical settings for interaction with public displays, starting from mobile devices [14], tablet-PCs, and finishing with AR-helms and stereoscopic glasses [7]. Since our work focuses on the settings available and familiar to a wide range of users, we consider two typical settings: only a public display (*PD-only*) and a public display assisted by a mobile device (*PD-mobile*). Other contexts, such as user activity, current task, etc. might also influence the protection necessity. However, they are often task-dependent and thus their impact is hard to generalize.

3   Studying the Relationship-Based Adaptation

To summarize, this paper aims to tackle the following questions:

- How does the relationship with the spectator influence user choice of protection strategy on public displays?
- How does privacy level of content influence this choice?
- How does presence of a mobile device in the setting influence this choice?

3.1   Prototypes

In order to address these questions, we arranged an experiment with two public display applications. The applications, called Friend Finder and Media Wall represent typical content for community public displays: support of a social network and a media gallery. Examples of these content types can be frequently encountered in research works [15, 16, 17, 18, 19], as well as in real-life projects, such as Interactive Video Wall in Copenhagen [20] or CityWall in Helsinki [19]. The examples show that despite the awareness of privacy issues [17, 21] caused by the personalized content, people do place their private data on public displays and do need to protect it. Below we describe our applications more in details.

Friend Finder visualizes a user's social network overlaid over a local map (see Fig.1). The users can browse through their peers and retrieve the directions to them. The public display can be operated via a mobile phone client or by means of gestures. An earlier conducted study [22] revealed that the peers' names, pictures, and locations are considered as privacy-critical data. Therefore, a privacy protection mechanism was integrated into Friend Finder: the display executed a uniform masking of peers' pictures and names once a spectator was detected in the proximity [23]. However, intermediate evaluations uncovered the need for a more flexible adaptation: users were willing to protect their data only from certain individuals.

 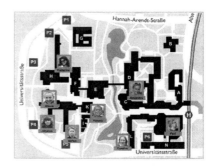

Fig. 1. Friend Finder visualizes user's social network on a public display

Media Wall presents a collection of media shared by community members. Users can upload and edit their media in the working space (see Fig. 2), view and rank the media of the others. Since privacy concerns are likely to arise when uploading the private media [17, 22], an adaptive protection was required. The need in protection depended on the privacy level of media content and on the spectator personality.

Fig. 2. Media Wall: start screen (left) and personalized working space (right)

For the experiment we created several prototypes of each system which differed by the privacy levels and by settings. For Friend Finder, two levels of privacy were provided. The higher privacy version (Friend Finder 2) showed peers' names and portrait pictures (see Fig. 1, right). The lower privacy version (Friend Finder 1) showed only names and uniform icons instead of the pictures. For Media Wall, three levels of privacy were created. The low privacy version (Media Wall 1) showed the personalized collection of neutral pictures, e.g. nature or sightseeing views containing no people or the user alone. The medium privacy version (Media Wall 2) showed the pictures containing the user and friends, but with no confusing content. Finally, the high privacy version (Media Wall 3) exposed the pictures with some compromising content: the user and friends in late party scenes, beach bikini scenes, etc.[1]

Each prototype provided five adaptive strategies aimed at privacy protection. Here, as private data we denote: peers' names for Friend Finder 1, peers' names and pictures for Friend Finder 2, personal collection for Media Wall. The adaptive strategies were executing the following actions:

1. Do Noting: private data remained on the display.

2. Minimize: private data was shrunk in size, but remained on the display.

3. Mask: private data was occluded with solid blinders.

4. Remove Private Part: private data was completely removed from the screen. The neutral elements, such as uniform icons (Friend Finder) and working space (Media Wall) remained on the public screen.

5. Remove All: all private data was removed; the screen showed only the map.

The prototypes were presented in *PD-only* and in *PD-mobile* settings. The *PD-mobile* setting supported the strategies *3-5* where private data was not visible on the public screen: the private data migrated to the mobile screen, enabling the users to continue interaction.

---

[1] Our estimation of privacy levels was verified during the experiment; it matched the estimation of the participants.

All in all, ten prototypes were presented to each test participant: Friend Finder 1 and 2, in *PD-only* and *PD-mobile* setting, and Media Wall 1,2, and 3, also in *PD-only* and *PD-mobile* setting.

3.2 Experiment Procedure

Seventeen persons participated in the experiment, 7 female and 10 male, aged from 23 to 37 (average 29,3). Among them there were Italians, Russians, Ukrainians, Chinese, Germans, and a Bosnian, working in banking, marketing, Engineering, Economics and Multimedia research, or studying at the University. All of them have experiences with social networks, such as Facebook, Studi-vz, XING, LinkedIn, myspace, InterNations; 12 persons have online photo collections.

At the beginning of the experiment we introduced shortly the topic of adaptation on public displays, demonstrated possible adaptation strategies, and presented our two applications, Friend Finder and Media Wall.

Then every participant was asked to imagine three individuals: a close friend, an acquaintance, and a stranger. The friend and the acquaintance should have been real persons (we asked to name them): the friend – a close trusted person and the acquaintance – a neutral familiar person, e.g. a colleague or a neighbor. The stranger was described by a uniform portrait: a male unfamiliar person, in his forties.

In the main part of the experiment the participants were asked to evaluate the adaptation strategies for the prototypes, first Friend Finder and then Media Wall. Every prototype was shown first in *PD-only* setting, and then in *PD-mobile*. The order of privacy levels within prototypes was counterbalanced. For every prototype we first demonstrated all five adaptation strategies. Then we asked the participants to imagine the following scenario. The participant interacts with the public display alone and uploads the private data. Then a spectator suddenly approaches the display. We asked which of the presented adaptation strategies would be preferred if the spectator was the friend, the acquaintance (named), or the stranger.

4 Results

The preferences of the participants were noted down as numbers from 1 to 5, referring to the strength of protection strategies (1 = *Do Nothing*, 5 = *Remove All*). The results were analyzed statistically, by comparing the preferences in various prototypes with pared t-test. Below we report on the results and give our comments.

4.1 Relationships Matter

As we assumed, participants consistently chose stronger protection strategies for less close relationships. Significant differences were obtained through all the results for Friend Finder and Media Wall, in *PD-only* and *PD-mobile* settings (see Fig. 3).

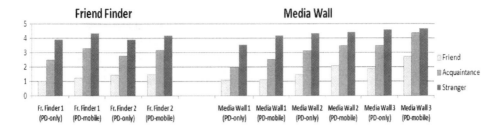

Fig. 3. Preferences in protection strategies for different relationships with spectators

Only for the stranger observing Media Wall 2 or Media Wall 3 in *PD-mobile* setting, the participants chose the strongest protection for both privacy levels.

4.2 Relationship Context in Friend Finder

Figure 4 summarizes the preferences in protection strategies for Friend Finder. The mean values are indicated above the graph bars.

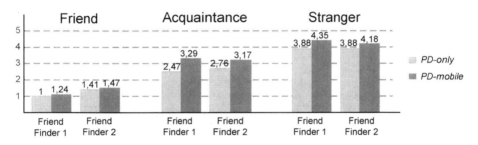

Fig. 4. Preferred protection strategies for Friend Finder in *PD-only* and *PD-mobile* settings

Spectator = Friend

Different privacy levels. The higher the privacy level of the content, the stronger protection strategy is chosen. Thus, the protection strategies for Friend Finder 2 were significantly higher than for Friend Finder 1 (p = 0.024). Friend Finder 2 discloses definitely more data on the social network: while just a name (Friend Finder 1) can stand for several persons, a picture and a name (Friend Finder 2) disambiguously points at a certain person. Often a spectator-friend shares some contacts of the user. The user might not be aware of private situation between the friends. Therefore, the user might prefer to hide the connections, in order not to confuse the common friends or the spectator: "Perhaps I have his [spectator's] ex-girlfriend in my network, and I have no idea what's their relationship now".

PD-only vs. PD-mobile Setting. The presence of a mobile device does not influence the choice of the protection strategy. If the users concern about the disclosure of their contacts, they choose a stronger protection in both settings.

Spectator = Acquaintance

Different privacy levels. No significant differences were found for privacy levels: similar strategies were chosen for Friend Finder 1 and Friend Finder 2.

PD-only vs. PD-mobile Setting. In *PD-mobile* setting the participants chose stronger protection than in *PD-only* setting. Friend Finder 1 (p = 0.0056) and Friend Finder 2 (p = 0.034). In the *PD-only* setting the users often sacrifice their privacy concerns for the sake of interaction comfort. Even under observation of an acquaintance, users choose less protective strategies which still enable them to proceed with interaction. The presence of a mobile device, however, eliminates the need to sacrifice the privacy; the mobile device enables further interaction and secures the private data. Therefore, a stronger protection is chosen on public display.

Spectator = Stranger

No significant differences were found for the stranger case. For both settings, *PD-only* and *PD-mobile*, independently on the privacy level, the preferences were spread between the stronger strategies *3-5*, which ensure invisibility of the private data.

4.3 Relationship Context in Media Wall

Figure 5 summarizes the preferences in protection strategies for Media Wall, showing the mean values above the graph bars.

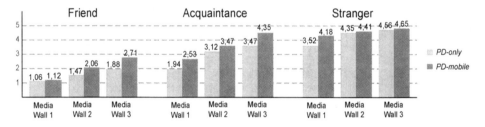

Fig. 5. Preferred protection strategies for Media Wall in *PD-only* and *PD-mobile* settings

Spectator = Friend

Different privacy levels. If a friend is observing the display, a strong protection is necessary only for highly private data. Thus preferences for Media Wall 3 were significantly higher than for Media Wall 1 (p = 0.0072) and for Media Wall 2 (p = 0.045). Highly private media often contain private information not only about the user, but also about their friends. Therefore, users prefer to hide the media in order not to confuse their friends who are even not aware of the possible disclosure.

PD-only vs. PD-mobile Setting. The protection preferences were significantly lower in *PD-only* setting than in *PD-mobile* setting, for medium (p = 0,038) and high (p = 0,015) privacy level. This result can be again explained by users' readiness to sacrifice their privacy concerns for the sake of interaction comfort: in *PD-only* setting users choose a weaker protection which does not impair the interaction. If a mobile device is available, the users continue the interaction on the mobile device and set a stronger protection on public display.

Spectator = Acquaintance

Different privacy levels. The higher the privacy level, the significantly stronger strategies were chosen, throughout all privacy levels.

PD-only vs. PD-mobile Setting. Low and high privacy levels require significantly stronger protection in *PD-mobile* setting than in *PD-only:* Media Wall 1 (p = 0,01) and Media Wall 3 (p=0,021). The protection for medium privacy level strongly depends on the role of the acquaintance. Users tend to decide once, if it is acceptable to show the content to the acquaintance and hold the decision for any setting.

Spectator = Stranger

Different privacy levels of content matter in *PD-only* setting. Medium and highly private data need significantly stronger protection than the low privacy level.

PD-only vs. PD-mobile Setting. The mobile device influences user decision only for low level privacy data: a stronger protection is chosen in PD-mobile (p = 0,043). For other privacy levels, the highest possible protection is chosen in either setting.

Discussion: Applying the Results

The results obtained in the experiment can be summarized as follows:

- **For a Friend-Spectator**, generally no protection is needed. The privacy concerns arise only if the display content can confuse the spectator-friend or compromise the persons involved in the content. In *PD-only* setting the users still keep the data opened, since hiding or removal is likely to impair the interaction process. In *PD-mobile* setting users tend to choose a higher protection: the mobile display serves as a safe depot for private data and enables further interaction with the content.

- **For an Acquaintance-Spectator**, a stronger protection is required. However, the preferences can be widely spread. Such distribution is caused by diverse roles of acquaintances. For instance, users may expose their holiday pictures to a neighbour, but prefer to hide them from a colleague. Having a mobile device available, the users tend to choose a stronger protection.

- **For a Stranger-Spectator**, the strongest protection is preferred. Since the users are not aware of intentions or interests of the stranger, they prefer to protect even the low privacy data. The presence of a mobile device barely influences the protection preference: the users choose the strongest protection in either setting.

The obtained results can inform the design of a real-time relationship-based adaptation. The relationship information can be retrieved from the structure of user's social network (such as Facebook), from the intensity of chat and phone conversations. The personality of the spectator can be identified in real time by camera-based face recognition or by means of mobile phone ID. Additional context analyzed in our experiment can be also retrieved automatically. The setting context can be derived from availability of a mobile device. The privacy level can be extracted from the display content. For instance, if several faces are detected on a picture, the picture is automatically set to medium or high privacy.

Privacy concerns vary greatly among the users; they depend on the personality, traits of the character, personal experiences and can be summarized as *trust disposition* [13]. In our experiment, we noticed that independently on nationality, gender, or age, participants showed some trust patterns, e.g. some of them concerned more about privacy in social networks, others – about private pictures. Therefore, the definition of "universally applicable" privacy levels still remains a challenging task.

The preferences found in the experiment can serve as recommendations for adaptation design for the diverse contextual settings. However, designers should always provide the users with leverages to override the automatic adaptation, so that the users feel the ultimate control over the system behaviour.

Conclusion

Relationship context can make the adaptation on public displays more flexible. By means of the literature review and the conducted experiment, we showed that personal relationships with spectator significantly impact the user's preference in adaptation strategy. Using example applications, we analyzed how this preference is influenced by privacy level of content and by the presence of an assisting mobile device. The reported results can guide the designers in creation of intelligent relationship-based adaptation mechanisms.

References

1. Cao, H., Olivier, P., Jackson, D.: Enhancing privacy in public spaces through crossmodal displays. Journal Social Science Computer Review 26(1), 87–102 (2008)
2. Vogel, D., Balakrishnan, R.: Interactive Public Ambient Displays: Transitioning from Implicit to Explicit, Public to Personal, Interaction with Multiple Users. In: UIST 2004 (2004)
3. Villar, N., Schmidt, A., Kortuem, G., Gellersen, H.: Interacting with proactive public displays. Computers and Graphics 27(6), 849–857 (2003)
4. McCarthy, J., McDonald, D., Soroczak, S., Nguyen, D., Rashid, A.: Augmenting the Social Space of an Academic Conference. In: Proceedings of the ACM Conference on Computer Supported Cooperative Work, CSCW 2004, pp. 39–48. ACM Press, New York (2004)
5. Rukzio, E., Mueller, M., Hardy, R.: Design, Implementation and Evaluation of a Novel Public Display for Pedestrian Navigation: The Rotating Compass. In: Proceedings of the Conf. on Human Factors in Computing Systems, CHI 2009. ACM Press, New York (2009)
6. Röcker, C., Hinske, S., Magerkurth, C.: Intelligent Privacy Support for Large Public Displays. In: Stephanidis, C. (ed.) UAHCI 2007 (Part II). LNCS, vol. 4555, pp. 198–207. Springer, Heidelberg (2007)
7. Boyle, M., Edwards, C., Greenberg, S.: The Effects of Filtered Video on Awareness and Privacy. In: Proceedings of the ACM Conference on Computer Supported Cooperative Work, CSCW 2000, pp. 1–10. ACM Press, New York (2000)
8. Shoemaker, G.: Supporting Private Information on Public Displays. In: Extended Abstracts on Human Factors in Computing Systems, CHI 2000, pp. 349–350. ACM Press, New York (2000)

9. Fraser, K., Rodden, T., O'Malley, C.: Trust, Privacy and Relationships in 'Pervasive Education': Families' Views on Homework and Technologies. In: LaMarca, A., Langheinrich, M., Truong, K.N. (eds.) Pervasive 2007. LNCS, vol. 4480, pp. 180–197. Springer, Heidelberg (2007)
10. Iachello, G., Smith, I., Consolvo, S., Chen, M., Abowd, G.: Developing Privacy Guidelines for Social Location Disclosure Applications and Services. In: Proceedings of the Symposium on Usable Privacy and Security, SOUPS 2005, pp. 65–76. ACM Press, New York (2005)
11. Palen, L., Dourish, P.: Unpacking "Privacy" for Networked World. In: Proceedings of the SIGCHI Conference on Human Factors in Computing Systems, CHI 2003, pp. 129–136. ACM Press, New York (2003)
12. Jones, S., O'Neill, E.: Feasibility of Structural network clustering for group-based privacy control in social networks. In: Proceedings of the Sixth Symposium on Usable Privacy and Security, SOUPS 2010. ACM Press, New York (2010)
13. Lumsden, J., MacKay, L.: How does personality affect trust in B2B e-commerce? In: Proceedings of the International Conference on Electronic Commerce, ICEC 2006, pp. 471–481. ACM Press, New York (2006)
14. Rukzio, E., Schmidt, A., Hussmann, H.: An Analysis of the Usage of Mobile Phones for Personalized Interactions with Ubiquitous Public Displays. In: Proceedings of the Workshop on Ubiquitous Display Environments (2004)
15. Congleton, B., Ackerman, M., Newman, M.: The ProD Framework for Proactive Displays. In: Proceedings of the ACM Symposium on User Interface Software and Technology, UIST 2008, pp. 221–231. ACM Press, New York (2008)
16. Huang, E., Mynatt, E.: Semi-Public Displays for Small, Co-located Groups. In: Proceedings of the SIGCHI Conference on Human Factors in Computing Systems, CHI 2003, pp. 49–56. ACM Press, New York (2003)
17. Holleis, P., Rukzio, E., Otto, F., Schmidt, A.: Privacy and Curiosity in Mobile Interactions with Public Displays. In: Adjunct Proceedings of the SIGCHI Conference on Human Factors in Computing Systems, CHI 2007 (2007)
18. Greaves, A., Rukzio, E.: View & Share: Co-Present Viewing and Sharing of Pictures using Personal Projectors. International Journal of Mobile Human Computer Interaction (2010)
19. Peltonen, P., Salovaara, A., Jacucci, G., Ilmonen, T., Ardito, C., Saarikko, P., Batra, V.: Extending large-scale event participation with user-created mobile media on a public display. In: Proceedings of International Conference on Mobile and Ubiquitous Multimedia, MUM 2007, pp. 131–138. ACM Press, New York (2007)
20. http://museummedia.nl/2011/04/museum-of-copenhagen-interactive-video-wall-housed-in-a-shipping-container/
21. Langheinrich, M.: A Privacy Awareness System for Ubiquitous Computing Environments. In: Borriello, G., Holmquist, L.E. (eds.) UbiComp 2002. LNCS, vol. 2498, pp. 237–245. Springer, Heidelberg (2002)
22. Kurdyukova, E. André, E., Leichtenstern, K.: Trust-centered Design for Multi-Display Applications. In: Proceedings of international conference on Advances in Mobile Computing & Multimedia, MoMM'10, pp. 415 – 420. ACM Press, New York (2010).
23. Kurdyukova, E.: Designing Trustworthy Adaptation on Public Displays. In: Konstan, J.A., Conejo, R., Marzo, J.L., Oliver, N. (eds.) UMAP 2011. LNCS, vol. 6787, pp. 442–445. Springer, Heidelberg (2011)

To Trust Upon That Someone Trusts Upon Yourself Influences of Trust and Other Factors on an Intranet Based Leader Strategy

Anette Löfström[1] and Mats Edenius[2]

[1] Uppsala University, ITC, Lägerhyddsvägen 2, Hus 1, 752 37, Uppsala, Sweden
anette.lofstrom@it.uu.se
[2] Uppsala University, Box 513, SE-751 20, Uppsala, Sweden
mats.edenius@im.uu.se

Abstract. In this paper we explore the theoretical concept of trust by putting it in to play empirically. Influences of trust on an Intranet based leader strategy in a big organisation are investigated. We also discuss other significant features that affect success or no success of such approach. The presentation builds on an interview study in one district of Stockholm, Norrmalm, and a survey committed in two districts of this city (Spånga-Tensta and Skärholmen). This paper is conducted in the field of Human Computer Interaction.

Keywords: Trust, Organisation, Human Computer Interaction.

1 Introduction

This paper builds on a three year long research project. Introductory we completed a pilot study in Norrmalm's district of Stockholm, Sweden. It resulted in 21 recorded and transcribed interviews plus 2 recorded and transcribed meeting lectures. While working with the interview results it appeared to us that feelings of trust, or no trust, affected respondents willingness to adapt an Intranet based leader strategy, called "the together modules". These modules consist of small videos, pictures and questionnaires. They aim at implementing a steering document, Vision 2030, in a consistent way to all 40 000 employees in the City of Stockholm [1]. For the reason that trust was revealed as a meaning carrying concept by the interviewees; we explicitly asked respondents how they viewed trust in the questionnaires. The survey was conducted in two districts of Stockholm, Spånga-Tensta and Skärholmen. It resulted in 118 responded questionnaires.

2 Trust in Prior Research

Trust has been defined in diverse ways. Fogg and Tseng, for example, write that: "Trust indicates a positive belief about the perceived reliability of, dependability of, and confidence in a person, object, or process [2]. Ben Schneiderman links trust to ancient traditions. He regards cultural phenomena like for example hand shaking as

D. Keyson et al. (Eds.): AmI 2011, LNCS 7040, pp. 238–242, 2011.
© Springer-Verlag Berlin Heidelberg 2011

elicitors of trust. However, in online activities of today new traditions are needed to enhance cooperative behaviors in electronic environments, he writes. Since users cannot make eye contact and judge intonations designers must create new social norms for professional services. He adds that consumer groups must be vigorous in monitoring and reporting deceptions and disreputable business practices [3]. Cyr et al combine discussions of trust with personalities along with cross cultural issues. They write that: "Disposition to trust is an enduring and personal characteristic that may also be embodied in culture" [4]. Three different perspectives are included in this view, and each one of them is immanent complex. These are trust, personal characteristics and culture.

Trust has also been enacted more or less as a tool among researchers in their ambition to classify and create knowledge [5]. It has also been about distinguishing between different kinds of trust, for example moral or strategic trust [3]. Friedman et al for example, handle trust by suggesting ten characteristics in online interactions. These are: Reliability and security of the technology, knowing what people online tend to do, misleading language and images, disagreements what counts as harm, informed consent, anonymity, accountability, saliency of cues in the online environment, insurance and finally performance history and reputation [6]. Furthermore; Pearl Pu and Li Chen investigate inherent benefits of using explanation interfaces for trust building. In their conclusions they claim that explanation interfaces have the greatest potential to build trust relationships that are inspired by competence with users [7].

It is shown that trust has been enacted and interpreted in different ways among researchers. Nevertheless; despite this richness of studies that explore meanings of trust; its influences on adaptation willingness concerning virtual/Intranet based leadership is unexplored. For that reason the aim of this short paper is: *to investigate and discuss influences of trust on willingness to adapt an Intranet based leader strategy.* Research questions are: *What features generate or hinder trust? Does trust influence respondent's adaptation willingness of the studied leader strategy? Are there any other influential factors? How can reflections on trust issues strengthen effects of Intranet based leader strategies in an organisation?*

The explicit asked questions of trust in the survey shows that among the respondents: 56 feel trust, 21 do not feel trust, 24 do not know and 17 did not answer the question. In the following section we describe generators and hinders of trust and how trust influences adaptation willingness among our respondents.

3   Generators and Hinders of Trust

Trust is: "To trust upon that someone trust upon yourself", a civil servant writes in a questionnaire. This quote suggests that trust must always involve at least two parts. Otherwise there is no counterpart to trust upon. It also proposes that feelings of trust reconstruct themselves when they are given to someone. This standpoint can be connected to leadership: "Trust for me is that leaders must trust the employees and vice versa" [8]. Hence; *trust in itself can be looked upon as a generator of trust.*

One comment from a leader is that she feels trust, but leaders must work harder to make Vision 2030 come true. So; trusted features must be connected to engagement among leaders. They also need to be visualised because: "It is excellent that good examples is visualised as it inspires everybody to get better" [11]. How the trusted message is implemented is important for creations of trust, or as a civil servant writes: "It is good to find a personal way to work with it, a way which employees find honest". Standardisation is mentioned as a generator of trust. A respondent writes that: "The method makes us move in the same direction to a higher grade" [8]. Another generator of trust is the mediated content. An employee writes that: "Since the content in Vision 2030 is good I think it leads to a good development". For one employee, feelings of trust are due to the (for her) obvious fact that: "of course Stockholm is everybody's city". So far we have presented explicit expressions of the feelings of trust. Now we will illustrate positive opinions that probably increase trust.

Willingness to develop is mentioned by some respondents. The very fact that leaders *want* to develop different aspects of the organisation might be a trust generating factor. Another factor that probably generates trust is that positive effects are mirrored in the close reality. One respondent writes that: "One of the most important [effects] of Vision 2030 in our activities is that we have increased our environmental thinking, for example by sorting garbage and by environmental friendly products" [8]. One leader appreciates the excitement it gives to be a part of the development. This standpoint suggests that involvement might be a generator of trust. If a person is given opportunity to take active part in the development process in an organisation it is likely that trust increase, since she/he has opportunity to influence features in the process.

An explicit mentioned hinder is that Vision 2030 is regarded as too abstract. Another comment is about (lack of) recourses, or as a respondent expresses it: "I can hope that we get the resources we need to do a good job for our families in the area but trust and resources is not the same thing" [8]. One employee writes that: "It is simply beautiful words articulated by higher civil servants who have no connection with me in my work" [8]. One employee writes that: "I do not think it makes any difference". These opinions are explicitly mentioned as hinders of trust. Features that probably diminish trust are experienced organisational distance between Vision 2030 and activities of respondent's daily routines. Distance in time is such an example, or as an employee writes: "It is too visionary and far away in time. I cannot find interest and motivation". Lack of anchoring is also mentioned as a problem by an employee, saying that: "It has not been rooted at our preschool yet. Visions are good but they need to be anchored". One employee simply describes this steering document as: "six feet under".

4 Influences of Trust on Adaptation Willingness

In this part we combine answers to the question: "Here I wonder about your willingness to work with the together modules with answers to the question: "Do you feel trust toward that Vision 2030 leads to something good"?

Among 118 respondents, 25 very much wanted to work with the together modules, 34 wanted to, 35 did not want to and 24 either did not know or did not answer the question. In each group, levels of trust were divided like this: Among respondents who very much want to work with the together modules 21 feel trust, 1 do not feel this trust and 3 do not know. Amid respondents who want to work with the together modules 25 feels trust, 2 do not feel trust and 7 do not know. Those who do not want to work with the together modules are divided like this: 9 feels trust, 11 do not feel trust and 15 do not know or no answer. Among respondents who did not answer the question of trust 1 feels trust, 6 do not feel trust and 17 do not know

These results show that among respondents who want to do this work a majority feels trust. On the other hand; among respondents who do *not* want to work with the together modules, the number of respondents who do not feel trust is in majority. *It is illustrated that willingness to adapt the explored Intranet based leader strategy is in parallel with levels of trust.* However; 9 respondents out of 35 who do not want to work with the together modules still feels trust towards it. Since this is a quite high number it is reasonable to believe that trust is an influential factor, but that adaptation willingness is influenced by other factors as well.

Time; or rather lack of time is a commonly mentioned factor that affects adaptation willingness among our respondents. "For me, it is only a matter of time and accessibility", a person writes [8]. Another time related issue is the 20 year long future view in Vision 2030. This is expressed with the following words by one respondent: "We live so intensively with solving close issues. The demands are high in the quality work so a vision 20 years from now does not feel obvious in our work, or rather it is difficult to make it obvious" [9]. Difficulties to see importance of the year 2030 in current time is common, which the following quote exemplify: "Improve *now* instead in 20 years from now" [8]. Another factor that probably affects adaptation willingness is technology issues. Many respondents describe technological obstacles, for example that: "Computer access and the long time it takes to log in, approximately 30-35 minutes make the work difficult" [9]. Computer access is also mentioned as a hinder. Some employees write that: "It does not work in practice, since we have one computer to be used by 22 persons" [8]. A more abstract influential factor is: "that is does not feel interesting" [8] to take part of this leader strategy. Instead the ordinary tasks it at focus. One employee writes that: "I work with humans. It takes lot of time to read mail, do documentation and so on. Who cares about them, the computers?"

In this paper we have illuminated influences of trust on adaptation willingness concerning an Intranet based leader strategy. Adding this we have revealed other factors of significance.

5   Conclusions

Our empirical results have illuminated that trust in itself is a generator of trust. If you are trusted, your own trust will increase. Engagement from leaders and visualisation of trusted features in the close reality generate trust. So do implementation methods and verifications of honesty. Standardisation and a common goal as well as a `good´ content generates trust. If a fact feels obvious it is regarded as trustworthy. Opportunity to be, and to feel, involved in a development process probably increases trust. One hinder of trust is about clarity. If the abstraction level is too high trust might decrease. This risk is also present when there is a lack of resources. Experienced distance between leaders/civil servants and employees as well as between a visionary future and present time hinders trust. Weak anchoring of the leader strategy at the local work place probably decreases trust.

It is shown that willingness to adapt an Intranet based leader strategy is parallel with levels of trust. However; since 9 respondents out of 35 who do not want to work with the explored leader strategy still feel trust towards it, we suggest that other factors than trust affect adaptation willingness among respondents.

Potential success, or nonsuccess, of an Intranet based leader strategy is due to factors like lack of time during the work day and difficulties to find meaning in current time of a vision 20 years from now. Technological issues like lack of computer access, slow computers and long log in times probably influence adaptation willingness.

Reflections on trust issues can strengthen effects of Intranet/web based leader strategies if it leads to clarifications of contents (decrease abstraction level), to decreases of experienced distance in the organisation, decreases of experienced lack of resources and to clearer anchoring's in local work contexts.

We have revealed generators and hinders of trust as well as other factors that might influence success or no success of an Intranet based leader strategy in an organisation. Methodologically we have interpreted positive views as generators and critical opinions as hinders. This way of analysing has coloured our results.

In the future each one of the presented conclusions might be operationalized as an analytical springboard in a number of studies; partly in order to validate or falsify their relevance in other contexts, and partly as grounds for new inquiries. For example one could ask: `if trust generates trust, how should leaders clarify their trust towards employees´, or: `how could leaders enhance apprehensions of time as a leader strategy´?

However; because potential success of an Intranet/web based leader strategy is influenced by more factors than trust, analytical methods must be chosen carefully in future studies. How, for example, should complexities be analysed as influential factors in future studies of trust?

References

1. http://www.stockholm.se/vision2030
2. Fogg, B.J., Tseng, H.: The elements of computer credibility. In: CHI 1999 Proceedings of the SIGCHI Conference on Human Factors in Computing Systems: the CHI is the Limit, pp. 80–87. ACM, New York (1999)
3. Schneiderman, B.: Designing trust into online experiences. Communications of the ACM 43(12), 57–59 (2000)
4. Cyr, D., Bonnani, C., Bowes, J., Ilsever, J.: Beyond trust: Website Design Preferences Across Cultures. Journal of Global Information Management 13(4), 24–52 (2005)
5. Corritore, C.L., Kracher, B., Wiedenbeck, S.: On-line trust: concepts, evolving themes, a model. International Journal of Human-Compter Studies 58(6), 737–758 (2003)
6. Friedman, B., Kahn Jr., P.H., Howe, D.C.: Trust online. Communications of the ACM 43(12), 34–40 (2000)
7. Pu, P., Chen, L.: Trust building with explanation interfaces. In: IUI 2006 Proceedings of the 11th International Conference on Intelligent User Interfaces, pp. 93–100. ACM, New York (2006)
8. Interview, employee
9. Interview, leader
10. Interview, civil servant

Free Play in Contemplative Ambient Intelligence

Douglas H. Fisher[1] and Mary Lou Maher[2]

[1] Vanderbilt University
douglas.h.fisher@Vanderbilt.Edu
[2] University of Maryland
mlmaher@umd.edu

Abstract. This paper introduces free play, a meaning making activity, as a desideratum of social and contemplative ambient intelligence. A contemplative AmI is not focused on easing routine human activities, but through free play and other mechanisms, will encourage humans to engage with each other and the AmI on thinking about and acting on societal issues over long time scales. These ideas are illustrated by the design of an interactive, intelligent art installation about adaptation to climate change. This approach to AmI extends the connotations of AmI along social, spatial, and temporal dimensions.

Keywords: Free play, collective intelligence, social intelligence.

1 Characteristics and Dimensions of Ambient Intelligence

"Digital environments that are sensitive and responsive to the presence of people" [1] is a Phillips' definition of ambient intelligence (AmI), which they further characterize as embedded, context aware, personalized, adaptive and anticipatory [1]. Moreover, many treatments of AmI further connote that embedding be 'invisible'; that 'personalization' be relative to an individual, rather than say a group; that 'anticipatory' actions be 'unobtrusive', seamlessly complementing human users.

Consider that 'calmness' and 'invisibility' are often forwarded as desiderata of pervasive technology generally [2], but the claim for invisibility is often limited to the technology's use phase. For example, sensors embedded in clothes may be invisible during the clothing's use, but this technology may be anything but invisible or calm if at the end of the clothing's life it is thrown into a garbage heap. To be truly invisible, the technology must be hidden and calm over its full lifetime, and over the lifetimes of many generations of the technology; otherwise it may in fact be harsh technology.

We seek to expand connotations of AmI in three spaces. Along *social* dimensions, AmI can be highly visible, proactively engaging participants in a larger community on critical social issues. Along *spatial* dimensions AmI is typically associated with appliances, rooms, homes, office buildings, and cities [2], but AmI can also extend to virtual worlds. Along *temporal* dimensions, latency of response can vary from instantaneous to the result of lengthy contemplation.

In most cases AmI is designed for an existing corpus of activities. However, a technology, even an 'invisible' one, can't help but to change human behavior. For example, environmentally 'smart buildings' may contribute to a glut of environmentally

D. Keyson et al. (Eds.): AmI 2011, LNCS 7040, pp. 243–247, 2011.

stupid people [3]; this is but one example of 'higher-order effects' on human behavior of pervasive computing [4], particularly when we look to larger social scales beyond the individual. Even simple changes to AmI designs may have important consequences on human participants; for example, an AmI that turns lights out after a period of no motion has possibly removed any concern with energy efficiency from the consciousness of the transitory occupant, whereas a more intelligent, context aware, and provocative AmI that turns lights out *as* (not after) the last person exits may actually raise human consciousness. In general, we can design AmI to be a proactive part of the social system, and design the activities with AmI in mind, all of which is consistent with activity theory and interaction design [5].

AmI that is 'calm' on small time and social scales may be negatively disruptive when viewed on larger scales. Inversely, it may be that AmI that is benevolent at large scales may be best achieved, at least in some cases, by technology that is visible and questioning, even provocative, at smaller scales.

In this landscape paper we introduce contemplative AmI, and given space constraints, we focus on but one design principle for social and contemplative AmI, the meaning making activity of *free play*. Section 2 introduces the free play paradigm and surveys some of its literature, with links to human-computer interaction (HCI) and experience design as appropriate. Section 3 illustrates free play in the context of an interactive art installation that is under development; this will be an AmI that engages in a kind of contemplative discourse with humans.

2   Free Play and Meaning Making

"Free Play is the creative activity of spontaneous free improvisation, by children, by artists, and people of all kinds." [6] The idea of free play has been described in contrast to competitive play: free play engages people to participate in playful activities that focus on meaning making and creativity, and competitive play engages people to participate in playful activities in which winning is the goal [7][8]. Free play has also been described as open-ended exploration, and an infinite game, played for the purpose of continuing the game [9]. Web 'surfing' is a good example of free play. While free play has open-ended aspects, this often includes goal driven activity in which the user selects and then pursues goals intermittent with exploration.

Gaver [10] has explored ludic engagement and ludic design of HCI-based interactive experiences, which favors design for pleasure, to include open-ended exploration, over function. In both HCI and AmI the emphasis has been to design for function, productivity and efficiency. Moving from function to pleasure has some precedents: environments and objects/toys can be designed specifically to encourage free play. For example, toys such as LEGO® provide objects that children can put together to create new objects or games. Virtual environments support free play by allowing people to build their own objects; the virtual world itself, appropriately instrumented, could be regarded as an AmI. In all of these contexts, goal-driven behavior frequently emerges, such as building an envisioned LEGO structure.

In contrast to toys and virtual worlds, we are beginning to see free play that invites participation, for example, in open-ended interactive art. The artist's intent behind the work is often to attract and initiate exploration by participants, that is, to invite free play, rather than to be invisible. Interactive art installations are often proactive AmIs, though they vary in the social, spatial and temporal extents that they engage humans. Goldberg [11] has created numerous robotic and internet-based art installations to provoke interaction and reaction. Goldberg's Robotic Tele-garden engaged thousands of people, many of them for years, in watering and seeding a common garden through tele-robotic controls available on a web page; on short time scales, individual actions like watering a plant are goal driven, but at large temporal scales the garden design 'dances' and the collective of gardeners can be viewed as engaged in free play. Merrick, Maher & Saunders [12] developed a curious information display that changed in response to its ability to attract the attention of the people in the room. Morrison, Miller & Viller [13] consider interactive art installations that provoke reflection through gesture.

HCI evaluation of interactive art is being explored in contrast to evaluating HCI for utility and efficiency [7]. Costello and Edmonds [14] focus on interactive art that stimulates playful behavior to achieve a deep level of engagement. They identify thirteen stages in a pleasure framework for interactive art. They used this framework to evaluate three installations, and the significant difference in experience occurred in the installation that has one open-ended play level. The participants reported that once they had "figured it out" they would move on. In contrast, we also want AmI to support infinite play, which engage people in exploration for long periods of time.

AmI that is designed to support, encourage and participate in free play can engage individual human thought and lead towards a collective intelligence with respect to social issues. Importantly, free play in AmI doesn't happen in a vacuum – the environment necessarily constrains the boundaries of exploration and play, facilitating constructivist human learning [15]. Finding the sweet spot between over and under constraint of exploration is a design challenge [10].

3   Encouraging Free Play on Ideas about Climate Change

To illustrate an AmI designed to provoke and affect our *thinking*, we describe a hypothetical knowledge-based, interactive art installation that promotes public dialog on climate change. Figure 1 shows the system (under development) in three layers: an artistic rendering (in front), a knowledge base (i.e., a concept or topic map), and an incoming content layer. Rather than being invisible, a large interactive display of the virtual world will be in a public location, giving both physical and virtual spatial extent to the AmI. When an observer approaches motion sensors will trigger activity, such as a meandering virtual tour. Beyond passive observation, the installation will encourage/support passersby' participation in several ways:

1. To explore the artistic rendering of climate change concepts by touching the screen and by moving an exhibit avatar through the virtual village; such exploration is one aspect of free play in this context.
2. To contribute commentary through online text and image messaging, which can be displayed in real-time; as well as substantive documents (e.g., class projects) offline to the installation's servers by email or Web interface (see below). These can all be the basis for asynchronous community dialogue.
3. User history informs AmI reactions, such as teleporting to a new location based on these histories with the exhibit; AmI reactions can be provocative, teleporting users to counterpoints of their own opinion, for example.

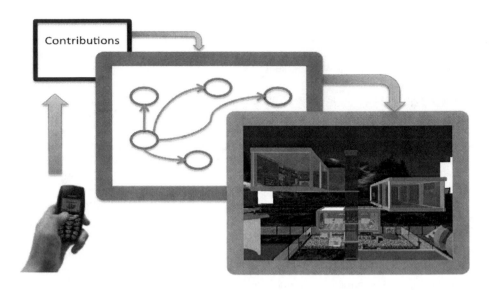

Fig. 1. An overview of an interactive art installation for engaging the public in creatively solving social issues (virtual world image is author and student created content in ActiveWorlds)

Machine learning methods of topic modeling and clustering (e.g., [16, 17]) will continually process commentary and substantive document contributions, deciding where they conceptually fit into the concept/topic map of the installation's middle layer, and changing those knowledge structures as a result. As the concept map evolves, so will the virtual village that organizes its content, since concepts will map onto virtual physical locations like different thematic rooms in a museum.

The virtual village and underlying concept map provide structure for exploring content and contributions of others. Individuals can "play" with ideas by touching, selecting, contributing and commenting. We intend "play" to extend well beyond fantasy and entertainment; we endeavor to create an environment for long-term socially responsive discourse. The proposed installation is similar in form and intent to Helsinki's CityWall [18], but there is no artificial intelligence in CityWall.

Context awareness is, in part, real-time, through motion sensors, touch and instant messaging identifiers of users. But context awareness also occurs in the realm of ideas (i.e., where do contributions fit relative to the concept map), and through these "thick" inputs, an awareness of where authors reside in this space. Response in this latter case takes the form of placing an author's work in a larger conceptual context, to be found later by the same authors and others; this response latency is not immediate, but based on machine-intelligent deliberation, all consistent with a desire for contemplation on issues of long-term planet sustainability. We anticipate that point/counterpoint works, as well as those exhibiting shared opinions, will be displayed side-by-side by the AI in the AmI, thereby provoking further human discourse over long time intervals.

4 Conclusion

AmI can be extended beyond supporting actions, to reinforce peoples' predispositions, to proactive environments in which free play and machine intelligence raise awareness in people and heighten their thinking. We suggest an extension of the original ambit of AmI, to include a highly visible social and collective intelligence, including machine learning that encourages thought and action on important societal issues. Generally, our *prescription* for contemplative AmI begs a more complete *description* as well – to characterize and distinguish current and future AmI along social, spatial and temporal dimensions.

References

1. Philips, http://www.research.philips.com/technologies/systsoftw/ami/background.html
2. Cook, D.J., Augusto, J.C., Jakkula, V.R.: Ambient intelligence: Technologies, applications, and opportunities. Pervasive and Mobile Computing 5(4), 277–298 (2009)
3. Peterson, J., Shunturov, V., Janda, K., Platt, G., Weinberger, K.: International Journal of Sustainability in Higher Education 8(1), 16–33 (2007)
4. Köhler, A., Erdmann, L.: Expected Environmental Impacts of Pervasive Computing. Human and Ecological Risk Assessment (10), 831–852 (2004)
5. Kaptelinin, V., Nardi, B.: Acting with Technology: Activity Theory and Interaction Design. MIT Press, Cambridge (2006)
6. Wikipedia, http://en.wikipedia.org/wiki/Free_Play:_Improvisation_in_Life_and_Art
7. Morrison, A., Mitchell, P., Brereton, M.: The lens of ludic engagement: Evaluating participation in interactive art installations. In: Proceedings of the 15th International Conference on Multimedia, pp. 509–512. ACM Press, Augsburg (2007)
8. Flemmert Jensen, A.: Time for Playful Learning? - A cross-cultural study of parental values and attitudes towards children's time for play. Lego learning institute, DK (2002)
9. Carse, J.P.: Finite and Infinite Games: A Vision of Life as Play and Possibility. Ballantine Books, New York (1987)
10. Gaver, B.: Designing for Homo Ludens. 13 Magazine (12) (June 2002)
11. Goldberg, http://goldberg.berkeley.edu/art/index.html
12. Merrick, K., Maher, M.-L., Saunders, R.: Achieving Adaptable Behaviour in Intelligent Rooms using Curious Supervised Learning Agents. In: CAADRIA 2008, Beyond Computer Aided Design, Chiang Mai, Thailand, pp. 185–192 (2008)
13. Morrison, A., Mitchell, P., Viller, S.: Evoking Gesture in Interactive Art. In: HCC 2008, Proceedings of the 3rd ACM International Workshop on Human-Centered Computing, pp. 11–18. ACM (2008)
14. Costello, B., Edmonds, E.: A study in play, pleasure and interaction design. In: DPPI 2007, Proceedings of the 2007 Designing Pleasurable Products and Interfaces (2007)
15. Brewer, J., Burke, M., Fenty, L., Patton, D., Post, J., Simpson, H.: Learning Methodology Reference Document, NAVSEA Performance Monitoring, Training and Assessment Program Office, PMS430 (1999), http://www.icte.org/T98_Library/LMREFDOC.PDF
16. Hoffman, M., Blei, D., Bach, F.: Online Learning for Latent Dirichlet Allocation. In: Proceedings of Neural Information Processing Systems (2010)
17. Fisher, D.: Iterative Optimization and Simplification of Hierarchical Clusterings. Journal of Artificial Intelligence Research 4, 147–179 (1996)
18. CityWall, http://citywall.org

A Student-Centric Intelligent Classroom

Margherita Antona[1], Asterios Leonidis[1], George Margetis[1], Maria Korozi[1],
Stavroula Ntoa[1], and Constantine Stephanidis[1,2]

[1] Foundation of Research and Technology – Hellas (FORTH)
Institute of Computer Science, Heraklion, GR-70013, Greece
cs@ics.forth.gr
[2] University of Crete, Department of Computer Science

Abstract. This paper discusses a line of research targeted to investigate and introduce innovative solutions for efficient learning in smart environments through integrating AmI technology in the learning process. Following a discussion of current approaches to technology integration in the classroom, the overall concept of the Student-Centric "Intelligent" Classroom and the related software are described. Potential future improvements are outlined.

Keywords: ambient classroom, student-centered design, natural interaction.

1 Introduction

The evolution of Information Technology (IT) for more than three decades has radically changed the way users interact with personal computers and has increased their expectations from technology. Towards this objective, novel concepts to provide content-rich invisible computing applications have been developed, eventually leading to the emergence of the Ambient Intelligence (AmI) paradigm and establishing it as a de facto key dimension of the Information Society, since many of the new generation industrial digital products and services are clearly shifted towards an overall intelligent computing environment.

As ICT is already permeating education in many ways, AmI has a significant potential to impact the domain of education by increasing students' access to information, enriching the learning environment, allowing students' active learning and collaboration, and enhancing their motivation to learn [1, 14].

2 Background Work

'Smart classroom' is used as an umbrella term meaning that classroom activities are enhanced with the use of pervasive and mobile computing, sensor networks, artificial intelligence, robotics, multimedia computing, middleware and agent-based software [3, 4]. Following the rationale of augmented technology in the educational environments, new means of interaction - such as interactive whiteboards, touch screens and tablet PCs - have gained popularity and have become a major tool in the educational process, allowing more natural interaction.

D. Keyson et al. (Eds.): AmI 2011, LNCS 7040, pp. 248–252, 2011.

Smart classrooms, for example, may support one or more of the following capabilities [1]: video and audio capturing in classroom, automatic environment adaptation according to the context of use, such as lowering the lights for a presentation [5], lecture capturing enhanced with the instructor's annotations, information sharing between class members, or even provide mentoring when a human mentor is not available [2]. Extensive progress was also made in the domain of Computer Assisted Collaborative Learning (CACL) in ambient environments where various collaborative platforms have been proposed based on either situation-aware interconnected handheld devices that facilitated content exchange [10], or on ubiquitous learning environments that promoted collaboration among the participants [11, 12]. Such features are considered to be fundamental for developing intelligent environments that augment the educational process. However, existing approaches still lack the dimension of environment intelligence and the adaptation to individual learner's needs.

3   A Student-Centric Ambient Classroom

In the technologically enhanced classroom, conventional classroom activities are enhanced with the use of pervasive and mobile computing through the replacement of the traditional artifacts (i.e., desks, boards) with technologically enhanced equivalents. In this context, the work presented in this paper encompasses the concept of student-centered learning, where focus shifts towards the individual needs and learning styles of the students, their responsibilities for educational activities are emphasized, and the teacher and the system act only as facilitators of learning. An intelligent classroom can be considered as a vehicle towards achieving these goals, as the presence of computer technology not only motivates learners' engagement in the various learning activities, but also establishes the ground for computer-assisted learning applications that benefit from context-awareness and deliver personalized content based on the needs of each individual student.

3.1   The "Intelligent" Classroom

The "Intelligent Classroom", as depicted in Figure 1, is a systematic approach to ambient intelligence in the classroom, suggesting a set of "intelligent" facilities to enhance the educational process. The key feature that differentiates the presented approach from similar work is the education-centric approach that has been adopted. Although the system mainly addresses activities which take place in the classroom, the software is general enough to support remote learning at home or elsewhere.

The architecture of the "Intelligent" Classroom is a stack-based model where the first layer, namely the middleware infrastructure, serves the interoperability needs of the classroom. The next two layers, namely the ClassMATE and the PUPIL frameworks, expose the core libraries and finally the remaining layer contains the educational applications. The ClassMATE [8] framework is an integrated architecture for pervasive computing environments that monitors the ambient environment and makes context-aware decisions in order to assist the student in conducting learning activities, and the teacher with administrative issues. The PUPIL system [7] delivers interaction workspaces customized to the needs of each "intelligent" artifact thus forming an educational-ecosystem across the entire class. The PUPIL framework offers a library of ready-to-use, adaptive, educational-oriented graphical components designed to optimally interact with the various educational applications of the ambient classroom on different devices.

Fig. 1. A glimpse of the "Intelligent" Classroom

3.2 The "Intelligent" Facilities

The presence of technology in the Ambient Classroom offers great potentials both from the interaction and the educational perspective. On the one hand, from the interaction perspective, it introduces innovative means of interaction with the various objects located in the classroom based on gestures performed either on the screen or on the physical objects themselves. On the other hand, from the educational perspective, computer technology paves the way for the augmentation of the learning process in a context-sensitive manner, by inferring information coming from the context of use (e.g., physical environment, current course, student preferences, etc.).

Inside the "intelligent classroom", every educational application can be launched, manipulated and migrated in any intelligent artifact. For that to be achieved a collection of adaptation-aware Classroom Window Managers (CWMs) was developed to host the various educational applications and automatically adapt them according to the needs of the targeted classroom artifact, thus ensuring their portability.

Considering that natural interaction in intelligent environments requires the elaboration of new concepts that extend beyond the current desktop and menu driven paradigms [13], new interaction techniques were introduced that seamlessly integrate the physical with the digital world, such as unobtrusive monitoring of the natural reading and writing process. The environment does not require any special writing device in order to monitor the student's gestures and handwriting, as it is able to perceive interaction with actual books and pens / pencils using computational vision [9] and through those modules gather information such as the page identification, the exact stylus' position on that page, its state and any recognized gestures.

The incorporation of "intelligent" technologies in the classroom does not automatically improve the learning process by itself. On top of the technological layer, a backbone infrastructure was built to exploit contextual awareness in order to augment the learning process to the benefit of the learners. The "intelligent" classroom features a sophisticated, unobtrusive, profiling mechanism that facilitates the classroom's students behavior monitoring and assessment, in order to provide user related data to the classroom's services and applications. The learners' record repository keeps track of every individual student's learning status from which statistics are produced for the teacher to drive potential adjustments to improve the learning curve. The latter is achieved by combining runtime information captured by monitoring student's interaction with semantic information coming from the context of use (e.g., a particular learning object). Such a combination enables, besides progress tracking, inference of potential correlations within various domains (e.g., the English course might provide information about the Physics course and vice versa).

Besides monitoring, user profile is extensively used to achieve personalized content delivery that addresses individual student's learning needs. The "intelligent classroom" incorporates an educational content classification and archiving mechanism where the necessary content-related rationale to data mining procedures are provided by enhancing the learning material with educational metadata based on IEEE Learning Object Metadata (LOM). Finally, taking into consideration that collaborative learning offers both a better learning experience and knowledge gain [6], the environment promotes collaboration by permitting the intelligent and efficient manipulation of such activities. Among others, the collaboration facility can suggest potential candidates that will form a coherent and motivated group of learners, monitor and guide the collaborative activities and finally assess the success of the applied collaborative strategy.

3.3 Educational Applications

On top of the "intelligent" facilities various applications were implemented and evaluated as a proof of concept. The "Augmented ClassBook" augments the physical book by integrating handwriting and supporting the learning process through context – aware content sensitive assistance. Elements of interest within a page are selectable and relevant content is dynamically gathered and displayed. Likewise, the "Exercise Assistant" enables students to solve an exercise electronically whilst context-sensitive help is available to assist them to accomplish their tasks. To develop critical thinking skills, help is presented gradually and the auxiliary "Multimedia Viewer" can also display relevant multimedia content to facilitate comprehension.

4 Conclusions and Future Work

This paper briefly summarizes the work conducted for the AmI classroom environment in the context of the ICS-FORTH AmI Programme. The results of the conducted studies confirmed that AmI technologies have the potential to enhance the classroom learning experience. Ongoing work aims to fully support the initial concept. Applications targeted to the teacher are currently under elaboration, while mobile devices are considered to be excellent candidates for incorporation in the classroom. Finally, following full implementation, a full scale evaluation experiment is being planned, aiming not only to assess the usability of the proposed environment, but its actual impact in the educational process as well.

Acknowledgements. This work is supported by the FORTH-ICS internal RTD Programme 'Ambient Intelligence and Smart Environments'.

References

1. Augusto, J.C.: Ambient Intelligence: Opportunities and Consequences of its Use in Smart Classrooms, vol. 8(2) (2009)
2. Augusto, J.C., et al.: Scoping the Potential for Anytime-Anywhere Support Through Virtual Mentors, vol. 9(4), pp. 74–85 (2010)
3. Cook, D.J., Augusto, J.C., Jakkula, V.R.: Ambient intelligence: Technologies, applications, and opportunities. Pervasive and Mobile Computing 5(4), 277–298 (2009)
4. Cook, D.J., Das, S.K.: How smart are our environments? An updated look at the state of the art. Journal of Pervasive and Mobile Computing 3(2), 53–73 (2007)
5. Cooperstock, J.: Classroom of the Future: Enhancing Education through Augmented Reality. In: Proc. Conf. Human-Computer Interaction (HCI Int'l. 2001), pp. 688–692. Lawrence Erlbaum Assoc., Mahwah (2001)
6. Feyzioglu, B., Akcay, H., Sahin-Pekmez, E.: Comparison of computer assisted cooperative, competitive and individualistic learning: An example of Turkey. In: Proceedings of Congrès International d'Actualité de la Recherche en Education et en Formation (2007)
7. Korozi, M.: PUPIL: pervasive UI development for the ambient classroom, Master's thesis (2010), available from e-Locus at:
   `http://elocus.lib.uoc.gr/dlib/a/e/2/metadata-dlib-81a07682706c2163d8f582245fd9edfd_1288689489.tkl`
8. Leonidis, A., Margetis, G., Antona, M., Stephanidis, C.: ClassMATE: Enabling Ambient Intelligence in the Classroom. World Academy of Science, Engineering and Technology (66), 594–598 (2010), `http://www.waset.org/journals/waset/v66/v66-96.pdf` (retrieved from February 16, 2011)
9. Margetis, G., et al.: A smart environment for augmented learning through physical books. In: Proceedings of the IEEE International Conference on Multimedia and Expo (2011)
10. Milrad, M., Perez, J., Hoppe, U.: C-notes: designing a mobile and wireless application to support collaborative knowledge building. In: Proceedings of IEEE International Workshop on Wireless and Mobile Technologies in Education 2002, pp. 117–120. IEEE Computer Society (2002)
11. Yau, S.S., et al.: Smart Classroom: Enhancing Collaborative Learning Using Pervasive Computing Technology, pp. 1–9 (2003)
12. Yang, S.J.H.: Context Aware Ubiquitous Learning Environments for Peer-to-Peer Collaborative Learning. Educational Technology & Society 9(1), 188–201 (2006)
13. Stephanidis, C.: Human Factors in Ambient Intelligence Environments. In: Salvendy, G. (ed.) Handbook of Human Factors and Ergonomics, 4th edn. John Wiley and Sons, USA (to appear, 2012)
14. Xu, P., Han, G., Li, W., Wu, Z., Zhou, M.: Towards Intelligent Interaction in Classroom. In: Stephanidis, C. (ed.) UAHCI 2009. LNCS, vol. 5616, pp. 150–156. Springer, Heidelberg (2009)

Sensing, Actuation Triggering and Decision Making for Service Robots Deployed in Smart Homes

Mortaza S. Bargh[1], Melvin Isken[2], Dietwig Lowet[3], Niels Snoeck[1],
Benjamin Hebgen[4], and Henk Eertink[1]

[1] Novay (NL)
[2] FASS (Gr.)
[3] Philips Research (NL)
[4] NEC Eurolabs (Gr.)
{1name.2name}@{novay.nl,offis.de,philips.com,neclab.eu}

Abstract. The Florence project develops a robot for elderly that provides multiple Ambient Assisted Living (AAL) and Lifestyle services with a consistent user-interface. The project success is measured by the acceptance of these services by the user group. Enabling such service robotics in (smart) homes requires a robust and flexible platform to collect, enhance and distribute sensory information; and to manipulate the actuators in the environment. A key characteristic of such an environment is that sensors and actuators are not always available, are distributed, and are mobile (due to e.g. the robot and phone mobility). This dynamicity requires a loose coupling between services and sensors/actuators. The paper describes the design principles and high level architecture of the Florence platform that hides the distribution, availability and mobility aspects from the services, and sketches some challenges that lie ahead.

1 Introduction

Recent demographical changes increase the demand for both professional and volunteer care in our society. The cost of care increases while the social inclusion of elderly decreases steadily. Enabling elderly to live independently as long as possible will significantly reduce the cost of care for our aging society. The Florence project is an EU FP7 project that uses robot technology to provide Ambient Assisted Living (AAL) services and to increase the level of independence of elderly. Provisioning of these services must be cost-effective, preserve the quality of life, increase the safety of elderly, and support the interaction among family-members/care-givers.

Robots are intelligent platforms that can move autonomously to interact with users, sense the environment, or perform actions. Both robots and AAL services, however, suffer from low acceptance by elderly [1]. Thus, the main challenges that the Florence project faces are cost effectiveness and user acceptance of AAL services and robots.

A key enabler of the Florence system is a platform component that makes it possible to use the sensors and actuators of the robot and those embedded in the environment (in the home, personal mobile devices, etc) by Florence-compliant services. The set of sensors and actuators available is dynamic and distributed at any time due to robot mobility, capabilities of the home infrastructure, and the load on

D. Keyson et al. (Eds.): AmI 2011, LNCS 7040, pp. 253–257, 2011.
© Springer-Verlag Berlin Heidelberg 2011

resources. The Florence platform provides a loose and location-transparent coupling between services and sensors/actuators whereby services do not need be configured with interfaces of specific sensors/actuators. This position paper describes our design principles, the high level architecture of the Florence platform, and the challenges to be addressed in upcoming implementation phases.

2   Background and Objectives

To enhance user acceptance, the Florence project offers social and fun services next to AAL services in order to persuade users to adopt the Florence robot early on, way in advance of needing AAL services. Early adoption of the Florence robot, i.e. when users are healthy, decreases the technology adoption barrier because users perceive robots as lifestyle devices and become proud of having one. The Florence services envisioned for the initial deployment of the system are: Fall Handling (to inform caregivers if elderly fall), Keep in touch (to enable social interactions with friends and family members), Lifestyle Improvement (to coach elderly about nutrition and physical activeness), Data Logging (to collect and analyse health related data), Advanced Home Interface (to enable the remote control of home appliances and actuators), Agenda Reminder (to remind elderly of agenda events, including medication reminders) and Collaborative Gaming (to promote social interactions via gaming). This basic set of services was determined by user studies, but it is extendable with new services. Florence will use consistent interaction mechanisms to reduce learning curves, increase usability, and improve the robot adoption.

To be cost effective, the Florence project uses an off-the-shelf robot [2] to which a touch screen is added. This Florence robot must work acceptably in homes with limited sensor and actuator capabilities and be able to integrate seamlessly with a home infrastructure that possesses enhanced capabilities. A key enabler of the system is a distributed software platform that federates sensors and actuators embedded in the environment with multiple Florence services in a dynamic setting, enhances the semantics and quality (e.g., accuracy, precision) of raw sensory information gathered, and coordinates among multiple services to share resources in a user acceptable way. This position paper covers design and specification of this Florence platform.

3   Guiding Design Principles

The setting in which the Florence system operates is dynamic. Sensors and actuators appear and disappear due to robot mobility and availability (e.g. when the robot is in the docking station charging its battery one cannot rely on the robot's mobility to monitor remote locations anymore). On another scale, the sensors and actuators in home infrastructure may be dynamic in the sense that they cannot be predefined during the design phase. Nevertheless, there might be a requirement on minimum set of home devices. The Florence system must adapt its service quality gracefully when the robot or home infra is (partly) unavailable or the robot is deployed in a new home.

Supporting *graceful performance degradation* requires that application services are able to adapt to these changes in an acceptable way for elderly and there exists an abstraction layer that hides the infrastructural changes from the applications as much as possible. This paper focuses on the latter requirement and describes the so-called Sensing Actuation Decision-making Enabling (SADE) service to realise the Florence abstraction layer. The SADE service is delivered by a *software platform* component that enables a *loose coupling* of application components with sensors/actuators. To this end, we have opted for the SOA (Service Oriented Architecture) paradigm, where applications should use device-discovery services and device independent semantics for accessing sensing and actuation services. We specifically will use QoC (Quality of Context) attributes [3] for describing the sensing services. For example, instead of asking for user location obtained from a specific ultrasonic sensor, the application asks the platform for user location with one meter accuracy. Similarly, we will describe actuating actions at a high abstraction level. For example, instead of asking for turning the light on at a specific room after somehow knowing in which room the user is, the application will ask the platform for turning the light on wherever the user is (i.e., without the application directly knowing the user location).

The SADE service continuously monitors the environment, makes a high-level task plan (i.e., makes decisions), and executes the plan by actuators. For complex systems as robots, decision making is a distributed functionality that takes place at different levels of the system. We distinguish between application specific decisions that are concerned with intra-application behaviours and generic decisions that are concerned with inter-application behaviours. Generic decisions affect shared resources like the GUI screen, robot location, and robot camera direction. Application specific decision making is up to application developers and out of scope of this paper. We consider planning of generic decisions as responsibility of the platform component that must be done delicately to enhance user acceptance. Competing for processing or user-interface resources is common for multiple services running concurrently on PCs. Competing for robot location or robot camera direction is quite unique for robotics, specially for the Florence setting that deals with multiple services concurrently.

4   High Level Architecture

Figure1 illustrates a high level functional architecture of the Florence SADE service. SADE can be decomposed into three components: Decision Making (DM), Context Management Framework (CMF), and Actuator Management Framework (AMF). The CMF manages all contextual information gathered by various sensors on the robot, in the home, on the mobile phone of the user, or on a remote system outside of the Florence home. The CMF coordinates *Sensing* components that collect, wrap and pre-process raw sensory data in a form usable for other system components. The *Sensor Access* component dynamically discovers the available sensors or context-sources and binds them with context consumers (proxy based, using publish-subscribe or request-reply modes). It also supports a *Reasoning* component that enhances the semantics and quality of the collected sensory information and wraps it into a format usable within SADE. User Localisation, Activity Detection, and Health Status Detection are three main sub-components of Reasoning that are derived from the requirements of the basic Florence services. For these components we envision to use Bayesian based reasoning. The CMF to be used in Florence is OSGi based, and originated from the EU Magnet Beyond project [4]. The CMF is designed as a distributed system that consists of one or more *Clusters*, each one located on the robot, home server, etc. Within a CMF Cluster, in turn, there is one or more so-called *Agents* which provide for local applications access to the context information of the whole CMF Cluster.

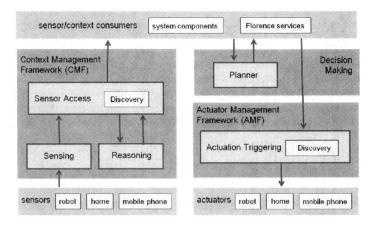

Fig. 1. High-level architecture of the Florence platform

The Florence AMF translates complex actuation tasks into elementary actuation tasks that can be executed by the actuators on the robot, home, etc. For example, a complex actuation task can be to prepare the room for doing physical exercises. The AMF will then make sure that the TV and radio are turned off, the curtains are closed, the lights are turned on, the robot is instructed to move to the appropriate position, etc. The AMF that will be developed in Florence is based on the concepts from the EU SENSEI project [5]. The AMF is distributed and uses OSGi tools to discover new actuators. Applications may use an API to request actuation tasks. In Florence we will have two types of actuation tasks: basic ones which are handled by individual actuators directly connected to the AMF (e.g., move the robot to the living room), and complex ones which are handled by composing some basic actuation tasks based on contextual information (e.g., prepare the room for doing physical exercises). This CMF-AMF architecture is similar to PERSONA's architecture described in [6].

The Florence DM component is responsible for the decision making process by decomposing high level goals into executable tasks and by prioritising and coordinating these tasks. For example, 'suggest activity X to the user' is a high level task that is decomposed to 'find the user location', 'check if the user is not busy at the moment', 'move the robot towards the user', and finally 'notify the user about the suggestion using the best available user interface'. We assume that every (application) service resolves its own internal scheduling, planning and conflicts. However, we must also ensure that application services can be developed independently. For that purpose we introduce a *Planner* component that determines the schedule of the Florence system/robot. It will prioritise competing services in a user acceptable way by taking into account the expected schedule of the user or the urgency of a particular request (e.g., an alarm or an incoming video call may be more urgent than other services). The Planner and application services will communicate via sockets and XML-RPC. With respect to the planning algorithm, we strive for a planning that is natural, intuitive and transparent for the user. The Planner in our first implementation will be "hand-coded" to handle the initial, predefined set of services. In next steps we will investigate whether and when use of Markov Decision Processes (MDPs) and Partially Observable MDPs (POMDPs) can provide more user acceptable results.

5 Conclusion and Future Work

The requirements of the Florence system and services guided us to make an initial design of a distributed platform component for sensing, actuation triggering and decision making. The platform offers two OSGi based frameworks for sensing and actuation triggering. As the set of embedded devices is dynamic, this approach enables a loose coupling of the Florence services and the devices embedded in the environment by adopting the service discovery principle of the SOA and relying on QoC semantics to bind applications with sensors or actuators. This approach, moreover, supports graceful performance degradation of applications and eases the job of application developers. For decision making we envisioned a central Planner to determine the schedule of competing Florence services in a user acceptable way.

The architecture described in this paper serves as the initial design of the Florence platform component. Currently we are implementing the architecture outlined here by extending an existing CMF with a robot side Agent and adapting an existing AMF to the robotic setting of the Florence project. A key challenge here is to make a robust system that operates satisfactorily in a setting where the resources appear and disappear dynamically. A silent characteristic of this work is to distribute the intelligence on the robot or on the home infrastructure such that the whole system works appropriately if the robot or other resources are unavailable momentarily.

Shortly, the first user trials will start and will be evaluated using the living labs methodologies. We will rigorously examine our design principles with respect to the user acceptance criterion. This examination may lead to new requirements for planning, reasoning intelligence/learning, and definition of complex actuations.

References

1. Vastenburg, M., et al.: Designing acceptable assisted living services for elderly users. In: European Conf. on Ambient Intelligence, Nürnberg, Germany, November 19-22 (2008)
2. Pekee II robot, Wany robotics, http://www.wanyrobotics.com/store/
3. Sheikh, K., Wegdam, M., van Sinderen, M.: Quality-of-Context and its use for Protecting Privacy in Context Aware Systems. Journal of Software 3(3), 83–93 (2008)
4. Magnet Beyond, http://magnet.aau.dk (retrieved on June 10, 2011)
5. Sensei project, http://www.sensei-project.eu (retrieved on June 10, 2011)
6. Tazari, M.-R., et al.: The PERSONA Service Platform for AAL Spaces. In: Handbook of Ambient Intelligence and Smart Environments, p. 1171. Springer, Heidelberg (2010)

Fusion of Radio and Video Localization for People Tracking

Massimiliano Dibitonto[1,2], Antonio Buonaiuto[1], Gian Luca Marcialis[1],
Daniele Muntoni[3], Carlo Maria Medaglia[2], and Fabio Roli[1]

[1] University of Cagliari, Dept. of Electrical and Electronic Engineering
{massimiliano.dibitonto,antonio.buonaiuto,
marcialis,roli}@diee.unica.it
[2] C.A.T.T.I.D. Sapienza University of Rome, Italy
carlomaria.medaglia@uniroma1.it
[3] Ambient Intelligence Laboratory – Sardegna Ricerche – Pula, Italy
muntoni@sardegnaricerche.it

Abstract. In this paper we introduce a hybrid people tracking system based on the combined use of RFID UWB technology and computer vision techniques. The proposed system takes advantage of the different characteristics of the vision and wireless subsystems to achieve better accuracy and reliability for people tracking. Moreover data gained from the subsystems can be used for a more complex context capture system and can be seen as an enabler of a number of application from video-surveillance to Ambient Intelligence scenarios. Different scenarios have been tested to assess the feasibility and performance of the system. Experimental results demonstrate advantages in people tracking tasks encouraging further researches.

1 Introduction

People identification and tracking, used traditionally for video-surveillance applications or human behaviour analysis, has become an enabler for Ambient Intelligence applications [1]. Many different approaches have been studied using various technologies and methods. Among them computer vision techniques and wireless localization systems can be successfully used to track and identify people. These two systems can offer a good accuracy but in real world scenario their performances can be affected by several environmental factors. Moreover the two systems strengths and weaknesses appear to be complementary and can be used to build hybrid system able to overcome performances of the single systems. To the best of our knowledge, no work presented so far an integrated system made up of a UWB-RFID-based remote localization system and a computer vision system. Previous works have investigated fusion strategies between RFID (non UWB) and computer vision technologies. In [2, 3] authors investigate the possibility to improve performances of object and people recognition systems. Authors bind the unique ID of the RFID to object/people data to store information related to color, shape or other parameters. This information is used by a computer-vision system to achieve a better

D. Keyson et al. (Eds.): AmI 2011, LNCS 7040, pp. 258–263, 2011.

accuracy in recognizing objects/people. Regarding to localization and tracking issues in [4], authors propose the use of RFID HF, Wi-Fi and visual tracking to locate people in a room. Data collected from each system are compared to define an area where a person is supposed to be. However it is not clear how ambiguous cases are solved (i.e. multiple people detection).

The main contribution of this work is the proposal of a hybrid system able to exploit data gained from an RFID UWB system and a computer-vision system in order to achieve a more reliable and robust tracking service and a more accurate context understanding. The system architecture and its characteristics make it an enabler for more complex Ambient Intelligence applications.

2 The Proposed System

The proposed system integrates a UWB-RFID-based remote localization system and a computer vision system. Current version of our system has been conceived for indoor applications.

The main motivation of such an integration is due to two elements: (1) the high level of precision given by the UWB-RFID system, and also the possibility to save ancillary information as the highness of the TAG and tracking people with TAG reliably; (2) the possibility to exploit advanced computer vision and pattern recognition tools for tracking people and also extracting important information as biometrics (faces) and other ancillary information.

2.1 High-Level View

In the following, we hypothesise that objects of interest in the scene are people, without loss of generality. Fig.1 shows the block diagram of the proposed system.

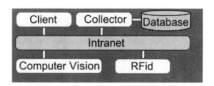

Fig. 1. Architecture of the proposed system

Two independent information sources about objects trajectories are collected by an intranet to a "collector", which is in charge of correlating such information. The collector tries to do a matching between the trajectory given by RFID system and the one given by the computer vision system. Since several people may occur in the scene, someone with an appropriate RFID-TAG and someone without it, the main problem is to associate correctly several pairs of trajectories. The computer vision system tracks people by focusing on embodied characteristic (blobs), but it is not able to identify person. The wireless system instead tracks people with an external object (a tag) but it provides a strong identification due to the unique ID of the tag. In that case, the two systems operate in a cooperative manner just comparing location data and in a collaborative way as the wireless system can provide accurate identification data. The collector uses a simplified version of the cross-tracking algorithm suggested in [5] to discriminate ambiguous cases. In fact computer vision system will always detect objects in the controlled area, whilst RFID system is able to detect objects if they have TAG. Moreover the areas controlled by the two systems may not perfectly overlap. Given the position of an incoming object, the algorithm predicts a new 2-D position hypothesis for every other know object in the system (assuming a constant velocity and a linear trajectory). The matching score calculated is proportional to the joint probability of the two positions (observation and object hypothesis).

Performance of this process has been evaluated though experimental activity explained in Section 4.

Once trajectories are correctly correlated, processed information is sent to a certain client (user), as an administrator system or an external video-surveillance operator. Processing may be related to detect some abnormal behaviour of detected people, for example related to its speed or some other ancillary biometrics (face), which are compared with other ones stored in the system database. Several actions and options may be performed, as sending warning messages related to the detect anomaly.

2.2 Low-Level View

In this Section, we briefly describe RFID- and computer vision-based systems, and the collector, which is in charge to fuse such information.

The RFID component has the task of propagating the events of both spatial and geometric localization from the system RTLS (Real-Time Location System) to the collector. The module uses the standard SOAP serialization of objects to communicate with the other end. To obtain real-time performances, SOAP messages are sent using UDP. The platform is based on UWB technology to determine the location of tags within range of the sensors. An Ubisense UWB "Research Package" [6] system was used during the present work. The system is composed by two elements: tags and sensors. Tags are active antennas that can communicate with sensors and to adjust power consumption using their own motion sensors and accelerometers. Sensors are antennas that receive and manage signals sent by the tags, but they have the capability of sending signals to them to manage the update rate or other features, including the power of LEDs on the tag. The communication technology involves the use of two carriers: one around 2.4 GHz as a channel for control and telemetry, the other from 6 to 8 GHz. It can exploit both TDoA (Time Difference of Arrival) and AoA (Angle of Arrival) information, as each antenna is actually made up of an array of antennas. The maximum updating frequency of each sensor is 135Hz, which allows receiving continuous position information of a tag every 7.4 ms. Obtained positions are filtered, in order to avoid outliers, and sent to the collector.

The computer vision system exploits frames coming from a fixed video camera. An object tracker detects people by assigning an ID to each blob (which is supposed to be a human being). The scene of interest is submitted to calibration. This allows an appropriate geometric transformation matrix projects the location of the blob to the correspondent 2D map of the scene. An additional face detection algorithm extracts frontal face from the blob. In order to avoid useless or noisy information, a quality evaluation algorithm for each extracted face is applied. Blob position and biometric information are finally sent to the collector.

3   Experimental Results

Test campaign have been undertaken to check the feasibility of automatic association of trajectories observed by the two subsystems and the reliability of high level information gained. This capability can be considered an essential function to build complex systems like video-surveillance o ambient intelligence applications. In this phase the locating accuracy is not evaluated, it will be subject of further investigations. Tests have been run inside the Ambient Intelligence Laboratory at Sardegna Ricerche (Sardinia, Italy), where the system is currently under development.

To perform tests 4 UWB sensors have been placed in the four corners of the room and a camera (640x480@30fps) was mounted in one corner. As seen in fig[2a] there is not a perfect matching between areas covered by the two subsystems. In this way is underlined how the two subsystems could be complementary.

A preliminary test phase focused in evaluating the static bias of the two subsystems. The test was performed asking to a user to walk in a given trajectory stopping for 10 seconds in given points. Results pointed out a scattered behaviour of the UWB subsystem, with a maximum accuracy of 15 cm. The CV subsystem presents an higher accuracy and a lower variance even if it can be affected by ambient conditions as environmental lights but also characteristic of the camera and of the Field of View (FoV). In fact the CV subsystem's accuracy decrease when the tracked person approaches the border of the image. Moreover the test was useful to evaluate the different behaviour of the UWB system in relation to the different radio coverage of the area.

After this we tested two different situations: (1) a person wearing a tag; (2) two person, one with the tag and one without it. As in the first case both systems can be used to track the person, in the second case it is evident how the vision system can act as a backup of the wireless system ensuring the overall system reliability.

In the first case results pointed out that the two trajectories detected have an average distance of 120 cm with a standard deviation of 89 cm. Different threshold have been set to check the positive matching rate. At 50 cm it is 16%, at 80 cm it is 46%, at 150 cm it is 70% and at 180 cm it is 80%. This behaviour is consequence of the bias and of the different behaviour of the two subsystems, however, considering the dimension of a human body, this accuracy can be considered acceptable for people tracking.

The second case presents another level of complexity. As described in 2.1 when multiple people are in the controlled area, the collector has to disambiguate data, by correctly associating the blob with the related TAG trajectory. Fig. 2b reports an example of two persons with tag, detected by RFID and computer vision system correlated each other by the collector. The detected trajectory of the UWB tag appears irregular, as a consequence of the bias of the system.

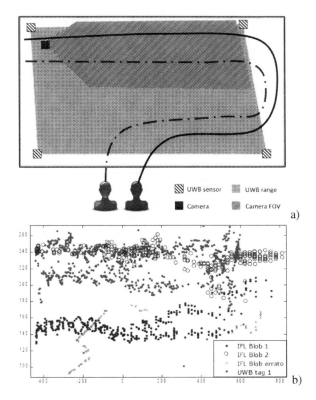

Fig. 2. The controlled area (a) and an example of trajectories (b) correlated by fusing RFID and computer vision systems information

The distance between the two persons during the experiment was about 100 cm. The association between tag-person was based upon a proximity criterion. The implemented classifier showed a false positive matching rate around 60, even if the equal error rate (EER) is at 147 cm thus underlying a non-optimal accuracy in matching trajectories. In general results highlight a non-optimal performance of the system, however they show the ability of the system to operate a matching at a "coarse" level. This is related mainly to the bias of the two subsystems and to the use of a punctual association algorithm. It can be overcome operating on the physical setting of the experiment via an improvement, a fine-tuning calibration of the two subsystems and a more efficient matching algorithm.

4   Conclusions

In this paper, we presented an integrated RFID-UWB system conceived for ambient intelligence applications where indoor areas must be under control of a human supervisor. The system is able to signal to an external operator several anomalies thanks to the fusion of information sent by two independent sources, namely, a UWB-RFID localization module and a computer vision module. Both subsystems are based on well-founded technology, even if people tracking are still lack of effectiveness under difficult video-surveillance scenarios, when multiple people can pass through the scene and cross each other. The main novelty of our system is in the joint use of UWB-RFID and computer vision technologies. In particular, thanks to the RFID tag, we can identify with high accuracy, and univocally, people that cross the scene. As the tag is associated to a certain blob in the scene: this is due to the possibility further confirmation is given by the computer vision system, since it may be able to extract several ancillary information as the users faces or information revealing their behaviour as their speed and the "pattern" related to their trajectory. In future developments the effectiveness of the system could be improved working on filtering and matching algorithms, as probabilistic models, especially to discriminate ambiguous cases. Further test campaigns will be undertaken evaluating also the locating accuracy compared to a ground truth system. In an Ambient Intelligence scenario the system could also be improved through the connection with other sensors, as a depth sensor, to have a better understanding of the ambient observed.

Acknowledgements. This work has been partially supported by Regione Autonoma della Sardegna, project no. CRP2-442 (Legge Regionale n.7 per la Promozione della Ricerca Scientifica).

References

1. Snidaro, L., Micheloni, C., Chiavedale, C.: Video security for ambient intelligence. IEEE Trans. on Systems. Man and Cybernetics, Part A: Systems and Humans 35(1), 133–144 (2005)
2. Jia, S., Sheng, J., Chugo, D., Takase, K.: Human recognition using RFID technology and stereo vision. In: IEEE Int. Conf. on ROBIO 2007, December 15-18, pp. 1488–1493 (2007)
3. Cerrada, C., Salamanca, S., Perez, E., Cerrada, J.A., Abad, I.: Fusion of 3D Vision Techniques and RFID Technology for Object Recognition in Complex Scenes. In: IEEE Int. Symp. on Intelligent Signal Processing, WISP 2007, October 3-5, pp. 1–6 (2007)
4. Matthieu, A., Crowley, J.L., Devin, V., Privat, G.: Localisation intra-bâtiment multi-technologies: RFID, Wi-Fi, vision. In: Ubimob 2005, Grenoble, France, pp. 29–35 (2005)
5. Collins, R.T., Lipton, A.J., Fujiyoshi, H., Kanade, T.: Algorithms for cooperative multisensory surveillance. Proc. of IEEE 89(10), 1456–1477 (2001)
6. Ubisense Research Package,
   http://www.ubisense.net/en/resources/factsheets/ubisense-research-package.html (last visit August 2011)

Evaluation of AAL Platforms According to Architecture-Based Quality Attributes

Pablo Oliveira Antonino[1], Daniel Schneider[1],
Cristian Hofmann[2], and Elisa Yumi Nakagawa[3]

[1] Fraunhofer IESE, Fraunhofer-Platz 1, 67663 Kaiserslautern, Germany
{pablo.antonino,daniel.schneider}@iese.fraunhofer.de
[2] Fraunhofer IGD, Fraunhoferstr. 5, 64283 Darmstadt, Germany
cristian.hofmann@igd.fraunhofer.de
[3] Dept. of Computer Systems, University of São Paulo, São Carlos, SP, Brazil
elisa@icmc.usp.br

Abstract. In the Ambient Assisted Living (AAL) domain, specific systems have been developed and applied to enable people with specific needs, such as elderly or disabled people, to live longer independently in their familiar residential environments. In order to support the development of such systems, a range of AAL platforms have been developed in recent years. However, there are considerable differences among these AAL platforms, particularly with respect to the treatment of important non-functional properties. This makes the selection of a suitable platform for a given AAL project very difficult. In order to support developers in this difficult task, we present an evaluation of relevant AAL platforms based on a selection of quality attributes that are important for AAL systems.

Keywords: Ambient Assisted Living, AAL Platform, System Architecture, Quality Attribute, AAL Platform Evaluation.

1 Introduction

Driven by demographical and societal changes in most industrialized countries, the development of Ambient Assisted Living (AAL) systems has emerged as a very promising application domain of Ambient Intelligence (AmI) systems. The main focus of AAL systems is to enable people with specific needs, e.g. elderly or disabled people, to live longer independently in their familiar residential environments [1]. From a technical perspective, an essential characteristic of AAL systems is their capability to react adaptively to dynamic changes in device/service availability, resource availability, system environment, or user requirements. Moreover, it is very important for the acceptance of such systems that they are able to assure both,functional and non-functional properties at any time. In order to tackle these challenges, it is indispensable to develop suitable AAL platforms that explicitly address openness, interoperability, adaptivity, and

D. Keyson et al. (Eds.): AmI 2011, LNCS 7040, pp. 264–274, 2011.

quality assurance. Recognizing these challenges, efforts have been aligned in national and European research projects in order to drive research into this direction [1,2]. As a result, a range of AAL platforms such as UniversAAL [13], OASIS [8], and OpenAAL [9] have been developed. However, each of these platforms has different foci and, correspondingly, different characteristics. In particular, there are considerable differences with respect to the treatment of relevant non-functional properties, such as security, maintainability, and safety. This obviously makes the selection of an adequate platform for a given AAL project very difficult. Even though the importance of non-functional properties has been widely discussed in the AAL research community (for instance, at the MonAMI project workshop in Passau, Germany [10]), there is no comprehensive survey on AAL platforms and their support of important non-functional properties.

Therefore, the main objective of this paper is to provide an evaluation of the currently most widely established and well-known AAL platforms with respect to their support of non-functional properties. To this end, we first identify and describe a set of relevant quality attributes for the context of AAL systems. Then we evaluate given AAL platforms by means of a qualitative analysis technique, describing to which degree the different quality attributes are fulfilled by each platform. The results are compiled into an evaluation of the platforms that should provide support for developers of AAL projects when faced with selecting an appropriate platform.

The remainder of this paper is organized as follows: In Section 2, we briefly discuss suitable quality attributes for our evaluation and provide a short overview of the selected attributes. Subsequently, we present the considered AAL platforms and their evaluation in Section 3. In Section 4, we conclude this paper with a discussion of our results, lessons learned, and limitations of this work.

2   Quality Attributes as Evaluation Criteria

As a basis for the platform evaluation, we first had to identify an appropriate (i.e., small enough to be described in this paper yet meaningful) set of quality attributes for the AAL domain. A general starting point was provided by established standards for software quality such as ISO/IEC 9126, ISO/IEC 14598, and the new ISO/IEC 25000 SQuaRE. From these comprehensive sets of quality attributes we extracted a subset that was well suited for assessing the considered AAL platforms from a quality assurance perspective (cf. Table 1). As the main categories (or, according to the wording used in the standards, as the top-level quality characteristics) to be considered, we mostly adopted those proposed in the ISO/IEC 9126 and ISO/IEC 25000 SQuaRE standards. However, we made some slight changes owing to our task of evaluating AAL platforms. In correspondence with the standards, we considered maintainability and efficiency because both play important roles in AAL systems and depend on the platform. As for the former, it is common for AAL systems to be continuously maintained over their life-time as the needs of the assisted person usually change. Efficiency is important because AAL systems consist of heterogeneous distributed devices, which might only have scarce resources. In contrast to the standards, we further chose to include safety and security as top categories in addition to reliability. This is because we believe that AAL systems need to be particularly trustworthy, with trustworthiness being a composite of different quality characteristics including (but not necessarily limited to) safety, reliability, and security [3,12]. Safety takes up a special position when compared to the other quality attributes considered, because it is always a system property. Thus, we considered the general eligibility of the platforms for safety-critical applications. More precisely, we evaluated if there are weak points within the platforms (i.e., single points of failure) or if the platforms offer mechanisms that are directed at or can be utilized for safety measures. As for security, we mainly focused on the protection of sensible information, hence considering confidentiality as a main quality characteristic. We consequently evaluated if there are suitable security mechanisms in place in the platforms. Also in contrast to the standards, we did not consider usability and portability. Usability is not a property of a platform but rather of the applications that run on a platform. The same argument is true for portability, which is mostly a characteristic of (application) software to be deployed in different contexts such as different platforms.

3   Overview and Evaluation of AAL Platforms

Due to the large number of existing platforms, we do not aim to provide a complete overview in this paper. We consider the following set of more consolidated and well-known AAL platforms: Alhambra [5], Hydra [6], OASIS [8], OpenAAL [9], PERSONA [11], and UniversAAL [13]. It is important to point out that these platforms are based on OSGi[1]. However, this was not a criterion in the selection process; we only realized this during the analysis. In the following, we first give a short overview of the platforms considered. Then we describe the method applied to gather the required platform-specific information. Finally, we describe the evaluation results and provide a table that shows the platforms based on the set of quality attributes identified in Section 2.

3.1   Overview of Evaluated AAL Platforms

Alhambra: This platform provides a comprehensive architecture for accessing and integrating heterogeneous devices, providing interoperability with different communication protocols, and using a uniform functional interface. Alhambra is a service platform for developing modular, service-oriented, hardware-independent applications. In this perspective, Alhambra provides modularization, enabling an exchange of applications.

Hydra: Hydra is a service-oriented platform built for operating in environments with limited resources, such as energy, memory, and computational processing. It is a peer-to-peer based system that offers, among others, mechanisms for allowing service discovery and for ensuring high interoperability.

---

[1] OSGi has been considered one of the most appropriate frameworks to be used as a basis for the development of AAL platforms - http://www.osgi.org/

Table 1. Quality Attribute Framework for the AAL Domain

Quality Attribute	Description
RELIABILITY	
Recoverability	Recoverability can generally be defined as the ability of the system to recover if a failure does occur. In our evaluation we assessed if and how good recoverability is supported by mechanisms of the respective platforms.
SECURITY	
Encryption Mechanism	Encryption Mechanisms are essential for providing end-to-end message security in Web Services based environments. The use of digital certificates can simplify access control for elderly and demented persons (as they do not need to remember usernames and passwords).
User Roles & Security Profile Definition	The interface to core management services (i.e., user management, access management, role management, and token management) should be defined for the developer.
MAINTAINABILITY	
Changeability	Changeability is a property that allows software engineers to easily perform a change in the system design. In the case of the AAL platforms, we especially considered their facilities to maintain them after deployment.
Installability	Installability is the capability of a software product to be installed in a specified environment. For AAL platforms, we considered the presence of installation mechanisms that allow both people with and without technical knowledge to effectively add new services and devices to the system, as well as mechanisms for assuring that external dependencies will be automatically downloaded to assure proper (re)installation of the system.
EFFICIENCY	
Adequacy for Small Devices	Given the heterogeneous nature of AAL systems, it is important for a corresponding platform to soundly incorporate devices ranging from sensor nodes to PCs. This can be particularly difficult for devices like sensor nodes, as resource scarcity might require special concepts in order to integrate them into a platform.
Resource Consumption	Here we considered the general resource efficiency of the platform (e.g memory, CPU).
Communication Overhead	AAL systems usually rely on numerous distributed devices and platforms are required to realize their communication in an efficient way.
SAFETY	
Presence of Single Point of Failure	A single point of failure corresponds to a system component that, if it fails, will compromise the proper functioning of the system.
Safety Pattern Usage	Safety patterns are measures applied to the system architecture that will assure that the system will always be in a safe state. Examples of safety patterns are Homogeneous/Heterogeneous Redundancy, Watch Dog, and Triple Modular Redundancy.

OASIS: OASIS is an ontology-driven, open reference architecture and platform that facilitates interoperability, seamless connectivity, and sharing of content between different services. Based on a service-oriented approach, it is open, modular, and standard-based. It includes a set of tools for content/services connection and management, for user interface creation and adaptation, and for service personalization and integration.

OpenAAL: The main goal is to enable an easy implementation and integration of flexible, context-aware, and personalized services. The OpenAAL middleware is a framework that supports integration and communication between AAL services. Furthermore, it provides generic platform services such as context management, workflow specifications of system behavior, and semantically enabled discovery of services. Both the framework and the platform services operate and communicate by means of a shared ontology.

PERSONA: The PERSONA project aims at developing a scalable, open-standard technological platform for building a range of AAL services. The relevant technical solutions include a middleware, a set of general-purpose components (forming the PERSONA platform), and a set of AAL services.

The middleware comprises a set of OSGi bundles organized in three logical layers: The Abstract Connection Layer handles the peer-to-peer connectivity between middleware instances, the Sodapop Layer realizes the peer and listener interfaces, and the PERSONA-specific Layer implements different busses, which are employed to enable the interaction between users and the general-purpose components.

UniversAAL: UniversAAL is based on a service-oriented architecture that reuses many components of PERSONA. The platform includes three main parts: (i) a runtime-support environment that provides core services for the execution of AAL services, (ii) a development support that provides documentation, tools, and development resources, and (iii) community support, including training and an online store, a one-stop shop for AAL services and applications.

3.2   Methodology for Collecting Information

Considering the characteristics of our work, we decided to conduct a survey in order to evaluate the AAL platforms. The conduction of surveys is an empirical strategy for a retrospective investigation about a topic of interest [14]. According to Wohlin et al. [14], a survey is a descriptive (to determine the distribution of attributes and characteristic), explanatory (to understand decisions that are made), and explorative (a preliminary study for a deeper future investigation) strategy. In particular, we adopted the interview technique, which is a qualitative analysis technique [7] widely used to conduct surveys [14] and is, in particular, sufficient to evaluate the selected quality attributes of software system architectures [4]. More precisely, we decided to conduct semi-structured interviews, guided by a script, but with interesting issues explored in more depth. The interviews were individually held more than one time so that bias could be minimized.

3.3   Result Evaluation

For each AAL platform, the quality attributes were discussed and analyzed. Table 2 summarizes the results of our analysis. In order to indicate if a platform addresses a specific attribute, we adopted these abbreviations: (i) HA (Highly Addressed), if the attribute is explicitly supported; (ii) A (Addressed), if the attribute is supported; (iii) PA (Partially Addressed), if the attribute is implicitly supported or limited to single features; (iv) NA (Not Addressed), if an attribute is insufficiently supported or is not addressed; and (v) INA (Information Not Available), if information about that attribute is not available. Bellow, we present more details about the platforms with regard to each quality attribute.

Recoverability: Since all platforms are based on the OSGi framework, on the level of single bundles, they are all protected by the recoverability mechanism provided by the hosting OSGi runtime environment. Besides the common protection, we identified that: (i) **Hydra** has a specific component for detecting

Table 2. Evaluation of the AAL Platforms

	Alhambra	Hydra	OASIS	OpenAAL	PERSONA	UniversAAL
RELIABILITY						
Recoverability	NA	A	NA	NA	HA	HA
SECURITY						
Encryption Mechanism	NA	A	A	NA	A	HA
User Roles & Security Profile Definition	A	A	PA	PA	A	HA
MAINTAINABILITY						
Changeability	PA	PA	PA	A	HA	HA
Installability	NA	A	A	NA	HA	HA
EFFICIENCY						
Adequacy for Small Devices	HA	HA	HA	NA	A	HA
Resource Consumption	A	NA	NA	INA	HA	HA
Communication Overhead	A	NA	NA	A	HA	HA
SAFETY						
Presence of Single Point of Failure	NA	NA	NA	INA	NA	HA
Safety Pattern Usage	NA	A	NA	NA	NA	A

failures in the system; (ii) **PERSONA** and **UniversAAL** address recoverability also at the hardware level; and (iii) **Alhambra**, **OASIS**, and **OpenAAL** do not provide additional mechanisms for recovery when failures occur.

Encryption mechanism: We observed that: (i) **Hydra** has an encryption mechanism addressed by the Trust Manager component; (ii) **OASIS** has an encryption mechanism in the Trust and Security Framework; (iii) **PERSONA** has an encryption mechanism where the necessary authorization for enabling a middleware instance (representing a PERSONA-aware node) to take part in a certain AAL Space requires manual installation of the AAL Space shared key on that node. The presence of such an encryption mechanism additionally ensures end-to-end security and integrity of messages exchanged among the middleware instances; (iv) **UniversAAL**'s encryption mechanism extends Persona's with additional public & private key pairs for communication beyond a single AAL Space (e.g., with another AAL Space or with Web services outside the AAL Space); and (v) **Alhambra** and **OpenAAL** do not offer any encryption mechanism.

User roles & security profile definition: We observed that: (i) **Alhambra** offers mechanisms for defining user roles and profiles; (ii) **Hydra** has a policy framework where user roles and security profiles can be defined. Overall confidentiality is assured by asymmetric encryption as mentioned before, combined with this policy framework; (iii) **OASIS**'s approach to linking user roles and security profiles can lead to user role conflicts (two roles with conflicting properties can be associated with the same user profile). Moreover, there is no mechanism to prevent user information (which should be strictly confidential) to be seen and manipulated by other users, which implies notable confidentiality issues; (iv) **OpenAAL** offers a possibility to define user profiles for different users that might also contain security information. However, such security-related profiles are currently not available; (v) **PERSONA**'s approach with respect to user roles and security profile definition is basically structured as an extensive ontology of different classes of users with the appropriate profile models and a profiling component for accessing profile data. PERSONA offers mechanisms for user and component authentication which, in addition to the two security points above, contribute to confidentiality; and (vi) **UniversAAL**'s approach was extended from PERSONA by adding policy-based security mechanisms integrated into matchmaking between offers and requests. With this extension, the confidentiality of UniversAAL is improved from PERSONA's solution, since the policy-based extension provides generalized mechanisms that might even eliminate the need for application-level access control.

Changeability: In general, because of the good modularity offered by OSGi, it is not difficult to perform changes in systems that are based on or use these platforms. Besides that, we identified that: (i) **Alhambra**, **Hydra**, and **OASIS** do not offer any additional mechanism for improving changeability; (ii) **OpenAAL** has a clear and quite simple architecture for a very specific set of applications that allow several extension possibilities. Additionally, OpenAAL's architecture exploits semantic technologies, which enhance changeability even further. On the other hand, documentation of these possibilities is rather sparse; (iii) **PERSONA** offers mechanisms for replacing components on the fly. The distributed implementation of the PERSONA middleware provides dynamic plug-and-play of hardware and software artifacts. Actually, the PERSONA middleware can be regarded as Communication Middleware. i.e., it is distributed on nodes that are PERSONA-aware. The distribution is hidden by the middleware, so that any building block is regarded in the same manner on the platform level; and (iv) **UniversAAL**'s changeability mechanisms are basically the same as PERSONA's, with improvements on the modularity of the PERSONA middleware as a result of enhancing the distribution function.

Installability: The main points are: (i) **Alhambra and OpenAAL** have no special mechanism for supporting installability. Service installations are done via simple copy and paste of bundles ; (ii) **Hydra** offers a wizard for guiding the user through the installation process; (iii) **OASIS** does not offer barriers for installing new devices and services in the existing systems. However, it is important to know the ontology of what the service is about to conduct a smooth installation; (iv) **PERSONA**'s approach regarding installability is based on dynamic dependencies checking. The installation of dependencies and other external components is facilitated by reusable and predefined OSGi configuration files that allow communication with external repositories where the newest versions of software artifacts are located; and (v) **UniversAAL**'s approach was improved from PERSONA. In particular, improvements were made to tools for the creation of an initial dataset as well as for facilitating the download and installation of applications from online stores, along with personalization tools.

Adequacy for small devices: With regard to this attribute, we observed that: (i) **Alhambra** can be easily integrated with small devices and sensor nodes in existing systems, since there are well-defined interfaces that allow smart integration of such elements; (ii) **Hydra** was explicitly designed to interoperate with small devices and sensor nodes. It has a hybrid approach for supporting the following scenarios: If the small device contains a Hydra implementation, it communicates directly via service invocation. If the small device does not have a Hydra implementation on it, communication is done via a proxy called Hydra Proxy; (iii) **OASIS**'s adequacy for small devices is also addressed using a proxy based approach consisting of the integration of two OSGi implementations: the one on which the whole system is structured and the other one that is dedicated to supporting integration of small devices; (iv) for **PERSONA**, a design pattern was specified in order to allow the integration of small device and sensor nodes. Based on this specification, PERSONA provides concrete implementation for well-known home automation standards such as KNX as well as the home automation and health profiles of ZigBee; (v) **UniversAAL**'s adequacy regarding the support of small devices and sensor nodes was improved from PERSONA by offering additional support for the IEEE-11073 standard, automatic generation of code for new device wrappers, and commissioning tools. This means that for each class of protocols (known to the system), UniversAAL offers the possibility to generate "virtual representations" compliant with the internal data/device model. In PERSONA, these internal representations had to be manually generated; and (vi) **OpenAAL** does not address this attribute.

Resource consumption: All of the analyzed platforms require a minimum resource for running OSGi, the Java Virtual Machine (JVM), and a database which, in general, is a lightweight one. In more detail, we observed that: (i) **Alhambra** has well-structured resource consumption management modules for ensuring that unnecessary resources will not be consumed. In general, resource consumption is very low; (ii) **Hydra**: Besides the resources needed for OSGi, JVM, and database, the Network Manager of Hydra consumes a considerable amount of physical memory; (iii) **OpenAAL** resource consumption was never evaluated in detail by the OpenAAL team. Nevertheless, the platform designers assume that the core parts are small enough to consume very few resources. The biggest resource consumers are memory and processor task; (iv) **PERSONA** and **UniversAAL** require 4MB of space and Java 1.3 running. It is important to point out that around 2MB are for OSGi. In order to achieve an optimal load balance, platform components can be distributed without restriction to the different available nodes in the AAL Space. Runtime measurements on memory and CPU consumption have not been performed so far; and (v) **OASIS** does not offer any management for resource consumption.

Communication overhead: Regarding this attribute, we observed that: (i) in **Alhambra**, on the Bus communication level, a Queue mechanism is used. The overhead depends on the size of the Queue. On the Service level, the OSGi mechanism takes care of this aspect and, in general, has very low overhead. For communication with external devices, there is a specific dedicated communication protocol for avoiding high communication overhead; (ii) in **Hydra**, the main cause of communication overhead is the Network Manager, which is based on JXTA; (iii) in **OASIS**, an the service level there is an overhead caused by a proxy-based approach to orchestrating the services. Another overhead is caused by the hybrid approach used in the data model: The most important information of the user profile is replicated in the central server and in the local node; (iv) in **OpenAAL**, communication is highly dependent on the OSGi communication framework, which results in little communication overhead; and (v) **PERSONA** and **UniversAAL** have a dedicated mechanism for dealing with communication overhead that is realized in two ways: Persona communicates through 4 busses. For 2 busses, n-1 (n = number of nodes) messages are broadcasted ONCE when a node throws a new event. The rest of the procedure is executed locally at each node. For the other two busses, communication is centralized, that are always optimized with respect to overhead). They introduce a "Coordinator", so that CONSTANTLY 0, 2, or 4 messages, in the worst case, are received. With other approaches, usually 2n messages are received.

Presence of single point of failure: We observed that: (i) in **Alhambra**, the Residential Gateway is a single point of failure for the whole platform; (ii) in **Hydra**, all communication is done via the Network Manager, which communicates via a single server called Super Node that, in turn, becomes a single point of failure; (iii) in **OASIS**, a single point of failure is the service registration component; if this component fails, service calls or registration will not be possible; (iv) **PERSONA**'s basic architecture and the distributed implementation of the middleware were explicitly designed to avoid single points of failure. Nevertheless, there are few mandatory platform components on top of the middleware that make the hosting node a critical one. The failure of such a node leads to the loss of certain functionalities. For instance, if the node hosting the PERSONA Dialog Manager fails, explicit interactions with the user will not work anymore; (v) in **UniversAAL**, there is no single point of failures; and (vi) regarding **OpenAAL**, no information is available.

Use of safety patterns: Regarding this attribute, (i) **Hydra** presents Redundancy as a safety pattern, through the use of different services with the same goal; (ii) for **UniversAAL**, explicit mechanisms are under development to support redundant installation of critical components; and (iii) the other platforms do not use any safety patterns.

Summarizing our analysis, we observed that the AAL platforms considered in this work are relevant and present different advantages in various contexts of use. Considering the analyzed set of quality attributes, the results point out that none of them fully addresses the quality attributes; however, overall, UniversAAL presented the best evaluation. Considering other quality attributes, the analysis might have a completely different result. With respect to our quality attribute set, it is important to point out that the use of safety patterns, in general, has not been taken in consideration, even knowing that their use could avoid failures leading to serious injuries to the assisted persons. It is worth highlighting that this type of analysis is not trivial, since it involves a huge amount of information from different sources and, beyond that, information analysis and summarization require considerable efforts and are time consuming. Thus, the performed evaluation per se demonstrates the necessity of a well-structured evaluation approach.

4 Conclusions

Selecting an adequate AAL platform is essential for the success of AAL projects. The main contribution of this paper is to present an evaluation of well-known AAL platforms, based on quality attributes analyzed on the architectural level and providing information that could provide guidance in the selection of the appropriate platform for a new AAL project. As future work, we intend to consolidate our analysis by performing scenario-based evaluations, also involving other AAL platforms and aiming at contributing to the effective development of AAL projects.

Acknowledgements. This work is supported by the OptimAAL and ProAssist4Life projects, and by the Brazilian funding agencies FAPESP and CNPq. We would also like to thank Saied Tazari from Fraunhofer IGD, Peter Wolf from FZI Karlsruhe, Marius Ofgen from TU Kaiserslautern, Mario Schmidt from Fraunhofer IESE, Lohrasb Jalali and Patrick Lukat from Fraunhofer IMS and Marc Jentsch from Fraunhofer FIT for serving as interview partners. We would also like to thank Sonnhild Namingha from Fraunhofer IESE for linguistic support.

References

1. AAL Joint Programme: Ambient Assisted Living (AAL) joint programme, World Wide Web (2011), http://www.aal-europe.eu/ (acessed May 16, 2011)
2. AAL Open Association: AAl Open Association - AALOA, World Wide Web (2011), http://www.aaloa.org/ (acessed May 16, 2011)
3. Avižienis, A., Laprie, J., Randell, B., Landwehr, C.: Basic concepts and taxonomy of dependable and secure computing. IEEE Trans. on Dependable and Secure Computing 1(1), 11–33 (2004)
4. Clements, P., Kazman, R., Klein, M.: Evaluating Software Architecture. The SEI Series in Software Engineering, Boston, MA (2002)
5. Dimitrov, T.: Design and Implementation of a Home Automation Service Gateway based on OSGi. Master's thesis, University of Duisburg-Essen, Düsseldorf, Germany (December 2005)
6. Hydra Project: Hydra open source middleware, World Wide Web (2011), http://www.hydramiddleware.eu/ (acessed May 17/2011)
7. Miles, M.B., Huberman, M.: Qualitative Data Analysis: An Expanded Sourcebook, 2nd edn. Sage Publications (1994)
8. OASIS Project: OASIS: quality of life for the elderly, World Wide Web (2011), http://www.oasis-project.eu/ (acessed May 11, 2011)
9. OpenAAL: OpenAAL: The open source middleware for ambient-assisted living, World Wide Web (2011), http://openaal.org/ (acessed May 16, 2011)

10. Passau Workshop on ICT & Ageing: Announcing the European Initiative for an AAL Platform: Which Features Should Be In AAL Platforms, World Wide Web (2010), http://www.hi.se/Global/monami/05PanelWhichFea turesShouldBeInAAL1Platforms.pdf (acessed May 13, 2011)
11. PERSONA Project: PERceptive Spaces prOmoting iNdependent Aging, World Wide Web (2011), http://www.aal-persona.org/ (acessed May 13, 2011)
12. Schneider, D., Becker, M., Trapp, M.: Approaching runtime trust assurance in open adaptive systems. In: SEAMS 2011 at ICSE 2011, Hawaii, USA (2011)
13. UniversAAL Project: The UniversAAL Reference Architecture, World Wide Web (2011), http://www.universaal.org/images/stories/deliverables/D1.3-B.pdf (access in March 25, 2011)
14. Wohlin, C., Runeson, P., Höst, M., Ohlsson, M.C., Regnell, B., Wesslén, A.: Experimentation in Software Engineering. Kluwer Academic Publishers (2000)

CommunityNet: Mediating Care
at the Local Community Level

Bas Stroomer, Martijn H. Vastenburg, and David V. Keyson

Faculty of Industrial Design Engineering, Delft University of Technology,
Landbergstraat 15, 2628 CE, Delft, The Netherlands
basstroomer@gmail.com, {M.H.Vastenburg,D.V.Keyson}@tudelft.nl

Abstract. Community care is expected to be increasingly important for seniors
in need of support towards prolonged independent living and higher quality of
life. Whereas people generally indicate they are willing to provide support
within their community, several barriers prevent elderly people from asking for
support. The present paper describes the design of CommunityNet, a social
network service that aims to bring together the local community and to lower
the barriers towards asking for help. Based on the findings from user research,
ambient awareness displays were developed and placed in the homes of seniors
and local community members. The awareness displays showed an overview of
the people, their requests for help, and the status of the requests. The concept
was evaluated in a field trial (n=4, 10 days). The participants indicated that they
preferred using CommunityNet compared to face-to-face contact and telephone
when the need for support was not urgent. According to the participants, the
barriers towards asking for help were lowered by the system. As a next step, an
automated match-maker mechanism will be developed which enables people to
extend their care network, and the system will be tested in a range of
communities.

Keywords: Independent living, community care, social network, awareness
display, communication system, peer-to-peer, field trial.

1 Introduction

Many elderly people in western countries prefer to live independently as long as
possible, but they need support in doing so [1, 2]. Care is nowadays generally
provided by professional caregivers, by family caregivers, and by the local
community. During the next decades, the number of professional caregivers per
elderly person in need of care is expected to decline in Western countries. Family care
and community care are thus expected to play an increasingly important role in
helping the elderly to continue living independently at home.

In interviews conducted in support of this study, as detailed below, people
generally indicated that they were willing to *provide* support within their local
community. Several barriers however prevent people from *asking* for support. First of
all, people find it hard to ask for help in a face-to-face setting, which could be caused
by the higher cost of denial in a face-to-face setting compared to a mediated setting.

D. Keyson et al. (Eds.): AmI 2011, LNCS 7040, pp. 275–284, 2011.

Secondly, the interviews showed that elderly people in particular experience a feeling of shame towards asking neighbors for help. Thirdly, seniors indicated that they often would not know who would be the best person to approach with a specific request. In short, barriers prevent people from asking for help, even though local community members may be able and willing to provide help.

Social networking mechanisms could be used to facilitate community care. By using a social network, people could ask for help via a mediated setting, which may lower the barrier as compared to face-to-face communication. Moreover, one may expect peer-to-peer social network systems to result in less stigmatization compared to traditional monitoring systems for independent living, since elderly people would not only ask for help, but also provide help. Additionally, a social networking system could help people find the best match when asking for help.

Whereas existing social network systems, such as Google+ and Facebook, could eventually be used as a platform for community care, in the current study the decision was made to explore the user needs and further design directions using a prototype communication system that was specifically developed in support of the study goals. This paper describes the design of CommunityNet, a social network service that aims to bring together the local community and to lower the barriers towards asking for help.

2   Related Work

Existing projects related to community care vary from phone-based match-making facilities, to web-based communication tools, to closed communication systems. As an example of phone-based match-making, Burenhulpcentrale[1] uses a database of over 17000 participating households to match care requests to care providers. An automated system was used to make a match between care requests and care providers. In many cases, however, no proper match was found, or the process of entering a request and finding a provider took too long [5]. Moreover, participants found it awkward and difficult to ask strangers for support.

There are several examples of systems that aim to improve social cohesion and enhance communication within a local community. I-neighbors[2], for example, is a website that aims to connect neighbors with similar interests. I-neighbors includes discussion boards, photo sharing, directories and a forum. Whereas I-Neighbors makes it possible to search for people with shared interests living nearby, the communication mechanisms seem inappropriate for communicating individual care requests, and it is unclear if users are able to translate the virtual ties into social ties in real life [3]. Likewise, Building Bridges, is a research project which aims to help older adults remain socially connected [4] by using communication technology to link users around broadcasts including news, documentaries, stories and music. A touch screen computer was combined with a phone handset using Skype. During or after a broadcast users could chat with other listeners. Whereas elderly users appreciated the system, it seems inappropriate for communicating individual care needs.

Well-known examples of closed communication systems are the Digital Family Portrait (DFP) [5] and the CareNet Display [6]. These awareness displays provide

---

[1] http://www.burenhulpcentrale.nl
[2] http://www.i-neighbors.org

peace-of-mind to distant family caregivers, and can be used to better assess what care is needed at what time. Whereas DFP and CareNet Display are basic automated monitoring systems by design, there are examples of systems that enable seniors to explicitly enter requests. ShareCare ZorgSite[3], for example, is a website that is used to coordinate care within an existing care network. Email and SMS are used to automatically distribute care tasks within the network. Since the website can only be accessed through a web browser, many elderly users are unable to access the system and post requests [7, 8, 9]. Moreover, since the system is based on the paradigm in which a caretaker is surrounded by caregivers, the system by design results in stigmatization, resulting in sub-optimal product adoption.

In short, barriers prevent elderly people from asking for support using existing communication systems. The present paper describes a design case that aims to lower the barriers towards asking for help by using a social network service to bring together the local community.

3 Approach

Figure 1 below shows the user-centered design approach that was followed in the present design case. The user research, as described in section 4, aims to better understand how people experience providing and receiving care in a local community setting, and to find out what barriers are preventing community care. In the design phase, an interactive concept was iteratively developed. Prototypes were built and evaluated in the evaluation phase.

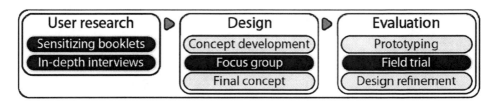

Fig. 1. A user-centered design approach was used to ensure that the interactive concept would properly address the user needs and that the concept would fit the context of use. The solid bars indicate the involvement of the user in each phase.

4 User Research and Context Analysis

Goal. User research was conducted to better understand how people approach providing and receiving care, to understand relationships with family, friends and neighbors, and to find out what barriers were preventing community care. The target group for the user research was defined as 'future seniors', i.e. people who are expected to be in need of care to continue independent living at a certain moment. The participants were two Dutch married couples and two Dutch widows, ranging from 58 to 65 years old. All of the participants held a part-time or fulltime job, and

---

[3] http://www.sharecare.nl

lived independently at the time of the study. Their education and computer experience levels vary.

Sensitizing Booklets. Booklets, as an element of context mapping [10], were developed to sensitize the participants for an in-depth interview on their personal and social life. The participants were asked to describe how active their social network was, how they currently receive care and what they expected in the future. The information collected from the sensitizing booklets was subsequently used as a guideline for developing the in-depth interviews. The booklets consisted of several assignments. The first assignment was to log contact moments for two days. This provided both the participants and the researchers an impression of the number of social contact moments per day. After this, a map of the social contacts was made, categorized by (a) family, (b) friends, (c) neighbors and (d) others. In the next assignments these contacts were placed on a circular map with stickers, axes meaning (a) distance (only family and friends), (b) the closeness of the relationship, (c) the expectation of these relationships for the future and (d) the experienced barrier to ask for support. The final assignment was to write down what support was provided by and received from the listed social contacts.

Interviews. Semi-structured interviews were conducted to better understand the participants' input in the sensitizing booklets, thus letting them clarify concerns about their personal situation.

Findings. In describing future care needs, the participants referred primarily to support from family and friends. The family-and-friends care network described tended to be rather small, often between 5 to 10 contacts. Since the family and friends referred to often lived nearby, most of the participants indicated they did not feel the need to build up a close relationship with neighbors in order to strengthen their care network. While the potential of the local community to strengthen the care network was mentioned, the participants indicated that they felt a barrier towards asking their neighbors for support; for example, fear of bothering or burdening their neighbors.

Based on the findings of the interviews and of the literature research, a categorized list of issues relevant for the design phase was created. Table 1 shows the list, which summarizes the explorative phase.

Table 1. Categorized issues that summarize the explorative phase, used as input in the design

Getting older	• Resistance towards new technologies (Adoption) • Difficulties with household activities • Afraid of stigmatization
Independent living	• Prefer to live independently as long as possible • Barrier towards asking for support • Don't want to give up privacy or provide personal information
Care potential	• Less care from children, more from local community • Communication systems as mediators • Self-management • Seniors are increasingly experienced in using computers (though for most seniors applications can soon become too complex)

5 Design

Based on the findings from the user research, the system should (a) avoid stigmatization, (b) include family and friends as well as neighbors, and (c) be easily-accessible and easy-to-use for people that have little experience with a computer.

Figure 2 below shows the design steps in the design phase. First, the design space was explored, and several explorative concepts were developed. The concepts were discussed in a focus group session. Based on the feedback from the participants, a final concept was created.

Fig. 2. Steps in the design phase

Since stigmatization was found to be a primary concern of the target users, the development of a peer-to-peer system was decided upon. A peer-to-peer system can be introduced before people are in need of care; users can then offer their help to other community members, and they can get used to the new device when they are still willing to adopt new technology.

Generating Concepts. The design space was explored using a series of provocative scenarios of interactions with future products.

Discussing Concepts. To understand how the target group would value potential design directions, the scenarios were discussed with the participants. Participants were asked to assess the scenarios based on (a) the barrier towards asking for support, (b) the information they would exchange through the system (c) preferred product initiative, (d) adaptation to the individual user, and (e) user motivation by the system.

Since users of all ages should be able to use the system, a variety of ways to communicate requests was explored. Ideas that were created include an application on a mobile device, an in-house product or application on a computer, or a central product in the neighborhood. Based on the discussions, creating new requests and responding to requests were considered to be the primary functions.

Elaborating Concepts. Three directions were explored: (a) a request-making product based on connecting physical objects, (b) an agenda-based request- and appointment-making product, possibly using awareness of presence, and (c) a combination of both.

Figure 3 shows three elaborated concepts. The first concept is based on connecting physical objects containing a contact, request, date or time. Seniors who experience the computer as a barrier, might be willing to and able to interact with physical objects, and thereby access the digital world through physical objects. Users can create a new request by connecting *contact* objects, *activity type* objects and a *date-time* object. The second concept combines the physical objects with an agenda on a (touch) screen. The agenda is used as a metaphor, since providing care can be seen as planning activities. The main advantage is that the user has an overview of its contacts, as well as all the appointments. In the third concept the agenda is the main functionality. An overview of contacts is shown, and requests can be entered using on-screen forms.

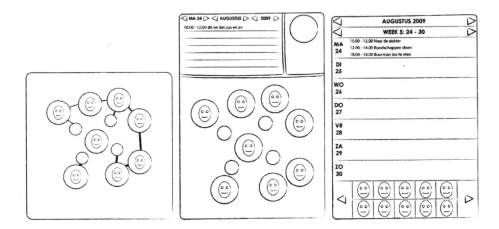

Fig. 3. Three concepts were studied: (1) Physical objects, (2) Physical objects and agenda on screen, and (3) Agenda and contacts on-screen

Focus Group Session. The three concepts were evaluated with 4 Dutch participants (1 male, 3 female participants, age 58-65) from the sensitizing booklets and interviews in a focus group session in the home of one of the participants. The project goal and the three concepts were discussed with the participants. The main findings were: (a) the participants indicated that it might be hard to set up and expand the network, since it was considered hard to approach their neighbors, (b) the participants did not want to have too many obligations in terms of supporting people with whom they do not have regular or frequent contact, providing support would depend on the urgency, frequency and expected commitment, (c) considering the concepts, the participants indicated that physical objects are difficult to keep organized, and when actively using the product there is little overview. However, the participants indicated that if the physical objects could be represented as digital elements, an overview could be kept, and the device could still be easy to use. The participants questioned whether they would use the agenda function in the device, since they usually already keep their own analog or digital agenda. The product should therefore not depend on the agenda function. Finally, regarding awareness of presence, the subjects reported that they did not want to share information about their personal life with people whom they would not frequently offer support to. If they were in need of regular support themselves, they reported that they would have no problem with providing information about their activities. However, there was a fear others would take too much of their time when they could see when they are available. Thus, in providing personal information a distinction has to be made between family and friends, and neighbors.

Final Concept. Based on the feedback from the focus group session, Concept 3 (Figure 3) was chosen as a basis for the final design, since the participants appreciated the usability and the flexibility. An interactive digital photo frame was chosen as an ambient awareness display in the living room, but that could draw attention if necessary. This method was proven to be successful in the DFP and the CareNet

Display. Presence information was not incorporated in the final concept, since the participants of the focus group session indicated that they did not want to give details about their personal life to relative strangers. The agenda function was replaced by a chronological overview of the requests, since the participants in the focus group indicated that they would not use an agenda on the device itself. An agenda function could however be synchronized with other digital agendas. Since it is unknown in advance when a request will be read, it is by nature unsuitable for emergency requests. Participants indicated that they would use the telephone or walk to the neighbor in case of an emergency.

Figure 4 shows the final concept, an ambient awareness display for community care. The user interface consists of (a) the contact area on the left side of the screen, (b) the request area and (c) the profile area on the right side of the screen. The contact area contains pictures of the user and its contacts, with request icons floating around the pictures. The user can switch between the request area and the profile area using tabs. When no picture is selected (mode a) the right side of the screen shows an overview of the appointments made. When the user selects himself/herself (mode b) an overview of the users requests is shown on the right side, with the options to add or remove a request. When a contact is selected (mode c) an overview of the contacts requests is shown on the right side, with the option to react on each request. When the user selects itself or a contact, the request icons are enlarged.

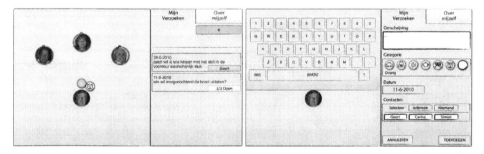

Fig. 4. In the main view (left), the user can see an overview of the request states of all pending requests. The panel on the right shows all accepted requests which are either initiated by the user, or accepted by the user. New requests can be added using the on-screen keyboard (right).

To enable quick responses and keep overview, a request can only be answered with 'yes' or 'no'. The user can select whom the request is sent to; by default all contacts are selected to stimulate users to ask as many contacts as possible for the request. Next to support requests, social requests can be placed. A distinction between support requests and social requests was made to stimulate users to also use the device for non-care-related aspects, thereby stimulating local community contact moments.

In the profile area, the user can enter his/her hobbies, interests, strengths and general support categories. Other users can search for new contacts based on these profiles, as well as on the location. This was added to stimulate users to find new contacts, and to share their interests and strengths.

6 Field Trial

Goal. A field trial was conducted in order to explore how target users use and experience the prototype system in a realistic setting, and thereby validate the design choices. A future extensive field study is needed to validate the concept.

Method. A group of 6 new Dutch participants (two married couples, a widow and a widower, age 45-93, with varying education levels and computer experience) was recruited for the field trial. They were part of an existing social network; three neighbors and a grandfather of one of them who lives close by.

First, the participants were asked to write down provided and received support in a period of 10 days. In interviews, the participants were asked to describe the relationship with the people they currently receive support from and provide support to, and if they think new communication products could be used to improve this.

Next, the prototype was placed in the homes of the participants for a period of 10 days (figure 5). During the trial the activities of the users were logged. The support activities before and during the trial were compared and discussed in exit interviews, and the participants were asked for feedback.

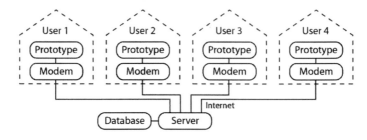

Fig. 5. Configuration of the system. Four prototypes were placed in the homes of the participants, connected through an Internet connection.

Results. Eleven requests were placed during the trial, of which only 4 lead to a match. The number of requests was in line with baseline measurement. The participants did however indicate that the perceived barrier to ask for support was lowered by the prototype, since it allowed them to ask multiple contacts for support at the same time, in a less direct way compared to face-to-face requests. They noted that they would like to have the product in their homes in the future, but only when it would be possible to have real-time contact. Requests varied from walking the dog to changing a lock. The eldest participant (93) did not place any requests, since the help that he received from his grandson was sufficient, and he preferred using the phone to contact his grandson.

The prototype was considered easy to use after it was used a couple of times. Placing a request was considered useful when it was not too urgent, since they were unsure whether they could expect a fast response. In that case phone calls were considered more adequate. The profile pages were only viewed once, and the social request function was hardly used as well. This was in line with our expectations since the participants already knew each other well. All participants indicated they would like audio feedback when a new request is received. The eldest participant would like replacing this device for the alarming device in his protected housing.

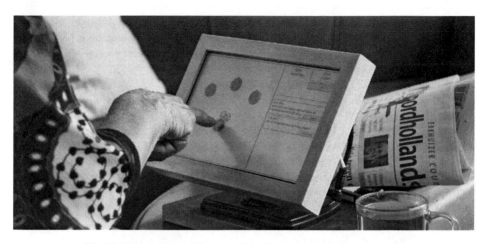

Fig. 5. One of the participants of the field trial using the prototype

Conclusions. Based on the findings from the field trial, one can conclude that a social network service could be used to lower the barriers in asking for support within a local community. Further studies are needed to quantify the effect of the service on support for a longer period of time. The field trial did however provide feedback on the design choices, which can now be used to improve the design.

The choice of a touchscreen interface was found to be successful, even though the eldest participant (93) had never used a touchscreen before. Although support requests could be made more anonymous than face-to-face contact, this appears to be useful when the request is not urgent, because of the uncertainty of response. The participants did not appreciate the option of being able to automatically send social requests to all contacts, since they did not always want to invite all of their contacts. The eldest participant (93) seemed to have problems with remembering how to use the device. This suggests that the current design may not be suitable for all ages. The feedback of the participants led to new requirements for a future version of the CommunityNet system, including audio feedback from the device itself or an e-mail or SMS notification when new requests or responses are received.

7   Conclusions

This paper presented a design case that aimed to stimulate community care using a social network with dedicated interfaces in every home. As observed during the interviews conducted, people may be willing to provide support within their community, proving the barriers are lowered in asking for support. The field trial demonstrated that a social network service could be used to lower barriers towards asking for help.

A key challenge in designing a community care system is the need to reduce stigmatization. By creating a peer-to-peer system, a community system can be introduced not only to people in acute need of care, but also to a larger group of people who in future might depend on the system. The peer-to-peer community approach enables seniors to offer their help to their neighbors, and thereby play an active role within their community. At the same time, they can get used to the new device at an age when they are still open to adopt new technology.

An interesting direction for future research would be to find mechanisms to extend social networks for community care, and to motivate people to be active participants within their network. Many seniors have rather small social networks. Social network mechanisms could be used to extend the networks, and thereby improve their means to prolong independent living.

Furthermore, it would be interesting to study how the system could be used on mobile devices. Whereas a dedicated device in the home of the elderly seems appropriate for present seniors with little computer experience, future seniors are expected to be experienced in using mobile devices. Future studies could for example focus on how to motivate seniors to offer and request support using a mobile service.

Finally, existing social network systems may be a good basis for community care in the future. A key design challenge seems to be to make these systems available to elderly users, who often have little experience with computers. A combination in which easy-to-use devices are available to seniors to access generic social network services seems a promising next step.

Acknowledgments. The work presented in this paper was part of the Independent at Home project, funded by AgentschapNL through the IOP-MMI program. We would like to thank all the participants for their input.

References

1. Vermeulen, J.: Langer zelfstandig wonen en hoe ICT daarbij kan helpen. PhD Thesis, University of Tilburg, The Netherlands (2006)
2. Consolvo, S., Roessler, P., Shelton, B.E., LaMarca, A., Schilit, B., Bly, S.: Technology for Care Networks of Elders. IEEE Pervasive Computing Mobile & Ubiquitous Systems: Successful Aging 3(2), 22–29 (2004)
3. Foth, M.: Facilitating Social Networking in Inner-City Neighborhoods. Computer 39(9), 44–50 (2006)
4. Wherton, J., Prendergast, D.: The Building Bridges Project: Involving Older Adults in the Design of a Communication Technology to Support Peer-to-Peer Social Engagement
5. Rowan, J., Mynatt, E.D.: Digital family portrait field trial: Support for aging in place. In: Proc. CHI 2005, pp. 521–530. ACM, New York (2005)
6. Consolvo, S., Roessler, P., Shelton, B.E.: The CareNet Display: Lessons Learned from an In Home Evaluation of an Ambient Display. In: Davies, N., Mynatt, E.D., Siio, I. (eds.) UbiComp 2004. LNCS, vol. 3205, pp. 1–17. Springer, Heidelberg (2004)
7. Dickinson, A., Newell, A.F., Smith, M.J., Hill, R.L.: Introducing the Internet to the over-60s: Developing an email system for older novice computer users. Interacting with Computers 17(6), 621–642 (2005)
8. Inoue, M., Suyama, A., Takeuchi, Y., Meshitsuka, S.: Application of a computer based education system for aged persons and issues arising during the field test. Computer Methods and Progress in Biomedicine 59(1), 55–60 (1999)
9. Docampo Rama, M.: Technology Generations Handling Complex User Interfaces. PhDThesis, Eindhoven University of Technology, The Netherlands (2001)
10. Sleeswijk Visser, F., Stappers, P.J., van der Lugt, R., Sanders, E.B.-N.: Contextmapping: Experiences from practice. Codesign 1(2), 119–149 (2005)

Experience Tags: Enriching Sensor Data in an Awareness Display for Family Caregivers

Martijn H. Vastenburg and Natalia Andrea Romero Herrera

ID-StudioLab, Faculty of Industrial Design Engineering
Delft University of Technology, The Netherlands
{m.h.vastenburg,n.a.romero}@tudelft.nl

Abstract. The design of awareness displays to support family care has been explored in many recent studies. Whereas user studies indicate that caregivers are interested to know seniors' subjective experiences regarding activities, events and general attitudes, product developers tend to focus on using sensors to automatically detect the state and context of seniors in time, resulting in systems that are unable to capture the seniors' experiences. This short paper presents *experience tagging*, a mechanism which enables end-users to enrich sensor data using subjective tags. A research concept of an awareness display for family caregivers is presented to illustrate how the mechanism can be integrated in the design of an awareness display. The preliminary findings from a 4-week field trial with three caregiver/senior couples are presented. As a next step, the use of experience tags could be studied in other settings where people or systems are interested to know the user perspective on sensor data.

Keywords: Interaction design, awareness displays, subjective tags.

1 Introduction

Awareness displays can be characterized as displays that continuously present information that is needed for a certain activity, task or goal, without distracting the user inappropriately from other tasks [1, 2]. Whereas the early research on awareness displays primarily targeted at office settings, awareness displays are increasingly being used in the care setting.

Awareness displays for family caregivers have been studied in several projects. A key example is Digital Family Portrait (DFP) [6]. DFP aims to improve peace of mind of remote caregivers by capturing observations that would naturally occur when someone lives in the same home or next door. Based on interviews with adult children, five key information categories were identified towards creating day-to-day assurance: health (mood, sleeping pattern, food intake, physical exercise), environment (home, weather), relationships (emotional wellbeing, social interactions), activity (physical activity) and events (planned and unplanned, richness and variety in life). In a 1-year field trial with one couple of participants, physical activity was used as the primary information source, since it could easily be measured using sensors. Perceived awareness was found to be stable for the duration of the study. Awareness

D. Keyson et al. (Eds.): AmI 2011, LNCS 7040, pp. 285–289, 2011.
© Springer-Verlag Berlin Heidelberg 2011

might have been improved by addressing the subjective information needs as identified in their user analysis, including emotional wellbeing and social interactions.

Consolvo et al. studied awareness displays to support day-to-day care of an elder by the local care network [3]. Exit interviews in their field trial indicated that caregivers experienced lower stress levels. The quality of communication increased since practical information was communicated through the display. Interestingly, even though moods were recognized as highly relevant in a day-to-day care setting, moods were not part of the CareNet display.

Affective messaging as part of an awareness display for family care was studied by Dadlani et al. [4]. Aurama was designed to create peace of mind and improve connectedness for adults that are peripherally involved in the care for their elderly parents. Sensors were used to detect presence, weight and sleeping patterns. Affective messaging through physical tokens (happy face, neutral face, sad face) was used to complement sensor information. A 6-month field trial showed that the participating couple enjoyed affective messaging, even though they did not communicate negative emotions. Sharing affective states was valued for achieving connectedness and peace of mind. Interestingly, communication of moods and communication of sensor data were provided as two independent communication channels within a single system.

The use of sensors in combination with self-reports was studied by Morris. Solar Display [5] aims to induce behavioral changes both for the elderly and for caregivers, by creating awareness of the changing quality and quantity of a social network of a senior. A 3-month field trial (6 dyads of seniors and caregivers) showed that self-reflection was encouraged and awareness improved. The improved awareness resulted in reflections on the social network by seniors and their caregivers. Based on the new insights, the elderly participants were more actively involved in strengthening their social network. Morris suggests studying the use of annotation tools to track subjective social satisfaction, next to the objective measures used in Solar Display.

MarkerClock [7] is an interesting example of how sensor data can be combined with abstract user annotations. MarkerClock aims to improve mutual awareness of living routines by visualizing the amount of activity detected by a webcam in time. Users can place abstract symbols on their own traces, as an additional form of communication. The field evaluation showed that the participants used the presence information for finding good times for visits or calls. Since the information display was limited to presence information and abstract symbols, it was however hard to communicate affective messages.

Next to the academic studies, there are examples of sensor-based systems commercially available that create awareness of the context and state of the elderly. The combination of sensor data and user input to clarify sensor data has not yet been applied in a commercial setting.

Existing awareness systems tend to focus on presenting data that can be automatically collected using sensors. Recent focus group sessions with family caregivers (publication pending) did however show that sensor data often raises new questions. For example, if the senior got out of bed late, would this indicate a need for care, or was the senior feeling fine? The present paper describes experience tagging, a mechanism that enables end-users to annotate sensor data using subjective tags. A research prototype was designed and evaluated in the field. The preliminary findings from a 4-week field trial with three caregiver/senior couples are presented.

2   Concept Development

User exploration: To better understand the context of family care and the information needs of the family caregivers, a focus group session was organized. Four participants (adult children who provide care to their parents) were asked to discuss how
they experience the family care activity, and to describe in detail what information
would help them be better prepared for the care activity. All participants indicated
that they felt responsible for their parents in need of care, and they had many worries
regarding the present needs of their parent and the changes in time. The worries can
be summarized in three categories: *physiology* (food intake, medicine intake, acute
physical problems, etc.), *safety* (whereabouts, environment, incidents/prevention,
etc.), and *love and belonging* (emotional state, social state).

These findings are in line with findings from related work [4, 6]. Family caregivers
express a need for information. Part of the information can be collected using sensors,
in particular the information related to physiology (e.g., medicine intake) and safety
(e.g., fall detection). The participants also expressed an interest in the emotional state
of the senior. Since present sensors are unable to accurately detect emotional states of
people in a home setting, the information needs to be collected in a different way.

To better understand the needs of the seniors, a focus group session was organized
with five participants (>65 years of age, living independently). We asked the seniors
their view on using a monitoring system to support family care, and their view on the
use of sensors as a privacy threat. Interestingly, all participants could imagine other
people using a monitoring system, whereas none of the participants found themselves
in need of a monitoring system. Furthermore, the participants indicated that they were
willing to accept sensors in their homes, as long as there would be a clear and direct
benefit for themselves.

The user exploration shows a basic need of family caregivers to be aware of the functional state and context of seniors. Family caregivers would also like to be aware of the
emotional state of the seniors, even in the early stages of the care process. At the same
time, seniors do see the value of communicating experiences and affective states. When
designing an awareness display for family care, one should however be aware that even
though seniors recognize the value of a monitoring system in the later stages of the care
process, they are skeptical towards using a monitoring system in the early stages of the
care process. When targeting 'younger' seniors, designers need to find new ways to
create benefit for seniors when using awareness displays and monitoring systems.

Design rationale: Family caregivers are interested to know the general attitudes and
the subjective experiences of the caretaker regarding activities, events, whereas
present sensor-based systems are unable to capture these subjective views. Experience
tags will enable end-users to annotate sensor data and thereby enhance awareness.

We decided to focus on 'younger' seniors who are capable of independent living.
The design aims to create meaningful awareness for both the caregivers and the
seniors, rather than providing 'functional' awareness and monitoring functions. A
symmetrical system design was selected, in which both the senior and the family
caregiver are treated as equal parties. The system can be regarded as a generic home
awareness display, which cannot only be used to support family care, but also to increase social connectedness.

Figure 1 shows a prototype of the experience-tagging awareness display. The display shows two activity traces, one for the family caregiver, and one for the senior in need of care. The activity traces are based on sensor data. In the prototype, passive infrared sensors are used to detect physical activity in the kitchen, living room and bedroom doorway, and tags are used to capture subjective experiences. The prototype thereby covers the information category *love and belonging* and partially covers the category *safety*. To support the later stages of the care process, the system would need to use additional sensors and monitoring functions.

Fig. 1. A touch-screen display was used as an interactive awareness display in the homes of participating seniors and family caregivers (left figure). The display shows an activity trace for both the family caregiver and the senior in need of care (right figure). Users can add subjective annotations to the local activity trace, and can add question marks to the remote activity trace.

Experience tags enable users to add a subjective view to the sensor data, and can be linked to the activity traces. Users select a mood from 9 predefined mood tags ranging from excited to sad [8], and they can add text. The senior in figure 1, for example, added an experience tag indicating that he felt happy because the weather was nice.

A key challenge is to motivate users to add experience tags. In the prototype, users could themselves motivate their remote partner by adding question marks. A question mark can be placed on the activity trace of the remote partner. The remote partner can click on the question mark, and will be asked to enter a mood and/or text.

Evaluation: A pilot study with two family caregiver/senior couples for approximately two weeks each was conducted to fine-tune the methodology and to test the technology. Next, a field trial was conducted with three couples of participants for 4 weeks each. Semi-structured intake-interviews and exit-interviews were used to better understand the care-relationship between the participants, to find out how participants experienced the prototype, and how the prototype affected the care relationship. Daily experience sampling questions were used to measure day-to-day changes in feelings of connectedness and awareness.

One couple actively used the experience tags. They appreciated the sensor-based presence information, and they were very positive about the system. They used the tags to ask both questions regarding the sensor data, and to communicate general messages. They felt the system indubitably improved their feeling of connectedness, they felt they were better aware of the remote setting, and they were sad to hand in the system at the end of the trial. Both participants indicated that the system contributed to their peace-of-mind, knowing that things were well at the remote location.

The second couple were inactive users of the system. The junior started by adding experience tags, but the senior did not react. After two weeks, it was decided to move the awareness display in the home of the senior to a different location of the living room, where the senior would more often glance at the display. Whereas more experience tags were added, the tags were generally used as short text messages without a link to the sensor data. Even though the use of the tags was limited, both participants did consider the system to be a valuable add-on to their life.

The third couple primarily used the system as a sensor-display. Tags were only used in a functional way ('are you home?'). In the exit interviews, though, both participants valued the improved awareness as created by the system.

3   Conclusions and Next Steps

The key innovation in the present project was the focus on experience tagging, which enabled seniors and their family caregivers to add their subjective experiences to sensor data. Moreover, the users were invited to elicit experiences from their counterparts. The project aimed to increase mutual awareness and ultimately improve connectedness and peace of mind. The user evaluation showed that participants varied in how often and in what way they used the experience tags. In general, however, participants appreciated the system and valued the system as a tool for family care.

As a next step, (1) motivational strategies to encourage users to enter subjective data will be studied, (2) mechanisms to allow for group communication will be explored, and (3) mechanisms for lightweight acknowledgement will be studied to avoid false expectations.

Acknowledgements. The work presented in this paper is part of the Independent@Home project, funded by Agentschap NL IOP-MMI.

References

1. Matthews, T., Mankoff, J.: A Toolkit for Evaluating Peripheral Awareness. In: Proc. CHI 2005 Workshop on Awareness Systems (2005)
2. MacIntyre, B., Mynatt, E.D., Voida, S., Hansen, K.M., Tullio, J., Corso, G.M.: Support for Multitasking and Background Awareness using Interactive Peripheral Displays. In: UIST 2001 (2001)
3. Consolvo, S., Roessler, P., Shelton, B.E.: The CareNet Display: Lessons Learned from an In Home Evaluation of an Ambient Display. In: Davies, N., Mynatt, E.D., Siio, I. (eds.) UbiComp 2004. LNCS, vol. 3205, pp. 1–17. Springer, Heidelberg (2004)
4. Dadlani, P., Sinitsyn, A., Fontijn, W., Markopoulos, P.: Aurama: Caregiver Awareness for Living Independently with an Augmented Picture Frame Display. AI & Society 25(2), 233–245 (2010)
5. Morris, M.E.: Social Networks as Health Feedback Displays. IEEE Int. Comp., 29–37 (2005)
6. Mynatt, E.D., Rowan, J., Jacobs, A., Craighill, S.: Digital Family Portraits: Supporting Peace of Mind for Extended Family Members. In: Proc. CHI 2001, pp. 333–340 (2001)
7. Riche, Y., Mackay, W.: PeerCare: Supporting Awareness of Rhythms and Routines for Better Aging in Place. CSCW 19, 73–104 (2010)
8. Vastenburg, M.H., Romero, N., van Bel, D.T., Desmet, P.: PMRI: Development of a Pictorial Mood Reporting Instrument. In: CHI 2011 Extended Abstracts, pp. 2155–2160 (2011)

Comparison of Health Measures to Movement Data in Aware Homes

Brian O'Mullane, Brennon Bortz, Ann O'Hannlon,
John Loane, and R. Benjamin Knapp

CASALA / Netwell, PJ Carrolls Building, DkIT, Ireland
{brian.omullane,brennon.bortz,john.loane,ben.knapp}@casala.ie,
ann.ohannlon@netwellcentre.org

Abstract. Detecting wellness in older adults with just ambient sensors is a challenging and difficult task, one that can only be address with large volumes of detailed annotated data and a diverse participant base. Presented here are early results comparing movement data to baseline depression and mobility data from a purpose built 16 unit ambient assisted living development in Ireland. With the goal of ultimately detecting health changes in an older population with ambient sensors, results here show that whereas there is some correlations between health measures and sensor data as well as some observable patterns, but more work needs to be done.

Keywords: AAL, Aware Homes, KNX, Depression, Mobility, PIR.

1 Introduction

The population is living longer and with this there is a push towards improving quality of life of older people as well as allowing them control and autonomy while aging. Nine years ago, female life expectancy in the record-holding country (Japan), had risen for 160 years at a steady pace of almost three months per year, and this upward trend has continued [1]. Ambient assisted living offers a potential solution to this problem and hence is an active area of research. It involves embedding low impact pervasive sensors, such as presence sensors and door usage sensors in homes. Using this technology to help build a picture of behaviour and detecting when this behaviour changes over time, and correlating this to indicators of decline is the ultimate goal of this research. But what does this behaviour presented by the sensors look like? How can we relate this behaviour to physical and mental health issues? In this paper we present data gathered from ambient sensors embedded the homes of 10 older people over a 3-month period. We look at the movement behaviour of the residents as well as baseline measures of their depression and mobility and try to identify commonalities between them.

2 Background and Related Work

A primary activity at the Centre for Affective Solutions for Ambient Living Awareness (CASALA) is our work with a number of older adults living at the Great Northern

D. Keyson et al. (Eds.): AmI 2011, LNCS 7040, pp. 290–294, 2011.
© Springer-Verlag Berlin Heidelberg 2011

Haven (GNH) demonstration housing project. GNH consists of 16 purpose-built aware homes in Dundalk, Ireland. Each home is equipped with a combination of sensor and interactive technologies to support ambient assisted living for older people. Currently there are 13 homes occupied by 11 men and 4 women. Using a total of 2240 sensors, actuators and higher level alerts throughout the development, we have collected close to 100million records of data to date. The sensors include presence sensors, contact sensors on all internal and external doors and windows, electricity, water and heating usage sensors, ambient light and temperature sensors as well as an array of other ambient sensors. For this study we are examining movement behaviour, using just the presence sensors in the hallway, bedroom, living room and the door sensor for the main entrance. The presence sensors are KNX passive infrared (PIR) sensors tuned to give readings of any small movement in a room with a reset interval of ten seconds.

This paper focuses on a first look at features that could be used as part of a behaviour recognition engine, currently in development[2], and compares them to baseline health measures taken from residents.

3   Data Description

The cohort for this study begun moving in to their homes in June 2010. Two of the three PIRs used for this study were moved from their location over the window to a new location over the entry door in the bedroom and livingroom on April 13th, to ensure capture of entry in to those rooms. Hence for this paper, only readings between 19th of April and 22nd of July 2011 are considered. All of the data used in this study was gathered KNX sensors and aggregated and logged by NETxAutomation OPC server software. Two of the homes are occupied by two residents—data for these homes were removed from the examination as the presence for each resident is difficult to determine and outside the scope of this study. Difficulties with incomplete data was observed on 3 of the 92 days, by examining a periodic sensor data (power sensor samples at 0.1Hz), these 3 days were moved entirely from the dataset.

The layout of the homes are show in figure 1. The resident must pass through the hall way sensor when moving between any of the rooms, such as when they are visiting the main bathroom from the living area during the day.

Fig. 1. Great Northern Haven home layout

Each presence sensor fired on average 155 times a day and the sensor firing times gave a characteristic that is easily identifiable by manual inspection. To help visualise behaviour patterns the sensor data was represented on a spiral plot called a "last clock"[3] that plots the data on a 24-hour clock with midnight at the top and spirals out from the centre. Each circuit represents a day.

The *outing data* was derived from both the front door sensor as well as the PIR inside home data. It was simply deduced from door firing and no movement inside house followed by another door firing. Outings group in to two very distinct groups which can be easily separated, outings of less than 5minutes are considered to be less significant and removed from this study. The design of the apartments is such that all of the residents on the ground flour have a second outside door operated by swipe card, the door sensor is located on the inside or apartment door, but inspecting the data shows unusually high number of firings for the apartment doors for 2 (ID4,5) of the 3 residents in the ground floor apartments. A characteristic of the KNX door sensors used is that they fire periodically if a door is left open, this high number of firings might suggest this internal door was left open. Additionally the hall PIR for apartment ID 25 reported no firings during this time, hence could be concluded as either damaged or incorrectly addressed.

 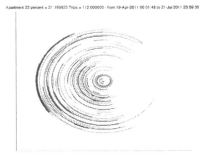

Fig. 2. Clock plot of time outside home for person with lowest depression score

Fig. 3. Clock plot of time outside home for person with highest depression score

Holiday data was derived from PIR data falling below a very low number for a resident in a day, the number chosen was 20, where normal daily average was 465. Holiday data was used to remove holidays from time outside and PIR firing analysis.

Mobility status: Mobility was assessed using the walking subscale of the Health Assessment Questionnaire Disability Index (HAQ-DI)[4]. The HAQ-DI assesses physical functioning in upper and / or lower extremities. The walking subscale, participants were asked about their ability to walk outdoors on flat ground and to climb up five steps. Response options ranged from zero (self-sufficient) to three (severely disabled).

Table 1. Mobility data. Understandably time outside show's strong correlation with mobility measure. P = .057

Apt ID	Mobility	Total PIR Records	Holidays	Time Outside (%)	Outings
4	1	25505	0	19.64	1775[1]
5	1	32649	4	16.67	1092[1]
20	1	47659	0	10.18	238
22	1	48222	2	21.16	112
25	1	28299	0	30.5	247
7	2	25381	0	1.79	59
11	2	17696	7	10.17	155[1]
8	2.7	41570	2	4.25	61
3	No Data	4048	52	4.29	112[1]
12	No Data	43012	0	3.04	83

Psychopathology: To examine mental health or well-being the General Health Questionnaire (GHQ-12) was used[5]. This measure consists of 12 items relating to common mental health experiences of depression, anxiety, somatic symptoms and social withdrawal. It is a screen to identify respondents likely to have or be at risk of developing psychiatric disorders. This scale is used widely in studies of well-being [6]. In the current study, higher scores equate with higher levels of psychopathology.

With the goal of comparing sleep patterns to depression scores bedroom PIRs sensor data was examined. It was hoped the standard deviation of bedroom presence data could help determine sleep times, but the data proved too inconsistent.

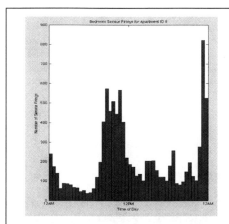	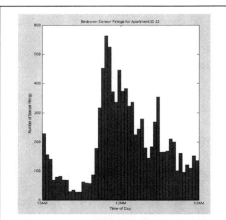
Bedroom PIR mean firing for participant with highest depression rating	Bedroom PIR mean firing for participant with lowest depression rating

---

[1] Ground floor apartment with extra security door allowing apartment door to be left open, outing data cannot be trusted.

Table 2. Depression Data. Only weak correlations to presence patterns observed

		Mean Daily PIR firing					
Apt ID	Depression	Time outside (%)	Outings	Bedroom	Hall	Living Room	STD of time in bedroom
8	19	4.25	61	113.82	71.23	292.77	0.27
5	22	16.67[1]	1092[1]	25.98	79.52	278.60	0.22
11	23	10.17	155	65.46	30.62	119.72	0.21
25	24	30.50	247	91.89	0.00[2]	226.08	0.20
3	25	4.29[1]	112[1]	319.65	236.89	535.57	0.27
22	30	21.16	112	110.01	120.11	324.15	0.23

4   Discussion and Further Work

It is dangerous to draw any firm conclusions on a test group with n=10, particularly where data is complete for only 3 residents, but with sensor data in this study of over 300,000 records some interesting results can be anticipated. Bedroom sensors show observable peaks in at bedtime and morning time, with further analysis sleeping hours may be determined. Outings and time out of home cannot be ruled out of correlations with depression, in fact the data tends towards the opposite. Mobility questionnaire correlates very well with what is observed by the sensors.

More baseline depression data will strengthen result conclusions, and better validation and monitoring of KNX sensors is required.

Acknowledgments. To Florian Le Touzé and Diane Fauré, research assistants at CASALA, for data analysis and Enterprise Ireland's Applied Research Enhancement Programme with support from EU Structural funds.

References

[1] Oeppen, J., Vaupel, J.W.: Broken limits to life expectancy. Science 296(5570), 1029 (2002)
[2] Loane, J., O'Mullane, B., Bortz, B., Knapp, R.B.: Interpreting Presence Sensor Data and Looking for Similarities Between Homes Using Cluster Analysis. Presented at the Pervasive Health 2011 (2011)
[3] Angesleva, J., Cooper, R.: Last clock. IEEE Computer Graphics and Applications 25(1), 20–23 (2005)
[4] Fries, J., Spitz, P., Young, D.: The dimensions of health outcomes: the health assessment questionnaire, disability and pain scales. J. Rheumatol. 9(5), 789–793 (1982)
[5] Goldberg, D.P.: Manual of the General Health Questionnaire. NFER Publishing
[6] Jones, M.: The burden of psychological symptoms in UK Armed Forces. Occupational Medicine 56(5), 322–328 (2006)

---

[2] Damaged PIR.

Context Assessment during Blood Pressure Self-measurement Utilizing the Sensor Chair

Stefan Wagner[1], Thomas Skjødeberg Toftegaard[1], and Olav Wedege Bertelsen[2]

[1] Department of Engineering
[2] Department of Computer Science,
Aarhus University, Helsingforsgade 14, 8200 Aarhus N
{sw,tst}@iha.dk, olavb@cs.au.dk

Abstract. Self-measurement of blood pressure requires the patient to follow a range of best practice recommendations in order to be considered valid for diagnostic use. We evaluate the feasibility of using a sensor-equipped chair to classify patient position during blood pressure measurement. Results indicate that this is feasible with over 89 % confirmed classification results.

Keywords: ambient assisted living, blood pressure self-measurement, ambient intelligence, pervasive healthcare, telemonitoring, telehealth, data quality.

1   Introduction

Blood pressure self-measurement (BPSM) is used to diagnose patients suspected of hypertension, as well as for long-term monitoring of a number of chronic patient groups. BPSM is considered a valid method for determining the blood pressure (BP) of such patient groups providing that the best-practice recommendations for obtaining the measurements are followed [1-3]. These recommendations are defined by a range of national and international clinical associations [4,5]. Recommendations include elements such as: patient should be sufficiently rested and seated correctly before and during measurement. The use of information technology for obtaining BPSM has been investigated in several studies without verifying patient adherence to the recommendations [6,7]. As only measurements following the recommendations are considered reliable [1-3], it may be argued that the quality of data from the reported studies [6,7] could be indeterminate and the clinical use of such systems could lead to over or under medication of the patient [1,7,8]. As a strategy for overcoming these challenges we suggest utilizing intelligent environments to detect user context to determine the level of user adherence. Context-aware technologies [9] have been used in a number of healthcare related studies [10-12], including as an intervention strategy for improving medical adherence [13,14]. Ambient assisted living research have pointed to the potential of using sensor-fusion and context-aware technologies for improved insights into user-behavior and context in the home setting [15-18].

   The aim of this study is to determine whether a sensor-equipped chair can be used to sense user-context and assess whether the user is correctly seated during BPSM as suggested by the recommendations.

D. Keyson et al. (Eds.): AmI 2011, LNCS 7040, pp. 295–299, 2011.

2   Suggested Solution

Sensing user context can be achieved in many ways including vision-based systems or body worn sensors such as accelerometer equipped wireless sensor nodes. We suggest equipping a chair with sensors using a minimum of sensor technology in order to keep complexity low, reduce cost, and allow for easier maintainability of the final solution. We propose that two piezoresistive force sensors embedded in the chair can be used for sensing user leg placement utilizing a computer based classification algorithm. The chair is intended to be part of a sensor network consisting additionally of a gateway computer and a BP measurement device, possibly combined with other sensors that could be useful for tracking other elements of the recommendations.

3   Methods and Materials

To evaluate the feasibility of the suggested solution, we have built an evaluation prototype consisting of an embedded Linux computer attached with two piezoresistive sensors (FlexiForce, Tekscan Inc., US) embedded in a chair (see Figure 1). The prototype communicates with a Windows computer for data extraction and real time evaluation feedback using Web services over a WiFi connection.

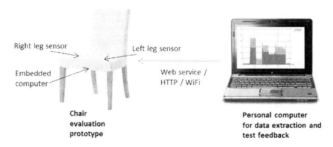

Fig. 1. The evaluation prototype (left) as part of the test bed. The chair computer is exposing sensor data via a web service to a dedicated data extraction and test feedback application.

The prototype is tested in the laboratory with users (n=10) performing a test scenario consisting of six test cases, changing between different positions: standing, seated with both feet on the ground, and seated with legs crossed. The test leader observes, evaluates and records the results of the computer classification of each change in user position. Users are instructed that deviations from the test protocol are allowed, shifting position more often, or in a different order, as classification runs independently of time and order of the test cases. A real time graph is depicted on screen during measurement with a guiding sound indicating when it is time to shift to the next test case. Data are automatically classified and reported visually on the real time graph by the test application. Concurrently, the test leader observes and verifies all classifications results and compares them to actual user position. All data are collected and stored in an XML file for future handling.

4   Results

Data was collected from 10 test users performing a total of 65 scenarios with a duration ranging from 31 to 82 seconds (average: 50 seconds). A total of 439 test cases spanning 248.848 samples were recorded (see Table 1). Test leader's manual observations were registered with the observations for each test case, providing the observed vs. classified percentage as the main evaluation parameter.

Table 1. Results overview

Parameter	Value
Total number of sensor readings and classified samples	248.848
Successful automated classification of samples, percentage	81.7 %
Observed changes in position (user changing position)	439
Observed vs. classified position change, percentage	89.5%

In Figure 2, a range of 6 test cases are presented illustrating the results of one test user completing a test scenario. The dots followed by arrows represent computer classification of changes in position into either: standing, seated, legs crossed or unknown. As can be seen in Figure 2: Test case 1 (TC1) is classified as "standing", lasting until TC2. The "unknown" state is only active for a short time due to sensor transition noise, then changing to "seated" in TC2. TC3 is classified as "legs crossed", TC4 as "seated", TC5 as "legs crossed" and finally TC5 as "standing".

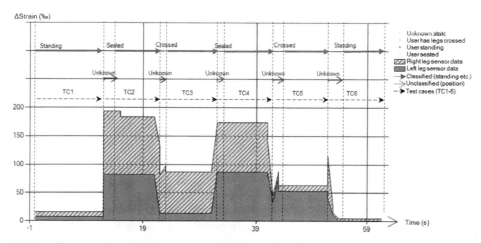

Fig. 2. Results from a sample test scenario. The diagonal and solid areas indicate the level of sensor strain on the left & right sensors respectively as a function of time. The arrows indicate a change of position: standing, seated, crossed, or unknown. TC1-6 have been added manually to the figure, in order to illustrate the timespan of the test cases 1 to 6.

5   Discussion

Results indicate that context-data on user position can successfully be obtained using seat sensors. Collected data was in 81.7% of the cases classified into either: standing (not seated), seated, and legs crossed. Of these, 89.5% were verified as correct by manual observations made by the test leader. However, results were obtained in a simulated setting prescribing the test subjects to constantly change position. In a real world scenario, we would rather expect subjects to remain seated for longer durations, and have fewer changes of position. To validate this we need further experimentation. Also, the system should be evaluated in situ, in the home setting and at the outpatient clinic, in order to detect the system's ability to detect actual user behavior.

There are several sources of bias including: sensor noise and drift, the physical construction of the chair, imperfect classification and filtering algorithms, and physical variations of the test subjects. Also, the presence of a test leader and location of the experiment may also result in observer bias. More accurate prototypes could be constructed, and more experiments could be carried out in order to evaluate alternative constructions, algorithms, sensors and sensor placement.

Requiring users to use a dedicated chair for healthcare measurements in the home setting may not be feasible for all patient types. Here, a small cushion or similar might be more appropriate as a sensor platform. In the outpatient clinic, the use of a dedicated chair appears more viable.

In conclusion, using intelligent and context-aware furniture for quantifying adherence levels during BPSM appears feasible. The deployment of such intelligent furniture alongside biomedical BP measurement devices could increase our understanding of user adherence to the recommendations and improve data quality.

The suggested solution might in the future also allow us to better guide patients through the measurement process in a relevant way to improve overall adherence levels, as well as assist caretakers to better assess the quality of data obtained in an unsupervised setting, such as in the home or at the outpatient clinic. This could lead to more reliable diagnosis of blood pressure related conditions in the future, which might reduce medication errors and optimize treatment efficiency.

6   Conclusion

We have suggested a system for assessing user position when performing BPSM. An evaluation prototype was built using a commercial chair and tested in the laboratory in order to determine the feasibility of the system. Evaluation indicated that such a system is feasible to construct and that it may be useful for physicians and patients using BPSM in order to obtain higher quality data: This could lead to more reliable diagnosis, reduce medication errors and optimize treatment efficiency.

Acknowledgments. Thanks to industrial designer Anders Bech Christensen, who helped conceive and build the prototypes and to students acting as test subjects.

References

1. Campbell, N.R., Chockalingam, A., Fodor, J.G., McKay, D.W.: Accurate, reproducible measurement of blood pressure. CMAJ 143(1), 19–24 (1990)
2. Pickering, T.G.: Ambulatory monitoring and blood pressure variability. Science Press (1991)
3. Pierdomenico, S.D., Di Nicola, M., Esposito, A.L., Di Mascio, R., Ballone, E., Lapenna, D., et al.: Prognostic value of different indices of blood pressure variability in hypertensive patients. Am J. Hypertens 22(8), 842–847 (2009)
4. Pickering, T.G., Hall, J.E., Appel, L.J., Falkner, B.E., Graves, J., Hill, M.N., et al.: Recommendations for blood pressure measurement in humans and experimental animals: part 1: blood pressure measurement in humans: a statement for professionals from the Subcommittee of Professional and Public Education of the American Heart Association Council on High Blood Pressure Research. Circulation 111(5), 697–716 (2005)
5. Frantz, J., Feihl, F., Waeber, B.: European Society of Hypertension. Practice guidelines of the European Society of Hypertension for home blood pressure measurement. Rev. Med. Suisse. 6(262), 1696–1699 (2010)
6. Huniche, L., Dinesen, B., Grann, O., Toft, E., Nielsen, C.: Empowering patients with COPD using Tele-homecare technology. Stud. Health Technol. Inform. 155, 48–54 (2010)
7. AbuDagga, A., Resnick, H.E., Alwan, M.: Impact of blood pressure telemonitoring on hypertension outcomes: a literature review. Telemed J. E. Health 16(7), 830–838 (2010)
8. Pickering, T.G., Miller, N.H., Ogedegbe, G., Krakoff, L.R., Artinian, N.T., Goff, D., et al.: Call to action on use and reimbursement for home blood pressure monitoring. Hypertension 52(1), 1–9 (2008)
9. Dey, A.K.: Ubiquitous Computing Fundamentals. CRC Press (2010)
10. Varshney, U.: Pervasive Healthcare and Wireless Health Monitoring. Mobile Networks and Applications 12(2), 113–127 (2007)
11. Bardram, J., Bossen, C., Thomsen, A.: Designing for transformations in collaboration: a study of the deployment of homecare technology. In: Proccedings of the 2005 International ACM SIGGROUP Conference on Supporting Group Work, pp. 294–303 (2005)
12. Bardram, J.E.: Pervasive healthcare as a scientific discipline. Methods Inf. Med. 47(3), 178–185 (2008)
13. Oliveria, R., Cherubini, M., Oliver, N.: MoviPill: improving medication compliance for elders using a mobile persuasive social game. In: Proceedings of the 12th ACM International Conference on Ubiquitous Computing. ACM, New York (2010)
14. Wan, D.: Magic Medicine Cabinet: A Situated Portal for Consumer Healthcare. Handheld and Ubiquitous Computing, 352–355 (1999)
15. Kidd, C., Orr, R., Abowd, G., Atkeseon, C., Essa, I., Macintyre, B., Starner, T., Newstter, W.: The Aware Home: A Living Laboratory for Ubiquitous Computing Research. Cooperative Buildings (1999)
16. Demiris, G.: Smart homes and ambient assisted living in an aging society. New Opportunities and Challenges for Biomedical Informatics. Methods Inf. Med. 47(1), 56–57 (2008)
17. Koch, S., Marschollek, M., Wolf, K.H., Plischke, M., Haux, R.: On health-enabling and ambient-assistive technologies. What has been achieved and where do we have to go? Methods Inf. Med. 48(1), 29–37 (2009)
18. Wagner, S., Toftegaard, T.S., Bertelsen, O.W.: Increased Data Quality in Home Blood Pressure Monitoring through Context Awareness. In: 2011 5th International Conference on Pervasive Computing Technologies for Healthcare, PervasiveHealth (2011)

Enhancing Accessibility through Speech Technologies on AAL Telemedicine Services for iTV

Héctor Delgado, Aitor Rodriguez-Alsina, Antoni Gurguí, Enric Martí, Javier Serrano, and Jordi Carrabina

Center for Ambient Intelligence and Accessibility of Catalonia, Campus UAB, 08193 Bellaterra, Spain
{hector.delgado,aitor.rodriguez,antoni.guirgui,enric.marti, javier.serrano,jordi.carrabina}@uab.cat
http://centresderecerca.uab.cat/caiac

Abstract. Ambient Assisted Living Technologies are providing sustainable and affordable solutions for the independent living of senior citizens. In this scenario, telemedicine systems enhance distance patient's health care through interactive audiovisual media at home. Today TV is becoming the main connected device at home. However, Interactive TV applications must be fully adapted, particularly to the available input device: the Remote Control (RC). Despite this adaptation, some tasks are still uncomfortable due to the RC limitations. Therefore, more user-friendly input modalities are strongly desired. Spoken language allows distance hands- and eyes-free operation within the room, providing an intuitive and natural interface. This paper presents some accessibility facilities based on speech technologies for an interactive TV telemedicine service. The specific layout for TV environments, the help of an avatar and the voice navigation will enhance the user access, while the speech-based creation of medical reports reduces dramatically the time physicians need to write reports.

Keywords: telemedicine, accessibility, multimodal interaction, natural user interfaces, interactive TV, speech technologies, avatar.

1 Introduction

Ambient Assisted Living (AAL) aims to produce technological support to help the aged to live independently, extending the time they stay in the environment where they are used to live. Telemedicine, understood as the deployment of telecommunication technologies to provide distance health care and health information to patients, can be extremely beneficial to provide close interactions between patients and experts. It is especially significant for people living in remote areas, people in dependant situations and even for senior citizens requiring an intensive use of medical assistance and careful monitoring [6]. Given the growth of Internet technologies, a number of Web applications to access to

D. Keyson et al. (Eds.): AmI 2011, LNCS 7040, pp. 300–308, 2011.

different health services have been developed to be used in home environments. However, accessing to these services usually depends on the availability of a computer or a specific device to connect to the health system. The rise of connected devices in people's daily lives such as smartphones, set-top boxes (STB) for digital TV, HbbTV and tablet PCs has generated a great variety of multimedia systems with Internet capabilities giving to the end-user (i.e. the patient) the possibility to access the health system anywhere, anytime. In the home environment, in spite of the rise of other connected devices, the TV is still the most used device for the consumption of multimedia contents and it is a realistic candidate to become, in a near future, the main platform to access to specific interactive services related to education, health and home automation [13]. In this context, the interactivity model of a TV environment must be taken into account to ensure proper access conditions for all users. People usually watch TV some meters away, interacting through a Remote Controller (RC) and sometimes in company. This implies, for instance, that the components and fonts of the interactive applications must be sized large enough for a comfortable readability and the navigation must be adapted to the RC instead of a pointer on the screen. In spite of these adaptations, some tasks such as introducing user data through the RC might be considerably tedious, frustrating and inefficient. Thus, the need of other input methods becomes practically indispensable for applications with a higher degree of complexity. The use of multimodal and more natural interfaces will facilitate the user navigation and, in the case of telemedicine systems, improve some medical procedures. Spoken language has several characteristics that make it a potential interaction method between user and computer. It allows distance hands- and eyes-free operation within the room, and provides an intuitive and natural interface. The use of speech technologies as user interface can result in very beneficial interactive TV applications. The user can give orders to the system using their voice, which will be obtained by the system through Automatic Speech Recognition (ASR). On the other hand, the system provides answers by means of speech synthesis.

This work is the result of a research and development project developed in collaboration with physicians to enhance the accessibility capabilities of a traditional telemedicine system. In this paper we present an interactive application for telemedicine in digital TV enriched with accessibility features based on speech technologies: (1) a spoken user interface that provides voice navigation and (2) a speech-assisted system for the creation of medical reports. In addition, we include the use of an avatar to provide the information to the user more effectively. The rest of the paper is organized as follows: section 2 describes the presented service, the main use cases and the system architecture; section 3 details the implementation issues for the used speech technologies and the avatar; finally, in section 4 we present the conclusions of our work.

2 System Overview

This section describes the AAL service, the use cases and the system architecture.

2.1   Service and Use Case Description

The implemented service is an interactive application for a digital TV environment that aims to enhance the accessibility in health and telemedicine systems. Here we refer to accessibility in a broad sense, as a set of measures that helps to improve access to everybody in general, mainly oriented to those people unfamiliar with technology (e.g usability enhancements). The service is connected to the Info 33 health system [2], which manages the clinical information of patients throughout their life. It allows an efficient monitoring of programs for prevention and health promotion through the clinical knowledge and a universal coding for clinical interventions. This information is certified by a health professional chosen by the user providing validity and reliability of the information recorded. The service presented in this work facilitates the access to the Info 33 system from a connected TV applying some accessibility techniques successfully used in traditional Web environments, such as the multimodal user interaction, the accessible design of web-based user interfaces based on the W3C Web Content Accessibility Guidelines (WCAG) [5], and the addition of an avatar for an assisted navigation and an ASR system for the user interaction. The service has been built as a Rich Internet Application (RIA) to improve its performance and the user experience [8].

In this scenario, two main use cases were defined: 1. An end-user accessing to his health information: A user is at home watching TV when he decides to consult his medical record and see if there is any automatic notification from the system (e.g. an appointment reminder or a vaccine alert). He starts the interactive application from the provided Media Center platform and an avatar welcomes him giving spoken information about the main navigation options. The user can browse the different sections in the service (e.g. personal data, clinical data, the record of vital signs, the lab test results, the medical reports and the automatic alerts) not only with the RC supplied with the platform, but also by saying the key words -giving orders- to navigate through the interactive interface. At any time, he can request help information about a specific section of the interface and the avatar provides it. 2. The professional user (e.g. the doctor) creating medical reports in a multimodal way: A doctor sees a patient at home to scan and diagnose his condition. The doctor accesses to the Info 33 health system through the generated TV interface identified as a doctor in order to be allowed to generate a new report. Thus, he selects the report section through his voice or the RC and opens a new report to edit it. During the exploration, the physician dictates the findings, which are being written semi-automatically (with confirmation and editing options) in a fully hands-free mode into the report. At all times, the report can also be modified manually by editing it directly with a connected keyboard.

2.2   System Architecture

The above described service has been built as a RIA into a custom Set-top Box (STB) platform, which will be provided to the system end-users. This platform connects to the Info 33 server through an IP network (e.g. Internet, IPTV networks). It contains the client application and only requests to the server the dynamic XML data related to the logged user. The application is shown on the TV through an HDMI interface and allows a multimodal user interaction through the support of different user input devices that are automatically detected by the user interface to interact consequently. Figure 1 depicts this overall architecture.

Fig. 1. Overall architecture of the presented telemedicine system

Due to the implementation of the RIA at the client platform, the interaction with the server is limited to the XML interchange of the specific health data, leaving the rest of the tasks for the STB platform in the client side. The middleware, which includes the RIA, the ASR module, the speech synthesis module, the avatar engine, the security module and a Web browser, as well as the built-in services have been built on top of an Intel Dual-Core Atom N330 @1.6GHz and a Linux OS. The STB architecture is described in Figure 2.

3   Speech Technologies for Multimodal Interaction

In an environment of digital TV, where the availability of a keyboard as input device is not always assured (a RC is usually used), other multimodal interaction methods are strongly desired to improve user interaction and accessibility. Speech is a natural way of communication. Due to its characteristics, it can be remotely used in hands- and eyes-busy situations. Previous work has been carried out in the application of speech recognition in medical environments [9]. On one hand, spoken dialogues systems for health care and telemedicine might empower users to introduce basic information and vital sign health data in order to perform self-monitoring tasks, or provide patients with useful information about appointments and other relevant issues. On the other hand, continuous speech

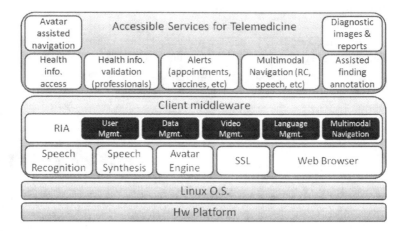

Fig. 2. The STB architecture of the presented telemedicine system

recognition dictation systems make the creation of medical reports lighter to the professionals of medicine [12].

The project aims to offer users an intuitive and easy way of accessing and introducing medical data into the interactive TV system, by means of their voice. On the patient's side, voice commands may be used to browse the application in a natural fashion. On the physician's side, medical information can be input through their voice without the need of an external device while the patient is being explored, providing an effective and efficient method for the generation of medical reports. This way, doctors save a significant amount of time writing reports and can pay attention to the patient, whose experience and degree of comfort will be improved.

Unlike dictation systems in medical domain, the presented approach focuses only on the subset of the medical findings. Limiting the ambit of application to the fixed list of findings implies an increment in terms of accuracy, since the task is significantly simpler than modeling more complex forms of language. In this situation, the language can be modeled through finite state grammars rather than statistical N-grams. The system also provides error correction. When the user pronounces a finding, the application will notify of the recognized utterance by means of speech synthesis, thus there is no need to look at the screen to check the result. With a simple error correction method via voice commands, incorrect findings can be easily removed, as well as corrected by re-speaking. More detailed explanations about the findings list and the error correction method are given in section 3.3.

The speech-based functionality developed in this work consists of two different parts: first, a spoken user interface that provides voice navigation through the application, and second, a system for speech-assisted creation of medical reports. In the subsequent subsections the training of the necessary infrastructure and development of the speech modules are explained in more detail.

3.1 ASR, Speech Synthesis and Avatar Setup

The current subsection gives an overview on the preparation of the necessary tools that are used later for the development of the speech-based functionality. It comprises the ASR training, the speech synthesis and the avatar.

ASR training. The acoustic models have been trained using the SpeechCon Catalan speech corpus [11]. The corpus consists of spontaneous and read speech from 550 speakers, recorded with four microphones at different distances. Each utterance is stored in 4 independent (one per microphone) 16 bit, 16 kHz uncompressed audio files. The audio files are then parametrized into a 39-dimensional feature vector consisting on 12 cepstral coefficients plus the 0th coefficient, deltas and delta-deltas.

The acoustic models consist in a set of cross-word tied-state triphone Hidden Markov Models (HMM) derived from 40 monophones HMMs, covering the sound units of Catalan language. The models were trained according to the standard Maximum Likelihood approach. Finally, the models are refined by applying the Discriminative Training technique. The whole training process has been carried out using the HTK toolkit [14]. Further information about the training process can be found in [7].

Speech Synthesis. Text-To-Speech (TTS) is utilized to generate the system responses dynamically. It makes possible to check results in eyes-busy situations. This way, the physician does not have to advert the eyes from the patient. The Festival [3] software is used for this purpose, combined with the Festcat [4] package that contains Catalan synthetic voices for Festival.

The Avatar. To improve interaction, we have included an avatar inside the interface. Here, avatar refers to a two-dimensional video representing a person or a virtual character. The main purpose of the avatar is to inform the user about the different navigation options available for each scene. Furthermore, there are many compelling reasons to include an animated agent in the interface. On one hand, avatars have demonstrated to be an effective way to improve user's understanding of synthetic voices [10]. On the other hand, it improves user's natural perception of the interaction, as the user acts as if they were both listening and speaking to a person. At the same time, a secondary purpose is to facilitate the learning and use of the interface. From the patient's point of view, the avatar can be seen as a medical assistant that takes notes and informs the patient about their medical condition and not as intrusion between him and his physician. At the same time, patient's confidence is very important when we talk about confidential or private information, as the user needs to feel comfortable to give or receive sensitive data and results. The avatar has been built off-line using AlterEgos [1]. This software generates the avatar's animation from a speech sound and the text speech files. For each scene, a text file with the scene presentation dialog is created. Using this file, a speech sound file is synthesized, using Festival. Then, the avatar facial animation is built, using both sound and text for lips synchronization. Afterward, the video is embedded in the scene. As the user navigates through scenes, the video is played accordingly.

3.2   Speech-Based User Interface

The speech-based user interface has been intended to facilitate access and browsing through the application, exploiting the naturalness of spoken communication as user input in ubiquitous systems.

The user can select the different options in the main menu through their voice. It allows a completely hands-free operation in order to navigate through the application. This method can be used by both end-users and professionals. The system implements a method for discarding the background speech based on 'universal' keywords. The system remains in 'wait' state, discarding speech input, until the universal keyword 'menu' followed by one of the possible menu entries is pronounced. Then, the best hypothesis is calculated. Next, a confidence measure is obtained to determine how likely the hypothesis is. If the confidence measure falls below an arbitrary threshold, the command is ignored and no action is performed. Otherwise, the menu entry corresponding to the hypothesis is accessed and shown in the graphic user interface.

3.3   Speech-Based Creation of Medical Reports

As said before, physicians spend a significant period of time writing medical reports. This fact makes patients feel uncomfortable, producing a feeling of impatience and inefficiency. The developed system offers the physician a way to generate the medical report while they are exploring the patient. It has important implications: doctors do not need to interrupt the exploration process, patients feel better treated, there is no dependency on other devices like a keyboard or RC, contact-time is optimized, etc.

Unlike conventional dictation systems in medial environment, the implemented module may be considered as a spoken dialogue system intended to introduce medical findings corresponding to the current appointment. The fact of considering only a subset of the medical language simplifies the task complexity noticeably. Although the system is not as flexible as a dictation system, the increment in accuracy is worth it, providing Word Error Rates (WER) next to 0%. The database of medical findings contains a list of 2144 sentences describing findings. Each one has a unique code within a whole categorization of findings.

The system consists of an ASR engine and a TTS module, as well as a simple dialogue manager that establishes the dialogue flow and deals with recognition errors and possible confirmations. Figure 3 depicts the dialogue flow. Once in new report mode, the system stays in 'wait' state until the keyword 'type' plus a medical finding is pronounced. Then, the best hypothesis from the database of the codified medical findings and a confidence measure are estimated. If the confidence measure reaches a set threshold, the hypothesis is considered correct, the TTS module pronounces it and the finding is stored. Otherwise, the system asks for confirmation by means of the TTS module. If the proposed hypothesis is correct, the user says "yes" and the finding is stored. If incorrect, the user can say "no" and the transaction is canceled, or can correct it proceeding with the finding, in which case the flow goes back to the hypotheses computation

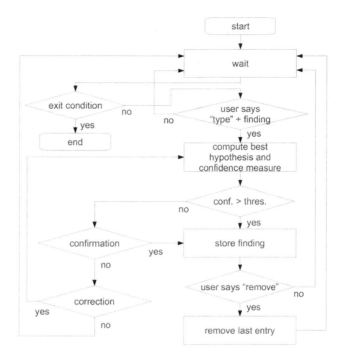

Fig. 3. Dialogue flow

state. In the event that an incorrect finding has been stored, the last entry can be deleted by saying 'remove'. The dialogue finished when the 'store' or 'cancel' report options are activated. In addition, the report can be edited at any time by means of the keyboard.

The speech recognizer has been tested in order to measure performance. A test corpus of 400 utterances from the whole set of 2144 sentences were recorded in quiet conditions. Due to the on-line constraints of the current application, the recognizer parameters have been tuned to achieve real time operation. In this situation, a word error rate of 0.7% has been obtained.

4   Conclusions

In the current scenario of connected interactive TVs, ambient intelligence and interactive applications anywhere and anytime, the accessibility issues for this kind of environments must be reviewed to ensure a proper access by everyone. This is especially important in health systems, which should be properly accessed by the largest possible number of users regardless of their age and condition. We have developed an interactive application for digital TV to access to the medical patient's record health system Info 33, in direct collaboration with physicians. We have applied speech recognition and synthesis techniques for voice navigation and medical report dictation, facilitating the data input in the TV environment.

The use of a specific speech recognizer based on finite state grammars instead of dictation systems based on N-grams has been demonstrated to be effective in the task of inputting medical findings into the system. Furthermore, the presentation of an avatar as a navigation help is an effective way to improve the user empathy with the interface.

Acknowledgments. This work has been partly founded by the Spanish Ministerio de Industria, Project Reference AVANZA TSI-020302-200.

This article is supported by the Catalan Government Grant Agency Ref. 2009SGR700.

References

1. Alteregos v1.2, http://www.alteregos.com
2. Info 33 Health System, http://www.mag.es
3. Black, A., Taylor, P., Caley, R.: The Festival Speech Synthesis System (June 1999), http://www.cstr.ed.ac.uk/projects/festival/manual/festival_toc.html
4. Bonafonte, A., Aguilar, L., Esquerra, I., Oller, S., Moreno, A.: Generation of Language Resources for the Development of Speech Technologies in Catalan. In: Proceedings of the Language Resources and Evaluation Conference LREC 2006, Genova, Italy (2006)
5. Caldwell, B., Cooper, M., Guarino Reid, L., Vanderheiden, G.: Web Content Accessibility Guidelines 2.0. W3C Working Draft (December 2007)
6. Cruz-Martín, E., del Árbol Pérez, L.P., Fernández González, L.C.: The teleassistance platform: an innovative technological solution in face of the ageing population problem. In: The 7th International Conference of the International Society for Gerontechnology (2008)
7. Delgado, H., Serrano, J., Carrabina, J.: Automatic Metadata Extraction from Spoken Content using Speech and Speaker Recognition Techniques. In: FALA 2010. VI Jornadas en Tecnología del Habla and II Iberian SLTech Workshop, Vigo, Spain, pp. 201–204 (2010)
8. Driver, M., Valdes, R., Phifer, G.: Rich Internet Applications are the next evolution of the Web. Tech. rep., Gartner (2005)
9. Jokinen, K., McTear, M.F.: Spoken Dialogue Systems. Morgan & Claypool Publishers (2009)
10. McGurk, H., MacDonald, J.: Hearing lips and seeing voices. Nature (December 1976)
11. Moreno, A., Febrer, A., Márquez, L.: Generation of Language Resources for the Development of Speech Technologies in Catalan. In: Proceedings of the Language Resources and Evaluation Conference LREC 2006, Genova, Italy (2006)
12. Rosenthal, D.I., Chew, F., Dupuy, D.E., Kattapuram, S., Palmer, W.E., Yap, R.M., Levine, L.A.: Computer-Based Speech Recognition as a Replacement for Medical Transcription. American Journal of Roentgenology (1998)
13. Tsekleves, E., Cosmas, J., Aggoun, A., Loo, J.: Converged digital TV services: the role of middleware and future directions of interactive television. International Journal of Digital Multimedia Broadcasting (2009), http://eprints.mdx.ac.uk/7809/
14. Young, S.: ATK - An Application Toolkit for HTK, 1.4.1 edn. (June 2007)

Touch versus In-Air Hand Gestures: Evaluating the Acceptance by Seniors of Human-Robot Interaction

Anouar Znagui Hassani[1], Betsy van Dijk[1], Geke Ludden[2], and Henk Eertink[2]

[1] Human Media Interaction, Twente University, Enschede, The Netherlands
a.znaguihassani@student.utwente.nl, e.m.a.g.vandijk@utwente.nl
[2] Novay, Enschede, The Netherlands
{henk.eertink,geke.ludden}@noyay.nl

Abstract. Do elderly people have a preference between performing in-air gestures or pressing screen buttons to interact with an assistive robot? This study attempts to provide answers to this question by measuring the level of acceptance, performance as well as knowledge of both interaction modalities during a scenario where elderly participants interacted with an assistive robot. Two interaction modalities were compared; in-air gestures and touch. A scenario has been chosen in which the elderly people perform exercises in order to improve lifestyle behavior. The seniors in this scenario stand in front of the assistive robot. The robot displays several exercises on the robot screen. After each successfully performed exercise the senior navigates to the next or previous exercise. No significant differences were found between the interaction modalities on the technology acceptance measures on effort, ease, anxiety, performance and attitude. The results on these measures were very high for both interaction modalities, indicating that both modalities were accepted by the elderly people. In a final interview participants reacted more positive on the use of in-air gestures.

Keywords: Robot Acceptance, Assistive technologies, Activities of daily Living (ADL's), Human Robot Interaction.

1   Introduction

Both touch modality and in-air gestures are candidates for serving as modality in Human-Robot Interaction (HRI). Recent developments in in-air gestures (Kinect) have made this modality a more likely candidate than before.

This thesis presents the results of an experiment on the technology acceptance of a multimodal interactive social robot. The work in this paper has been done at Novay for the EU FP7 project Florence (http://www.florence-project.eu/) that focuses on personal assistive robots for Ambient Assisted Living (AAL) at home. The research involves an experiment using an assistive robot called *Florence*[1] and

---

[1] The project is named after Florence Nightingale, who is seen as the founder of nursing sciences. When she worked as a nurse, she wandered through the hospital during the nights to look after her patients, why she became known also as the lady with the lamp.

D. Keyson et al. (Eds.): AmI 2011, LNCS 7040, pp. 309–313, 2011.

the evaluation of this system by seniors in a local care home. The knowledge that has been gained may be applied in the development of automatic gesture recognition systems that fit typical or natural human behavior and capabilities.

The main question which will be answered in this study is: What is the influence of interaction modality in the context of HRI on user acceptance and preferences? Simply said, when an elderly person performs a gesture/tactile command towards a robot screen, does that have influence on the users acceptance? And is there a preferred modality? The research question to some extent was inspired by the preliminary research regarding the acceptance of social robots by seniors [5], but predominantly they were chosen because of the importance to learn more about the perception by seniors of a social robot with multi modal interaction capabilities. The main research has been split in the following subquestions:

1. Does the HRI context afford a certain type of modality e.g. touch or gestures?
2. Which of the two modalities is preferred by the senior participants, or what are the objections for a particular modality against the other?
3. Is there a difference in gesture performance? Does the notion of *'Next'* or *'Previous'* lead to different gesture performances?

An experiment has been performed addressing these questions. In the experiment, participants were given the task to perform physical exercises to improve or maintain a healthy lifestyle. In order to move to the next exercise, the participants were asked to either *press a screen button which says next* (in case of the touch interface) or give a 'Next' In-Air gesture. No information was provided *a priori* about how to perform such a *'Next'* or *'Previous'*. Thus, insight was gathered into human gesture perception of the actions *'Next'* and *'Previous'*.

2   Design

For this comparative study between interaction modalities, a simple prototype of an assistive robot and an application have been developed. Both the application and the robot will be described in more detail here.

For this application a scenario has been chosen in which the elderly person performs exercises in order to improve lifestyle behavior. The senior in this scenario stands in front of the assistive robot. On the screen of the robot several body postures are presented that have to be copied by the senior. After each successfully performed posture (as recognized by the recognition part of the software) the senior navigates to the next or previous exercise.

HRI may be realized using different modalities such as speech, head pose, gesturing and touch or a combination of these modalities. This study compares two modalities namely touch and gestures. The main concern regarding the design and implementation of the software application was gesture recognition.

Gesture recognition is a very popular research area ([3,2])in which the implementation of various kinds of feature extraction algorithms finally result in the recognition of the points of interest such as a human hand.

Instead of traditional gesture recognition software, a contemporary approach is used in this research: The Microsoft Kinect 3D sensor array. (see figure 1a).

This 3D sensor was originally designed for the game console Xbox 360. But the 3D sensor is also usable when connected with the PC. The Kinect is mounted on a stand. The stand is mounted on top of the mobile platform PeekeeII [4]. A touchscreen, which essentially is a touchscreen enabled laptop is mounted below the Kinect(See figure 1b). By having the depth-of-field camera and the RGB camera a calculated distance apart, the Kinect is able to perform immediate, 3D incorporation of real objects into on-screen images.

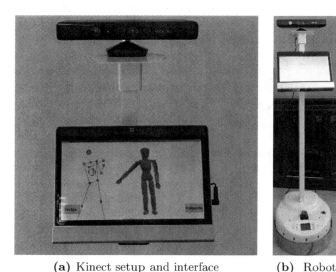

(a) Kinect setup and interface   **(b)** Robot

Fig. 1. Setup

3   Methodology of the Experwhereiniment

3.1   Subjects

Participants in the experiment were 12 elderly people who participated voluntarily in this study, and signed a consent form. The average age of the participants was $77,17 (\sigma = 7.19)$ with the youngest being 71 and the oldest 96. Of the 12 participants 7 were female. 8 participants had mobility problems. Most of participants reported to never have used a computer before. The most frequent appliances used by the participants were the TV, coffee machine and microwave.

3.2   Experimental Setup

The gesture recognition system is implemented in such a way that it even if the 'Next' or 'Previous' gesture is not performed precisely as suggested it can be recognized correctly. Not only differences between modalities can be measured. Agreements in the way that gestures are performed may become visible as well as the different notions which the participants have towards the notion of *gestures* in general. Each participant was asked whether he or she knows what gestures are, and how he or she would perform a *'Next'* or *'Previous'* gesture before showing how the actual gesture should be performed in order for the system to be recognized.

3.3 Data Acquisition, Procedure and Analysis

The participant is recorded during the experiment. The Technology Acceptance Model(TAM) is used to investigate Effort, Ease & Anxiety (EEA) and Performance & Attitude (PA) [1]. Together with a short interview which is recorded on video, insight in the preferences and acceptance of the interaction modalities is obtained. A within subject design is chosen to measure differences between the modalities gestures and touch. Counterbalancing of the two modalities is a applied to avoid order effects. The participant started with filling in a pre-test with questions regarding their daily use of appliances. A questionnaire including questions regarding a modality was filled in after each modality experiment. A final interview was held in which comparing questions were asked regarding preference, effort, ease and attitude.

4   Results

An item in the gesture questionnaire asked whether the participants found the gestures easy to perform. Using a 7 -point Likert scale 12 subjects answered with a mode of 7 (6 out of 12 answered with a 7) and an average of 6.4. The exact same result is discovered after the analysis of the question regarding the touch modality wherein the question was asked whether the participant found it easy to press the screen buttons. Testing these results with a Wilcoxon signed-rank test to a neutral result, yielded $Z = -.587, p = 0.557$. No significant differences were found on the other questions of the questionnaire either.

The interview yielded valuable information concerning alternative gestures by the participants for the concepts 'Next' and 'Previous'. Also interesting behavior was noticed after the preliminary question about the notion of gestures. 4 out of 12 participants knew instantly what gestures and they even gave examples of gestures which they used back in the days during work or sports. Although they had different ideas about the performance of the gestures *'Next'* and *'Previous'*, they did not have any problems understanding and relating the specified gestures to the concepts *'Next'* and *'Previous'*.

In the final interview participants reacted more positive towards the use of in-air gestures. 9 out of 12 participants preferred the gesture interface. They also reported that they have little knowledge about assistive robots. They were inquisitive and felt the need to have more information which is expected to result in a overall higher level of robot acceptance. Many participants (7 out of 12) argued that they could express themselves more using in-air gestures as opposed to pressing screen buttons. Physical constraints of the participants was also a cause of the before mentioned preference, as they had to walk towards the robot in order to touch the screen.

5   Conclusion and Future Work

Two interaction modalities were compared; in-air gestures and touch. No significant results were found regarding the variables Effort, Ease & Anxiety (EEA) and Performance & Attitude (PA). The results on these variables were very high for both interaction modalities, indicating that both modalities were accepted by the elderly people.

The results on questions in the final interview where people were asked to compare the use of the two modalities indicate that the participants reacted more positive towards the use of in-air gestures. Most participants had a preference to use in-air gestures for the interaction with the robot because they could express themselves more using gestures as opposed to pressing touch screen buttons. An extra reason to prefer gestures were the physical constraints of many of the participants. In the touch interface they had to walk towards the robot in order to touch the screen. In-air gestures can be further applied in for instance *calling* the robot, as well as *interrupting* the robots activity.

Acknowledgements. This research is supported by the Florence project. Florence is supported by the European Commission in the FP7 programme under contract ICT-2009-248730.

References

1. Heerink, M., Kröse, B., Wielinga, B., Evers, V.: Measuring the influence of social abilities on acceptance of an interface robot and a screen agent by elderly users. In: Proceedings of the 23rd British HCI Group Annual Conference on People and Computers: Celebrating People and Technology, BCS-HCI 2009, Swinton, UK, pp. 430–439. British Computer Society (2009)
2. Keskin, C., Erkan, A., Akarun, L.: Real time hand tracking and 3d gesture recognition for interactive interfaces using hmm. In: Joint International Conference ICANN/ICONIP. Springer, Heidelberg (2003)
3. Park, C.-B., Lee, S.-W.: Real-time 3d pointing gesture recognition for mobile robots with cascade hmm and particle filter. Image and Vision Computing 29(1), 51–63 (2011)
4. Wany-Robotics. PekeeII Essential package (2011), http://www.wanyrobotics.com
5. Znagui-Hassani, A.: Discovering the level of robot acceptance of seniors using scenarios based on assistive technologies. Technical report, University of Twente (HMI) (2010)

Classification of User Postures with Capacitive Proximity Sensors in AAL-Environments

Tobias Alexander Große-Puppendahl, Alexander Marinc, and Andreas Braun

TU Darmstadt, Karolinenplatz 5, 64289 Darmstadt, Germany
Fraunhofer IGD, Fraunhoferstr. 5, 64283 Darmstadt, Germany
t_groae@rbg.informatik.tu-darmstadt.de,
{alexander.marinc,andreas.braun}@igd.fraunhofer.de

Abstract. In Ambient Assisted Living (AAL), the context-dependent adaption of a system to a person's needs is of particular interest. In the living area, a fine-grained context may not only contain information about the occupancy of certain furniture, but also the posture of a user on the occupied furniture. This information is useful in the application area of home automation, where, for example, a lying user may effect a different system reaction than a sitting user. In this paper, we present an approach for determining contextual information from furniture, using capacitive proximity sensors. Moreover, we evaluate the performance of Naïve Bayes classifiers, decision trees and radial basis function networks, regarding the classification of user postures. Therefore, we use our generic classification framework to visualize, train and evaluate postures with up to two persons on a couch. Based on a data set collected from multiple users, we show that this approach is robust and suitable for real-time classification.

Keywords: AAL, capacitive proximity sensors, classification, user context

1 Introduction

Population aging in many industrial countries is posing various challenges to society, where a shrinking number of working persons has to care for an ever growing number of seniors. Assistive health-care applications, designed for elderly users, are trying to counteract the shrinking budgets in public health care. The paradigm of Ambient Assisted Living (AAL) represents methods, concepts, systems and services that unobtrusively support a person in daily life. User-centric technologies and concepts are integrated into the immediate environment of the person requiring assistance, and customized to individual needs and capabilities.

To support the adaptation of the environment to a user, it is necessary to determine an application context, particularly information about a person and any interaction with the environment. Typical examples include acquiring the location of a user within the premises or measuring relevant medical data, e.g. blood pressure. Determining a user's posture on furniture generates additional

D. Keyson et al. (Eds.): AmI 2011, LNCS 7040, pp. 314–323, 2011.

contextual information that can be used within AAL applications, for example safety features in home automation. If a user is lying on a bed, the system can deduct that he will remain there for a while, causing lighting and heating in adjacent rooms to be adjusted. If the user is suddenly sitting at night, the system may anticipate that the user is going to the toilet, thus activating dimmed lights to prevent tripping and falling.

The aim of this work is to classify the posture of a person using capacitive proximity sensors that are embedded into the living area. Classification refers to making a discrete observation, e.g 'a person is lying on a couch', derived from a set of incoming sensor readings. We have created a generic framework that is able to interface multiple sensor classes and classification methods. In this work we will present a system based on capacitive proximity sensors that can be unobtrusively integrated into existing furniture, while providing reliable information about the presence of a subject.

Capacitive proximity sensors use oscillating electric fields between an emitter and a ground electrode. The properties of an electric field change if a conductive object is brought into it. The human body, or bio mass in general, falls under this class, thus it is possible to unobtrusively detect a person or body parts of a person that approach such a sensing device [16]. Combining several sensors, we are able to fuse their outputs, in order to obtain information about the body posture.

We have chosen a couch in a living room to test our system. The generated context can be used for energy saving purposes, e.g. shutting off lighting in other rooms, but also for controlling ambient parameters like lighting and multimedia equipment that may react differently to sitting and lying persons. We have equipped an ordinary couch with eight capacitive proximity sensors and applied various classification techniques to the generated data. We have evaluated different classifiers by testing the prototype system on a diverse group of persons. Results show that such a system is reliably able to recognize various user postures, even if body mass and height differ strongly. Moreover, interviews performed with our test persons strongly indicate that the unobtrusive nature of capacitive proximity sensors will increase the user acceptance in actual applications, compared to camera-based systems. The interviews revealed that, using camera-based systems, people feel particularly observed and consider popular recent data leaks.

2   Related Work

Intelligent environments have been a research focus in the past decades [15]. Industry has started using developed technologies to link various technical devices in the living area. The property 'intelligent' refers to systems that are able to manipulate the environment without explicit user interaction, only using the implicit context a user generates, based on presence. To acquire this context, it is necessary to place various sensing devices in the living area. In order to manipulate the environment, actuators are required. Systems that include cognitive capabilities like perception, learning, reasoning, planning or executing tasks are denoted as *Cognitive Technical Systems* (CTS)[3].

Every element of a living area can be part of the CTS. For example, Beetz et al [4] have equipped a kitchen with several types of sensors, realizing various scenarios based on a robotic assistant for supporting activities of daily life. Indoor localization methods are an important part of many CTS. They allow the system to provide services like energy saving, home security and fall prevention. Methods include GSM triangulation [12] or capacitive sensors [13]. Capacitive sensors are applicable in various AAL-related scenarios, e.g. the detection of spine strain and subsequent user feedback on appropriate lying positions using an array of capacitive proximity sensors in a bed [7]. Kivikunnas et al [8] have equipped a couch with capacitive proximity sensors for future application in posture recognition.

The fusion and interpretation of data generated by various sensors is one of the main application areas of machine learning [10]. Specifically they can be used to map the continuous input sets to discrete classes. Amoretti et al describe example applications in AAL [1]. As proof-of-concept for our posture recognition in AAL environments we have tested the system by building a prototype based on a couch augmented with capacitive proximity sensors.

3   User Posture Classification

3.1   Sensors

By using capacitive proximity sensors, we can measure the proximity of a person's body. A typical capacitive sensor consists of an electrode, emitting an electric field that oscillates at 10 - 200 KHz and a receiving electrode that measures certain properties of this electric field. Other designs, like ours, are based on a single electrode that creates a field with other electric potentials within reach, for example a ground node. When body mass enters this electric field, the displacement current, measured in the emitting node, changes. This effect makes it possible to detect the proximity of body mass[16]. Furthermore, it is possible to gather information about the distance of the object entering. If an object is uniformly sized, the displacement current will increase when it is brought closer to an electrode. The operating range and resolution of this sensor type strongly depends on the electrode size, material used, emitter frequency and emitter voltages, resulting in achievable distances between a few nanometers and several meters [2]. The generated electric fields will progress through any non-conductive material. Thus it is possible to install these sensors unobtrusively, e.g. underneath the upholstery of wooden elements or furnishing. This makes them less prone to mechanical influences in the operating and setup time, as well as hiding active system parts from the user allowing a free external design of the furnishing.

3.2   Preprocessing and Feature extraction

The sensors deliver continuous signals, which are sampled with a low frequency, e.g. 10 Hz, and normalized to an interval between 0 and 1. In the next step, overlapping short-time windows (e.g. with a length of 1 second), containing samples from all sensors, are built. Due to the high amount of data contained in a window, a direct classification is computationally complex or even impossible. Thus, we must focus on relevant information for classification, the features of a short-time window.

Typical features for user posture classification are the empirical mean and the standard deviation of a short-time window. For example, we may extract the empirical mean from each sensor and use it for classification. A feature vector $X_i = (x_1, ..., x_n)^T$; $X_i \in \Re^N$ consists of all extracted features, whereas the feature space contains all these vectors. In order to be able to uniquely identify the classes in the classification step, the extracted features must build a compact and bounded subspace for each class [11].

3.3   Classification

We aim to recognize a discrete class $z_k, k \in \{0, 1, ..., K\}$ from the extracted feature vector X_i. A class may be represented by a statement like *'one person is sitting at the right side of the couch'* that reflects an observation of the actual system.

To cope with the complex task of classification, we need to learn from experience, making use of an annotated training set of feature vectors and the corresponding classes. The main goal of classification is to reliably identify a class for unknown feature vectors. Thus, generalization is a very important property of a classifier. In the following, we will present three suitable classifier models for user posture classification.

Naïve Bayes models are very popular models in machine learning applications due to their simplicity and computational efficiency. The classifier assigns the most likely class z_k to a given feature vector X_i. The classifier's model structure is simplified by the assumption that the distributions of all features for a specific class are conditionally independent. This assumption of conditional independence of features is often seen as a weakness of the Naïve Bayes model. However, this property makes the Naïve Bayes model very fast and efficient for testing and evaluation purposes [5].

Unlike the Naïve Bayes model, Decision tree classifiers can overcome the problem of conditional dependence of features. A decision tree consists of nodes, which represent logic rules and leafs, which represent the final decision, as shown in figure 1 at the right. Classifications are made by traversing the tree structure, evaluating a decision function in each node, until a leaf is reached. In practice, binary decision trees with threshold decision functions for a single feature are commonly used (e.g. $x_j <= r$; $x_j, r \in \Re$). The advantage of decision trees is the input-dependent traversal of its nodes. Decision trees can be built with algorithms like the C4.5 algorithm, which selects the feature with the highest information gain for each decision node [9,5].

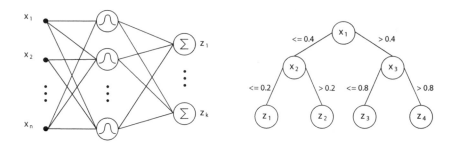

Fig. 1. Left: Layout of an RBF network. Right: An example decision tree

Radial basis function (RBF) networks, as shown in figure 1 at the left, are a specialization of artificial neural networks and are often applied on classification problems. RBF networks consists of three layers, one input layer, a hidden layer with radial activation functions and an output layer, that implements a weighted sum over the hidden unit's outputs. The number of chosen basis functions is essential for the network's generalization abilities. RBF networks, or artificial neural networks in general, face the problem that their output behaviour is often not easy to comprehend, especially when a transparent functioning is required [9,6].

4   The Smart Couch Scenario

4.1   SenseKit: A Generic Approach

Since there are numerous scenarios for applying user posture classification, we have developed a generic framework called *SenseKit* for posture classification tasks. Different scenarios, e.g. posture-detecting chairs or beds require different types and numbers of capacitive sensors, in order to reliable detect the required postures. Sensekit tackles these classification tasks and provides additional functionality, most notably visualization and evaluation of the processing pipeline. Sensekit is based on a configurable dependency injection framework that allows all components (classifiers, sensors, feature extractors, etc.) to be dynamically combined, corresponding to the individual application scenario.

Apart from SenseKit's classification and digital signal processing abilities it also implements training and visualization components. Sensor readings, as well as the final classification results, may be visualized and presented in an effective way. We have integrated various machine learning algorithms into our framework. Most algorithms are adapted from the WEKA Machine Learning Project [14]. Moreover, we integrated WEKA's explorer into our framework, a comprehensive tool that provides functionality to evaluate recorded training data.

Our prototype is an ordinary couch augmented with capacitive proximity sensors hidden underneath the upholstery. In order to prove our methodology, we

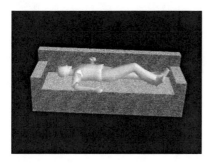 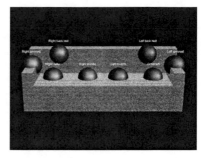

Fig. 2. Left: Visualization of a classification. Right: Visualization of sensor readings.

intended to classify a high amount of potential postures, various sitting and lying positions (2 at the left) for one and two persons. We deemed eight sensors to be sufficient in establishing a good data basis for classification of the various postures. The final design consists of two sensors, placed underneath both armrests, two sensors in the back rests and another four sensors underneath the sitting area, as shown in figure 2 at the right. Even though the sensors are up to 15 centimeters away from the user and covered by upholstery and wood (see 3), we are still able to retrieve good measurements of body mass proximity, supported by the fact that some electrodes have pressure applied to them, causing a geometric deformation that also affects the output signal.

Fig. 3. An ordinary couch has been equipped with capacitive proximity sensors that have been set up under the upholstery and wooden elements

In order to determine a suitable test set, we are distinguishing nine different possible postures on a couch that can be performed by one or two persons. The 18 test persons were given simple written instructions to perform the desired postures. The persons performed all postures, relaxed and without restrictions in their movements, for approx. 30 seconds. Similar postures were always interrupted by unrelated postures. The data set contains a training set, with data from 9 test persons, and a test set with data of another 9 persons. Both, the training and test data set, were recorded on different days with different test persons. Additionally, we recorded body weights and sizes (figure 4), since those are the main properties affecting sensor measurements. Our training set consists of 2829 instances (about 24 minutes), whereas our test set consists of 2312 instances (about 20 minutes).

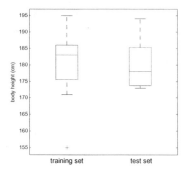 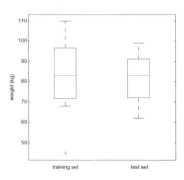

Fig. 4. A box plot of body heights and weights in our data set. The blue box denotes data from lower to upper quartile, the red dash denotes the median and red crosses mark outliers.

In the regarded scenario, we use the empirical means of our eight sensors, which are extracted from a short-time window, as feature vector. Overlapping short-time windows are passed to the classifier every second, containing the last 2 seconds of sensor readings.

4.2   Evaluation

Three classifiers were evaluated on our data set. We evaluate the performance of the Naïve Bayes classifier, decision trees and RBF networks. To measure the performance, we consider the metrics of precision and recall. As each sensor has individual characteristics, e.g. caused by different electrode sizes, the evaluation results are not symmetrical concerning the geometry of the couch. Furthermore, each sensor produces an individual amount of noise that has to be taken into account. The performances of the three classifiers are shown in table 1.

Our evaluation results show that the Naïve Bayes model does deliver inferior results compared to more sophisticated models, such as RBF networks. This fact is mainly caused by the very strong assumption of conditional independence, which is not satisfied in user posture classification scenarios. However, the Naïve Bayes model provides sufficiently precise results, as well as efficient training and data analysis. We retrieve an overall recall of 92.2% and a precision of 90.6%.

The evaluation of decision trees, built with the C4.5 algorithm, shows similar results as the Naïve Bayes model. Classes like 'two persons sitting together with a gap' were sometimes classified as lying postures. Moreover, many activities with lower sensor measurements, e.g. caused by a low body weight, have been classified as 'no person', resulting in a poor precision of 66.4% for this particular class. The overall recall is 87.3%, whereas the overall precision is 90.7%.

Table 2 shows the confusion matrix of an RBF network, evaluated on our test set. We can see that some sitting postures on the right of the couch have been classified as *lying head right* postures, leading to a lower precision for this

Table 1. Evaluation results for the three classifiers

	Naïve Bayes		Decision Trees		RBF network	
Class	Prec	Rec	Prec	Rec	Prec	Rec
sitting outer left one person : OL	0.92	0.97	1.0	0.84	1.0	0.99
sitting middle left one person : ML	0.99	0.60	0.99	0.90	0.98	0.88
sitting outer right one person : OR	1.0	0.78	1.0	0.63	1.0	0.96
sitting middle right one person : MR	0.96	0.93	0.93	1.0	1.0	0.95
lying head right one person : LR	0.77	1.0	1.0	0.89	0.92	1.0
lying head left one person : LL	0.85	1.0	0.7	0.95	0.98	0.99
two persons sitting together : TT	0.77	1.0	0.95	1.0	0.87	1.0
two persons sitting gap : TG	1.0	0.99	0.98	0.64	1.0	0.99
no person : NP	1.0	0.92	0.66	1.00	1.0	1.0
Weighted average	0.92	0.91	0.91	0.87	0.98	0.97

class. Moreover, we retrieve a low recall for *sitting middle left* postures, as they are often misclassified as *sitting together* postures. However, in general, RBF networks perform very well on the test set with an overall recall of 97.5% and a precision of 97.2%. Furthermore, the determined clusters and their corresponding weights indicate that all sensors contribute equally to classification.

Table 2. Confusion matrix for the RBF network classifier

	OL	ML	OR	MR	LR	LL	TT	TG	NP	Prec	Rec
sitting outer left one person : OL	296	1	0	0	0	2	1	0	0	0.99	0.987
sitting middle left one person : ML	3	227	0	0	0	0	28	0	0	0.98	0.88
sitting outer right one person : OR	0	0	253	0	11	0	0	0	0	1.0	0.958
sitting middle right one person : MR	0	0	0	243	12	0	0	0	0	1.0	0.953
lying head right one person : LR	0	0	0	0	260	0	0	0	0	0.91	1.0
lying head left one person : LL	0	3	0	0	0	254	0	0	0	0.98	0.988
two persons sitting together : TT	0	0	0	0	0	0	197	0	0	0.87	1.0
two persons sitting gap : TG	0	0	0	0	0	3	0	212	0	1.0	0.986
no person : NP	1	0	0	0	0	0	0	0	306	1.0	1.0

We can conclude that RBF networks are a robust classifier model with a high accuracy for user posture classification in our scenario. The generalization abilities of this classifier are coping well with the variation of body heights and weight of the different test persons. We have identified a decent generalization ability as an essential requirement for classifiers in user posture classification.

5 Summary

5.1 Conclusions

We have shown that capacitive proximity sensors are well-suited to give robust and reliable information about a user's context, proven in an evaluation with

18 different test persons of diverse body height and weight. Using only eight sensors in our couch example we have achieved a reliability of more than 97% in eight different postures using RBF network based classifiers. The classification based on machine-learning methods is easily implemented, trained and can be visualized by using the created SenseKit framework. We have achieved a fine-grained and reliable detection of user application context that can be used by intelligent systems to control the environment.

5.2 Future Work

Open issues are the reliable detection of nearly similar postures, e.g. one person lying and two persons sitting. Most issues related to this topic can be solved by simply using more sensors. Even though SenseKit is supporting this the higher costs and complexity of the used hardware are undesirable. We intend to test other physical sensor configurations that could achieve better results as our current prototype. However, a well-defined theory and methodology, that describes the ideal distribution of sensors within the furniture, based on number of sensors and desired posture classes, is highly desired. Given the nature of capacitive proximity sensors and the highly complex distribution of electric fields, another option would be to use a simplified model to simulate the sensor values within the furniture and apply optimization strategies to achieve a good sensor configuration. We are planning to integrate some of this functionality in future versions of our easily extendable SenseKit. Another topic of interest is testing our system on different types of furniture and integrating other types of sensors that might provide more diverse applications while achieving the same reliable results.

Acknowledgments. We would like to thank the students of TU Darmstadt and the employees of Fraunhofer IGD that lent us their sitting and lying abilities for the evaluation.

References

1. Amoretti, M., Wientapper, F., Furfari, F., Lenzi, S., Chessa, S.: Sensor data fusion for activity monitoring in ambient assisted living environments. In: International Conference on Wireless Sensor Network (WSN) Systems and Software 2009, pp. 206–221 (2009)
2. Baxter, L.K.: Capacitive Sensors: Design and Applications. IEEE Press (1996)
3. Beetz, M., Buss, M., Wollherr, D.: Cognitive Technical Systems — What is the Role of Artificial Intelligence? In: Hertzberg, J., Beetz, M., Englert, R. (eds.) KI 2007. LNCS (LNAI), vol. 4667, pp. 19–42. Springer, Heidelberg (2007)
4. Beetz, M., Jan, B., Kirsch, R., Maldonado, A., Müller, A., Rusu, R.B.: The assistive kitchen a demonstration scenario for cognitive technical systems. In: Proceedings of the 4th COE Workshop on Human Adaptive Mechatronics (2007)
5. Bishop, C.M.: Pattern Recognition and Machine Learning (Information Science and Statistics). Springer-Verlag New York, Inc. (2006)

6. Buhmann, M.D.: Radial Basis Functions: Theory and Implementations. Cambridge University Press (2003)
7. Hamisu, P., Braun, A.: Analyse des schlafverhaltens durch kapazitive sensorarrays zur ermittlung der wirbelsäulenbelastung. In: Proceedings of the Conference of Ambient Assisted Living 2010. VDE Verlag GmbH (2010)
8. Kivikunnas, S., Strömmer, E., Korkalainen, M., Heikkilä, T., Haverinen, M.: Intelligent furniture and their ubiquitous use scenarios. In: Proceedings of the AALIANCE Conference (2010)
9. Kotsiantis, S.B.: Supervised machine learning: A review of classification techniques. In: Proceeding of the 2007 Conference on Emerging Artificial Intelligence Applications in Computer Engineering: Real Word AI Systems with Applications in eHealth, HCI, Information Retrieval and Pervasive Technologies, pp. 3–24. IOS Press (2007)
10. Mitchell, T.M.: Machine learning and data mining. Commun. ACM, 30–36 (1999)
11. Niemann, H.: Klassifikation von Mustern. Universität Erlangen-Nürnberg, Lehrstuhl für Mustererkennung (2003)
12. Otsason, V., Varshavsky, A., LaMarca, A., de Lara, E.: Accurate GSM Indoor Localization. In: Beigl, M., Intille, S.S., Rekimoto, J., Tokuda, H. (eds.) UbiComp 2005. LNCS, vol. 3660, pp. 141–158. Springer, Heidelberg (2005)
13. Steinhage, A., Lauterbach, C.: Sensfloor(r): Ein aal sensorsystem für sicherheit, homecare und komfort. In: Proceedings of the Ambient Assisted Living Congress 2008 (2008)
14. University of Waikato: Weka machine learning project (May 2011), http://www.cs.waikato.ac.nz/ml/weka
15. Wren, C.R., Sparacino, F., Azarbayejani, A.J., Darrell, T.J., Starner, T.E., Kotani, A., Chao, C.M., Hlavac, M., Pentland, A.P.: Perceptive spaces for performance and entertainment: Untethered interaction using computer vision and audition. Applied Artificial Intelligence, 267–284 (1997)
16. Zimmerman, T.G., Smith, J.R., Paradiso, J.A., Allport, D., Gershenfeld, N.: Applying electric field sensing to human-computer interfaces. In: Proceedings of the SIGCHI Conference on Human Factors in Computing Systems, CHI 1995, pp. 280–287 (1995)

"Maybe It Becomes a Buddy, But Do Not Call It a Robot" – Seamless Cooperation between Companion Robotics and Smart Homes

Claire Huijnen[1], Atta Badii[2], Herjan van den Heuvel[1],
Praminda Caleb-Solly[3], and Daniel Thiemert[2]

[1] Stichting Smart Homes, P.O. Box 8825, 5605 LV Eindhoven, The Netherlands
{c.huijnen,h.vdheuvel}@smart-homes.nl
[2] Intelligent Systems Research Laboratory, University of Reading, White Knights Campus,
Reading, RG6 6AY, United Kingdom
{atta.badii,daniel.thiemert}@reading.ac.uk
[3] Bristol Institute of Technology, University of the West of England, Frenchay Campus,
Bristol BS16 1QY, United Kingdom
praminda.caleb-solly@uwe.ac.uk

Abstract. This paper describes the findings arising from ongoing qualitative usability evaluation studies on mobile companion robotics in smart home environments from two research projects focused on socio-technical innovation to support independent living (*CompanionAble* and *Mobiserv*). Key findings are described, and it is stated that the robotic companion, the smart home environment, and external services need to be seamlessly integrated to create a truly supportive and trusted system. The idea of *robot personas* is introduced, and based on our empirical observations, it is argued that the robot persona, rather than the physical embodiment, is the most important determinant of the degree of users' acceptance in terms of users' perceived trustability and responsiveness of the robot and therefore their sense of enhanced usability and satisfaction with such personal assistive systems.

Keywords: companion robotics, smart homes, ambient assisted living, independent living, human-robot interactivity, social robotics, man-machine mixed initiative taking, user-centred co-design, UI-REF, robo-humatics.

1   Introduction

Independent living, enhanced quality-of-life, wellbeing, and not feeling isolated or alone are generally viewed as amongst our shared values and goals. As life expectancy in the EU and other countries is continuously increasing [1], the percentage of older adults in the population is growing, and more and more older persons live alone and desire to age at home. The move from 'home' via 'protected living' to 'nursing home' is often regarded as heralding a trend towards reduced independence which is not viewed positively by most since staying as independent as (long as) possible gives satisfaction to individuals and reduces societal costs.

D. Keyson et al. (Eds.): AmI 2011, LNCS 7040, pp. 324–329, 2011.

ICT can play an important role in responding to the personal and societal needs for prolonging this (active) independent living and improved quality-of-life and health outlook [2]. Smart home technology proved to have positive impacts on people's lives as well as on the lives of the informal caregivers [13]. In this paper, we focus on the seamless semantic integration and cooperation between social assistive robotics with smart home environments.

2   Robotics and Smart Homes

An emerging trend in smart home technology is that such environments become increasingly capable of inter-operation with many assistive devices and services within and outside the home [3]. A personal assistive robot could be one of these devices. Such robots are becoming a realistic expectation of user-adaptive assistive technology of the future, supporting comfort and companionship within the home; particularly for older or impaired persons but potentially for all citizens. There are a number of related national and European projects; e.g. *Care-O-Bot*, a mobile service robot focussed on the execution of fetch-and-carry tasks to support the personnel of older persons nursing home in their daily tasks [4]; *RoboCare,* a multi-agent human assistance system, composed of a robotic agent, sensors for continuous monitoring, and additional reasoning systems [5]; *K-SERA,* a social robot that monitors, helps and alerts persons with COPD during their daily activities, to facilitate effective self-management of their disease [6]; and *Florence*, a robot with existing home automation infrastructures and local and remote communication services, to improve home care for older persons [7]. Similarly, projects like *CompanionAble* [8] and *Mobiserv* [9] recognize that the next frontier towards close and sensitive cooperation between a smart home and a social companion robot would be via improving natural and inspiring interaction, and addressing more user needs in a trusted manner. Due to the nature of this close cooperation, interaction possibilities will be numerous. The user would expect to interact through touch screens around the home and on the robot, as well as through other interaction modalities, e.g. through voice or gestures.

3   The Companions

The vision motivating the authors' work under the *CompanionAble* and *Mobiserv* research programmes is to design and validate an architecture for semantically integrated companion robotics and ambient intelligence technologies so as to provide for a socio-technically acceptable assistive companion environment. Using a robot that understands you when you speak and engages in a meaningful dialogue seems more motivating, engaging, and fun than using a (tablet) screen. Moreover, another dimension is added when the possibilities of embodiment are exploited.

Our work has included advanced relationship-centred co-design approaches (e.g. UI-REF [8]) requiring close contact with end-users, their proxies, and end-user organisations in several European countries. Accordingly, the insights gained through extensive   user-centred   research   (such   as   cultural   probes,   focus   groups, semi-structured interviews, use-context studies) have build a consistently integrated requirements formalisation and usability evaluation of the resulting smart-home companion systems. From these results and through several user-centred design cycles, in both projects a set of key functionalities have been defined.

Fig. 1. CompanionAble Robot 'Hector'   **Fig. 2.** Mobiserv Robot 'Kompaï'

CompanionAble serves the needs of persons with mild cognitive impairments (MCI) and provides a cognitive assistive companion to support their wellbeing, lifestyle management and security. This includes a range of use-cases such as cognitive training, games, social inclusion mechanisms, home-care such as intelligent day-time-management, context-aware reminders for medication intake and appointments, safety reminders, analysis of emotions, prevention of dangerous situations, recognition of distress signals, and the ability to remotely control the robot.

Mobiserv is targeted at older persons with early dementia and/or physical disabilities and provides health-care support, wellness monitoring, safety protection, and social support through nutrition assistance and dehydration prevention. This includes a health-coach providing a self-check platform and motivational advice for physical activities as well as games for social and cognitive stimulation responsive to the user's emotions. Mobiserv also provides a mobile remote control for the home and a panic responder with audio/video communication to a service centre, family/friends.

4   User Trials

Extensive trials were conducted with the two prototypes integrated with a smart home environment. Both trials took place in a fully functional smart home, including living room, kitchen, etc. [10]. A range of potential end-users took part in the trials and their views on the performance and usability of the systems were elicited.

For *Mobiserv*, realistic video prototypes of the functions were shown to the test participants on the actual robot prototype. Participants performed basic tasks with the autonomously running robot. Five persons participated in this trial (age; 67 – 76).

For *CompanionAble*, a partly autonomous robot prototype was used in combination with a 'Wizard-of-Oz'-controlled smart home. A number of scenarios where conducted: welcome home, medicine reminders; wellbeing monitoring, fridge-door-left-open warning, cognitive training, remote control. A total of ten MCI persons participated in these trials (age; 52 – 88). Through analysis of the feedback from 25 trial sessions, key findings were as follows:

Interaction and Usability: The perception of comfortable interactivity-usability was associated with factors such as the quality/tone of voice, dialogue style (reminding or encouraging), turn-taking behaviour i.e. optimal control of robotic pro-activity in man-machine initiative taking [9,10] and the level of surprise / predictability in user-system interactions.

Being a Companion: The perceived level of companionship was strongly influenced by the capability of the system to adapt to the situated preferences of the user in the given use-context. This implies context-aware responsiveness; i.e. knowing when to react, what to do and how to best present information to a given user based on their abilities and preferences. Smart dialogue management and different 'characters' of the companion system where strong user needs.

Control and Trust: The perceived level of trust influences the potential for user-system inter-working. Cooperation and co-design of the system involving the professional carers can build trust. Furthermore, expectation management, offering appropriate support, intelligent dialogue, and positive reinforcements increase the feeling of enhanced autonomy and trust. Trust is relationship-based and as is the case with human relationships, it is experientially informed; e.g. already during the two hours of the user trials, users indicated that they gained trust in the system.

Acceptance and Privacy: Privacy protection assurance and technology acceptance are needs influenced by the capability of the system for social situation awareness, context-sensitive and helpful responses, as well as transparency of the interactivity logic (e.g. the system making it clear to the user the reason for its recommendations/ actions/state in a given context). This includes context-aware privacy, as privacy dynamically depends on the time, place, purpose, social setting, and conditions.

5   Conclusions

Companion robotics pose a number of challenges as well as opportunities. Our user trials with such systems have led to the following observations:

Advanced Interactivity: The users' expectations of such companionable systems are much more exacting than the capabilities of current ICT technologies. Challenges include a safety and security protective operation, advanced personalisation, highly responsive context-and-privacy-awareness, emotionally-intelligent dialogue, safe navigation, mixed-initiative taking, and invitational tone of voice, and pro-active and context-sensitive assistance (e.g. reminding, alerting).

Powerful Synergy: The above capabilities can be best realised given the semantic integration of ambient devices within a smart environment. Companion robots, when part of a bigger infrastructure of external sensors and actuators, become empowered to deliver their functionalities more intelligently and effectively. It is of utmost importance that the smart home and the robot are fully integrated and are thus both aware of the status and needs of the inhabitant(s), social setting and the outside world.

Robot Personas: Obviously users differ in their personal preferences regarding the roles, responsibilities and thus the type of persona they would like to see in their companion robot [10]. Therefore there is a need for the companion robot to be capable of (re)instantiation of its own character to match user-specified robot personas. Note the differences in the style of a companion as a butler/servant, a friendly helper, an entertainer, or a guardian angel. Our empirical evidence, based on our user trials, suggests that users care significantly less about the robot's design and physical embodiment, than about its functionality and 'character' or interaction style.

Future Work: There are several areas of outstanding challenges relating to the co-design of user-centred companion-social robot personas and their graceful integration with smart homes. For example, technically, it is feasible to tell a person where the keys that he may be looking for are located. We should question ourselves, as to whether we are really giving them what they need or just what they want. There may be occasions when the deeper value of such assistive intervention may lie in a smarter dialogue that triggers users to deploy their own intellectual resources.

Acknowledgments. This work is developed within the CompanionAble (IP 216487 www.companionable.net) and Mobiserv (STREP 248434 www.mobiserv.eu) projects, partly funded by the European Commission (7th Framework Programme on ICT & Aging). The authors thank the Commission and extend their appreciation to all the project members of CompanionAble and the Mobiserv consortia.

References

1. Mortality and life expectancy statistics (August 2010), http://epp.eurostat.ec.europa.eu/statistics_explained/index.php/Mortality_and_life_expectancy_statistics
2. Sixsmith, A., Meuller, S., Lull, F., Klein, M., Bierhoff, I., Delaney, S., Savage, R.: SOPRANO – An Ambient Assisted Living System for Supporting Older People at Home. In: Mokhtari, M., Khalil, I., Bauchet, J., Zhang, D., Nugent, C. (eds.) ICOST 2009. LNCS, vol. 5597, pp. 233–236. Springer, Heidelberg (2009)
3. Chan, M., Campo, E., Esteve, D., Fourniols, J.: Smart Homes - Current features and future perspectives. Maturitas 64(2), 90–97 (2009) ISSN 0378-5122
4. Graf, B., Parlitz, C., Hägele, M.: Robotic Home Assistant Care-O-bot® 3 Product Vision and Innovation Platform. In: Jacko, J.A. (ed.) HCI International 2009. LNCS, vol. 5611, pp. 312–320. Springer, Heidelberg (2009)
5. Cesta, A., Cortellessa, G., Giuliani, M.V., Pecora, F., Scopelliti, M., Tiberio, L.: Psychological Implications of Domestic Assistive Technology. PsychNology Journal 5(3), 229–252 (2007)
6. KSERA, http://ksera.ieis.tue.nl
7. Meyer, J., Brell, M., Hein, A., Gessler, S.: Personal Assistive Robots for AAL at Home - The Florence Point of View (2009)

8. Badii, A., Etxeberria, I., Huijnen, C., Maseda, M., Dittenberger, S., Hochgatterer, A., Thiemert, D., Rigaud, A.: CompanionAble- Graceful integration of mobile robot companion with a smart home environment. Gerontechnology 8(3), 185 (2009)
9. Badii, A.: Man-Machine Mixed Initiative Taking Architecture for Shared Action (Robo-Humatics-Llemex_Rb): Graceful Human-Robot Co-operativity Support Framework. In: 5th CRI Research Workshop, Brussels, Belgium, March 8 (2011)
10. Badii, A., Khan, A.: Real-time Cognitive-Capacity-Sensitive Multimodal Information Exchange for the Cockpit Environment. In: MOBILITY, Barcelona, Spain, October 23-29 (2011)
11. Nani, M., Caleb-Solly, P., Dogramadgi, S., Fear, C., Van den Heuvel, H.: MOBISERV: An Integrated Intelligent Home Environment for the Provision of Health, Nutrition and Mobility Services to the Elderly. In: 4th Companion Robotics Workshop, Brussels, Belgium, September 30 (2010)
12. De Slimste Woning van Nederland, Stichting Smart Homes, http://www.smart-homes.nl/Kennisoverdracht/De-Slimste-Woning.aspx
13. Huijnen, C.: The Use of Assistive Technology to Support the Wellbeing and Independence of People with Memory Impairments. In: Intelligent Technologies for Bridging the Grey Digital Divide, pp. 65–79 (2011)

Ambient Monitoring from an Elderly-Centred Design Perspective: What, Who and How

Marije Kanis, Sean Alizadeh, Jesse Groen, Milad Khalili, Saskia Robben, Sander Bakkes, and Ben Kröse

Amsterdam University of Applied Sciences, Duivendrechtsekade 36-38, 1096 AH, Amsterdam, The Netherlands
{M.Kanis,Sean.Alizadeh,S.M.B.Robben,B.J.A.Krose}@hva.nl

Abstract. This paper describes a participatory design-oriented study of an ambient assisted living system for monitoring the daily activities of elderly residents. The work presented addresses these questions 1) What daily activities the elderly participants like to be monitored, 2) With whom they would want to share this monitored data and 3) How a monitoring system for the elderly should be designed. For this purpose, this paper discusses the study results and participatory design techniques used to exemplify and understand desired ambient-assisted living scenarios and information sharing needs. Particularly, an interactive dollhouse is presented as a method for including the elderly in the design and requirements gathering process for residential monitoring. The study results indicate the importance of exemplifying ambient-assisted living scenarios to involve the elderly and so to increase acceptance and utility of such systems. The preliminary studies presented show that the participants were willing to have most of their daily activities monitored. However, they mostly wanted to keep control over their own data and share this information with medical specialists and particularly not with their fellow elderly neighbours.

Keywords: Ambient Assisted Living, ambient interaction, information sharing, elderly-centred design, data visualization, participatory design.

1   Introduction

The growth of the elderly population and the exponential increase of medical expenditure have stimulated interest in Ambient Assisted Living (AAL), an emerging field that promotes independency in the old age with the support of advanced technologies. Residential monitoring is particularly being explored for this purpose. Typically, it is focused on monitoring elderly Activities of Daily Living (ADL); a set of activities used by physicians to benchmark physical and cognitive decline. Although the governmental and clinical perspective is dominant in the design of monitoring technology, designing such systems should indeed be accompanied with the elderly acceptance and understanding. A recent study amongst elderly care specialists [1] supports the foremost importance of including elderly input in the telemonitoring process. However, the exact workings of novel, ambient intelligent systems in the home might not be entirely clear to the user. This makes it difficult to

D. Keyson et al. (Eds.): AmI 2011, LNCS 7040, pp. 330–334, 2011.
© Springer-Verlag Berlin Heidelberg 2011

gather honest and true opinions and attitudes that can rightly inform the design of a monitoring system. The work described in this paper, is therefore focused on gathering insights and means to include elderly in this process of designing a system for monitoring their daily activities. The following sections introduce the what, who and how issues of designing a system for monitoring ADL's.!

What: Ambient Monitoring. Ambient monitoring systems [2] (also referred as tele- or residential monitoring) are particularly under investigation as to gather and analyze information about elderly's activities of daily living in the home. Ambient monitoring involves placing sensors in the environment to be monitored, rather than on the user themselves. In our current investigated home aged care scenario, this involves placing 15 simple sensors such as motion detectors and switches on doors throughout elderly homes that track the user's activities of daily living. Deviations in ADL (e.g. bathing, toileting and eating) may reveal information that leads to preventive measures. Researchers have progressed on the rather techno-centric issue of activity recognition [3] and clinical-centric issues such as the importance of the various ADL from the medical specialists view [1]. Though important for acceptance, an underexplored issue is elderly's perceptions on what kind of activities to monitor.

Who: Sharing Information. The elderly in the context of this study reside within assisted living environments and are considered independent in terms of performing their activities of daily living. Given the personal nature of behavioural information that may be monitored and transmitted, the general belief is that such data needs to be carefully dealt with. A study on user acceptance issues from the elderly perspective [2] specifically suggests control as an important factor for elderly acceptance of sensor technology. One may argue that to be in control, the elder needs to be aware and able to make sense out of the incoming data. Yet, the difficulty of ambient technology and the almost invisible interaction and data streams it facilitates, is that it becomes difficult to know what information is being collected, and with which party or person such data is being shared. In this context, it is unclear whether the elder want to share ambient data with medical specialists, friends, family or neighbours and leaving the interpretation of ambient data to expert others. As the desired level of sharing of information has obvious design and ethical implications, this needs to be clarified first, particularly as this has not been studied to a large extent.

How: An elderly-centred design approach. Researchers [4-6] argue that when designing care systems for the elderly, end users should be very much involved in the process. They suggest that human-centred design methods such as participatory design and value sensitive design, which emphasize the values and opinions of direct and indirect stakeholders, are key to upholding the ethical and democratic standards of the design process. Participatory design also plays a valuable role in creating more useful and better technology for end users [4] and hence acceptance of technology. However, some argue [5, 7] that strategies and methods on how to involve seniors in technology design are still unclear. Furthermore, the near invisibility and novelty of ambient technology makes it difficult to imagine residential monitoring systems and the (sensor) data streams it can produce. This has obvious consequences for engaging users in the design of the system. Providing users with example scenarios (e.g., via theatrical techniques [8], dollhouses [9] or smart home environments (such as Ambient kitchen [10]) are imaginative ways for requirements gathering. The challenge is to develop novel methods for AAL requirements gathering, particularly ones that fit within the daily life [4] of the citizen, and cater for the diverse ideas and agendas of multiple stakeholders and users involved [8]. Furthermore, enabling users to experience technology in the home and present appropriate feedback on monitored data would help to improve understanding of the system, and so help its acceptance.

2   Study

Through conducting participatory design activities, as well as in-depth interviews with additional questionnaires, the study's aim was to better understand the needs of the elderly within the context of residential monitoring and consequently address acceptance issues. Specifically, the study aimed to address the following issues: (1) What: Activities from the elderly point of view, (2) Who: Investigate seniors' attitudes on the sharing of data with different parties, and (3) How: Employ participatory design techniques to aid the elderly in having a better understanding of residential monitoring. The scope of the study was restricted to the anticipated users of the system and directly related to monitoring seniors living independently in their own homes in a residential care environment. The participants included six senior citizens residing in an assisted living environment in Naarderheem, The Netherlands. Though some participants had partial physical or cognitive impairments, the elderly in question were able to live and perform their daily activities independently. The participants had no prior experience with a monitoring system in their home. However, prior to the present study they had expressed an interest in having such system installed. The study involved: (1) Frequent (in)formal discussions between the researchers and different stakeholders (such as the technical specialists and care staff), (2) Participatory design activities (i.e. co-creation sessions and iterative prototyping) to critique, build and evaluate the monitoring system being designed and installed, (3) Semi-structured interviews with the senior participants in their home, (4) A questionnaire investigating what kind of activities the interviewees wanted to be monitored (similar to the one used in previous study [2]) and with which party (just themselves, medical specialists, friends, family and/or neighbours) they wanted to share this information.   The participants rated the importance of monitoring each ADL and preferred sharing party using a 7-point Likert scale.

2.1   Results

This study uncovered several what, who and how issues with regards to designing a monitoring system for the elderly. General issues involving the design of telemonitoring have been explored as well as developing participatory design techniques to aid the elderly in understanding monitoring technology.

What: Monitoring Activities from the Elderly Point of View. The results from the interviews indicate that the majority of the participants are currently familiar with some form of telemonitoring system, such as wearable panic buttons. However, the elderly were not very keen on such wearable devices. Furthermore, the majority of the interviewees (5/6) discarded the idea of using video and audio recordings for monitoring as being too invasive. As one participant explained *"Imagine if I have guests over, will you be monitoring them as well?"* On the other hand, the elderly felt that such system could be useful in acute situations, such as heart failure or fall accidents. When regarding the importance of activities as rated by the elderly in the questionnaire and expressed in the interviews, the participants found telemonitoring useful for a number of activities, such as taking medication, movement and continence. Still, the elderly all found that being able to have their own say when regarding their personal state was most important.

Sharing Information with Others. From the interviews and questionnaires it was found that the participants were generally not very willing to share one's daily living routine with others, except when it concerns sharing with a medical specialist. Results reveal less willingness to share information with friends and family members. Particularly so, willingness to share information with neighbours was rated lowest in the questionnaire, but also in the interviews the participants made it clear that they were particularly not interested in sharing information with their neighbours. As a participant expressed *"I do regularly greet the lady next door, but I don't want her to know anything about my personal life."*

Participatory Design for Ambient Assisted Living: An Interactive Dollhouse. The participatory design process resulted in an interactive dollhouse as a new tool to aid users' understanding of telemonitoring and engage users in the desired workings of such system. This dollhouse (a scale model copy of the participants' home) has been equipped with simple sensors that are able to track movement and so simulate the actual monitoring environment. The dollhouse communicates with a graphical user interface that displays simple feedback on what is being monitored in the dollhouse. Representations of sensor data derived from monitoring technology are often designed and visualized in a way that only allows a trained professional to interpret and act, but the interface of the dollhouse was designed with the elder user in mind. The dollhouse (Fig. 1.) has already been used in five participatory design sessions and was found to be a helpful tool in giving the elderly and other stakeholders a better understanding of the desired workings of the system and its output. The dollhouse has also been found effective in helping discussion and reaching more common understanding between the elderly, researchers and other parties involved.

Fig. 1. Dollhouse prototype and participatory design with the elderly

3   Conclusion

Senior citizens represent a growing base of users that can benefit from an engagement with monitoring technology. Considering the pilot study results, it can be concluded that the elderly find ambient monitoring useful for a number of activities. According to the study, their considerations and input is most important, and thus key in creating a monitoring system that is accepted by the end users. However, traditional user-centred design methods provide little guidance in how to involve the elderly in accepting ambient assisted living scenarios. To address this, an elderly-centred approach was taken to discuss challenges for designing monitoring technology. The interactive dollhouse was found a useful technique to engage the elderly and appeared to be an effective tool to familiarize the end user with monitoring technology currently being installed, and so to engage them in accepting and influencing the proposed monitoring solution. The study was also fruitful in terms of increasing awareness of the workings of the system and long-lasting partnerships formed with the elderly and other stakeholders involved. This is valuable and essential to progress further study. As to draw more reliable and insightful conclusions, a larger group of participants is required and recommended for future work. Furthermore, issues such as data visualization, activity recognition, information sharing and acceptance need to be further considered and explored in-situ to bring real value to the users. In doing so, it is recommended to be sensitive to the attitudes of the elderly and exemplify ambient scenarios to aid democratic engagement in ambient technology design.

Acknowledgments. This research has been supported by SIA and CCCT. We thank Marijn Rijken (TNO), Vivium Naarderheem and all other research contributors.

References

1. Alizadeh, S., Bakkes, S., Kanis, M., Rijken, M., Kröse, B.: Telemonitoring for assisted living residences: The medical specialists' view. In: Proceedings of Med-e-Tel 2011, pp. 75–78 (2011)
2. Steele, R., Secombe, C., Brookes, W.: Using Wireless Sensor Networks for Aged Care: The Patient's Perspective, pp. 1–10 (2006)
3. Kasteren, T.v., Noulas, A., Englebienne, G., Kröse, B.: Accurate activity recognition in a home setting. In: Proceedings of UbiComp 2008 (2008)
4. Ballegaard, S.A., Hansen, T.R., Kyng, M.: Healthcare in everyday life: designing healthcare services for daily life. In: Proceedings of CHI 2008 (2008)
5. Duh, H.B.-L., Do, E.Y.-L., Billinghurst, M., Quek, F., Chen, V.H.-H.: Senior-friendly technologies: Interaction design for senior users. In: Proceedings of CHI 2010 (2010)
6. Davis, J.: Design methods for ethical persuasive computing. In: Proceedings of Persuasive (2009)
7. Newell, A.F., Arnott, J.L., Carmichael, A., Morgan, M.: Methodologies for involving older adults in the design process. In: Proceedings of HCI International, pp. 982–989 (2007)
8. Morgan, M., Martin, C., McGee-Lennon, M., Clark, J., Hine, N., Wolters, M., Arnott, J.: Requirements gathering with diverse user groups and stakeholders. In: Proc. of CHI 2008 (2008)
9. Tore, U., Asmund, W., Anne, Z., Solveig, E., Julie Kleppen, R.: Pivots and structured play: stimulating creative user input in concept development. In: Proceedings of NordiCHI (2002)
10. Olivier, P., Monk, A., Xu, G., Hoey, J.: Ambient Kitchen: Designing situated services using a high fidelity prototyping environment. In: Proceedings of the PETRA (2009)

Poetic Communication: Interactive Carpet for Subtle Family Communication and Connectedness

Mili John Tharakan, Jose Sepulveda, Wendy Thun, and Adrian David Cheok

Keio-NUS CUTE Center, National University of Singapore
21 Heng Mui Keng Terrace, Singapore 119 613
{militharakan,sepulveda,adriancheok}@mixedrealitylab.org
u0706004@nus.edu.sg

Abstract. Recent research in Human Computer studies have shown that smart and efficient technology alone is not what people desire for in their homes. The Interactive Carpet project aims to produce a new kind of interaction - Poetic Communication, enabling remote communication through the creation of a sense of sharing, co-presence, and connectedness. This technology connects two carpets in remote locations enhancing communication through more meaningful aesthetic interactions.

Keywords: Poetic Communication, Kinetic Textiles, Interactive carpet, Co-presence, Family communication, Technology adoption.

1 Introduction

In the past decade, there has been a rush to embed technology into our daily lives to help us be more efficient, connected and informed. Recent research in Human Computer studies have shown that smart technology alone is not what people desire for in their homes [1]. People look for products that allow them to reflect, objects that blur the boundaries between gadgets and crafts, creating aesthetical, emotional and informative experiences. According to Dunne, "the most difficult challenges for designers of electronic objects now lie not in technical and semiotics functionality, where optimal levels of performance are already attainable, but in the realms of metaphysics, poetry and aesthetics, where little research has been carried out" [2]. This research is the beginning of a series of products that look to explores the realm of poetry and aesthetics through technology and products. We define this kind of technology for communication as 'Poetic communication' and have developed an interactive carpet that explore and test these ideas further..

The etymology of the word Poetry in Arabic and Greek helps us to better understand *Poetic communication*. The English word poetry is derived from the Greek 'poiein' meaning 'to make' and in Arabic, the word for poetry is derived from the work 'Shi'ir' which means 'to feel' [3]. Poetic communication combines both the meanings - 'to make' and 'to feel' and this needed to be the essence of the technology that enables Poetic communications. In the German language, two words are used for 'experience' – *Erlebnis* and *Erfahrung*. *Erlebnis* is used to describe everyday events

D. Keyson et al. (Eds.): AmI 2011, LNCS 7040, pp. 335–339, 2011.

in our life whereas *Erfahrung* is used to describe an experience that is a turning point in ones life such as having a baby, surviving through war etc. [4]. Poetic Communication is about expressing *Erlebnis*. The interactive carpet is a tool for Poetic Communications of everyday experiences. Research has shown that the bond between family members living apart is strengthened through small acts of daily life or shared presence [5]. The interactive carpet enables shared presence or connectedness through poetic and aesthetic expressions and interactions.

Carpets are common at homes; they demarcate space - public, private, scared, provide warmth and comfort, symbolises power and wealth etc. The conscience choice of textiles as a medium to integrate digital technology was due to its seamless use and affordance offered. The goal of this project is to use technology to enhance interaction and to evoke emotions and memories through familiar home products. With the Interactive carpet, movements and activities on one carpet will be reflected in real time by actuated movements of carpet tufts on a remote carpet, thus enabling motion and gestural communication between two separate spaces.

HCI research in Family communication has shown that adoption of domestic communication technology happens through small imperceptible steps from the edge of existing products such as furniture [6]. In a study done with parents to understand their most valuable awareness information, it showed that one of the three key information they required was the activity and location information of their dependant children [7]. The interactive carpet is a surface that allows for this kind of information exchange that is subtle, silent and non intrusive.

2 Related Works

Woolgar, writes that technologies should act as a supplement rather than substitute [8]. Extending the same concept, a Bonner found that technologies should be adopted in a slow manner to reduce to produce gradual awareness [9]. The concept of ambient intelligence to support the awareness of elderly living alone has been much investigated by various people. Dadlani et al. research has confirmed the potential of awareness systems intertwining with expressive communications [10]. *Aurama* is a system for monitoring elders using non-obstructive sensor technology, this system has indicated a need for information on the health and well-being of the ageing parents [11]. Khan and Markopoulos study concluded that, awareness information needs to vary in contexts and be sent in a non-obstructive manner, to avoid adding burden to others' busy lifestyles [12].

In the research of interactive motions through fabric or fur, *Surflex* used the Shape Memory Alloy (SMA) composite and successfully created a three – dimensional movement. However, *Surflex* is limited to homeographic shape changes and this prevents any performance on its surface or edges [13]. In addition, SMA uses the concept of heating and cooling, which is not suitable for the application of the interactive carpet. In *Sprout I/O* by Coelho and Maes, the structure was made to resemble grass blades in a 6 x 6 array. Each strand was made of fabric and SMA composite that can bend in two directions, mainly forward and backward bending. This restricted movement made the movement less natural [14]. Furukawa et al. embedded vibration motors under a layer of fur, which created bristling effect on its surface [15]. The fur movement was non reversible with only mechanical vibration. *Tabby*, by Ueki, is a lamp with a breathing-like feature, where it is being controlled by a pressure fan within the lamp [16]. Raffle and Joachim developed the Super *Celia Skin*. Super *Celia Skin* can be applied to various planar or non-planar objects, but just like the fur the movement is not reversible and cannot be flattened as it is controlled by magnetic force between each cilium actuator and the displacement and deflected angles are limited [17].

3 Systems Description

Durability, natural movement of tufts and inaudible hardware technology are the three main factors that needed to be addressed in the design of this system.

3.1 Experiments

The aim of the experiment was to find out which actuation methods provide the smoothest, uninterrupted actuation needed for the interactive carpet.

Experiment set up - Four experiments were conducted, the first adopting the concept used in *Tabby* [16]. Plastic strips, representing tufts were attached to a base with openings combined with a fan. The results are shown in Figure 1.

The second method used the approach by Nils [18], using a single straw to suck and inject air into the plastic tubes, as it can be seen in Figure 2.

Fig. 1. (a) Initial position, (b) Strips raised 90* **Fig. 2.** (a) Deflated tubes, (b) Inflated tubes

The next method of actuation was modified from *I/O Sprouts* [14], with fishing line as a substitute for shape memory alloy (SMA). The heat produced by the SMA was not suitable for a household application. Results shown in Figure 3.

The final method of for actuation originated from Furukawa [15]. Tamiya motor was placed under the carpet and the continuous rotation of axles generated ruffling movement on the carpet as shown in Figure 4.

Fig. 3. (a) Onset, (b) Actuation position   **Fig. 4.** (a) Onset, (b) Motor movement

Actuation Results - The experiments showed that motor actuation was the most suitable method for the interactive carpet. The first and second methods presented control problems. The third method was unable to create the desired sweeping effect. Based on the evaluation, motor was chosen as the best solution.

Motor Selection - The selection of motor was done based on the noise level. The noise level of three types of motors: Direct Current (DC) motor, gear motor and stepper motor were measured using the TrueRTA Audio Analyzer Level 1. The stepper motor was chosen because of its low noise level, with the range between 22 dB and 28 dB.

3.2 Hardware Design

The interactive carpet system consists of two carpets, which were designed to communicate wirelessly using XBee modules. The design combines Force Sensing Resistors (FSRs) with six stepper motors. Data collected from FSRs controls the motor's movement using the pre-defined Pulse Width Modulation (PWM) frequencies. The interactive carpet uses two hard acrylic sheets, with the circuit and motors sandwiched between the two sheets for protection. FSRs were placed on the top acrylic sheet and were covered by the carpet.

3.3 Programming of Stepper Motors

Three methods have been used to control the stepper motors movement. The first method used a single pulse for every step desired. The second method modified the built-in *Stepper Library* in Arduino, to allow a modification of the speed. The last method produced a wave of pulses using the pre-defined PWM frequencies in the microcontroller to generate movement.

From the three methods, methods 1 and 2 generated jerky movements on the carpet, due to the delay produced by running six motors continuously. In method 3 the jerky movement was solved.

4   Future Work

The future work will include conducting a user study where we analyse how families would use the carpet for interaction and to understand the poetic and aesthetics value of this communication. The interactive carpet should also be further programmed to create different patterns/movements to be tested by users to obtain the statistics on the effectiveness of the carpet to display awareness and emotions through sensing and actuation. it is important to relate human emotions through the carpet, and more user studies are required to develop the transmission of feelings and emotions using a carpet. This information will drive the creation of a second prototype that will refine the kinetic resolution to further enhance Poetic communication, thereby improving our experience of shared awareness, subtle communications and connectedness in aesthetic and poetic ways.

Acknowledgement. This research is partly a CUTE Project No. WBS R-7050000-100-279 partially funded by a grant from the National Research Foundation (NRF) administered by the Media Development Authority (MDA) of Singapore.

References

1. Olivier, P., Wallace, J.: Digital Technology and emotional families. International Journal of Human-Computer Studies 67, 204–214 (2009)
2. Dunne, A.: Hertzian Tales: Electronic Products, Aesthetic Experiences and Critical Design. MIT Press, Cambridge (2005)
3. Abdul-Settar, A.: The Etymology of the Word "Poetry" in Arabic and Indo-European Languages,
   http://www.shvoong.com/humanities/1779651-etymology-word-poetry-arabic-indo/ (retrieved from May 18, 2010)
4. Boswijk, A., Thomas, T., Peelen, E. (eds.): The Experience Economy: A New Perspective. Pearson Education, Beneleux (2007)
5. Itoh, Y., Miyajima, A., Watanabe, T.: 'TSUNAGARI' Commincation: Fostering a Feeling of Connection Between Family members. In: CHI 2002 Human Factors of Computing Systems, pp. 810–811 (2002)
6. Bonner, V.H.J.: Adding critical sensibilities to domestic communication technology. International Journal of Human-Computer Studies 67, 215–221 (2009)
7. Khan, V.J., Markopoulos, P.: Busy families awareness needs. International Journal of Human-Computer Studies 67, 139–153 (2009)
8. Woolgar, S.: Five rules of virtuality. In: Virtual Society?: Technology, Cyberbole, Reality. Oxford University Press, Oxford (2002)
9. Bonner, J.V.H.: Adding critical sensibilities to domestic communication technologies. International Journal of Human-Computer Studies, 215–221 (2008)
10. Dadlani, P., Markopoulos, P., Aarts, E.: Intertwining Implicit and Explicit Awareness of Wellbeing to Support Peace of Mind and Connectedness. In: Tscheligi, M., de Ruyter, B., Markopoulus, P., Wichert, R., Mirlacher, T., Meschterjakov, A., Reitberger, W. (eds.) AmI 2009. LNCS, vol. 5859, pp. 153–158. Springer, Heidelberg (2009)
11. Dadlani, P., Sinitsyn, A., Fontijn, W., Markopoulos, P.: Aurama: Caregiver awareness for living independently with an augmented picture frame display. AI & Society 25, 233–245 (2010)
12. Khan, V., Markopoulos, P.: Busy families awareness needs. International Journal of Human-Computer Studies 67, 139–153 (2008)
13. Coelho, M., Ishii, H., Maes, P.: Surflex: a programmable surface for the design of tangible interfaces. In: Human Factors in Computing Systems (CHI 2008). ACM, Florence (2008)
14. Coelho, M., Maes, P.: Sprout I/O: a texturally rich interface. In: Tangible and Embedded Interaction Conference. ACM Press, Bonn (2008)
15. Furukawa, M., Uema, Y., Sugimoto, M., Masahiko, I.: Fur Interface with Bristling effect induced by vibration. In: 1st Augmented Human International Conference, pp. 1–6 (2010)
16. Ueki, A., Kamata, M., Inakage, M.: Tabby: designing of coexisting entertainment content in everyday life by expanding the design of furniture. In: Int. Conf. on Advances in Computer Entertainment Technology, vol. 203, pp. 72–78 (2007)
17. Raffle, H., Joachim, M.W., Tichenor, J.: Super Cilia Skin: An Interactive Membrane. In: Conference of Human Factors in Computing Systems (2003)
18. Volker, N.: One Hundred and Eight-Interactive Installation. In: Vimeo,
    http://vimeo.com/16558492 (retrieved from October 11, 2010)

Selective Inductive Powering in Hardware-Based Paper Computing

Kening Zhu*, Hideaki Nii, Owen Noel Newton Fernando,
and Adrian David Cheok

Keio-NUS CUTE Center,
NUS Graduate School for Integrative Sciences and Engineering,
National University of Singapore
ken@cutecenter.org

Abstract. We present a method of selective wireless power transferring for paper computing. The novelty of this method lies in the power transmitter can be controlled to selectively activate different receivers in the context of wireless power transferring with multiple receivers. This was achieved by changing the output frequency of the power transmitter and the impedance of the receivers. With this method, users could easily design new types of paper-computing system without worrying about the arrangement of the massive wire connection to power supply. This technology combining with paper computing can become a physical rendering system using paper-crafts, such as paper folding and cutting.

1   Introduction

Since its invention, paper has been used as not only the medium of writing to communicate information, but also given rich cultural value and treated as a source of inspiring various forms of artworks from its plain surface, such as drawing, folding, cutting, and so on [1]. Although the society is gradually turned paperless along with the rapid development of digital technology, research has shown that there are still rich advantages of paper in our daily life. Since the rise of ambient intelligence is driving the technology disappearing into everyday objects and environment, researchers who are interested in paper material brought up the concept of Paper Computing, which appreciates paper, the traditional information medium, as a good candidate for ambient human computer interaction. In PaperComp 2010 [2], the first International Workshop on Paper Computing, the participants claimed that far from a paperless world, paper could become ubiquitous interfaces in everyday interaction with digital information, and this is the dawn of paper computing.

In this paper, we present a new method of wireless powering for hardware-based paper computing. While the traditional powering methods connected interactive paper system to external power source through massive wires, in our method, the power is provided throught changing eletromagnetic field wirelessly

---

* Corresponding author.

D. Keyson et al. (Eds.): AmI 2011, LNCS 7040, pp. 340–344, 2011.

and selectively to individual embedded electrical components inside the paper material.

In the rest of this paper, an overview of related works will be presented and compared with our method, followed by the detailed description of our method and example of application. Finally we will discuss our future works and how the presented technology can be applied to other areas of ambient intelligence.

2   Related Works

In the related literatures, there are three main powering method applied in hardware-based paper computing. The first and the most common method is connecting the interactive system to external power source through wire. In Easigami [3], Yingdan Huang et al. presented a novel tangible interface with embedded sensors on the edge of paper whose power is provided by external power supply through wire connection.

The second method is using batteries embedded in paper material. In the project of Electronic Popables [4], the authors developed an interactive pop-up book which integrates electronics and pop-up mechanisms as a whole user interface. In order to make the pop-up book a standalone interface, magnetic battery module was embedded in the paper to power up LEDs.

However, these existing methods sacrficed the tangibility of paper material because of either massive wire connection or bulky embedded batteries. Compared to these methods of powering in paper computing, we present a new technology which utilizes selective inductive powering to create interactive papercraft platform. Taking one step further over the existing works, our method eliminates the massive external power connection, and makes the paper-based interaction merge into daily environment more seamlessly, and keeps the custumizability and the exibility for users to directly interact with these paper-crafts with hands.

3   System Description

3.1   Prototype Implementation

The fundamental principle of our method is based on the theory of electromagnetic power generation. A physical prototype of selective wireless powering has been built based on the results of software simulation as shown in 1(a). The transmitter was built with a high output power push/pull MOSFET oscillator setup. The LC tank in the system generates the oscillation, and two power MOSFETs amplifies it to enable the system to transfer more energy wirelessly. Ten polypropylene capacitors are respectively controlled by a relay and a switch so different capacitance value can be included at runtime to generate a variety of frequencies. Finally, the system can generate discrete frequencies in the range from 50KHz to 1.24 MHz.

In the prototyping of the receiving coils embedded in the paper, we used LC tank to harvest energy at its resonance frequency. The inductor L in the system refers to coil made of 0.5mm enameled copper wire; it is circular with diameter 2.5cm and has only 4 turns to match the small resistance of the heating wire. The capacitor and the load resistor are attached to 2 nodes of the copper coil. Each coil will have a different value capacitor attached, thus each will have different resonance frequency. The physical prototype of the receiving part is shown in Figure 1(b). Two receiving coils with capacitors rated 10 nF and 33nF respectively are used in the experiment. They are placed 2 cm from the transmitting coil.

(a) Power Transmitter   (b) Receiving   Coils
                             with Actuators embed-
                             ded in Paper

Fig. 1. Selective Wireless Power Transmitter and Paper with Embedded Receiving Coils

3.2   Experiment Results

Actual experiments with the prototype were conducted with 14 different values of capacitance. The peak value of the inductive voltage was attained from the oscilopescope, and the power was calculated using Equation 1. The experimented results were shown in Figure 2.

$$P = \frac{V_{peak}^2}{2R_{load}} \tag{1}$$

It is easily observed that different values of the capacitor result in different frequencies to achieve peak inductive power, especially from 68nF to 10uF showing that for one specific capacitance the peak power is higher than the other values of power for other capacitance. This means multiple receivers can be distinguished using different output frequencies and different capacitors. This concluded that the proposed method of selective inductive powering can be done and embedded in Paper Computing.

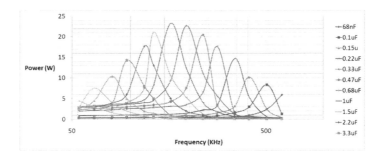

Fig. 2. The Experiment Result

4   Application

By combining the technology of computer-vision-based origami recogntion [5] and selective wireless powering, we developed a initial prototype for physical origami sharing through Internet. Here shape-memory alloy (SMA) was used as the load resistor for receiving coils embedded in paper. Array of receiving coils with SMA acutators are embedded in important folding positions in paper, and basic foldings can be generated by activating different receiving coils selectively.

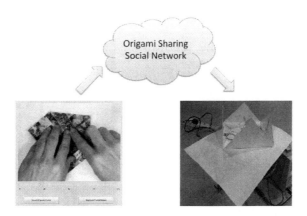

Fig. 3. Online origami sharing by the automatic folding paper

Figure 3 illustrates the overall flow of the origami-sharing system. Users can record and share their videos of making origami to the online server. Meanwhile they can also download their friends' videos, and the video is analyzed to extract the steps of folding and recreate the origami with paper folding automatically. Therefore users can share their origami as permanant physical gifts with friends through Internet, even if they are not physically together.

344 K. Zhu et al.

5 Conclusion and Future Works

There are still several possible improvements and interesting directions for this proposed technology. Firstly we are further researching in increasing the resolution of the powering system as the current size of the transmitter is limited to the diameter of 20cm. In the near future, larger transmitter with smaller receivers will be presented. Secondly, the effciency of power transferring is also a critical issue in the current stage. The low efficiency in current system can be improved by introducing the system of automatic frequency tuning. Meanwhile we are also focusing on developing a programmable toolkit for this technology being utilized in paper computing as a physical rendering interface. With our toolkit every designer can create his/her own transmitter and receivers, further develop more paper-based rendering system.

Besides paper computing, our method can also be used in other applications in ambient intelligence. For instance of wireless power charging, multiple devices can be placed on the powering surface which can sense the charging progress of each device and decide to match the frequency and charge the device with less power. In another application, this technology can be applied to intelligent textile which has the property of changing color or shape. Therefore, by developing the technology of selective inductive powering, we hope to open a new perspective not only in paper computing, but also in the whole area of ambient intelligence.

Acknowledgement. This research is carried out under CUTE Project No. WBS R-705-000-100-279 partially funded by a grant from the National Research Foundation (NRF) administered by the Media Development Authority (MDA) of Singapore.

References

1. Sloman, P. (ed.): Paper: Terar, Fold, Rip, Crease, Cut. Black Dog Publishing (2009)
2. Kaplan, F., Jermann, P.: Papercomp 2010: first international workshop on paper computing. In: Proceedings of the 12th ACM International Conference Adjunct Papers on Ubiquitous Computing, Ubicomp 2010, pp. 507–510. ACM (2010)
3. Huang, Y., Gross, M.D., Do, E.Y.-L., Eisenberg, M.: Easigami: a reconfiguralbe folded-sheet tui. In: TEI 2009: Proceedings of the 3rd International Conference on Tangible and Embedded Interaction, pp. 107–112. ACM, New York (2009)
4. Qi, J., Buechley, L.: Electronic popables: exploring paper-based computing through an interactive pop-up book. In: TEI 2010: Proceedings of the Fourth International Conference on Tangible, Embedded, and Embodied Interaction, pp. 121–128. ACM, New York (2010)
5. Zhu, K., Fernando, O., Cheok, A., Fiala, M., Yang, T.W.: Origami recognition system using natural feature tracking. In: 2010 9th IEEE International Symposium on Mixed and Augmented Reality, pp. 289–290 (2010)

Digital Taste: Electronic Stimulation of Taste Sensations

Nimesha Ranasinghe, Adrian David Cheok, Owen Noel Newton Fernando,
Hideaki Nii, and Ponnampalam Gopalakrishnakone

Keio-NUS CUTE Center, Department of Electrical and Computer Engineering,
National University of Singapore,
{nimesha,adriancheok,newtonfernando,nii}@mixedrealitylab.org,
gopalakrishnakone_pon@nuhs.edu.sg
http://www.mixedrealitylab.org

Abstract. With the continuous advancements in ubiquitous computing and media, the technology has widened to include the multisensory experiences. Although there are quite a lot of systems in auditory, vision, and haptic domains, remarkably few attempts have been made in smell and taste senses in order to facilitate ambient intelligence. We present a novel control system that enables digital stimulations of the sense of taste (gustation) to enhance remote multisensory interactions on human. The system uses two approaches to actuate taste sensations digitally: the electrical and thermal stimulations on tongue. At present, the initial experimental results suggested that sourness and saltiness are the main sensations that could be evoked besides several evidences of sweet and bitter sensations.

Keywords: Taste, Gustation, User interfaces, Control systems, Virtual reality, Input devices.

1 Introduction

Over the last decade, numerous research works have been conducted to engage main five human senses; the touch, sight, taste, smell, and hearing in ambient intelligence. Among the five main human senses, taste is one of the most prominent senses, which motivate human beings to consume varieties of foods [1]. However, the sense of taste is undermined in the ambient intelligence paradigm due to the incomplete understanding of the fundamental form of human taste. The existing methods of stimulating the sense of taste are analog and involve distinct scalability and digital controllability issues. Hence, the sense of taste remained as an unexplored territory in ubiquitous computing, ambient intelligence, and digital communication realms currently dominated by vision, audition, and haptic.

To overcome these shortcomings, we propose a novel method, Digital Taste Actuating System (Figure 1), to achieve the electronic actuation of human taste sensations thus to promote ubiquitous taste experiences. The digital control system itself and the method of stimulating (electrical and thermal combined)

D. Keyson et al. (Eds.): AmI 2011, LNCS 7040, pp. 345–349, 2011.

the taste sensations are the two main novelties of this technology. The control system applies different stimuli to the tip of the tongue by changing current, frequency, and temperature through the silver electrodes.

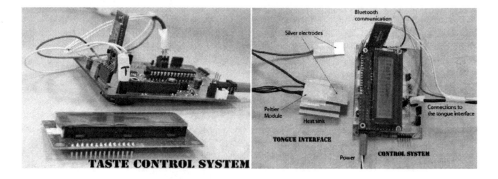

Fig. 1. The digital taste (gustatory) actuating system

The system is capable of generating taste sensations digitally based on electrical and thermal stimulations on human tongue. As illustrated in Figure 2 (A), two plates of electrodes are attached to the users tongue, which are also attached to the electronic control system. Electrical stimulations with predetermined magnitude of current (20, 40, 60, 80, 100, 120, 140, 180, 200 μA), frequency (50, 100, 200, 400, 600, 800, 1000 Hz), and duration (manual control through serial commands) are then applied to the tip of the tongue through the electrodes to produce taste sensations.

1.1 Related Work

Several interactive systems are presented related to taste interfaces in literature. Two such systems are the BeanCounter and TasteScreen [2]. The BeanCounter is a computer memory profiling application and a network monitoring application, which dispense jellybeans (with different flavors) based on the events of memory and data transmissions. The TasteScreen let its users lick their screens to taste food items on their computer monitors. It has flavor cartridges that mix and sprinkle the chemical flavors to the screen based on the contents. The users then are able to taste the flavors on their screens by licking their screens.

Furthermore, related to non-traditional methods of stimulating the sense of taste, Cruz et al. introduced the thermal stimulation of tongue and its results [4]. They have shown that although the tongue is not sensitive for thermal stimulations, heating or cooling small areas on the tongue may actuate taste sensations. In addition, there were few attempts and experiments conducted in the medical field on electrical stimulation of human tongue. Lawless et al. presents the metallic taste generation from electrical and chemical stimulation [3]. This study was conducted to examine the similarities and differences of stimulation with metals, electrical stimulation, and solutions of divalent salts and ferrous sulphate. They have investigated the results of electrical stimulation across the oral locations with metal electrodes and confirmed that a weak electric pulse on the tongue induces metallic taste sensations. The control system is developed by combining those two stimulation methods to finally generate taste sensations digitally.

2 System Description

The taste actuating methodology of the proposed system consists of three sub modules; the electrical and thermal output control systems and the tongue interface. As in Figure 2 (B), the tongue interface acts as an interface between the control system and the tongue. Furthermore, the system makes use of serial commands through Bluetooth communication to configure the output on the tongue interface.

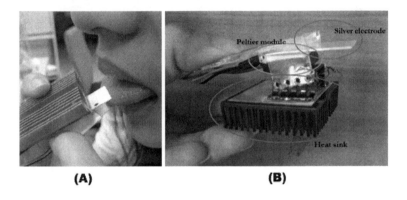

(A)   **(B)**

Fig. 2. Set up of the tongue interface module

In electrical stimulation subsystem, we use a digital potentiometer with a constant current source to provide constant current to all the participants. Because, the impedance of the tongue is varying person to person due to the differences in the density of papillae on the tongue surface. The electrical stimulation module provides square wave pulses to the silver electrode with diverse current from $0\mu A$ to $200\mu A$ and frequency from 50Hz to 1000Hz. In thermal stimulation subsystem, we use a Peltier semi-conductor module (Peltier Junctions) to rapidly change the temperature of the tongue. The thermal stimulation module controls (both cooling and heating) the Peltier module within 20°C   35°C, which attached to silver electrodes.

The tongue interface consists of two silver electrodes (each has dimensions of 40mm x 15mm x 0.2mm), a Peltier module, and a thermister. Moreover, It requires a heat sink for effective temperature control through the Peltier module.

3 Preliminary Experiment and Results

To investigate and analyze the effectiveness of this approach, an initial user experiment was conducted with eighteen subjects (ten males and eight females, age range from 21-27). Electrical stimulations with predetermined magnitude of current (20, 40, 60, 80, 100, 120, 140, 180, 200µA), frequency (50, 100, 200, 400, 600, 800, 1000Hz), temperature (cooling and heating between 20°C 35°C), and duration (manual control through serial commands) are then applied to the tongue through the electrodes to produce taste sensations. Subjects rinse their mouth with deionized water and rested 10 minutes between each stimulus. Participants were asked to provide a verbal descriptor after each stimuli and rate their sensation in a 5 level Likert-type scale.

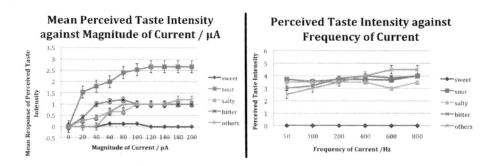

Fig. 3. The perceived intensity of taste sensations during electrical stimulation

Figure 3 reveals the intensities of taste sensations reported during the electrical stimulation. The strength of sour and salty sensations increased when the magnitude of the current increased. Responses from all the participants were quite similar and continuous for sour sensation. However, few indicated (60%) that salty and bitter sensations are also increased when the magnitude of the current increased. All the participants indicated that the change of frequency has not affected on the intensity of the sensation.

Although the rate of successful generation of sweet sensation was low, it implied the possibility of being able to produce the sweet sensation using the thermal stimulation (Figure 4), especially when cooling down the tongue from 35°C. Furthermore, several subjects reported that they felt the minty taste, refreshing

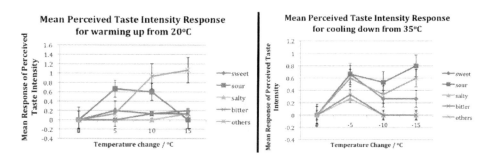

Fig. 4. The perceived intensity of taste sensations during thermal stimulation

taste (cooling down from 35°C to 20°C), and also slight spiciness (heating up from 20°C to 35°C).

Additionally, we understood the ethical issues behind this research and already secured the necessary approval from Institutional Review Board (Approval No: NUS 1049) before the experiments.

4   Conclusion and Future Works

Up until now, most of the systems, generating taste sensations are based on blending several chemicals respectively, and there was no definite strategy to stimulate the sense of taste digitally. In the presented system, effects of most persuading factors such as current, frequency, and temperature have been accounted for digitally actuating the sense of taste by digitally actuating the tongue. The results of the initial experiment suggested that sourness, saltiness, bitterness, and sweetness are the main sensations that could be evoked at present. Further studies will have to do with the characterization of the human tongue for electrical and thermal stimulation. Furthermore, it will facilitate developing innovative systems to stimulate taste sensations digitally, for example, electronic lollipops. It will also enable embedded, context aware, personalized, adaptive, and anticipatory taste interactions on ambient intelligence environments.

Acknowledgements. This research is carried out under CUTE Project No. WBS R-7050000-100-279 partially funded by a grant from the National Research Foundation (NRF) administered by the Media Development Authority (MDA) of Singapore.

References

1. Drewnowski, A.: Taste preferences and food intake. Annual Review of Nutrition 17(1), 237–253 (1997)
2. Maynes-aminzade, D.: Edible Bits: Seamless Interfaces between People, Data and Food. In: ACM Conference on Human Factors in Computing Systems (CHI 2005), pp. 2207–2210 (2005)
3. Lawless, H., Stevens, D., Chapman, K., Kurtz, A.: Metallic taste from electrical and chemical stimulation. Chemical Senses 30(3), 185 (2005)
4. Cruz, A., Green, B.G.: Thermal stimulation of taste. Nature 403(6772), 889–892 (2000)

NOCTURNAL Ambient Assisted Living

J.C. Augusto[1,*] W. Carswell[1], H. Zheng[1], M. Mulvenna[1], S. Martin[2],
P. McCullagh[1], H. Wang[1], J. Wallace[1], and P. Jeffers[3]

[1] School of Computing and Mathematics, University of Ulster, UK
jc.augusto@ulster.ac.uk
[2] School of Health Sciences, University of Ulster, UK
[3] Fold Housing Association, UK

Abstract. There is increasing interest in the development of ambient assisted living services to increase the quality of life of the increasing older population. Little consideration has been given to the specific problem of providing such services and systems at night. We report on the NOCTURNAL project which provides specialised night time support to people at early stages of dementia.

Keywords: Ambient Intelligence, Ambient Assisted Living, safety critical, Multi-Agent Systems.

1 Introduction

Assisted living systems for healthcare are being developed as part of the fundamental shift from hospital-centred to home-centred models of care within health services. Most of the contributions reported in the technical literature focus on the most active period of the day (daylight time). Our project NOCTURNAL (Night Optimised Care Technology for UseRs Needing Assisted Lifestyles) assumes that the night period and daylight periods of the day are different enough to require separate analysis [1]. It is estimated that 10 million people across Europe and 35.6 million people worldwide have dementia [2].

The environment at night is very different and disorientation is more likely for a person with dementia due to low light conditions. A person with dementia is also more likely to be confused and disorientated on awakening, either naturally as they awake from sleep, or if they are exhibiting 'sundowning', where the behaviour of people with dementia changes as the evening and night falls [3]. Older people generally experience changes in their sleeping behaviours. This includes going to sleep early but awaking earlier as well, having more fragmented sleep patterns, suffering from insomnia, and from sleep apnoea, which is "increasingly seen among older people and is significantly associated with cardio- and cerebrovascular disease as well as cognitive impairment" [4]. People with dementia may also be likely to move around their home and beyond causing distress to themselves and their carers [5]. Finally, a person with dementia is more likely to be alone, or not have as immediate access to carers as during the daytime. This can cause any stress and

---

* Corresponding author.

D. Keyson et al. (Eds.): AmI 2011, LNCS 7040, pp. 350–354, 2011.
© Springer-Verlag Berlin Heidelberg 2011

anxiety experienced, as they awake in the dark, to be significant and to increase unchecked and more rapidly than would otherwise be the case if a carer was with them. A literature study [6] shows that technology can play a pivotal role providing assistance to people with dementia during night time. However, these studies focused on monitoring only one specific aspect of the night time activity or on applying a single technology to aid people with dementia during the night. Our work builds upon the current setup commercial telecare offerings of our partner company[1] and provides additional features in what is a more holistic approach to night time care.

2   Technological Infrastructure of the NOCTURNAL System

The NOCTURNAL infrastructure has been designed so that the technology is transparent, user friendly, and cost effective. This has been achieved by focusing on the visualisation of the information in the interface for use by carers, and by using existing, common off-the shelf telecare and computing components. Our system (Figure 1) assumes only one house occupant is monitored at night time (i.e. around 11PM to 7AM) and it passes direct control to our telecare service provider partner when more than one person is inside the house.

(a) Typical dwelling with sensing

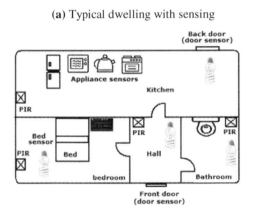

(b) Bedside unit interface. The default mode is to show the time. It also shows pictures and music previously selected by the client and video clips recorded by carers.

Fig. 1. Technological Infrastructure of NOCTURNAL system

The basic sensing set consists of Passive Infra-Red (PIR) sensors, and a bed movement sensor. The basic actuation set consists of a set of lights switches and dimmers and a tablet PC bedside unit, which can deliver time information and textual messages to assist the occupant with understanding of their context, as well as music and pictures for reminiscence and relaxation. Other technologies such as door sensors and appliance sensors can also be used but they are optional and the explanation of the system provided in this work will be focused on the behaviour of the system which is based on the basic configuration.

---

[1] Fold Housing Association(http://www.foldgroup.co.uk/), a not-for-profit organisation delivering telecare/telehealth services to UK/Ireland.

3 Design of the System

The multi-agent based platform was implemented in Jade and has three main roles: detect situations of interest with help of the sensing platform, decide whether the situation requires intervention, and delivering/follow up actuations to assess if the situation has improved.

Our system is organised around the monitoring of three main situations: restlessness, bed occupancy and movement around the home. Activities of the client trigger sensors which are recorded as events in a database. These events are fed to a group of three monitoring agents specialised on detecting those situations. When the number of episodes of interest detected by any single agent is above an acceptable threshold, which is dynamically adapted to the client and the context, the agent involved contacts a coordinating agent (CA) which has a holistic view of the context informed by all the single agent's reports. If appropriate, CA can order the Therapeutic Intervention Agent (TIA) to act helping the client. If subsequent reports from the monitoring agents show there is still reasons for concern the coordinating agent can issue a new intervention through the TIA or eventually, if the situation requires it, the call centre at the service provider can be contacted so that a human deals directly with the situation.

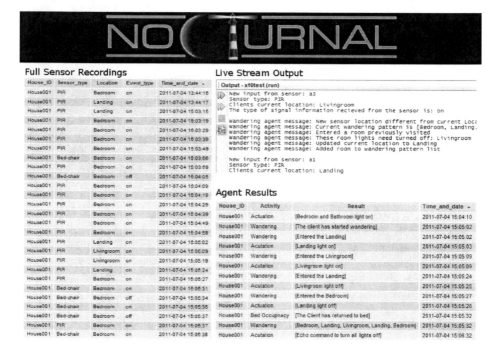

Fig. 2. Example of the system at work, clockwise from left to right: gathering information from sensors, a log of events and recording actuations

The strategy of the system to deal with situations can be described as a stack of situations upon which the system has to act. When there are no noticeable problems the stack is empty. If restlessness is detected, the system puts that in the stack and starts dealing with it. If this is dealt with effectively the system then empties the stack. If, instead, the person gets out of bed then this situation is put on top of the stack and becomes the focus of actuation. Should this be successfully addressed then this concern is removed and the focus return to the remaining one (restlessness), but if the person continues to move through many rooms this problem becomes the top priority. If at any stage a situation persists despite several attempts from the system, then the company is alerted and the contextual information is passed to the operators. Figure 2 shows the Multi-Agent System (MAS) at work whilst detecting movement after the occupant left the bed and visited a number of rooms. The system delivered actuations turning on/off relevant lights and using the bedside unit. The aim was to encourage the person back to bedroom, to return to bed to sleep. All the main components of the system including the four agents described above have been modelled using Promela and simulated and model checked with SPIN to verify the correctness of our strategy and algorithms. We recently reported in detail our models and findings [7].

4 System Services

The system provides several services, while safety assessment in real time is the main focus. If the system believes the actuation is not being successful on dealing with one of the three specific situations of interest (restlessness, bed occupancy or movement) then it will contact the company which delivers the service.

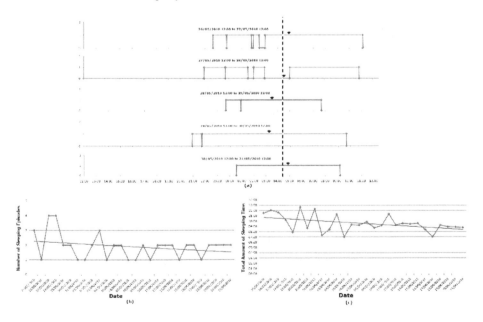

Fig. 3. Patterns of sleep for individual days, week and month

The procedures are the typical ones with an alert being raised at the call centre where human operators will decide on the best course of action (e.g., calling the client or a formal/informal carer). Also important is the information the system can provide on the lifestyle of the house occupant and the variations of some relevant parameters through time [8]. For example, the system can produce profiles of the sleeping and movement patterns of a specific person in a specific period of time (Fig. 3).

5 Conclusions

At night, a person with dementia is often likely to be confused and disorientated as they awake from sleep. It can be argued that for them a need for assistive technology may be as important as those that lead to the development of assistive technology to support independent living during daylight time. The opportunities for research for nocturnal care of people with dementia using holistic assistive technologies are for more specialised algorithms; specially designed interventions that provide therapeutic support to people to reduce anxiety through a multimedia device; and sophisticated guidance, through the use of lightning. Our system differs fundamentally from previous, narrower, approaches to the problem. We provide a more holistic and state-of-the-art extensible framework with a combination of cost-effective infrastructure supported by intelligent agents which can detect and act upon meaningful situations.

References

[1] McCullagh, P., Carswell, W., Augusto, J., Martin, S., Mulvenna, M., Zheng, H., Wang, H., Wallace, J., McSorley, K., Taylor, B., Jeffers, W.: State of the Art on Night-Time Care of People with Dementia. In: Proc. of the Conf. on Assisted Living 2009. IET, London (2009)
[2] Prince, M., Jackson, J. (eds.): Alzheimer's Disease International World Alzheimer Report, ADI (2010)
[3] Scarmeas, N., Brandt, J., Blacker, D., Albert, M., Hadjigeorgiou, G., Dubois, B., Devanand, D., Honig, L.: Disruptive behavior as a predictor in Alzheimer disease. Archives of Neurology 64(12), 1755–1761 (2007)
[4] Wolkove, N., Elkholy, O., Baltzam, M., Palayew, M.: Sleep and aging: 1. Sleep disorders commonly found in older people. CMAJ 176(9), 1299–1304 (2007)
[5] Hermans, D.G., Htay, U.H., McShane, R.: Non-pharmacological interventions for wandering of people with dementia in the domestic setting. Cochrane Database System Review (1), CD005994 (2007)
[6] Carswell, W., McCullagh, P., Augusto, J.C., Martin, S., Mulvenna, M., Zheng, H., Wang, H., Wallace, J., McSorley, K., Taylor, B., Jeffers, P.: A Review of the Role of Assistive Technology for People with Dementia in the Hours of Darkness. Technology and Health Care 17(4), 281–304 (2009)
[7] Augusto, J.C., Zheng, H., Mulvenna, M., Wang, H., Carswell, W., Jeffers, P.: Design and Modelling of the Nocturnal AAL Care System. In: Novais, P., Preuveneers, D., Corchado, J.M. (eds.) ISAmI 2011. AISC, vol. 92, pp. 109–116. Springer, Heidelberg (2011)
[8] Wang, H., Zheng, H., Augusto, J.C., Martin, S., Mulvenna, M., Carswell, W., Wallace, J., Jeffers, P., Taylor, B., McSorley, K.: Monitoring and Analysis of Sleep Pattern for People with Early Dementia. In: KEDDH 2010, Hong Kong, China (December 2010)

Just Saying 'Hi' Means a Lot: Designing Subtle Interactions for Social Connectedness

Thomas Visser, Martijn Vastenburg, and David Keyson

ID-StudioLab, Industrial Design Engineering, Delft University of Technology,
The Netherlands
{t.visser,m.h.vastenburg,d.v.keyson}@tudelft.nl

Abstract. In the domain of assisted living, the majority of the work on awareness systems focuses on communicating information on health and security for functional purposes: to provide better care and peace of mind. When aiming for improved well-being, awareness systems could also be used to stimulate a sense of connectedness. Not much is known on how awareness systems for well-being should be designed. This paper describes several design explorations that illustrate how communication of subtle, low-bandwidth information may be leveraged to support a mutual feeling of social connectedness between people. We discuss the gained insights, which are useful for the design of ambient displays and interactions. The insights presented in this paper are useful for the future design of assisted living services, and for awareness systems in general.

Keywords: Awareness systems, tangible interaction, computer mediated communication, ubiquitous computing.

1 Introduction

Awareness systems support people in their awareness about the things that are going on in specific places or with specific people [1]. Originally rooted in the domain of Computer Supported Collaborative Work, the first systems were designed to provide mutual awareness of workers between two different workplaces (e.g. Portholes [2]). More recently, awareness systems have been designed for many different purposes, one of them being the increase of feelings of safety, security and health between patients and caregivers. Such systems, including the CareNet Display [3] and Digital Family Portrait [4], communicate information about a patient to family or medical care givers, in order to improve care, and to support peace of mind. Awareness systems have primarily focused on communicating functional information, for the end purpose of physical well-being of the patient.

The design of systems for social well-being has received less attention from both designers and researchers in the past decade. Although several examples are known of social awareness (SA) systems, such as the work by Gaver [5] and Vetere [6], these have not focused particularly on the care-domain. Also, more recent examples, such as ASTRA [7] and VIO [8], have aimed primarily for families or romantic relationships.

D. Keyson et al. (Eds.): AmI 2011, LNCS 7040, pp. 355–359, 2011.

The present paper discusses how SA-systems can support social connectedness (a key determinant of social well-being [9]) using subtle communication. Several design explorations have been made, based on key considerations found in literature on SA-systems. We first outline the four SA-systems that were designed to connect independently living seniors with their close relationships in a subtle and ambient way. Based on the findings from these designs and the design process, we evaluate the design parameters, and we present three new insights, relating to communication intention, abstract information, and network size. We discuss the value of these insights for designing embedded interaction, and how they may be leveraged to enhance social connectedness. Finally, opportunities for future work and development of SA-systems for assisted living are outlined.

2   Exploring Social Awareness

As part of a design course, teams of post-graduate design students were given the task to design an SA-system that connects seniors with people that are close to them. Based on a review of literature on SA-systems and connectedness, three key considerations were given to the students as a background for their designs:

1. **Foreground / background.** To allow systems to blend in the daily lives of users, without moving out of sight, they should be able to move from background to foreground of the user's attention [6, 8]. In this sense, not just modalities should be considered, but also the aesthetics and appearance of the device.
2. **Tangible interaction.** The use of tangible interfaces supports an easier blend with the home environment. Moreover, tangible interaction with an SA-system is considered to be more intimate [1].
3. **Subtle communication.** Previous research [7, 9] suggests that subtle communication of awareness information can be powerful in supporting 'thinking about each other' and 'closeness', which are dimensions of social connectedness.

The first exploration considers an SA-system, called WeDo, which connects two homes. One device would be installed in the senior's home, and the other one in the home of the relative or friend. Motion detection is used to collect presence information, which is displayed in the remote device by the small opening lighting up. Users may choose to open the box and will then receive more information through snippets of sound from the other room.

Three other awareness systems that were designed are examples of social network awareness, which allow connecting to more than one user. In the case of ScatteredConnected (Fig. 2), motion measured in the room of another user was indicated by the picture frame (representing that user) lighting up. Having more picture frames, and more users involved, this would generate a light pattern on the wall, showing the network activity. Users may also wave at the photo frames to make their own picture blink in the room of their relatives. For both examples, awareness information is displayed in an abstract way, with a possibility to engage in deeper communication.

Fig. 1. and 2. WeDo (left) and ScatteredConnected (right) social awareness systems

KeyPing, a second SA-system with network awareness, is a communication board with magnetic tokens, each representing other users in the network. Using a token on their key ring, users activate the board, integrating interactions in a homecoming routine. The brighter the tokens light up on the board, the closer the other people are to their home. Also, users may 'ping' a person by pressing that person's token. The token representing the user at that person's board will then light up.

WallTree is the final exploration, which supports network awareness of up to 8 relatives. Whenever someone is at home, his or her branch lights up in green in the other homes. A user may stroke a branch representing a person, to light their branch in that person's house, similar to 'pinging' in the KeyPing design.

Fig. 3. and 4. WallTree (left) and KeyPing (right)

The four systems were evaluated in an open-house exhibition, with about 40-60 visitors per system. The visitors were able to experience working prototypes of the designs, and they were informally interviewed about their experiences.

3   Design Insights

The design process, and the results from the interviews enable a discussion of the considerations introduced at the start of the design process. A primary observation was that the approach to refrain from using (touch)screens or key-interfaces helped to make the designs blend with the home context. Similar to [6], the systems were designed as decorative elements for the living room. In terms of tangible interaction (and in line with [1]), users experienced pressing (KeyPing) and stroking (WallTree) meaningful interaction for supporting intimate communication. Also, the key-ring-based design of KeyPing allowed successful integrations in daily routines.

Through the explorations, also several new design insights were gained:

1. **Intention.** The designs show that awareness information can be communicated unintentionally (measurement and display of movement) or intentionally (pinging). Users indicated that the absence of a 'ping'-function makes it unclear whether communication is intentional or not, leading to misinterpretation.
2. **Abstract information.** The abstract displays were found to work well for maintaining a sense of privacy. Moreover, contrary to what was expected, users suggested that this type of display might support connectedness more, as it stimulates them to imagine what is going on in the other location, thus thinking more of the other.
3. **Network size.** Awareness systems have traditionally focused on one-on-one communication, or on communication in a small network. Users indicated that, for assisted living purposes, they would be interested in linking the systems to existing social network platforms (e.g. Facebook), to make them less stand-alone.

4   Discussion and Future Work

This paper presented an overview of four design explorations that aim to mediate subtle social cues to support social connectedness. Instead of aiming for 'peace of mind' or communicating information on patient health, the designs focused on enhancing social well-being through social connectedness. The design principles that were taken as a starting point have been explored through the design process and evaluation. Also, we presented three new insights that were generated in the process.

The insights were gained through informal evaluations, and should therefore be further validated in more extensive case studies. The first two insights (*intention* and *abstract information*) were integrated in a system called SnowGlobe, which was evaluated in a longitudinal field study. The results of this study will described in detail in [10].

Future work should also focus on addressing the third new insight, which relates to linking awareness systems to existing online social networks services. Studies into this direction are in development and the first results point towards systems being considered to be less stand-alone, and thereby also commercially more interesting. Additionally, such systems are likely able to generate a broader user base, as it's not restricted to physical products and systems only. Eventually, one might envision the physical SA-systems to become a feature of existing (social) care-networks.

The current work provides a background for discussing ambient mediated social interaction. The insights could serve as a frame of reference for future designs of awareness systems. Although the presented insights cannot yet be supported with formal empirical evidence, we consider them to be a valuable contribution to the field, as they may help designers of such systems to better understand how awareness systems may support connectedness, and how they can be integrated in our daily lives.

Acknowledgements. This work is part of the Independent@Home project, funded by Agentschap NL (IOP-MMI program). We would also like to thank the students that supported the work in their design courses and graduation projects, as well as Marc de Hoogh and Rob Luxen, for their support on programming and electronics.

References

1. Rittenbruch, M., McEwan, G.: An Historical Reflection of Awareness in Collaboration. In: Markopoulos, P., de Ruyter, B., Mackay, W.E. (eds.) Awareness Systems: Advances in Theory, Methodology and Design, pp. 3–48. Springer, London (2009)
2. Dourish, P., Bly, S.: Portholes: supporting awareness in a distributed work group. In: Proc. CHI 1992. ACM, New York (1992)
3. Consolvo, S., Roessler, P., Shelton, B.E.: The Carenet Display: Lessons Learned from an in Home Evaluation of an Ambient Display. In: Davies, N., Mynatt, E.D., Siio, I. (eds.) UbiComp 2004. LNCS, vol. 3205, pp. 1–17. Springer, Heidelberg (2004)
4. Mynatt, E.D., Rowan, J., Jacobs, A., Craighill, S.: Digital family portraits: Supporting peace of mind for extended family members. In: Proc. CHI 2001, pp. 333–340. ACM, New York (2001)
5. Vetere, F., Gibbs, M., Kjeldskov, J., Howard, S., Mueller, F., Pedell, S., et al.: Mediating intimacy: designing technologies to support strong-tie relationships. In: Proc. CHI 2005, pp. 471–480. ACM, New York (2005)
6. Gaver, B.: Provocative awareness. CSCW: An International Journal 11(3-4), 475–493 (2002)
7. Romero, N., Markopoulos, P., Baren, J., de Ruyter, B., IJsselsteijn, W., Farshchian, B.: Connecting the family with awareness systems. Pers. and Ubiq. Computing 11(4), 299–312 (2007)
8. Kaye, J.: I Just Clicked To Say I Love You: Rich Evaluations of Minimal Communication. In: Extended Abstracts of CHI 2006, pp. 363–368. ACM, New York (2006)
9. van Bel, D.T., IJsselsteijn, W.A., de Kort, Y.A.W.: Interpersonal connectedness: conceptualization and directions for a measurement instrument. In: Proc. CHI 2008. ACM, New York (2008)
10. Visser, T., Vastenburg, M.H., Keyson, D.V.: Designing to Support Social Connectedness: The Case of SnowGlobe. International Journal of Design (accepted)

Aesthetic Intelligence:
Designing Smart and Beautiful Architectural Spaces

Kai Kasugai[1], Carsten Röcker[1], Bert Bongers[2],
Daniela Plewe[3], and Christian Dimmer[4]

[1] Human Technology Centre, RWTH Aachen University, Germany
{Kasugai,Roecker}@humtec.rwth-aachen.de
[2] Faculty of Design, Architecture and Building, University of Technology Sydney, Australia
Bert.Bongers@uts.edu.au
[3] University Scholars Programme, National University of Singapore, Singapore
DanielaPlewe@nus.edu.sg
[4] Research Center for Advanced Science and Technology, University of Tokyo, Japan
Chris@ud.t.u-tokyo.ac.jp

Abstract. This paper reports on the first international workshop on Aesthetic Intelligence. The focus of the workshop is on the relevance of beauty and aesthetic values for Ambient Intelligence and the meaning of aesthetically pleasing design for usability, technology acceptance, and well-being in technology-enhanced spaces.

Keywords: Ambient Intelligence, Ubiquitous Computing, Smart Spaces, Aesthetics, Design, Architecture, Urban Informatics.

1 Towards Intelligent Spaces

Ambient Intelligence describes the integration of a multitude of tiny microelectronic processors and sensors into almost all everyday objects, which enables an environment to recognize and respond to the needs of users in an almost invisible way (see, e.g., [1]). The envisioned technologies "will weave themselves into the fabric of everyday life until they are indistinguishable from it" [2]. Through the integration of information, communication and sensing technologies into existing architecture, smart environments will emerge, which offer context-adapted services and assist their inhabitants in everyday activities. In a very general sense, the concept of Ambient Intelligence implies that some sort of intelligence surrounds us – somehow. But how does Ambient Intelligence manifest itself? Where does it show up and how do people, who the services are intended for, notice and interact with it? Should it stay invisible or should it form a perceptible digital layer augmenting the physical space? While many of these almost philosophical questions are still actively discussed in our research community, the integration of technology into physical spaces is already happening and changes our environment both visually and functionally.

Urban screens are a good example for this ongoing change. As large displays increasingly move into sight of our everyday city landscape, they are not limited anymore to the public places of metropolises like New York or Tokyo. With the rapid

D. Keyson et al. (Eds.): AmI 2011, LNCS 7040, pp. 360–361, 2011.

advances in display technology in terms of size and cost, ambient displays are gaining increased presence in everyday life and in all kinds of environments. Less than ten years ago, for example, any public viewing of a sport event would have taken place inside pubs on large television sets. Today, we gather in public space and watch such happenings live on display walls. Information screens in airports or train stations are not located exclusively in the waiting hall anymore, but large, medium, and small sized displays are distributed across those places to provide helpful information for travelers. In trains, displays broadcast advertisements and show passenger information. This is just one of many examples illustrating how digital technology changes physical space. The focus of the workshop will be on the visual and perceptual possibilities that arise from the use of Ambient Intelligence technology both in public and private space. Another focus will be the relevance of beauty and aesthetic values for Ambient Intelligence and the meaning of aesthetically pleasing design for usability, and acceptance of the technology as well as for the well-being in technologically mediated spaces.

2 Aesthetics as a Design Criterion

Ambient Intelligence is still a relatively young research field and previous work mainly focused on questions of technical feasibility and more general aspects of human-computer interaction. While those are important aspects, it seems to be time to extend ongoing research activities and also include hedonic and aesthetic dimensions of design and usage. A variety of authors like, e.g., Hassenzahl [3] showed that users wish for more than the pure technical functionality and prefer devices with a high social and hedonic value. And as smart technical devices will be increasingly used within home environments, these aspects are likely to gain additional importance in the future. The first international workshop on Aesthetic Intelligences addresses this challenge by bringing together researchers from different disciplines to discuss the interrelation of functional, architectural, and aesthetic factors and their consequences for the design, use and acceptance of smart environments.

References

1. Aarts, E., Marzano, S.: The New Everyday - View of Ambient Intelligence. 010 Publishers (2003)
2. Weiser, M.: The Computer for the Twenty-First Century. Scientific American 265(3), 94–104 (1991)
3. Hassenzahl, M.: Experience Design – Technology for All the Right Reasons. Morgan & Claypool, San Rafael (2010)

The Role of Ambient Intelligence in Future Lighting Systems

Dzmitry Aliakseyeu[1], Jon Mason[1], Bernt Meerbeek[1], Harm van Essen[2], and Serge Offermans[2]

[1] Philips Research Europe, 5656 Eindhoven, The Netherlands
[2] TU Eindhoven, Industrial Design department, Eindhoven, The Netherlands
{dzmitry.aliskseeyeu,jon.mason,bernt.meerbeek}@philips.com,
{h.a.v.essen,s.a.m.offermans}@tue.nl

Abstract. LED-based lighting systems have introduced radically new possibilities in the area of artificial lighting. Being physically small the LED can be positioned or embedded into luminaires, materials and even the very fabric of a building or environment. The light switch therefore in many situations will need to be enhanced or fully replaced by intelligent controls and smart environments that are sensitive to the context and responsive to the presence of people. Future lighting systems will become a part of the Ambient Intelligence (AmI). This workshop explores how the vision and principles of the AmI paradigm can be applied to future lighting controls, where lighting is not anymore only a functional on/off system, but a flexible system capable of creating a large range of functional/decoration and ambient light effects.

Keywords: Ambient Intelligence, Lighting, User Interaction, LED.

1 Introduction

The Light Emitting Diode (LED) has caused a profound change within the lighting industry. This is due in part to the LED's key properties of being physically small, highly efficient, digitally controlled and soon, very cheap to manufacture. Being physically small the LED can be positioned or embedded into luminaires, materials and even the very fabric of a building or environment [1]. Our future lighting systems will be *ambient*.

In the past, the single light bulb was controlled using a single switch; on and off. LED-based lighting systems can easily consist of hundreds of separate light sources, with each source having many individually controllable parameters including colour, intensity, and saturation. The price to pay for all this functionality and flexibility is complexity. It is unreasonable and unrealistic to assume that end users of such lighting systems will be able or willing to manage this complexity. The ratio of the effort required to obtain the reward of beautiful and advanced LED lighting needs to be carefully managed. One direction that is being explored is to enrich lighting systems with sensor networks that will enable automatic lighting control that is based on contextual information [2]. However, other directions will need to be defined and explored also. Future lighting systems will need to be *intelligent*.

D. Keyson et al. (Eds.): AmI 2011, LNCS 7040, pp. 362–363, 2011.

In many situations, such as setting up an atmospheric light, an explicit user interaction may still be required. Moreover, as functionality and complexity of light systems grow, the mapping between the sensors data and the desired light outcome will become fuzzy and may require an explicit user interaction for fine tuning the outcome or for adjusting the mapping between sensor input and light output. Thirdly, explicit interaction can be desired to allow users to feel in control while interacting with intelligent lighting systems. The light switch therefore in many situations will need to be replaced by novel forms of interactions that offer richer interaction possibilities such as tangible, multi-touch, or gesture-based user interfaces. As proliferation of LED light continues, it becomes more important to go beyond scattered design efforts [2, 3] and systematically study user interaction with emerging lighting systems. The goal of this workshop is to take the first steps in this direction.

2 Goal of the Workshop

The goal of this workshop is to explore how the vision and principles of the Ambient Intelligence paradigm (i.e. embedded, context-aware, personalized, adaptive, and anticipatory) can be applied to the interaction with future lighting systems. This exploration should help to formulate the key research challenges for Ambient Intelligent Lighting Systems and new product opportunities.

From this workshop we aim to identity:

1. Key research challenges for Ambient Intelligent Lighting Systems.
2. New user interaction solutions.
3. New product opportunities and ideas for how to realize the AmI vision.

References

1. Price, C.: Light Fantastic. Digital Home Magazine (November 2003)
2. Bhardwaj, S., Ozcelebi, T., Lukkien, J.: Smart lighting using LED luminaries. In: Proc. of PERCOM Workshops, pp. 654–659. IEEE (2010)
3. Lucero, A., Lashina, T., Terken, J.: Reducing Complexity of Interaction with Advanced Bathroom Lighting at Home. I-COM 5(1), 34–40 (2006)

Interactive Human Behavior Analysis in Open or Public Spaces

Hayley Hung[1], Jean-Marc Odobez[2], and Dariu Gavrila[1,3]

[1] University of Amsterdam, The Netherlands
[2] Idiap Research Institute, Switzerland
[3] Daimler Research and Development, Germany

Abstract. In the past years, efforts in surveillance and open space analysis have focused on traditional computer vision problems like scene modeling or object detection and tracking. Research on human behavior recognition have tended to work on predefined simple activities such as running, jumping or left luggage, and single-person trajectory analysis. The goal of the workshop is to bring together experts and researchers from different fields to share their experience and expertise about the opportunities on the development of tools for automated social analysis in open and public spaces. Humans exhibit a rich range of behaviors, from their interaction with the environment such as how groups of people occupy the space or how they manipulate or use objects within it, to the way they communicate with each other. Such behaviors can be captured from multiple sensors. Automatically interpreting interactive behavior provides a richer foundation for ambient intelligent environments.

Keywords: Human Behavior, Interaction, Multimodal Sensing, Computer Vision, Surveillance, Sensor Fusion.

Introduction

Automatically understanding interactive human behavior in public spaces is the next step for ambient intelligent environments that can sense our needs with both the objects within the space but also with other people around us. By understanding human interactive behavior in public spaces, we can facilitate a richer interaction between ourselves and the world around us. If we are at a social event and we do not know anyone there, we may want help identifying who we can talk to and the appropriate time to approach a group of people so that we are not ignored. We may want to measure the success of a party or social event based on observing people's social behavior, or indeed change the atmosphere such as the lighting if the mood of the party changes. We can use automated methods to understand how a space is used and how interventions can change its use. It also provides a tool for retailers, sociologists, public planning authorities, architects, as well as surveillance and security industries.

D. Keyson et al. (Eds.): AmI 2011, LNCS 7040, pp. 364–366, 2011.

Themes of the Workshop

Submissions for this workshop[1] embraced the ambient nature of automated interactive behavior analysis using a wide range of sensor types including inertial sensors [3], mobile phones [6], thermal cameras [5], infrared sensors,video cameras [2,1], microphones, as well as depth sensors [4]. Some of the papers addressed technological building blocks that are important for behavior analysis, like the detection of people in video images [2], or the detection of individual motion activity from body sensors [3]. Others have studied the understanding of and how to influence the urban mobility behavior of individuals [6], while another paper evaluated the feasibility of a shopping assistant that recognizes the need for help when observing shopping activities[4].

Of particular note was the work of Cristani et al. [1], who asked the question of whether it was possible to use distant sensors to estimate who was speaking in a conversation when extracting audio data is ethically questionable, and sometimes impractical. Under such circumstances, research on whether aspects of vocal behavior can be estimated from gestural cues becomes particularly important. Their results show promise not only for estimating when people are speaking but also that vocal pitch exhibits some correlation with body motion.

Another paper of interest came from the architectural domain by Skouboe et al. [5] and showed a case study of how simple but effective automated techniques could be used to analyze the use of a space and therefore understand how a space can be enhanced or modified by placing new features within it. This study motivates further work to understand how longer-term observations can be used to help understand how temporal context may affect urban space design. With such a diverse range of topics covered, we are optimistic that this research field will grow and benefit future ambient intelligent systems.

Acknowledgments. The organization of this workshop was partially supported by the European Community through FP7/2007-2013 under grant agreement nr. 218197 (ADABTS), nr. 248907 (VANAHEIM), and a Marie Curie Research Training fellowship in the project "AnaSID" (PIEF-GA-2009-255609).

References

1. Cristani, M., Pesarin, A., Vinciarelli, A., Crocco, M., Murino, V.: Look at who's talking. In: Workshop on Interactive Human Behaviour in Open and Public Spaces, InterHuB (2011)
2. Descamps, A., Carincotte, C., Gosselin, B.: Person detection for indoor videosurveillance using spatio-temporal integral features. In: Workshop on Interactive Human Behaviour in Open and Public Spaces, InterHuB (2011)
3. Muhammad, S.A., Klein, N., Laerhoven, K.V., David, K.: A feature set evalution for activity recognition with body-worn inertial sensors. In: Workshop on Interactive Human Behaviour in Open and Public Spaces, InterHuB (2011)

---

[1] http://www.idiap.ch/workshop/interhub2011/

4. Popa, M., Rothkrantz, L., Shan, C., Wiggers, P., Kemal-Koc, A.: Kinect sensing of shopping related actions. In: Workshop on Interactive Human Behaviour in Open and Public Spaces, InterHuB (2011)
5. Skouboe, E., Andersen, H.J., Jensen, O.B.: Using human motion intensity as input for urban design. In: Workshop on Interactive Human Behaviour in Open and Public Spaces, InterHuB (2011)
6. Teeuw, W., Koolwaaij, J., Peddemors, A.: User behaviour captured by mobile phones. In: Workshop on Interactive Human Behaviour in Open and Public Spaces, InterHuB (2011)

Workshop on User Interaction Methods for Elderly People with Dementia

Felix Kamieth[1], Kathrin Kim[2], and Hester Bruikman[3]

[1] Fraunhofer Institute for Computer Graphics Research IGD, Darmstadt, Germany
Felix.kamieth@igd.fraunhofer.de
[2] User Interface Design GmbH, Ludwigsburg, Germany
Kathrin.kim@uid.com
[3] Philips Research, The Netherlands
Hester.Bruikman@philips.com

1 Background

The development of dementia happens to a large part of elderly people. Since the condition is – so far – without a cure, the only means of dealing with it, currently, is personal or institutional care. Basically, as dementia progresses, the affected person tends to forget more about his or her immediate surroundings and regresses into early memories from childhood, for example. The results are disorientation, confusion and the inability to perform many daily life tasks like keeping appointments or even a regular way of life. The high prevalence of the condition in conjunction with the very personnel-consuming means of treatment poses a direct challenge to existing health care systems in the near future.

As a very widespread cognitive disease, the care of dementia patients is provided right now by relatives and professional caretakers alike. The quality of this care usually depends on the time and financial resources available to the caretakers. Proper care of the rising numbers of dementia patients in the future will require an improvement on the use of these scarce resources for the benefit of the patient. As an assistive means for the caretakers as well as support for the dementia patients themselves, the use of AAL systems can offer a platform based on which such improvements are made possible.

To tackle the issue of dementia, AAL systems need to provide solutions to the common problems of affected patients. Core issues include forgetfulness, disorientation and a lack of connection to the present moment. Using ICT solutions for dementia patients requires taking these issues into account during development.

This poses a challenge to the user interfaces designed for such AAL systems. End users need special care in the presentation of information and in the interaction with the system to minimize disorientation and confusion. In addition to common requirements for technology-averse elderly people, dementia patients thus require special guidance and user-friendly interaction metaphors and techniques. It shall be also noted that the workshop focuses on early stages of dementia when the user is able to retain abilities with proper care. Later stages of dementia, as it is understood by the workshop organizers, require close human care and cannot be handled with technological support solutions alone. Possible support solutions at later stages are meant to support already existing close care, but value in terms of more efficient use

D. Keyson et al. (Eds.): AmI 2011, LNCS 7040, pp. 367–368, 2011.

of professional caretaker time, for example, is diminishing with the disease's progression.

2 Scientific Aim of the Workshop

AAL-solutions for dementia sufferers can be an important step in providing better care to dementia patients. Also, they allow the development of cost-effective solutions aimed at a specific set of end-user needs.

This workshop aims at the development of a set of guidelines for the development of such solutions. It draws on existing developments being done in this field, ranging from end-user research to interaction development and evaluations.

The workshop poses these questions to its participants and collects current research results on the following topics:

- User research with dementia patients (Focus groups and interviews to inquire about the needs of these patients)
- Research from care personnel (health care staff or caring relatives giving insight into their requirements for providing better care)
- Interaction development for dementia patients (Development of user interfaces, input metaphors, design principles, etc.)
- Presentations of integrated systems aimed at supporting dementia patients
- Presentations of software/hardware solutions aimed at helping dementia patients in everyday life (medication dispensers, reminder systems, monitoring systems, alarm and control units, relevant sensory equipment, etc.)

Based on the collection of current work in the field, guidelines are extracted to support the development of cost-effective support systems for caretakers and dementia patients. These guidelines provide a set of the most important challenges faced by caretakers and patients. They also provide benchmarks for the financing power available for these solutions. They list feasible solution approaches as well as areas for future work where helpful support system elements cannot be carried financially or require additional technological development. Finally, the guidelines provide a reference for researchers in the field to existing projects and available solutions to be used to tackle the problem and give future researchers an easy entry-point into this area of research.

The workshop results will be used in the AAL Joint program project CCE (Connected Care for Elderly People with Dementia) as input from the scientific community to improve upon the developed AAL solution for dementia sufferers, which will also be presented on the workshop.

Empowering and Integrating Senior Citizens with Virtual Coaching

Andreas Braun[1], Peter H.M.P. Roelofsma[2],
Dieter Ferring[3], and Milla Immonen[4]

[1] Fraunhofer Institute for Computer Graphics Research IGD, Darmstadt, Germany
andreas.braun@igd.fraunhofer.de
[2] VU University, CAMeRA, Amsterdam, The Netherlands
p.h.m.p.roelofsma@vu.nl
[3] Université de Luxembourg, Luxembourg
dieter.ferring@uni.lu
[4] VTT Technical Research Centre of Finland, Oulu, Finland
milla.immonen@vtt.fi

1 Background of the Workshop

With Europes aging population and an increasing number of older people living alone or geographically distant from kin, loneliness is turning into a prevalent issue. This might involve deleterious consequences for both the older person and society, such as depression and increased use of healthcare services. Virtual coaches that act as friend in a para-social relationship but also as mentor that helps the elderly end- user to create meaningful relationships in his actual social environment are a powerful method to overcome loneliness and increase the quality of life in the elderly population. The AAL Joint Programme projects A2E2 (AAL-2008-1-071) and V2me (AAL-2009-2-107) are exploring virtual coaches and their application in AAL scenarios, including the use of user avatars, virtual self-representations that allow the user to be represented in communication scenarios. Other European research projects that focus on social integration of the elderly are e.g. ALICE (AAL-2009-2-091) or WeCare (AAL-2009-2-026). Outside the European Union the negative implications of population aging can be observed in Japan, having an even larger proportion of senior citizens, using individual-centred devices, such as robot pets,[1] to improve the quality of life of lonely elderly persons.

The user groups involved often are not acquainted with modern ICT systems and therefore it is a challenge to create intuitive, adaptive platforms that cater to the individual needs and allow the user to interact easily.

2 Aim of the Workshop

The workshop will discuss the effects of virtual coaches on elderly users and how they can be used to improve the quality of life by aiding in planning daily life

---

[1] Wada, K.; Shibata, T., Living With Seal Robots - Its Sociopsychological and Physiological Influences on the Elderly at a Care House, IEEE Transactions on Robotics, Oct. 2007.

D. Keyson et al. (Eds.): AmI 2011, LNCS 7040, pp. 369–370, 2011.
© Springer-Verlag Berlin Heidelberg 2011

activities and mediating meaningful relationships to maintain and expand the social network of the elderly persons. Additional applications of virtual coaches and avatars in AAL specific context will be discussed. Furthermore it will explore intuitive interaction between the user and virtual entities, leading to the following collection of topics:

1. Realistic virtual characters in AAL applications
2. Adaptive virtual self-representation in AAL applications
3. Emotional expressiveness of virtual characters
4. Intuitive interaction devices for elderly end-users
5. User interface design for interaction with virtual entities
6. Virtual entities in smart, sensor-equipped environments
7. Mediating social contacts by means of virtual coaching
8. Technology use and aging: Inhibiting and facilitating factors
9. User experience and acceptance evaluation: Results of pilot studies and prototype testing from end-user perspective

3 Organisation of the Workshop

The full-day workshop consists of two parts. In the first part, the different approaches to above topics are collected to create a set of current solutions, dealing with the socio-psychological and technical aspects of virtual coaches in AAL environments. In the second part, a forum will provide workshop participants with the possibility to evaluate the solutions collected in the first part to find common aspects and determine further applications scenarios for virtual characters in AAL. The workshops aims at creating a shared set of knowledge gathering the current state of virtual coaching for elderly persons and collecting novel approaches for further applications in AAL context.

The workshop is aimed at experts in ambient assistant living services, socio-psychological methods, usability engineering and smart-environments. Psychologists, researchers and engineers working on the implementation of technical platforms, as well as usability and evaluation studies are called to join us in this workshop.

Each participant is expected to submit a position paper of 2-4 pages, describing experiences and results in research on the area of application scenarios of virtual coaches and virtual self-representations, intuitive interaction with virtual characters and integration of these into smart environments.

Workshop: Integration of AMI and AAL Platforms in the Future Internet (FI) Platform Initiative

Antonio Kung[1], Francesco Furfari[2], Mohammad-Reza Tazari[3],
Atta Badii[4], and Petra Turkama[5]

[1] Trialog, Paris, France
[2] ISTI-CNR, Pisa, Italy
[3] Fraunhhofer-IGD, Darmstadt, Germany
[4] U.Reading, UK
[5] U.Aalto, Finland
antonio.kung@trialog.com, francesco.furfari@isti.cnr.it,
saied.tazari@igd.fraunhofer.de, atta.badii@reading.ac.uk,
petra.turkama@aalto.fi

Abstract. The digital agenda of the European Commission includes plans for the building of Information and Communication Technology (ICT) based on a new generation of networks, or the Internet of the Future. To this end, the Future Internet Private Public Partnership (FI-PPP) has been established with the help of the European Commission. It will involve the building of a proof of concept FI platform in the coming two years. One of the main challenges of this platform is to be generic while serving the needs of specific application sectors. This workshop will focus on the challenges of integrating Ambient Intelligence (AmI) and Ambient Assisted Living (AAL) platforms with this kind of platform. Participants in the workshop will include members of the AmI/AAL platform community, members of the FI community, and policy makers.

Keywords: AmI, AAL, Future Internet, Platforms.

1 Workshop Context

In March 2008, the ICT community in Europe produced the Bled declaration calling for a concerted European action to redesign the Internet [1]. The result was the Future Internet Public Private Partnership programme (FI-PPP) [2] which is coordinated by the CONCORD facilitation project [12]. It includes three phases as shown in Figure 1 and will involve a public budget of 300 MEuro. The first phase has started in April 2010 and consists of a technology foundation project focusing on the provision of an FI platform that will be used by up to eight use case scenario projects. The second phase will focus on further validation of this platform through five use case scenario pilots. The third phase will be dedicated to the expansion and enlargement of many test beds and pilots.

Ambient Assisted Living refers to "intelligent systems that will assist elderly individuals for a better, healthier and safer life in the preferred living environment and

D. Keyson et al. (Eds.): AmI 2011, LNCS 7040, pp. 371–373, 2011.
© Springer-Verlag Berlin Heidelberg 2011

covers concepts, products and services that interlink and improve new technologies and the social environment" [3]. AAL is supported by the European Commission's ageing well action plan [4] as well as a series of measures that involve more than one billion Euros in research and development between 2006 and 2013. Realising that many collaborative projects were dedicating resources to the development of platform features, the European Commission decided in 2009 to launch a call for proposals for the development of a common platform. This led to UniversAAL, an FP7 project [5] which is now coordinating AALOA, an initiative for an open source platform [6]. In parallel, work related to accessibility has led to the launch of the OpenURC initiative [7]. AAL is a compelling use case scenario for the Future Internet. Furthermore, the AAL community has accumulated a wealth of platform requirements [8,9] that could directly benefit the Future Internet. The vision of the FI-PPP is that the technology foundation project will provide generic enablers which would be associated with specific enablers developed within a domain to allow for the design, development and deployment of applications. The question is, can the FI-PPP enablers give leverage to the AAL community?

Further to technical integration, the FI PPP and AAL communities share the same development priorities: smartness, sustainability and inclusiveness, as well as similar social, regulatory and economic implementation barriers. This workshop discusses joint methodologies and instruments for collaborative research, development and innovation contributing to the European growth strategy. Such methods include user driven open innovation, public sector innovation, policy coordination methods, as well as living lab experimentation.

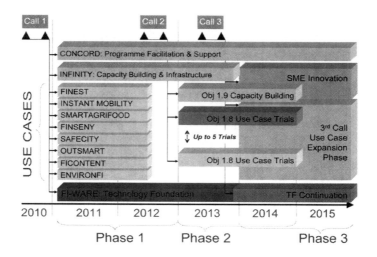

Fig. 1. FI-PPP Phases

2   Workshop Content

This workshop will focus on the challenges of integrating AmI and AAL platforms with the FI-PPP initiative. In this respect the workshop provides information on concrete means to engage with the FI PPP future calls and experiments, either as a user or as a co-developer. A secondary objective is to explore the opportunities for joint statements and declarations addressing the grand societal challenges of aging, e-inclusion and e-competences, as well as the implementation of Digital Agenda.

The following topics will be discussed:

- Architecture of an FI platform. Challenges from an FI viewpoint.
- Architecture of existing and to come AmI/AAL platforms. Challenges from an AmI/AAL viewpoint.
- How can integration take place? What are the hurdles?
- What are the means of experimentation? Can AAL be a usage area for the Future Internet?
- What is the impact of evaluation? How can we move towards a European digital single market?
- Identification of measures and instruments.
- Actions.

Participants of the workshop will include members of the AmI/AAL platform community, members of the FI community, and policy makers.

References

1. Bled declaration,
   http://www.future-internet.eu/publications/bled-declaration.html
2. Future internet FI-PPP,
   http://www.fi-ppp.eu/,
   http://ec.europa.eu/information_society/activities/foi/lead/fippp/index_en.htm
3. Ambient Assisted Living Roadmap. AAliance, http://www.aaliance.eu
4. Action Plan on Information and Communication Technologies and Ageing, June 14 (2005),
   http://eur-lex.europa.eu/LexUriServ/site/en/com/2007/com2007_0332en01.pdf,
   http://eur-lex.europa.eu/LexUriServ/site/en/com/2007/com2007_0332en01.pdf
5. UniversAAL IST project, http://www.universaal.org/
6. AALOA, http://www.aaloa.org
7. OpenURC, http://www.openurc.org
8. Kung, A., Jean-bart, B.: Making AAL Platforms a Reality. In: de Ruyter, B., Wichert, R., Keyson, D.V., Markopoulos, P., Streitz, N., Divitini, M., Georgantas, N., Mana Gomez, A. (eds.) AmI 2010. LNCS, vol. 6439, pp. 187–196. Springer, Heidelberg (2010), http://portal.acm.org/citation.cfm?id=1926762
9. Fagerberg, G., Kung, A., Wichert, R., Tazari, M.-R., Jean-Bart, B., Bauer, G., Zimmermann, G., Furfari, F., Potortì, F., Chessa, S., Hellenschmidt, M., Gorman, J., Alexandersson, J., Bund, J., Carrasco, E., Epelde, G., Klima, M., Urdaneta, E., Vanderheiden, G., Zinnikus, I.: Platforms for AAL Applications. In: Lukowicz, P., Kunze, K., Kortuem, G. (eds.) EuroSSC 2010. LNCS, vol. 6446, pp. 177–201. Springer, Heidelberg (2010), http://portal.acm.org/citation.cfm?id=1940178
10. MonAMI project, http://www.monami.info/
11. CompanionAble, http://www.companionable.net/
12. CONCORD, http://www.fi-ppp.eu/projects/concord/

First International Workshop on Ambient Gaming (AmGam'11)

Janienke Sturm[1,2], Stine Liv Johansen[3],
Mark de Graaf[1], and Ben Schouten[1,2]

[1] Dept. Industrial Design, Eindhoven University of Technology,
P.O. Box 513, 5600MB Eindhoven, The Netherlands
[2] Serious Game Design / Ambient Intelligence & Design lectorate,
Fontys University of Applied Sciences,
P.O.Box 347, 5600AH Eindhoven, The Netherlands
[3] Institute for Information and Media Studies,
Aarhus University, Helsingforsgade 14, 8200 Arhus N, Denmark
{j.sturm,bschouten,m.degraaf}@tue.nl, imvslj@hum.au.dk

1 Workshop Description

New technologies create opportunities to enrich people's experience while playing games. In recent years we have seen many examples of technological advances opening up new player experiences, for instance new controllers (e.g. Nintendo's Wii), new sensor technologies (e.g. GPS), and new forms of play (e.g. multi-player online games and open-ended play), etc. Another novel technology offering ample opportunities to derive new properties for games and play is *ambient intelligence*. Ambient intelligence refers to electronic networked environments that are sensitive and responsive to the presence of people, with the following characteristics [1]:

- Context aware: game devices can recognize you and your situational context;
- Personalized: they can be tailored to your needs;
- Adaptive: they can change in response to you;
- Anticipatory: they can anticipate your desires without conscious mediation.

'Ambient games', i.e. innovative game designs incorporating these ambient intelligence characteristics, may lead to a whole new player experience [2,3]. Several existing games and genres include some aspects of ambient intelligence, for example, pervasive and locative games [4]. These games blend the virtual and real world and are interacted with through multiple ubiquitous devices and as such offer context-aware and personalised features. Ambient games allow players to move around freely, without being bound by a computer screen or another device, by using information coming from sensors. Ambient games support casual play, i.e. play and games are seamlessly integrated with daily activities. Ambient gaming implies taking the everyday stuff of life and turning it into a game, and yet that gaming is not limited to a single device at a single time, but is intertwined with daily activities.

Ambient gaming offers promising opportunities for creating novel and unique player experiences. However, there are still many unanswered questions related to this

D. Keyson et al. (Eds.): AmI 2011, LNCS 7040, pp. 374–375, 2011.
© Springer-Verlag Berlin Heidelberg 2011

new field of research, such as what are promising scenarios for ambient game design? Which technologies are available that can be used for ambient gaming? How to design and evaluate ambient games? In this workshop on Ambient Gaming we intend to discuss these issues from different perspectives and uncover the potential of ambient technology for play and games, by bringing together people who are active in this field (game designers, game researchers, and game developers). The workshop objectives are:

- To share experiences, research, insights and best practices regarding issues related to design, theory, technology, and methodology;
- To unfold the challenges and opportunities of this interesting emerging area and develop a common research agenda for future studies;
- To come to a strategy and research agenda in the field of Ambient Gaming for the forthcoming years
- To stimulate participants to form collaborations to advance the field further in a multidisciplinary manner.

The workshop will be a half-day workshop, with about 15 participants from different disciplines both from academia and industry. Participants were selected on the basis of a position paper describing their area of research and their specific interest in the topic of ambient gaming. All position papers were peer reviewed by an international program committee.

References

1. Aarts, E., Marzano, S. (eds.): The New Everyday: Visions of Ambient Intelligence. 010 Publishers, Rotterdam (2003)
2. Schouten, B.: Play as Source for Ambient Culture. Inaugural speech Professor of Serious Gaming, Fontys University of Applied Science (2008)
3. Eyles, M., Eglin, R.: Ambient Games, Revealing a Route to a World Where Work is Play? International Journal of Computer Games Technology (2008)
4. Montola, M., Stenros, J., Waern, A.: Pervasive games: theory and design. Morgan Kaufmann (2009)

Second International Workshop on Human Behavior Understanding: Inducing Behavioral Change

Albert Ali Salah[1] and Bruno Lepri[2,3]

[1] Dept. of Computer Engineering, Boğaziçi University,
Istanbul, Turkey
salah@boun.edu.tr
[2] Fondazione Bruno Kessler
Trento, Italy
lepri@fbk.eu
[3] Media Lab, Massachusetts Institute of Technology
Cambridge:MA, USA

Abstract. The HBU workshop is organized for the second time, with a focus theme of *inducing behavioral change*. The general aim of the workshop is to bring together researchers developing and using computer analysis tools for learning and modeling human behavior, covering both hardware or software aspects. As such, the topics link areas like pattern recognition, sensor technologies, social signal processing, and interaction design.

Keywords: human behavior analysis, persuasive technologies, pattern recognition, serious gaming, social signal processing, smart environments, affective computing, ambient intelligence, sensors, interaction design, human-computer interaction.

1 Description

New technologies and algorithms empower computers with ways to analyze human behavior[1]. Hence, in many research fields, such as ubiquitous computing, multimodal interaction, ambient assisted living and assisted cognition, as well as computer supportive collaborative work, the awareness is emerging that endowing the computer with a capacity to attribute meaning to users attitudes, preferences, personality, social relationships, etc., as well as to understand what people are doing, the activities they have been engaged, their routines and lifestyles, has the potential to re-define the relationship between the computer and the interacting human, moving the computer from a passive observer role to a socially active participating role and enabling it to drive some kinds of interaction, such as influencing attitudes and behaviors of people in their everyday natural environments. The second HBU workshop aims to see where this change is taking us,

---

[1] Description taken from Workshop website: http://hbu2011.fbk.eu

D. Keyson et al. (Eds.): AmI 2011, LNCS 7040, pp. 376–377, 2011.
© Springer-Verlag Berlin Heidelberg 2011

and how computers can be used to change human behavior in order to promote individual and societal values.

2 Content

The first HBU was organized in 2010, as a satellite to ICPR [1]. This workshop gathers researchers dealing with the problem of modeling human behavior under its multiple facets (expression of emotions, display of complex social and relational behaviors, performance of individual or joint actions, etc.), with particular attention to systems that aim to induce behavioral change in their users. Concrete examples are intelligent tutoring systems that rely on analysis to provide feedback (e.g. sign language tutoring based on gesture analysis), healthcare systems that improve the patients physical or cognitive well-being, interactive games that serve beneficial purposes (e.g. improving fitness), technologies that promote positive behavioral change (e.g. environmental sustainability and better life-styles), to name a few.

The Workshop received 32 submissions, all of which were peer-reviewed by at least two program committee members [2]. 13 papers were accepted as oral presentations. Two invited keynote talks are scheduled by Dr. Nuria Oliver from Telefonica Research and Dr. Wijnand Ijsselsteijn from Eindhoven University of Technology, respectively. We have solicited papers in the following areas:

1. **Design and Applications:** Human-computer interaction, interaction design, systems to observe and promote health, technologies to promote sustainable behavior, interactive and immersive games, interactive marketing, human-computer dialogue, persuasive systems design, art and creative applications, educational technologies, behavioral biometrics
2. **Behavioral Analysis:** Reality mining, action and gesture recognition, recognition of daily living activities and lifestyles, spatio-temporal models, behavior semantics, social behavior analysis, social signal processing, affect and emotion recognition, corpora for behavioral analysis
3. **Devices for Capturing Behaviors:** Smart cameras, audio technology, mobile phones, wearable sensors, new sensory modalities, integration

References

1. Salah, A.A., Gevers, T., Sebe, N., Vinciarelli, A. (eds.): HBU 2010. LNCS, vol. 6219. Springer, Heidelberg (2010)
2. Salah, A.A., Lepri, B. (eds.): HBU 2011. LNCS, vol. 7065. Springer, Heidelberg (2011)

Privacy, Trust and Interaction in the Internet of Things

Johann Schrammel[1], Christina Hochleitner[1], and Manfred Tscheligi[1,2]

[1] CURE, Center for Usability Research & Engineering
Modecenterstraße 17 / Objekt 2, 1110 Wien, Austria
[2] HCI Unit, ICT&S, University of Salzburg
Sigmund-Haffner-Gasse 18, 5020 Salzburg, Austria
{schrammel,hochleitner,tscheligi}@cure.at

Abstract. This workshop addresses topics of increasing importance in the emerging area of the Internet of Things (IoT): privacy, trust and related interaction concepts. The aim of the workshop is to bring together experts from different areas to cover the complexity of the questions involved and to provide a forum for developing new ideas on how to address the major challenges in the field considering both a scientific and an industrial viewpoint. The workshop targets to identify pressing questions and to develop a research agenda for trusted and privacy-respecting computing in the IoT. Special attention within the workshop is given on whether and how experiences with privacy and trust from related areas can be applied to the IoT, where existing conceptualizations need to be extended or modified and where radically new concepts are required.

The Internet of Things (IoT) is an umbrella term covering a number of different base technologies aimed at linking physical objects and their virtual representation with the goal to utilize this link for improved service and interaction concepts [3]. The IoT approach combines concepts and paradigms informed by Ambient Intelligence, Ubiquitous Computing, Sensor Networks, Grid Computing, etc. Even though the IoT is still a vision and far from being a reality, more and more aspects of it become already tangible. For example, objects are equipped on large scale with RFID-tags for logistics purposes, formerly stand-alone devices become connected to the net and the "smart home" knows where a user left his glasses.

Looking a little closer into potential effects and implications of such scenarios it becomes immediately evident that there are serious privacy, trust and related interaction issues that need to be addressed to allow taking full advantage of the potentials of the IoT. For example, being able to find a specific book within your library at once is a nice feature. However, providing others the possibility to know, analyze and interpret when you were reading which book might be far less desirable.

Privacy issues have been researched in many related areas e.g. [3][4][5]. In the IoT however new sets of potentially sensitive data becomes available through profiling of "things", and questions regarding what this data is telling about the user and who should be allowed to see and use this information have to be raised. The key issue is "how one is being read (and interpreted in a possibly mismatching context) by someone else" [4]. Another new dimension of privacy aspects in the internet of things is the vast amount of objects and data that has to be dealt with. Whereas the related ubicomp scenarios typically only deal with selected subsets of actions and dedicated

D. Keyson et al. (Eds.): AmI 2011, LNCS 7040, pp. 378–379, 2011.

devices in the IoT literally everything in the users environment needs to be considered with regard to privacy aspects. Due to the amount and hiddenness of information new dimensions of complexity in the formulation of privacy concepts, the engineering of privacy policies, and the management of information privacy emerge. Research has shown that the information on social networking sites has the potential for severe consequences, and that users have difficulties to correctly understand possible long-term effects of their behavior [1]. Even more severe problems have to be expected for a wide-scale application of IoT-concepts.

Closely related to these privacy issues is the question on how a basic level of trust can be supported and achieved within the IoT. Little is known on how models of trust that are formed both in interaction in human society and in the context of desktop computing can be transformed towards the IoT, which specific difficulties, misconceptions and challenges might arise, and how they can be accounted for from a design perspective. Currently, trust is often anchored in a strictly technological context, which is easily misinterpreted by humans and miscommunicated by system vendors and owners. Therefore we want to further develop the understanding of relevant factors for the perception and formation of trust in the context of the IoT.

Another specifically challenging aspect of the IoT is that only very limited feedback and interaction possibilities are available to communicate the current status of the system and the data exchange. Due to the pervasive and ubiquitous nature of the everyday objects they only can be enhanced with little information bits, thereby making it extremely challenging to communicate complex patterns of data transmission and privacy status. The typical communication bandwidth of an object within the IoT might be one bit: on or off, possibly displayed by use of a LED or similar means. Here the question is how much (status) information regarding privacy issues can be communicated with such restricted possibilities, and what other means to keep user informed and aware of what's going on can be utilized in the IoT context.

In detail the workshop addresses the following questions and objectives: What are the main (new) privacy challenges arising from the IoT-concept? How do existing solutions for privacy scale within the IoT? What are the mental models of trust that users form with regard to the IoT? Which metaphors can be used to support users in developing helpful and reality-conform mental models in IoT-settings? Which (simple) interaction mechanisms and concepts are suited best for providing feedback in the IoT? What supporting measures and mechanisms are available to help users to form a proper understanding of the IoT?

References

1. Acquisti, A., Grossklags, J.: Privacy Attitudes and Privacy Behaviour. In: Camp, J., Lewis, R. (eds.) Economics of Information Security, pp. 165–178. Springer, NY (2004)
2. Fritsch, L.: Profiling and Location-Based Services. In: Hildebrandt, M., Gutwirth, S. (eds.) Profiling the European Citizen, pp. 147–160. Springer, Netherlands (2008)
3. Gershenfeld, N., Krikorian, R., Cohen, D.: The Internet of Things. Scientific American 291, 76–81 (2004)
4. Hildebrandt, M.: An Ecosystem of Legal and Technological Protections, on: Trusted e-services for the citizen session. In: ICT Event 2010, Brussels (2010)
5. Langheinrich, M.: Privacy in Ubiquitous Computing. In: Krumm, J. (ed.) Ubiquitous Computing. Chapman & Hall / CRC Press (2009)

Author Index